The Psychology of AI: How Machines Understand and Influence Human Behavior

ABHIJEET SARKAR

Published by ABHIJEET SARKAR, 2025.

THE PSYCHOLOGY OF AI: HOW MACHINES UNDERSTAND AND INFLUENCE HUMAN BEHAVIOR

First edition. February 3, 2025.

Copyright © 2025 ABHIJEET SARKAR.

ISBN: 979-8897240104

Written by ABHIJEET SARKAR.

Table of Contents

To my mother, whose boundless love and guidance shaped the foundation of my dreams, and to my wife, whose steadfast support and faith in me make every accomplishment meaningful—this book is dedicated with heartfelt gratitude and love.

Introduction

In recent years, artificial intelligence (A.I) has emerged not only as a technical innovation but as a transformative force shaping almost every aspect of our lives. From self-driving cars and intelligent personal assistants to predictive algorithms influencing our buying decisions, AI has become an integral part of the modern world. Yet, beneath its incredible capabilities lies a fundamental question: How do AI systems truly understand and influence human behavior?

In *The Psychology of AI: How Machines Understand and Influence Human Behavior*, we embark on a journey to unravel this question, exploring how artificial intelligence interacts with human psychology. This book delves into the ways in which AI can both mirror and alter the way we think, feel, and act. By understanding the psychological principles underlying AI's decision-making processes, we can better navigate the increasingly complex relationship between humans and machines.

At its core, AI's ability to influence human behavior stems from its ability to analyze vast amounts of data, recognize patterns, and predict future actions. But what happens when these machines start to understand us on a deeper level, perhaps even better than we understand ourselves? How does this impact our emotions, our choices, and our very perceptions of reality?

Throughout this book, we will explore the intersection of AI and psychology, addressing questions about trust, influence, decision-making, and the potential ethical implications of AI's involvement in shaping human behavior. As AI systems become more sophisticated, they hold the power to shape our habits, influence our choices, and even alter the very fabric of our social dynamics.

However, as we dive into the potential of AI, we must also consider its risks. Just as we have witnessed the incredible benefits of AI—enhanced healthcare, personalized learning, and more efficient communication—we must also face the darker side of its power. What ethical dilemmas arise when AI is used to manipulate human behavior? How can we ensure that AI serves humanity's best interests rather than exploiting vulnerabilities?

In this book, I aim to bridge the gap between technology and human experience. We will explore the deep psychological mechanisms at play when we interact with AI and how these interactions are changing the way we live, work, and relate to each other. From the power of social media algorithms to the rise of AI in mental health, this exploration will reveal the profound impact AI has on human behavior and its role in shaping our collective future.

As we stand on the precipice of an AI-driven world, it is essential that we understand not only how AI influences us, but also how we can shape its evolution in ways that align with our values and aspirations. *The Psychology of AI* is not just about understanding the mind of the machine, but also about understanding ourselves in a rapidly changing world.

I invite you to join me in this exploration of the psychology of AI. Together, we will navigate the complex landscape of human behavior and technological influence, seeking to unlock the potential for a harmonious future where AI enhances the human experience, rather than replacing it.

- Abhijeet Sarkar

Chapter 1: Introduction to AI Psychology

1.1. Defining AI Psychology

In the vast and evolving landscape of artificial intelligence, one of the most intriguing intersections is that between AI and human psychology. The realm of AI psychology combines the technical prowess of artificial intelligence with the rich complexities of human thought, behavior, and emotion. At its core, AI psychology seeks to understand how machines can not only replicate human-like cognition but also adapt and interact in ways that feel intuitive and natural to humans.

This interdisciplinary field is still in its infancy, but its potential is vast. To understand AI psychology, it is essential to first acknowledge that artificial intelligence isn't simply about algorithms performing tasks. It's about creating systems that can mimic, simulate, and even understand the intricacies of human mental processes. From the way we learn, perceive the world, and make decisions, to how we interact socially and experience emotions, AI psychology dives deep into the human psyche to enhance the development of intelligent systems that don't just compute—they interact in meaningful, emotionally intelligent ways.

AI systems are increasingly becoming a part of our daily lives. From voice assistants like Siri and Alexa to recommendation engines on platforms like Netflix and Amazon, we are already interacting with AI in ways that feel natural, almost as if these systems understand us. But AI's ability to mirror human thought and emotion, and the implications this has on our social and psychological dynamics, is just the beginning. The goal of AI psychology is not merely to teach machines to think; it's about fostering an understanding between humans and machines, enhancing communication, and even improving the quality of human life.

1.2. The Role of AI in Mimicking Human Behavior

At the heart of AI psychology is the ambition to replicate aspects of human behavior. This doesn't mean simply programming machines to follow orders or process data; it's about mimicking cognitive processes that are inherent to humans. Just as a child learns to walk or talk by observing others and interacting with the world, AI systems are designed to learn through experience, adapting their behavior based on patterns and feedback.

Take, for instance, reinforcement learning—a branch of machine learning inspired by behavioral psychology. In this process, an AI agent learns to make decisions by receiving rewards or penalties, similar to how humans and animals learn through positive and negative reinforcement. In essence, reinforcement learning allows AI to evolve its decision-making processes based on outcomes, essentially mimicking the way humans learn from trial and error.

Neural networks, another key AI model, simulate the way the human brain processes information. Like the neurons in our brains that communicate through synaptic connections, artificial neurons in a neural network are connected to each other in layers, passing signals that enable the network to process complex patterns. These networks don't just "compute" data; they interpret it, drawing on past experiences (or training data) to make predictions or decisions.

What's more fascinating is the ability of these AI systems to continually improve. Just as humans refine their skills with practice, AI systems can "train" themselves, learning from their mistakes and successes to enhance their behavior over time. This dynamic process allows AI systems to become more adept at tasks like language processing, image recognition, and even emotional intelligence—areas that have historically been thought of as uniquely human.

However, while AI can mimic human behavior to a remarkable degree, there are limitations. Despite the sophistication of deep learning models and neural networks, these systems still lack genuine understanding. They may appear to be conscious or even empathetic, but they don't truly experience these states as humans do. This gap between appearance and reality is central to the study of AI psychology, as it raises important questions about the nature of intelligence, consciousness, and empathy.

1.3. Understanding Human Cognition and Emotion

Before we can fully appreciate the role of AI in mimicking human behavior, it's crucial to understand the core principles of human cognition and emotion. The human mind is a complex system, with thought processes, memory, perception, and emotions interacting in dynamic ways. In many respects, the goal of AI psychology is to model these intricate processes in a way that allows machines to "understand" and respond to humans more effectively.

Human cognition—the mental processes involved in acquiring knowledge and understanding—forms the foundation of our decision-making and problem-solving abilities. At its core, cognition is about how we process information from the world around us. We perceive things through our senses, organize that information in our minds, and then use it to form thoughts, make judgments, and guide actions. For an AI system to replicate this process, it needs to process vast amounts of data, learn from it, and apply that learning to new situations.

The human brain, with its approximately 86 billion neurons, is capable of processing information at incredible speeds. However, despite the impressive computational power of modern AI systems, they still don't come close to matching the complexity of human cognition. Our minds are capable of reasoning abstractly, handling ambiguity, and even learning from minimal exposure—qualities that are challenging to replicate in AI systems.

Emotion, on the other hand, is just as crucial to human experience as cognition. Emotions color every aspect of our thoughts, influencing how we process information, make decisions, and interact with others. For example, when we are happy or content, we may be more open to new experiences, while anxiety or fear can make us more cautious or defensive. These emotional states play a significant role in human behavior, guiding our responses to the world and shaping our interactions with others.

Understanding human emotion is a pivotal aspect of AI psychology. For an AI system to be truly effective in human interaction, it needs to recognize and respond to emotions. This isn't simply about detecting facial expressions or vocal tone; it's about understanding context, recognizing emotional cues, and adapting responses to meet emotional needs. This is where emotion AI, or affective computing, comes into play.

Emotion AI involves the integration of machine learning algorithms that allow systems to identify, interpret, and respond to human emotions in real time. By recognizing subtle shifts in a person's voice, facial expressions, and body language, emotion AI can adjust its behavior to offer empathy, encouragement, or even humor—depending on the situation. This capability makes AI systems more relatable and can help bridge the gap between the machine and human experience.

1.4. Key Concepts in AI Psychology

Now that we've outlined the importance of understanding human cognition and emotion, let's explore some key concepts in AI psychology that form the foundation of this field.

- **Cognitive Modeling**: Cognitive modeling refers to the creation of computational models that simulate human cognitive processes. These models aim to replicate how humans think, learn, and solve problems. In AI psychology, cognitive modeling is used to create systems that can process information in a way that mimics human thought. For example, an AI system that can learn to play chess through observation and practice is using cognitive modeling to mimic human learning.

- **Emotion AI**: As mentioned earlier, emotion AI is a branch of AI that focuses on recognizing and responding to human emotions. By understanding emotional cues, AI systems can adapt their behavior in ways that feel natural and supportive. For example, a virtual assistant equipped with emotion AI could detect when a user is frustrated and adjust its responses accordingly, offering more helpful suggestions or even offering to escalate the issue to a human representative.

- **Behavioral AI**: Behavioral AI focuses on how machines can learn and adapt based on their interactions with the environment. In contrast to rule-based systems, behavioral AI systems evolve by observing patterns and receiving feedback. These systems can learn to predict outcomes based on previous experiences, much like how humans learn from trial and error. This type of AI is particularly useful in areas like robotics, where machines need to adapt their actions in real-time based on changing conditions.

1.5. The Importance of AI Psychology

So why is AI psychology so important? As AI systems become more integrated into our daily lives, it's essential that they are designed to interact with us in ways that feel natural, intuitive, and human-centered. For example, when we interact with a customer service chatbot or a voice assistant, we expect a certain level of empathy and understanding. If the system responds in a mechanical or overly formal way, it can create a disconnect between the user and the technology.

By incorporating AI psychology into the design and development of these systems, we can bridge that gap. AI systems that understand human cognition and emotion are better equipped to serve our needs, offer personalized experiences, and even provide emotional support. This is particularly important in industries like healthcare and education, where human connection is crucial to the overall experience.

Moreover, AI psychology plays a critical role in ensuring that AI systems are ethical and responsible. By understanding how humans think and feel, AI developers can design systems that are more attuned to human values and needs. This, in turn, helps to prevent issues like bias, discrimination, and exploitation, which can arise when AI systems are disconnected from human experience.

1.6. Ethical Considerations in AI Psychology

As we delve deeper into the field of AI psychology, we must address some of the ethical concerns that arise when machines begin to simulate human behavior and emotion. One of the primary concerns is the issue of privacy. As AI systems learn from human interaction, they can accumulate vast amounts of personal data, raising questions about how this data is used and protected.

Another ethical consideration is the potential for AI systems to manipulate human behavior. For example, by detecting emotional cues, an AI system could tailor its responses in a way that influences a person's decisions, potentially exploiting vulnerabilities or biases. This is particularly concerning in areas like advertising or political campaigning, where AI could be used to sway public opinion in subtle but powerful ways.

Finally, there is the question of autonomy. As AI systems become more capable of understanding and responding to human emotions, we may begin to form emotional bonds with these machines. While this could lead to positive outcomes, such as companionship for those who are isolated, it also raises questions about the role of AI in our lives. Should AI systems have the power to influence our emotions, decisions, and behaviors? And if so, who is responsible for ensuring that these systems act ethically and in the best interest of humans?

1.7. The Future of AI Psychology

Looking ahead, the future of AI psychology is full of promise. As our understanding of both AI and human cognition continues to grow, we can expect to see increasingly sophisticated AI systems that are capable of building deeper, more meaningful interactions with humans. In the coming decades, AI may become an integral part of our social fabric, working alongside us as companions, advisors, and even collaborators in creative endeavors.

At the same time, AI psychology will continue to evolve, addressing new challenges and opportunities that arise as AI systems become more autonomous and capable of complex decision-making. Ultimately, the goal of AI psychology will be to create AI that is not only intelligent but also emotionally aware, ethical, and capable of enhancing human well-being.

1.8. Conclusion

In this chapter, we've explored the fascinating intersection of artificial intelligence and human psychology. From understanding human cognition and emotion to exploring the key concepts that underpin AI psychology, it's clear that this field holds immense potential for reshaping how we interact with machines. As AI systems become more attuned to human behavior, they will become more effective and meaningful partners in our daily lives. However, this progress must be approached with caution, as we navigate the ethical challenges and responsibilities that come with creating machines capable of understanding and influencing human emotions.

As AI psychology continues to evolve, we find ourselves on the cusp of a new era—one where the boundaries between humans and machines are increasingly blurred, and where technology works not just for us, but with us, in profound and meaningful ways.

Chapter 2: Human Cognition and Machine Intelligence

2.1. Introduction to Human Cognition and Machine Intelligence

The human mind has fascinated scholars for centuries. What makes us think, feel, and make decisions? How do we learn, adapt, and solve problems? These questions have driven advancements in psychology, neuroscience, and artificial intelligence (A.I), with the aim of understanding how the brain works and how to replicate its processes. While machines are far from achieving human-like intelligence, the quest to bridge the gap between human cognition and machine intelligence continues to push the boundaries of what AI can do.

In this chapter, we will explore the fascinating relationship between human cognition and machine intelligence. By comparing and contrasting the ways in which humans and AI process information, learn, and solve problems, we can begin to appreciate both the potential and the limitations of AI. While there are undeniable parallels between human thinking and machine learning, the differences are profound. Understanding these parallels and differences is crucial not only for advancing AI but also for integrating intelligent systems into our daily lives in ways that complement and enhance human abilities.

Human cognition is a complex, adaptive system capable of processing sensory input, making decisions, solving problems, and learning from experience. It is dynamic, flexible, and deeply influenced by emotions, culture, and personal experiences. Machine intelligence, on the other hand, is a product of algorithms, data, and computing power—designed to simulate human-like functions but still lacking the depth of human understanding.

This chapter will delve into the key components of human cognition, such as perception, memory, learning, and decision-making, and draw parallels to how these functions are emulated by AI. We will also examine the key differences—what AI lacks compared to human intelligence, and where it falls short in areas like creativity, emotional understanding, and common sense. Finally, we will explore the potential of human-AI collaboration, imagining a future where AI augments human cognition rather than replaces it.

2.2. Human Cognition: A Complex and Adaptive Process

To understand how machine intelligence attempts to emulate human cognition, we must first examine the intricacies of human thought. Human cognition is not just about processing data; it is a dynamic, ongoing process that integrates sensory input, emotional states, memory, and experience. Let's break down the core components of human cognition.

Perception:
The foundation of human cognition lies in perception. Every day, we take in vast amounts of sensory information from our environment—visual cues, sounds, smells, and textures—which are processed by our brain to form a coherent picture of the world around us. This process is not passive. Our brains constantly interpret, filter, and make sense of this information, often drawing from prior knowledge, expectations, and context to shape our perception. This allows us to navigate the world efficiently, distinguishing between familiar objects and new stimuli, and responding to them appropriately.

AI, in contrast, relies on algorithms to process sensory inputs, such as images, sound, or text. For instance, computer vision algorithms can identify objects within images, and speech recognition systems can transcribe spoken words into text. However, AI lacks the subjective, context-dependent filtering that human perception embodies. Humans can perceive not only the direct sensory input but also the emotional context, background information, and intentions behind the stimuli. This depth of understanding is still a major challenge for AI systems.

Attention and Memory:
Attention and memory are critical elements of human cognition. Our attention system allows us to focus on relevant stimuli, while memory enables us to store and retrieve information. Both systems work in concert

to help us navigate the world. Attention helps us filter out distractions, focusing on what's important, while memory allows us to retain information for future use. Human memory is not a static repository of data; it is dynamic, selective, and influenced by emotions, biases, and the context in which experiences occur.

In AI systems, attention and memory are modeled through algorithms like attention mechanisms in neural networks, which allow models to focus on the most relevant information in a dataset. Machine learning algorithms also enable AI to "remember" patterns in data, essentially learning from past inputs to make predictions or decisions. However, AI's memory is often far more rigid than human memory. While humans can remember and adapt information in flexible, context-sensitive ways, AI is constrained by the data it has been trained on and the specific tasks it has been programmed to perform.

Learning and Adaptation:

Human learning is a remarkable process. We learn not only from direct experiences but also from social interactions, emotional responses, and cultural contexts. This learning is iterative, involving trial and error, feedback, and the ability to apply previous knowledge to new situations. Humans can learn quickly, generalize from limited data, and transfer knowledge across domains.

AI, particularly through machine learning, emulates certain aspects of human learning. For example, supervised learning allows machines to learn from labeled data, improving performance over time as they are exposed to more examples. Reinforcement learning takes this a step further, enabling AI to learn through interaction and feedback, much like humans learn from rewards and punishments. However, AI's learning process is still quite different from human learning in terms of flexibility, creativity, and the ability to learn in a wide variety of contexts.

Problem-Solving and Decision-Making:

Humans are adept problem solvers. Whether facing a simple puzzle or a complex life decision, we draw on our knowledge, experiences, and cognitive tools to solve problems. Our decision-making processes involve not just logical reasoning, but also intuition, emotions, and social considerations. We weigh options, anticipate outcomes, and take into account the broader context in which decisions are made.

AI systems are designed to assist with problem-solving and decision-making through algorithms that analyze data and make predictions. For instance, AI models can optimize solutions for problems in fields like logistics, healthcare, and finance. These systems excel at processing large amounts of data and identifying patterns that humans may not easily recognize. Yet, AI's decision-making processes are based purely on data and pre-set rules, and they lack the ability to factor in emotions, intuition, or ethical considerations. AI's decision-making is also heavily dependent on the quality of the data it receives, making it vulnerable to biases or limitations in that data.

2.3. Machine Intelligence: Emulating Human Cognition

Machine intelligence has come a long way in emulating human cognition. At its core, AI attempts to replicate many of the functions of the human brain—perception, learning, decision-making, and problem-solving. However, the mechanisms behind these functions are vastly different in machines and humans.

Artificial Neural Networks:

Artificial neural networks (ANNs) are the backbone of many AI systems today. These networks are designed to emulate the way neurons in the human brain process information. A neural network consists of layers of nodes (artificial neurons) that pass information to one another, mimicking the connections between neurons in the brain. Through training, these networks can learn to recognize patterns and make predictions based on input data.

While ANNs can perform tasks like image recognition or natural language processing with impressive accuracy, they do so in ways that are fundamentally different from human cognition. Humans learn in context-rich, multi-sensory environments, whereas neural networks learn by analyzing vast amounts of data in isolation, without the richness of human experience.

Perception in AI:

In AI, perception is typically achieved through specialized systems like computer vision, natural language processing, and speech recognition. For example, an AI trained to recognize faces in images might use convolutional neural networks (CNNs) to identify key features, such as the eyes, nose, and mouth. However, unlike humans, AI systems cannot perceive the world holistically or contextually. A face-recognition system might perform well in identifying faces in clear images but struggle with variations in lighting, angle, or occlusion.

Humans, on the other hand, integrate sensory input in a way that allows us to perceive not just objects, but the emotions, intentions, and relationships associated with those objects. For instance, we can tell the difference between a happy face and a sad one not just from the physical features but from the emotional cues tied to those features. AI, while capable of recognizing patterns, still falls short in interpreting the emotional context behind what is perceived.

Learning in AI:

Machine learning (ML) is a subset of AI focused on enabling systems to learn from data. There are various forms of machine learning, including supervised learning, unsupervised learning, and reinforcement learning. In supervised learning, AI systems learn from labeled data, making predictions or classifications based on examples provided by humans. In unsupervised learning, AI systems try to find patterns and relationships in data without explicit labels. Reinforcement learning allows systems to learn by interacting with an environment, receiving feedback in the form of rewards or penalties.

While machine learning mimics certain aspects of human learning, it is often limited in its capacity to generalize across tasks. Humans, in contrast, can learn new concepts and apply them flexibly to a wide variety of situations. An AI trained to play chess, for example, would struggle to apply its knowledge to a completely different domain, such as cooking or music. This difference highlights the limitations of current AI systems and their reliance on large amounts of data and specific training environments.

Decision-Making in AI:

AI systems make decisions by analyzing data and following algorithms. Machine learning models, for example, use statistical techniques to predict outcomes based on historical data. AI can excel at tasks where patterns are clear and data is abundant, such as recommending products or diagnosing medical conditions. However, decision-making in AI is limited by the data it receives. Unlike humans, who make decisions based on a combination of reason, intuition, and ethical considerations, AI decisions are based purely on data-driven models that do not take emotions or morals into account.

2.4. Parallels Between Human Cognition and Machine Intelligence

Despite the vast differences between human cognition and machine intelligence, there are fascinating parallels that have emerged as AI has developed. These parallels offer insights into how AI can be used to augment human intelligence and serve as tools to enhance cognitive processes. Let's examine some of the key similarities.

Pattern Recognition:

At the core of both human cognition and machine intelligence lies the ability to recognize patterns. In the human brain, pattern recognition occurs almost instantaneously. When we see a familiar face, for example, we instantly recognize it, even from an unusual angle or in poor lighting. This ability to process and identify patterns helps humans navigate the world with remarkable efficiency. The human brain is particularly adept at recognizing complex patterns, such as emotions or social cues, which often guide our interactions and decision-making.

AI, particularly in the realm of deep learning, excels at recognizing patterns too. Deep neural networks, especially convolutional neural networks (CNNs), are designed to identify patterns in data—whether it's in images, text, or sound. These AI models can be trained to recognize faces, objects, and even complex trends in large datasets. The more data they are exposed to, the better they become at identifying patterns. However, the distinction lies in the fact that AI systems are typically constrained by the data they are trained on. If a pattern is not part of the training set, AI systems can struggle to generalize. Humans, by contrast, can recognize patterns across vastly different contexts and in ways that are often flexible and adaptive.

Learning from Experience:

Both humans and machines learn from experience, but the mechanisms are different in significant ways. Human learning is deeply tied to experiences—emotional, social, sensory, and intellectual. We learn through trial and error, observation, and social interaction. For instance, a child learns not just by being taught but also through interaction with the world, adapting to new situations, and testing hypotheses about how things work. Machine learning, specifically supervised and unsupervised learning, also relies on experience, but the process is fundamentally data-driven. In supervised learning, algorithms learn from labeled datasets, while in unsupervised learning, systems identify patterns in unlabeled data. Reinforcement learning adds another layer, where an AI learns by receiving feedback from its environment and adjusting its behavior accordingly. AI systems can improve their performance based on exposure to more data, but unlike humans, this learning process is more rigid. Machines may excel at performing specific tasks but often struggle to generalize across new, unfamiliar contexts.

Memory Systems:

Memory plays a pivotal role in both human cognition and machine intelligence. In humans, memory is multifaceted, consisting of short-term memory, long-term memory, and working memory, among others. These memory systems allow us to retain and retrieve information, adapt to new situations, and make decisions based on prior experiences. Human memory is not just a storehouse of facts; it is dynamic and influenced by emotions, context, and meaning. We can forget irrelevant details, prioritize information, and retrieve memories based on emotional salience or personal significance.

AI systems, too, have memory—though it works in a fundamentally different way. Machine learning models store learned knowledge in weights and parameters that are updated over time through training. In neural networks, this memory is encoded in the connections between artificial neurons. Some AI systems, like recurrent neural networks (RNNs), are designed to process sequential information, allowing them to "remember" previous inputs in order to make predictions about future ones. However, AI memory is far more limited and precise compared to human memory. While humans can recall memories based on context or emotional triggers,

AI's memory is more mechanical and can only draw from the data it has been trained on.

Adaptability:

Adaptability is one of the key strengths of human cognition. Humans can quickly adjust to new circumstances, learn new skills, and adapt to a wide range of environments. This flexibility allows us to thrive in complex, dynamic situations, from navigating a new city to learning a new language. Our ability to adapt is not only cognitive but emotional and social—humans can adjust their behaviors based on shifting emotional states or social dynamics.

AI, in contrast, can be adapted but in a more limited sense. When new data is introduced, machine learning models can be re-trained or fine-tuned to adjust to the new information. Reinforcement learning allows AI systems to learn from interaction with their environments, enabling them to adapt over time. However, AI is still relatively inflexible compared to human adaptability. Machines can only adapt based on their programming and the data they are exposed to. They lack the general cognitive flexibility that humans demonstrate in adjusting to entirely new situations or environments.

2.5. Key Differences Between Human Cognition and Machine Intelligence

While there are clear parallels between human cognition and machine intelligence, the differences are even more striking. These differences underscore the limits of current AI technology and highlight the unique qualities that make human cognition irreplaceable.

Consciousness:

One of the most significant differences between humans and machines is consciousness. Human cognition is inseparable from our conscious awareness of the world. We experience thoughts, emotions, and sensations in a subjective, first-person way. We can reflect on our thoughts, make self-conscious decisions, and engage in metacognition—thinking about thinking.

AI, on the other hand, is not conscious. Machines do not experience the world; they simply process data. While AI systems can mimic certain aspects of cognition—such as pattern recognition or decision-making—they do so without any understanding or awareness of the implications. A self-driving car might make decisions about navigation, but it has no awareness of the consequences of those decisions, nor does it have any sense of self. The lack of consciousness means that AI systems cannot truly understand or interpret the world in the way humans do.

Emotional Intelligence:

Humans are deeply influenced by emotions, which play a critical role in decision-making, learning, and social interaction. Emotional intelligence allows humans to recognize, understand, and manage their own emotions, as well as empathize with the emotions of others. Emotions inform our judgments, guide our moral decisions, and shape our relationships.

AI, in contrast, does not possess emotional intelligence. While there are attempts to design AI systems that can recognize and respond to emotional cues (such as detecting facial expressions or tone of voice), these systems do not actually feel emotions. An AI may be programmed to recognize a sad face and offer comforting words, but it lacks any true understanding of sadness or empathy. Emotional intelligence is uniquely human, rooted in our biology and psychology.

Creativity and Flexibility:

Humans are capable of profound creativity, not just in artistic expression but in problem-solving, innovation, and thinking outside the box. Human cognition is flexible and abstract. We can generate new ideas, imagine future possibilities, and approach problems from entirely new perspectives. While AI systems can be designed to generate new content—such as composing music, writing poetry, or even generating artwork—these creations are based on patterns learned from data. AI-generated outputs may appear creative, but they lack the spontaneous, unstructured nature of human creativity. AI does not generate ideas independently; it relies on predefined models and algorithms. True creativity in humans involves the ability to draw connections between seemingly unrelated ideas, something that current AI systems cannot replicate on their own.

Common Sense and Context:

Humans possess a deep understanding of context and common sense knowledge. We know, for instance, that a hot stove is dangerous, that we should not interrupt people while they are speaking, or that water flows downhill. These basic, everyday facts are not explicitly taught to us but are instead ingrained through our experiences and socialization. Common sense allows humans to navigate the world effectively, even in novel situations.

AI, by contrast, struggles with common sense. While machine learning models can process vast amounts of data and make predictions, they often lack the broader context that would allow them to apply knowledge in real-world scenarios. An AI system may correctly identify a stove as an object in a kitchen, but it may not understand that the stove could be hot, even if it has been used recently. Similarly, AI systems lack a deep understanding of human social norms and may struggle with tasks that require nuanced judgment or empathy.

Ethical Reasoning:

Humans possess ethical reasoning that informs our decisions. We consider the moral implications of our actions and make judgments based on a variety of factors, including empathy, fairness, and justice. Ethical reasoning is deeply tied to our values, cultural norms, and social context.

AI, however, lacks inherent ethical reasoning. While AI can be programmed with ethical guidelines, it does not have an innate understanding of morality. Decisions made by AI systems are based on algorithms and data, not on ethical principles. This raises important questions about the role of AI in decision-making, especially in areas like healthcare, law enforcement, and autonomous systems, where moral considerations are critical.

2.6. The Limits of Machine Intelligence in Replicating Human Cognition

Despite significant progress in artificial intelligence, the limitations of machine intelligence in replicating human cognition are still glaring. AI has made impressive strides in specialized tasks—such as playing chess, diagnosing diseases, or identifying images—but it falls short when it comes to the breadth and depth of human cognition.

Human cognition is not confined to specific tasks or domains. It is holistic, adaptive, and deeply integrated with our emotions, experiences, and social interactions. Machines, by contrast, are highly specialized. A machine that excels in one domain may struggle to perform in another. For example, a machine trained to play chess cannot simply apply that knowledge to understanding natural language or recognizing emotions in a photograph. The idea of general AI—machines that can perform any intellectual task a human can—is still far from realization. While narrow AI is highly effective in specific contexts, the vision of AI that can match or exceed human general intelligence remains an elusive goal.

2.7. The Future of Human-AI Collaboration

While understanding the differences between human cognition and machine intelligence is essential, it's equally important to explore how these two can complement each other. As AI continues to advance, we are entering an era where human and machine capabilities can work in synergy, creating new possibilities in fields ranging from healthcare to education, business, and beyond.

Enhancing Human Decision-Making:

One of the most promising aspects of AI is its potential to enhance human decision-making. AI systems can process and analyze vast amounts of data at speeds and scales far beyond human capabilities. This can provide valuable insights in situations where human cognition might struggle with information overload. For instance, in medical diagnosis, AI can analyze thousands of medical records to identify patterns that may not be immediately apparent to a doctor. By presenting these insights to medical professionals, AI enhances their decision-making process, allowing them to make more informed choices, faster.

In business, AI-driven analytics can help managers sift through enormous datasets to identify trends, forecast future outcomes, and make data-driven decisions. When humans and AI collaborate in this way, AI serves as a tool to augment cognitive abilities, enabling us to make better, more informed decisions across industries.

Personalized Learning and Education:

AI's ability to personalize education is another exciting area of human-AI collaboration. Traditional education systems often struggle to cater to the unique learning needs of each student. However, AI can tailor learning experiences to individual students by analyzing their performance, identifying areas of weakness, and adapting the material accordingly. This personalized approach ensures that each student progresses at their own pace, receiving the support they need in real-time.

Furthermore, AI-powered tutoring systems can provide students with immediate feedback, allowing them to learn from mistakes and correct misconceptions. In this way, AI does not replace human teachers but rather supports them, allowing educators to focus on fostering creativity, critical thinking, and emotional intelligence in their students.

Creative Collaboration:

AI has also proven to be a powerful tool for creative professionals. In the realms of art, music, and writing, AI can act as a collaborator, generating new ideas or providing inspiration. For instance, AI algorithms can create visual art by learning from existing styles, offering artists new ways to express themselves. In music, AI can generate melodies or harmonies that human musicians can build upon, sparking creative innovation.

This partnership between human creativity and AI capabilities allows for more diverse and dynamic forms of artistic expression. However, it is essential to recognize that while AI can generate new ideas, it does not possess the emotional depth or cultural context that human creators bring to their work. The collaboration between human intuition and machine intelligence enriches the creative process, allowing for a fusion of the best of both worlds.

Complex Problem-Solving:

Many of the most pressing challenges facing humanity today, from climate change to global health crises, require innovative solutions that demand human creativity, empathy, and collaboration. AI has the potential to assist in solving these complex, multidimensional problems by providing powerful tools for analysis and optimization.

For example, AI can model climate change scenarios, helping scientists understand the potential impacts of various interventions. In healthcare, AI can assist researchers in discovering new treatments by identifying patterns in biological data that may go unnoticed by human researchers. In these instances, AI serves as a valuable partner, accelerating progress and offering new insights that humans alone might not uncover.

By working together, humans and AI can tackle challenges that would be insurmountable for either alone. The key lies in recognizing the strengths and limitations of both, ensuring that AI complements human ingenuity, empathy, and creativity.

2.8. Ethical Considerations in Human-AI Collaboration

As AI becomes more integrated into various aspects of human life, it is essential to address the ethical implications of this collaboration. While AI offers numerous benefits, it also raises important questions about fairness, privacy, and accountability.

Bias and Fairness:

One of the most significant ethical concerns in AI is bias. AI systems learn from data, and if the data they are trained on is biased, the AI can inherit and perpetuate those biases. For example, in hiring algorithms, if the training data includes biased hiring decisions, the AI may discriminate against certain demographic groups. In healthcare, biased AI models could lead to unequal access to medical treatments or misdiagnoses for underrepresented groups.

To mitigate these biases, AI developers must ensure that their models are trained on diverse and representative data. It is also crucial to regularly audit AI systems for fairness and transparency, ensuring that they operate without discrimination.

Privacy and Data Security:

As AI systems become more integrated into our lives, they collect vast amounts of personal data. This raises concerns about privacy and data security. It is essential to establish clear guidelines and regulations around how AI systems collect, store, and use data. Individuals must be informed about how their data is being used and must have control over how it is shared. Transparent policies and strong data protection practices will help ensure that AI systems respect user privacy.

Accountability and Transparency:

Another key ethical concern is accountability. When an AI system makes a decision, such as recommending a loan, diagnosing a medical condition, or directing an autonomous vehicle, it is crucial to understand how and why the decision was made. AI systems can often operate as "black boxes," meaning their decision-making processes are opaque and difficult to interpret.

In these cases, accountability becomes a complex issue. Who is responsible when an AI system makes a harmful decision? Is it the developer, the company using the AI, or the AI itself? Clear regulations and guidelines are necessary to ensure that AI systems are transparent and that accountability is maintained.

2.9. The Road Ahead: Integrating AI into Society

The integration of AI into society offers enormous potential, but it also requires careful thought and consideration. As we continue to develop more advanced AI systems, we must ensure that these technologies are designed and used in ways that benefit humanity.

Education and Workforce Development:

As AI becomes more prevalent in the workplace, there will be an increasing demand for workers with the skills to interact with and leverage AI systems. Education will need to adapt to ensure that students are equipped with the necessary technical skills and an understanding of the ethical, social, and philosophical implications of AI. In addition, lifelong learning programs will become essential as the workforce continues to evolve in response to AI-driven change.

Collaboration between Researchers, Policymakers, and Technologists:

The development of AI should not happen in isolation. Collaboration between researchers, policymakers, and technologists is crucial to ensure that AI benefits society as a whole. Ethical guidelines, regulations, and frameworks will need to be established to guide AI development and integration. These frameworks should prioritize human well-being, fairness, and accountability, ensuring that AI technologies are used for the greater good.

Public Engagement and Awareness:

Public understanding of AI is another critical aspect of its successful integration into society. As AI systems become more ubiquitous, it is important that people understand what these technologies can and cannot do. Public engagement and education will help demystify AI, reducing fear and uncertainty and fostering a more informed dialogue about its potential.

2.10. Conclusion

The exploration of human cognition and machine intelligence provides both an exciting glimpse into the future and a reminder of the complexities that lie ahead. While AI systems can replicate certain aspects of human cognition, such as pattern recognition and decision-making, they remain fundamentally different from the human mind in terms of consciousness, creativity, and emotional intelligence.

As we move forward, it is crucial to focus on how AI can complement and enhance human capabilities. By collaborating with AI, humans can address some of the most pressing challenges of our time, from climate change to healthcare. However, this collaboration must be guided by ethical principles that prioritize fairness, transparency, and accountability.

Ultimately, the future of AI lies not in replacing human cognition but in augmenting it—creating a world where both human and machine intelligence work in harmony to solve complex problems and improve the quality of life for all.

Chapter 3: Emotion Recognition in AI Systems

3.1. Introduction to Emotion Recognition in AI

The ability to recognize and interpret human emotions is one of the most fascinating and complex challenges in the development of artificial intelligence (A.I). Historically, machines were designed to perform specific tasks that required logical reasoning or pattern recognition. But as AI systems have evolved, there has been a growing need for these machines to understand the more nuanced aspects of human behavior, such as emotions. This chapter delves into the mechanisms by which AI systems are learning to recognize emotions, explores the various methods they employ, and highlights the challenges and potential applications of emotion recognition technology.

Emotion recognition in AI refers to the ability of machines to detect and interpret human emotions from various cues, including facial expressions, speech, physiological responses, and written text. This capability can significantly enhance human-computer interactions, making them more natural, empathetic, and responsive. While the concept of machines understanding human emotions might seem like science fiction, it is rapidly becoming a reality thanks to advancements in machine learning, natural language processing (NLP), computer vision, and biometrics.

The importance of emotion recognition in AI cannot be overstated. In many areas, from customer service to healthcare and entertainment, the ability to understand human emotions can revolutionize the way we interact with technology. Imagine a virtual assistant that not only responds to your queries but also adjusts its tone based on your emotional state, or a chatbot that can sense when you're frustrated and escalates the issue to a human agent before things worsen. This chapter will explore these possibilities and the technology behind them, as well as the ethical and societal implications.

3.2. How AI Recognizes Human Emotions

Emotion recognition in AI is grounded in the analysis of various types of data. By leveraging sophisticated algorithms and vast datasets, AI can learn to detect emotional cues that humans may express through facial expressions, vocal tones, body language, and written language. The underlying mechanisms that enable emotion recognition often rely on machine learning techniques, particularly supervised and unsupervised learning, which allow AI systems to improve their ability to interpret emotional data over time.

Data Sources for Emotion Recognition: AI systems rely on several types of data to recognize emotions. The most common sources include:

- **Facial Expressions**: The human face is one of the most expressive ways to convey emotion. AI systems can capture facial movements and use them to identify emotions like happiness, sadness, anger, surprise, and disgust. Facial recognition technology uses computer vision to detect facial features and match them to pre-trained models of emotional expressions.

- **Speech and Tone**: The tone of voice can provide a wealth of emotional information. By analyzing speech patterns, pitch, speed, volume, and intonation, AI can detect emotions such as joy, sadness, frustration, or excitement. This technique is often referred to as "prosody analysis."

- **Textual Data**: Sentiment analysis is a widely used method in which AI systems analyze the words, phrases, and structure of written text to determine the sentiment behind it. By identifying key emotional words and phrases, AI can classify text as positive, negative, or neutral and sometimes more specifically as joyful, angry, or sad.

- **Physiological Signals and Body Language**: Biometric sensors, such as those used in wearables, can provide additional data to detect emotions. Changes in heart rate, skin conductivity, and even body posture can reveal how a person is feeling, and when integrated with other data types, they can enhance the accuracy of emotion detection.

Machine Learning and Deep Learning Techniques:
The algorithms behind emotion recognition often rely on machine learning models, particularly deep learning, which allows systems to learn from large datasets and improve their accuracy over time. For example, convolutional neural networks (CNNs) are commonly used for facial expression recognition because of their ability to process image data and detect patterns in facial features.

AI systems learn by being trained on large annotated datasets containing thousands or even millions of labeled emotional examples. These datasets are built using images, audio files, or text, each tagged with the corresponding emotion. The more data these systems have access to, the more accurate their predictions become. Through repeated training, AI can refine its understanding of emotional cues, eventually developing the ability to detect and interpret emotions with remarkable precision.

3.3. Methods of Emotion Recognition in AI

Emotion recognition in AI involves several key methods, each with its own strengths and limitations. Below, we explore the primary methods employed to detect and analyze emotions in humans.

Facial Expression Analysis

One of the most intuitive ways AI recognizes emotions is through facial expressions. The human face has a complex array of muscles that allow individuals to express a wide range of emotions. Six basic emotions—happiness, sadness, anger, surprise, fear, and disgust—are universally recognized across cultures, although the intensity and expression of these emotions can vary.

Computer Vision and Facial Recognition: AI uses computer vision to detect facial features, including the eyes, eyebrows, mouth, and overall facial structure. Machine learning models are trained to identify the slight movements and changes in these features that correspond to different emotions. For example, a smile is associated with happiness, while furrowed brows often signal anger or confusion.

One of the key challenges in facial emotion recognition is the variation in how individuals express emotions. Age, gender, cultural background, and even individual personality can affect how emotions are displayed. To account for these differences, AI models must be trained on diverse datasets that include a wide range of faces and emotional expressions.

Speech and Tone Analysis

The human voice is another powerful indicator of emotional states. Emotional tone is reflected in changes to the pitch, volume, speed, and rhythm of speech. For example, a person speaking in a high-pitched tone may be perceived as anxious or excited, while a slow, deliberate voice might indicate sadness or contemplation.

Acoustic Analysis: AI systems use acoustic analysis to detect these changes and correlate them with specific emotions. By analyzing the frequency and intensity of speech, AI can identify feelings of joy, anger, sadness, or fear. This method is especially effective in real-time applications, such as virtual assistants or customer service bots, where immediate emotional feedback is crucial.

However, speech-based emotion recognition faces several challenges, including the difficulty of accurately detecting emotion in noisy environments, interpreting emotions in languages with less overt prosodic cues, and accounting for cultural variations in speech patterns.

Textual Emotion Recognition

Text-based emotion recognition, or sentiment analysis, is a method used to identify emotions in written communication. It plays a vital role in applications such as customer service, social media analysis, and content moderation. By analyzing the words, syntax, and context of text, AI can determine whether a message conveys a positive, negative, or neutral sentiment.

Natural Language Processing (NLP): At the core of textual emotion recognition is natural language processing, a field of AI that enables machines to understand and generate human language. Sentiment analysis models are trained on vast amounts of text, using algorithms that detect emotional indicators such as keywords (e.g., "happy," "angry," "sad"), punctuation, and sentence structure.

Despite its success, NLP faces challenges, particularly when interpreting complex or ambiguous emotions. For instance, sarcasm, irony, and humor can be difficult for AI to interpret correctly, as they often require deep contextual understanding.

Physiological Signals and Body Language

Physiological signals, such as heart rate, sweat levels, and pupil dilation, provide additional clues about a person's emotional state. Wearable technology, such as fitness trackers and biometric sensors, can collect this data in real time, offering AI systems a deeper understanding of human emotions.

Integrating Body Language: AI also examines body language—such as posture, gestures, and movements—to assess emotions. For instance, crossed arms might indicate defensiveness or discomfort, while a relaxed posture may suggest calmness. By integrating these physical cues with other data sources, AI can achieve a more comprehensive understanding of a person's emotional state.

While this method can be highly accurate, it requires specialized hardware, and its effectiveness can vary depending on the individual's level of awareness or control over their physiological responses.

3.4. Challenges in Emotion Recognition

Despite the progress made in emotion recognition technology, there are several significant challenges that must be overcome for AI systems to reliably and accurately detect human emotions. These challenges stem from the complexity of human emotions, the diversity of emotional expression, and the limitations of current technology. Below are some of the key challenges in emotion recognition for AI systems:

Cultural and Contextual Differences

One of the most notable challenges in emotion recognition is the variation in emotional expressions across cultures and individuals. While certain emotions—such as happiness, sadness, and anger—are universally recognized, the way these emotions are expressed can differ widely. Cultural norms play a significant role in shaping how emotions are conveyed, and this diversity can lead to inaccuracies in emotion detection. For example, in some cultures, showing emotions like anger or frustration in public is considered inappropriate, while in others, these expressions may be more openly displayed. Similarly, a smile may indicate happiness in one culture but could represent discomfort or nervousness in another. AI systems that rely on facial recognition or body language may struggle to accurately interpret emotions without a deep understanding of cultural context.

Moreover, the context in which an emotion is expressed is crucial for its accurate interpretation. A person's emotional state may change depending on their situation, surroundings, or the people they interact with. An AI system that fails to account for the context of an emotional expression might misinterpret the emotion itself. For instance, a person might express frustration in a calm voice because they are in a professional setting, even though they are actually quite upset.

Subjectivity of Emotions

Emotions are inherently subjective, and individuals experience and express them in ways that are deeply personal. This subjectivity presents a challenge for AI systems, which must account for the vast spectrum of emotional experiences that may not always be clearly articulated or expressed in recognizable ways. For example, one person may show signs of anxiety through fidgeting, while another may remain completely still but still be anxious.

The complexity of mixed emotions further compounds this issue. A person may feel both happy and sad at the same time, such as during a bittersweet moment, or they may express multiple emotions in quick succession. AI must not only be able to recognize primary emotions but also understand the subtleties of mixed or fluctuating emotions.

Additionally, emotions are often influenced by internal states, such as hormonal fluctuations or mental health conditions, which can further complicate AI's ability to accurately detect emotions. For instance, someone with depression might express emotions differently than someone with anxiety, even though both may be experiencing emotional distress.

Ethical Concerns

The ability of AI systems to recognize and interpret human emotions raises significant ethical concerns, particularly around privacy, consent, and fairness. The collection of emotional data—whether through facial recognition, speech analysis, or physiological sensors—can be highly invasive. People may be unaware that their emotions are being monitored, and even when they are aware, they may not fully understand the implications of this data being collected.

Privacy and Consent:
Emotion recognition technology relies heavily on data collection, which can raise privacy concerns. In many cases, individuals may not be informed that their emotional expressions are being tracked, which could lead to feelings of vulnerability or mistrust. Even when individuals consent to having their emotions monitored, there is the question of how this data will be used and who will have access to it. There is also the risk of data being misused or exploited for commercial, political, or surveillance purposes.

Bias and Fairness:
Bias is another critical ethical concern in emotion recognition. AI systems are only as good as the data they are trained on, and if the datasets used to train emotion recognition algorithms are not diverse, the system may

fail to accurately recognize emotions in certain populations. For example, AI systems trained primarily on datasets of white, middle-class individuals may have difficulty accurately recognizing emotions in people of different racial or ethnic backgrounds, leading to biased outcomes.

Similarly, AI systems may struggle to interpret emotions in people with disabilities or those who express emotions in non-traditional ways. This could result in unfair treatment or misunderstanding of certain individuals, exacerbating existing societal inequalities. To ensure fairness, it is essential that emotion recognition systems are trained on diverse, representative datasets and that their application is continuously monitored for bias.

Manipulation and Emotional Exploitation:

As AI becomes more adept at recognizing human emotions, there is the potential for emotional manipulation. For example, marketers could use emotion recognition to craft personalized advertisements that exploit an individual's emotional vulnerabilities. Similarly, governments or other entities could use emotion detection systems to influence public opinion or manipulate individuals' emotional states for political gain.

There is also the risk that emotion recognition technology could be used to exploit emotional weaknesses in vulnerable populations, such as those suffering from mental health issues. This highlights the need for strong ethical guidelines and regulations surrounding the use of emotion recognition technology, particularly in sensitive contexts like healthcare and therapy.

3.5. Applications of Emotion Recognition in AI

Despite the challenges, emotion recognition in AI has found numerous applications across a variety of fields. These applications enhance user experiences, improve outcomes in healthcare and customer service, and help create more empathetic, responsive AI systems. Below, we explore some of the most promising and impactful uses of emotion recognition in AI.

Customer Service and Support

One of the most immediate and widespread applications of emotion recognition is in customer service. AI-powered chatbots, virtual assistants, and customer support systems can use emotion recognition to assess the emotional state of customers during interactions. For instance, if a customer expresses frustration or anger, an AI system can detect this emotion through text analysis or speech recognition and escalate the issue to a human agent before it escalates further.

This ability to recognize and respond to emotions in real-time can lead to improved customer satisfaction, as customers feel that their emotional needs are being acknowledged. Additionally, emotion-aware AI systems can adapt their responses to be more empathetic, tailoring their tone and approach based on the emotional state of the user. This creates a more personalized and human-like interaction, which is crucial in building customer trust and loyalty.

Healthcare and Therapy

In the healthcare field, emotion recognition technology is being used to monitor patients' emotional well-being, particularly in mental health care. By analyzing facial expressions, speech patterns, and physiological signals, AI systems can detect early signs of emotional distress, such as depression or anxiety, which may not be immediately obvious to human caregivers.

Emotion recognition systems are also being integrated into telemedicine platforms to provide real-time emotional feedback during virtual therapy sessions. For example, if a therapist's virtual assistant detects that a patient is becoming upset or anxious, it could prompt the therapist to adjust their approach accordingly. In this way, emotion recognition technology can help ensure that therapy remains effective, even in remote settings.

Moreover, AI systems are being used in mental health diagnostics, where detecting subtle changes in emotional expression could help identify individuals at risk of developing mental health conditions. AI can play a vital role in providing continuous monitoring for patients, allowing for early intervention and better mental health management.

Marketing and Consumer Behavior

Emotion recognition in AI has also made waves in marketing, where companies use the technology to better understand consumer sentiment and tailor their marketing efforts accordingly. By analyzing consumers' facial expressions, vocal tones, or social media posts, businesses can gain insights into how people are emotionally responding to advertisements, products, or services.

This emotional feedback allows brands to create more targeted, emotionally resonant campaigns that appeal to their audience's feelings and desires. For instance, a company might analyze how viewers react emotionally to a commercial, adjusting its content or tone based on the observed emotional responses. Additionally, AI-powered emotion recognition can help businesses track customer satisfaction, enabling them to fine-tune their strategies in real time.

Autonomous Systems

Emotion recognition is also being integrated into autonomous systems, such as self-driving cars and robots, to enhance human interaction and safety. In autonomous vehicles, AI systems can analyze the emotional state of the driver to detect signs of stress, fatigue, or distraction. For instance, if a driver appears anxious or exhausted, the system could alert them to take a break or offer calming suggestions to improve their focus and well-being.

In the context of robotics, emotion recognition can help create more empathetic robots that interact with humans in a socially intelligent way. For example, robots designed to assist the elderly or those with disabilities can use emotion recognition to assess the emotional state of the person they are interacting with and adapt their responses accordingly. This makes the interaction more comfortable and supportive, improving the overall experience.

3.6. Future Directions of Emotion Recognition in AI

As AI continues to evolve, the field of emotion recognition is poised for rapid advancements. While current systems have made significant strides in detecting basic emotions, the future promises even more sophisticated and nuanced capabilities. These developments will likely be driven by innovations in machine learning, multimodal data integration, and human-centered design. In this section, we explore the potential future directions of emotion recognition in AI, focusing on enhanced accuracy, new applications, and the ethical considerations that will accompany these advancements.

Multimodal Emotion Recognition

One of the key trends in the future of emotion recognition is the integration of multimodal data. Currently, many emotion recognition systems rely on a single source of input—such as facial expressions, speech, or text. However, emotions are complex and multifaceted, and no single data source can capture the full range of human emotional experience. The future of emotion recognition will likely involve combining multiple modalities—facial expression analysis, speech prosody, text sentiment analysis, and physiological signals—into a unified system that provides a more accurate and holistic understanding of emotional states.

For example, if a system detects a person's facial expression showing signs of sadness, it could corroborate that information with the tone of their voice, their speech content, and physiological signals (like heart rate or skin conductivity) to confirm that they are indeed feeling sad. This approach would reduce the likelihood of misinterpretation and improve the overall effectiveness of emotion recognition systems.

Context-Aware Emotion Recognition

As mentioned earlier, understanding the context in which emotions are expressed is crucial for accurate interpretation. The next generation of emotion recognition systems will likely become more context-aware, taking into account not only the emotional cues themselves but also the surrounding circumstances that influence emotional expression.

For instance, an AI system might be able to assess whether a person is smiling because they are genuinely happy or because they are engaging in polite social behavior. By considering factors like location, social setting, and recent events, AI could develop a deeper understanding of the emotional context and respond more appropriately.

In addition, AI systems could become better at recognizing the dynamic nature of emotions. Instead of simply classifying emotions into discrete categories (e.g., happy, sad, angry), future systems might be able to track shifts in emotional states over time, identifying patterns and offering insights into emotional trends. This would be particularly valuable in contexts like mental health care, where monitoring emotional fluctuations can be crucial for understanding an individual's emotional well-being.

Emotion Recognition in Virtual and Augmented Reality

Another exciting frontier for emotion recognition technology is its integration with virtual reality (VR) and augmented reality (AR). As VR and AR technologies continue to gain traction in fields such as entertainment, education, and training, emotion recognition could play a significant role in creating more immersive and emotionally resonant experiences.

In virtual environments, AI systems could analyze users' emotional reactions to various stimuli in real-time and adapt the experience accordingly. For instance, in a VR-based therapy session, an AI system could detect signs of distress in a patient's facial expressions or voice and adjust the content or pace of the session to alleviate anxiety. Similarly, in gaming, emotion recognition could be used to create dynamic storylines that respond to players' emotional engagement, leading to a more personalized and immersive experience.

Additionally, in AR applications, emotion recognition could be used to enhance user interactions with the real world. For example, a virtual assistant could detect that a user is frustrated by a task and offer help or adjust its responses to provide a more soothing, supportive interaction. This would elevate the user experience by making technology feel more intuitive and responsive.

Ethical Guidelines and Regulation

As emotion recognition technology becomes more advanced and widespread, it will be essential to establish clear ethical guidelines and regulations to protect users' privacy and rights. The ability of AI systems to track and analyze emotional data raises significant concerns about surveillance, manipulation, and discrimination. Therefore, it will be crucial for governments, regulatory bodies, and industry leaders to collaborate in creating ethical frameworks that address these challenges.

One of the primary ethical considerations is the issue of consent. Users must be informed when their emotional data is being collected, and they should have the option to opt-out of this data collection if they choose. Moreover, clear guidelines should be established on how emotional data can be used and who has access to it. For example, businesses may not be allowed to use emotion recognition data to manipulate consumer behavior without explicit consent.

Another ethical issue is the potential for emotional data to be misused in ways that harm vulnerable individuals or communities. As AI systems become more adept at detecting emotions, there is the risk that individuals with mental health conditions, for example, could be unfairly targeted or manipulated by companies or organizations seeking to profit from their emotional vulnerabilities. Ethical guidelines should be designed to protect these individuals and ensure that emotion recognition technology is used in ways that promote well-being and social good.

Additionally, transparency in AI decision-making will be crucial. Users must understand how AI systems interpret their emotions and what actions those systems may take based on their emotional data. Ensuring that emotion recognition systems are explainable and accountable will be vital to maintaining public trust and ensuring that these technologies are used responsibly.

3.7. Conclusion

Emotion recognition in AI represents a profound leap forward in how machines understand and interact with humans. By giving AI the ability to detect and interpret human emotions, we open up new possibilities for more empathetic, responsive, and personalized human-computer interactions. From healthcare and customer service to entertainment and autonomous systems, emotion recognition technology has the potential to enhance our daily lives in ways that were once unimaginable.

However, as we continue to develop and deploy emotion recognition systems, it is essential to remain mindful of the challenges and ethical considerations that accompany this technology. From cultural and contextual differences to privacy concerns and the risk of bias, emotion recognition in AI is not without its complexities. As we move toward a future where AI systems are better equipped to understand and respond to human emotions, it will be crucial to strike a balance between technological progress and ethical responsibility.

Looking ahead, emotion recognition in AI will likely become an integral part of many applications, helping machines and humans communicate in more nuanced, empathetic ways. With continued research, innovation, and thoughtful regulation, AI can harness the power of emotional intelligence to improve the way we interact with technology and each other.

Chapter 4: Behavioral Predictions: How AI Reads Us

4.1. Introduction to Behavioral Predictions

In an era defined by data, one of the most fascinating and powerful capabilities of artificial intelligence (A.I) is its ability to predict human behavior. From understanding our buying habits to foreseeing how we might respond in social or professional situations, AI systems are increasingly able to offer predictions that seem almost eerily accurate. But what makes these predictions possible? How do AI systems "read" us, and how reliable are their conclusions?

At its core, behavioral prediction refers to the use of data-driven models to forecast future human actions based on past behavior and other contextual variables. The realm of behavioral predictions extends across a variety of sectors, including marketing, healthcare, finance, security, and beyond. Through the power of machine learning algorithms, AI is able to sift through vast amounts of data, discerning patterns, relationships, and trends that would otherwise remain hidden to the human eye.

AI's ability to predict behavior isn't just a scientific curiosity—it's becoming a driving force in shaping our interactions with technology, the decisions we make, and even the way businesses and governments engage with us. Yet, this ability to predict human behavior also raises significant questions: What are the implications of these predictions on our autonomy, privacy, and society at large? Can AI truly understand the complexity of human behavior, or is it simply an advanced form of guesswork? And perhaps most importantly, how do we ensure that AI's power to predict is used ethically? This chapter seeks to examine how AI reads us—how it predicts our behaviors, what data it uses, and the techniques that power these predictions. We'll explore the ways in which AI analyzes behavioral data, from simple consumer habits to complex emotional and social dynamics. We will also delve into the ethical considerations surrounding these predictions, offering insight into how these technologies are reshaping our world.

4.2. Foundations of Behavioral Data

To understand how AI can predict human behavior, it's crucial to first grasp the concept of behavioral data itself. Human behavior is multifaceted, influenced by emotions, cognitive processes, societal norms, and a host of other factors. Yet, despite its complexity, human behavior is not entirely random. Patterns emerge, and these patterns can often be quantified through data.

Understanding Human Behavior

Human behavior is the result of an intricate web of internal and external factors. Internally, our emotions, thoughts, and psychological states shape our actions. Externally, societal pressures, environmental factors, and social interactions play a huge role in how we behave in different situations. Predicting human behavior, therefore, requires understanding not only these individual elements but also how they interact.

For instance, a person's decision to purchase a particular item may be influenced by a range of factors: their emotional state, the time of day, their past purchasing history, and even external factors like advertisements or social media trends. AI systems aim to understand these complex webs of causality to predict future actions.

Types of Behavioral Data

AI systems rely on several types of behavioral data to make predictions. These can be broadly categorized into:

- **Transactional Data**: This includes purchase history, browsing behavior, and other actions related to consumer behavior. For example, if someone frequently buys fitness-related products, an

AI system might predict that they will continue making similar purchases in the future.

- **Psychological and Physiological Data**: This includes data gathered through wearables, sensors, and other technologies that track physical responses like heart rate, sleep patterns, and even facial expressions. This type of data can give insights into an individual's emotional and psychological state, which can be factored into predictions about future actions or needs.

- **Social and Contextual Data**: Social interactions and contextual information—such as the time and place of an action or what is happening in the user's life at a given moment—can also be valuable sources of behavioral data. This includes data from social media platforms, text messages, and online communications.

Data Collection Methods

Behavioral data collection has come a long way. The advent of the internet, mobile devices, and connected technologies like smart homes and wearables has created an unprecedented opportunity to collect detailed, real-time data on human behavior.

- **Social Media**: Platforms like Facebook, Instagram, and Twitter provide vast amounts of data about people's emotions, preferences, and social interactions. AI algorithms can analyze these data points to predict behavior, such as how likely someone is to respond to an advertisement or share certain content.

- **Wearables and IoT Devices**: Devices like smartwatches, fitness trackers, and home assistants (e.g., Amazon's Alexa, Google Home) track a wide range of activities—sleep, physical exercise, daily routines, and even moods. This data is invaluable for predicting behavior related to health, fitness, and lifestyle choices.

● **Surveys and Interaction Data**: Direct interactions with users, such as surveys or customer service chat logs, are another critical source of behavioral data. These interactions often provide more explicit insights into people's preferences, attitudes, and intentions.

Together, these sources of data help AI systems form a comprehensive picture of human behavior, enabling more accurate predictions.

4.3. AI and Machine Learning Techniques in Predicting Behavior

The ability of AI to predict human behavior is primarily powered by machine learning (ML) techniques, which allow the system to learn patterns from historical data. These techniques range from basic supervised learning to more advanced methods like reinforcement learning, each with its own strengths and applications.

Supervised Learning

Supervised learning is perhaps the most common method used in behavioral prediction. In supervised learning, an AI system is trained on a labeled dataset—data that includes both input features (such as age, location, or previous purchase behavior) and the corresponding outcomes (such as the purchase of a product or attendance at a specific event). The system learns from these examples to make predictions about future behavior based on new, unseen data.

For example, a retail company might use supervised learning to predict whether a customer will purchase a particular item based on their previous purchasing habits. The system is trained on past customer data and learns to recognize patterns that indicate a likelihood of purchase.

Unsupervised Learning

In situations where labeled data is not available, unsupervised learning techniques are employed. Unsupervised learning algorithms analyze data without predefined labels, searching for hidden patterns or groupings within the data. These patterns can then be used to make predictions about future behavior.

For instance, clustering algorithms can group customers into segments based on similarities in their behavior, such as people who are likely to buy the same types of products or people who engage in similar social activities. This segmentation can help companies target specific customer groups with tailored marketing strategies.

Reinforcement Learning

Reinforcement learning (RL) is another key technique used in behavioral prediction, particularly when predicting actions that occur in dynamic environments. In reinforcement learning, an AI system learns through trial and error, receiving feedback in the form of rewards or penalties based on its actions. This technique is particularly useful for predicting decisions that involve a sequence of actions over time, such as how a user might navigate a website or make purchasing decisions across multiple touchpoints.

For example, RL can be applied to recommendation engines that suggest products to users based on their past interactions. Over time, the system learns what types of recommendations lead to successful conversions and adjusts its behavior accordingly.

Natural Language Processing (NLP)

Natural Language Processing (NLP) allows AI to analyze and understand human language, whether in the form of text, speech, or other forms of communication. By analyzing written or spoken language, AI systems can gain insights into people's thoughts, emotions, and intentions.

For instance, sentiment analysis—an NLP technique—can be used to assess whether a customer's feedback is positive or negative. Based on this analysis, the AI system can predict how likely the customer is to make a repeat purchase or recommend the product to others.

4.4. Predicting Human Behavior in Different Contexts

As AI's ability to predict behavior has advanced, its applications have become increasingly diverse. Today, AI is used in multiple contexts—consumer behavior, healthcare, social interactions, and even workplace dynamics. Let's examine some of these fields and see how AI-driven predictions are reshaping each.

Consumer Behavior

One of the most prominent areas where AI excels in behavioral predictions is in consumer behavior. Retailers and businesses are leveraging AI to forecast what products consumers will buy, when they will buy them, and even how much they are willing to pay. By analyzing vast quantities of transactional data, AI systems can make highly accurate predictions about future purchases and preferences.

Recommendation Systems: Many e-commerce giants, such as Amazon and Netflix, use recommendation engines powered by machine learning to suggest products or media based on a customer's previous behavior. These systems can also predict what a customer is likely to purchase next or even when they are likely to make a purchase, allowing businesses to time promotions and advertisements effectively.

For instance, if a customer frequently browses fitness equipment, the AI system might predict they are in the market for new workout gear and show them targeted ads for new products. If a customer watches a lot of romantic comedies, a streaming service like Netflix will suggest similar films based on the user's preferences. These personalized experiences are powered by sophisticated AI algorithms that analyze not just past behavior, but also patterns from similar customers to predict future actions.

Customer Retention: Predictive AI models can also help businesses anticipate when a customer may be about to stop using a product or service. Through behavioral patterns such as reduced website visits, lower engagement, or past cancellation history, AI can identify "at-risk" customers and prompt companies to intervene with personalized offers or support.

Healthcare

In the healthcare sector, AI's predictive abilities are transforming patient care. AI systems are used to analyze patient history, genetic data, and even real-time health metrics to forecast future health risks and guide treatment plans. These predictions can help doctors take proactive measures, improving health outcomes while reducing costs.

Predicting Patient Behavior: One major application of AI in healthcare is predicting patient adherence to treatment plans. AI systems analyze data such as appointment attendance, prescription refills, and even behavioral indicators like social media posts to determine the likelihood that a patient will follow their prescribed treatment. For instance, AI may predict that a diabetic patient is at risk of not taking their medication regularly based on patterns such as missed appointments or failure to refill prescriptions. This prediction can trigger alerts to healthcare providers, allowing them to intervene early and help the patient stay on track with their treatment.

Preventive Healthcare: Beyond individual behavior, AI is also used to predict public health trends and outbreaks. By analyzing large datasets—ranging from vaccination rates to patterns of symptoms reported in emergency rooms—AI can forecast the spread of diseases and recommend preventive measures. For instance, predictive models have been used to forecast flu seasons, helping healthcare providers prepare for demand spikes and allocate resources more effectively.

Social Behavior

AI is increasingly being used to predict and analyze social behavior, particularly in the realm of social media and digital communication. By monitoring and analyzing online interactions, AI can not only predict individual actions but also broader social trends and group behaviors.

Social Media Analysis: Platforms like Facebook, Twitter, and Instagram provide a treasure trove of data that AI systems can use to analyze individual user behavior. AI algorithms analyze user activity, comments, likes, and shares to predict future posts or content preferences. These predictions are valuable for businesses that want to target specific audiences with ads or promotional content, but they can also be used to predict broader social trends.

For example, AI systems can analyze patterns in online discussions about political events or social movements, forecasting public opinion shifts. By tracking the sentiment and frequency of certain keywords or hashtags, these systems can predict how public sentiment may change over time and how different groups might react to emerging events.

Group Behavior and Trends: Beyond individual behavior, AI can predict collective social behaviors, such as the spread of information or the formation of trends. This is especially relevant in areas like marketing, where businesses need to anticipate the direction of popular trends in order to capitalize on them early. If an AI system detects a growing trend in a particular type of fashion or lifestyle, it can predict that this trend will soon be mainstream, guiding companies to develop products and campaigns that align with these predictions.

Workplace Behavior

In the workplace, AI's ability to predict human behavior can help businesses optimize their workforce and improve employee satisfaction. By analyzing various data points—ranging from employee performance to social interactions—AI systems can offer valuable insights into how employees are likely to perform, which teams will work well together, and even which individuals are at risk of burnout or leaving the company.

Employee Performance: AI can analyze employee performance data, such as productivity metrics, attendance, and historical performance reviews, to predict future outcomes. For example, AI can identify patterns indicating that an employee is likely to excel in a particular role or that a team is likely to achieve success in an upcoming project. This can help managers make data-driven decisions about assignments, promotions, or potential career development opportunities.

Employee Retention: Predictive models can also be used to forecast employee turnover. By analyzing historical data about employees who left the company, AI can identify patterns related to job satisfaction, work-life balance, and career growth opportunities. For instance, if employees in a particular department are leaving at a higher-than-average rate, AI could flag this as a potential issue, prompting management to investigate further and take preventive measures.

4.5. Ethical Considerations in Behavioral Predictions

While the potential for AI to predict human behavior offers exciting opportunities, it also raises significant ethical concerns. The ability to predict how we will behave or what decisions we will make touches on deep questions about privacy, autonomy, and fairness.

Privacy and Data Security

The collection of data necessary to predict human behavior inevitably raises concerns about privacy. AI systems require vast amounts of personal data to make accurate predictions—whether it's data from social media, wearable devices, or medical records. This data is often deeply personal, revealing intimate details about an individual's lifestyle, health, and emotions.

The ethical question arises: who owns this data, and how can it be used responsibly? While companies can use data to provide better services and products, there is a risk that personal information could be exploited for commercial gain or, worse, fall into the wrong hands due to data breaches or inadequate security measures.

Regulations such as the General Data Protection Regulation (GDPR) in Europe attempt to address some of these concerns by setting clear guidelines on how personal data should be handled. However, questions about data ownership, transparency, and informed consent continue to be debated.

Bias and Fairness

Another pressing ethical issue is the potential for bias in behavioral prediction models. AI systems are only as good as the data they are trained on, and if that data is biased, the predictions will be biased as well. For example, if an AI model is trained on data from a specific demographic—say, young urban consumers—its predictions may not generalize well to older or rural populations, leading to discriminatory outcomes.

To mitigate bias, AI developers must ensure that training datasets are diverse and representative of all relevant demographic groups. Moreover, efforts must be made to regularly audit and test AI systems for fairness, ensuring that they do not unfairly disadvantage certain groups of people.

Manipulation and Autonomy

AI's ability to predict human behavior also raises concerns about manipulation. For example, if companies use predictive models to anticipate consumer behavior, they may use this information to manipulate customers into making purchases they wouldn't otherwise make. Similarly, political campaigns could use predictive models to target vulnerable voters with highly personalized messages that play on their emotions and biases.

This introduces a question of autonomy: if AI systems can predict our behavior with high accuracy, to what extent does that limit our freedom of choice? Do we retain control over our decisions, or are we merely following a path that has been mapped out for us by machines?

Regulation and Oversight

Given the potential ethical concerns surrounding behavioral prediction, it is essential that governments and regulatory bodies put in place safeguards. These could include clear guidelines on data usage, requirements for transparency in AI decision-making, and protocols for addressing potential harm caused by AI predictions.

As AI systems become more integrated into everyday life, creating a robust framework for the ethical use of these technologies will be crucial in maintaining public trust and ensuring that AI serves society in a fair and beneficial manner.

4.6. The Future of Behavioral Predictions in AI

The future of behavioral prediction in AI is bright, but it also presents significant challenges and opportunities. As AI systems become more sophisticated, they will be able to predict human behavior with ever-increasing accuracy, offering new possibilities for businesses, healthcare providers, governments, and individuals.

Advancements in Predictive Accuracy

The accuracy of behavioral predictions is expected to improve significantly in the coming years. As AI systems are exposed to larger datasets and more diverse data sources, they will be able to make predictions that are more nuanced and tailored to individual behaviors. The integration of AI with other technologies, such as the Internet of Things (IoT) and augmented reality (AR), will allow for even more precise predictions.

The Role of Emotional and Cognitive Factors

The future of behavioral predictions will also see a greater emphasis on understanding the emotional and cognitive factors that drive human behavior. AI systems will increasingly analyze not just physical actions but also psychological states, allowing for more accurate predictions of how people will behave in emotionally charged or complex situations.

Integration with Other Technologies

AI-driven behavioral predictions will also be integrated with other emerging technologies, creating new possibilities for personalized experiences. For example, AI could predict a user's needs in a smart home environment, adjusting temperature, lighting, and even entertainment options based on the user's mood and behavior. Similarly, predictive AI in healthcare could allow for more personalized treatment plans, adjusting recommendations based on how a patient responds to previous treatments.

The Balance Between Prediction and Free Will

As AI continues to refine its ability to predict human behavior, questions about free will and autonomy will become even more pressing. How much control do we retain over our actions when machines can predict and influence our decisions? These philosophical questions will be central to the ongoing debate about the role of AI in society and the ethical implications of predictive technologies.

4.7. Conclusion

AI's ability to predict human behavior is one of its most powerful and transformative features. By analyzing vast amounts of data, AI systems can forecast future actions with remarkable accuracy, providing valuable insights into consumer behavior, healthcare, social dynamics, and workplace trends. However, the rise of behavioral prediction also brings with it significant ethical concerns related to privacy, bias, and manipulation.

As AI continues to evolve, it will be essential to balance the incredible potential of predictive technologies with responsible and ethical practices

. Ensuring that AI serves the best interests of society requires thoughtful regulation, transparency, and ongoing reflection on the moral and philosophical implications of this technology.

Ultimately, AI's ability to predict human behavior offers a window into the future, providing a glimpse of a world where our actions, decisions, and desires are understood in ever-greater detail by the machines we create. Whether this future will be one of empowerment or exploitation depends on how we choose to navigate the challenges and opportunities that lie ahead.

Chapter 5: Human Bias in AI Systems

5.1. Introduction to Human Bias in AI

Bias is an inherent feature of human psychology—shaping our perceptions, judgments, and actions. From early childhood, we are taught to make sense of the world by drawing from a limited set of experiences. While these mental shortcuts help us navigate complex environments, they also create patterns of prejudice, favoritism, and even discrimination. Human bias has always been a part of social dynamics, but with the advent of Artificial Intelligence (A.I), this issue has evolved into a major societal concern.

AI, in its quest to mimic human intelligence, learns from data generated by human behavior. The very data that trains AI systems often reflects the biases embedded in society—be it through historical inequalities or unconscious preferences. AI systems, although non-human in nature, can thus inherit and perpetuate human biases, creating outcomes that can negatively impact marginalized communities, perpetuate stereotypes, and reinforce existing societal disparities.

In this chapter, we will examine how human bias influences AI systems, how biases in human psychology can shape AI outcomes, and the wide-reaching implications of these biases for ethics, fairness, and society at large. Understanding the roots of bias in AI is not just a technical concern—it is a moral imperative. As AI technologies increasingly govern decision-making in areas such as hiring, healthcare, criminal justice, and beyond, the potential consequences of biased AI systems demand immediate attention.

5.2. Types of Bias in AI

AI systems, like their human counterparts, can exhibit a range of biases, often resulting from the way they are designed, trained, and implemented. To understand the complexities of bias in AI, we must first break down the types of biases that can occur.

5.2.1. Data Bias

At the heart of AI's ability to function lies the data it is trained on. Data is the lifeblood of AI systems—without it, these systems would be incapable of learning or making predictions. However, if the data used to train AI systems is biased, the resulting outputs will inevitably reflect those biases. Data bias is one of the most common types of bias found in AI, and it can stem from a variety of sources.

- **Historical Data**: One of the most significant contributors to data bias is historical data, which often carries the weight of societal inequalities. For example, if an AI system is trained on hiring data from a company that has historically discriminated against women or people of color, the AI is likely to replicate those biased hiring decisions. Similarly, if an AI algorithm is trained on criminal justice data from a system that has shown bias against certain racial groups, the AI may perpetuate those same biases when making decisions about parole or sentencing.

- **Sampling Bias**: Sampling bias occurs when the data used to train AI systems is not representative of the population it is meant to serve. For example, a facial recognition system trained on predominantly white faces will struggle to identify individuals with darker skin tones, leading to inaccuracies and potential harm. Similarly, if an AI system used in healthcare is primarily trained on data from one demographic group, it may not accurately predict health outcomes for people from different racial or socio-economic backgrounds.

- **Labeling Bias**: Labeling bias arises when the human annotators tasked with labeling data bring their own biases into the process. For example, if a set of images is labeled by humans with cultural or racial biases, the AI will learn to associate those biases with certain categories. This is particularly problematic in areas like sentiment analysis, where human emotions are subjective, and the labels assigned to data can be influenced by the annotators' own experiences and preconceptions.

5.2.2. Algorithmic Bias

Even when the data is as unbiased as possible, biases can still emerge from the algorithms used to process that data. Algorithmic bias refers to the ways in which the mathematical models and decision-making frameworks that power AI systems can produce biased outcomes. This type of bias is often a result of the design choices made by developers or the limitations of the algorithms themselves.

- **Model Assumptions**: Algorithms often make assumptions based on the data they are trained on. If the assumptions embedded in an algorithm are faulty or overly simplistic, they can result in biased outcomes. For example, an algorithm designed to predict job performance may assume that all candidates are equally likely to have had the same opportunities in their careers, ignoring the impact of systemic inequalities such as gender, race, or class.

- **Optimization Goals**: Many AI algorithms are optimized to maximize certain outcomes, such as accuracy or profit. However, this can lead to biased outcomes if the optimization goal does not take fairness or diversity into account. For instance, a recommendation algorithm that optimizes for user engagement may end up favoring content that is sensational or polarizing, reinforcing existing stereotypes and biases in media consumption.

- **Opaque Decision-Making**: Some AI systems, particularly those powered by deep learning models, operate in ways that are not easily interpretable by humans. This lack of transparency—often referred to as the "black box" problem—means that even if biases are present in an algorithm, it can be difficult to identify and correct them. The opacity of these systems raises concerns about accountability, as it may be unclear who is responsible for biased decisions made by AI.

5.2.3. Feedback Loops and Amplification

Once AI systems are deployed, they can create feedback loops that reinforce and amplify existing biases. This occurs when biased predictions or decisions made by AI systems influence future data, which, in turn, perpetuates the cycle of bias.

- **Reinforcing Bias in Predictive Policing**: In the criminal justice system, predictive policing algorithms use historical crime data to predict where crimes are most likely to occur. However, if these algorithms are trained on biased data from neighborhoods with disproportionately high arrest rates among minority communities, they may predict that these areas are at higher risk for crime, leading to more policing in these areas. This, in turn, can lead to more arrests in those communities, creating a feedback loop that further skews the data and perpetuates the bias.

- **Algorithmic Bias in Hiring**: Similarly, algorithms used in hiring can create feedback loops that favor certain groups over others. For example, if an AI system is trained on data from previous hiring decisions that favored male candidates, the system may predict that male candidates are more likely to succeed in the role, leading to more male hires and further reinforcing the bias.

5.2.4. Cognitive Biases in Humans and Their Impact on AI

Human cognitive biases are deeply ingrained psychological patterns that affect how we perceive and interpret information. These biases can significantly influence the development and deployment of AI systems.

- **Confirmation Bias**: Confirmation bias occurs when individuals search for or interpret information in a way that confirms their pre-existing beliefs or assumptions. In the context of AI, this can manifest when developers or data scientists inadvertently select or emphasize data that supports their preconceived notions, leading to biased AI systems. For example, if a developer believes that a certain demographic group is more likely to commit crimes, they may subconsciously design an AI system that is more likely to flag individuals from that group.

- **Implicit Bias**: Implicit bias refers to the subconscious associations we make about people based on their race, gender, age, or other characteristics. In AI development, implicit bias can affect how data is labeled, how algorithms are designed, and how results are interpreted. For example, an AI system trained on biased data may not be able to identify or address the needs of marginalized groups, leading to unfair outcomes.

- **Attribution Bias**: Attribution bias occurs when we make assumptions about the causes of other people's behavior. This bias can influence AI systems when they make judgments about human actions. For example, if an AI system is used to assess job performance, it may attribute poor performance to personal characteristics, such as laziness, rather than to external factors such as systemic inequalities or lack of resources.

5.3. The Psychological Roots of Bias in AI

Human biases are not just abstract concepts—they are deeply rooted in our psychology. Our minds are wired to make judgments quickly and efficiently, which often means relying on mental shortcuts. While these cognitive shortcuts, or heuristics, can be useful for navigating a complex world, they also lead to systematic errors in thinking. These errors often manifest as biases, influencing how we interact with others and how we process information.

When it comes to AI systems, these psychological biases—whether conscious or unconscious—can creep into the development process and the data collection phase, shaping the outputs of machine learning models. To understand how bias enters AI systems, we must look at the cognitive biases that influence human behavior and decision-making.

5.3.1. Cognitive Biases in Humans

Our minds are shaped by a range of cognitive biases that affect the way we perceive reality. These biases affect our judgment, memory, and decision-making, and they are often subtle and unconscious. Some of the most influential cognitive biases that impact AI development are:

- **Confirmation Bias:**

This bias refers to the tendency to search for, interpret, and remember information in a way that confirms pre-existing beliefs. Developers working on AI systems may unintentionally select data that supports their assumptions, thus reinforcing biases within the model. For example, if an AI system is designed to predict success in a particular field, and the developer believes that one demographic is more likely to succeed, they may subconsciously prioritize data from that demographic, skewing the model's predictions.

- **Anchoring Bias:**

Anchoring bias occurs when people rely too heavily on the first piece of information they receive when making decisions. In the context of AI, this bias can impact the training of machine learning models. For example, if a certain feature of the data (such as gender or ethnicity) is given disproportionate weight during training, the AI system may anchor its predictions based on that feature, leading to biased outcomes.

- **Implicit Bias:**

Implicit bias refers to the unconscious attitudes or stereotypes that influence our perceptions and actions. In AI, implicit bias can manifest in both the data collection process and algorithmic design. If the individuals who collect or label data bring their own biases into the process, these biases are reflected in the training data, ultimately impacting the AI's decision-making.

- **Attribution Bias:**

This bias happens when we attribute other people's actions to their personality or inherent traits, rather than considering external factors. In AI systems, attribution bias can affect the way the model interprets human behavior. For example, an AI used for employee performance evaluation might attribute poor performance to a lack of ability, ignoring factors like systemic discrimination or lack of opportunity.

5.3.2. Unconscious Bias in Data Annotation

Human annotators are often tasked with labeling data that will be used to train AI systems. These annotators are not immune to the biases that shape human cognition. Unconscious bias in data annotation can have a profound impact on the AI system's ability to accurately understand and process data.

- **Cultural Bias:**

Data annotators come from different cultural backgrounds, and their interpretations of data may be influenced by cultural norms or stereotypes. For example, a facial recognition system may struggle to accurately identify individuals from diverse cultural backgrounds if the annotators labeling the data do not account for cultural nuances in facial expressions or behaviors.

- **Gender and Racial Bias:**

Gender and racial biases are among the most common forms of unconscious bias that influence data labeling. In the context of image recognition, for instance, annotators may be more likely to label images of women with certain stereotypical tags, such as "emotional" or "nurturing," which can lead to biased outcomes when the AI system is deployed.

- **Class and Socioeconomic Bias:**

The socioeconomic status of data annotators may also influence the way they label data. For instance, if annotators come from affluent backgrounds, they may unintentionally overlook the challenges faced by individuals from lower-income communities, leading to skewed data that doesn't represent the full spectrum of human experiences.

5.3.3. Bias in Decision-Making Processes

AI systems are designed to assist in decision-making, but they are not immune to the biases that affect human decision-makers. The biases inherent in human cognition can be transferred to AI systems at various stages of their development and deployment.

- **Confirmation Bias in Algorithm Design:**

Developers may unintentionally design algorithms that reflect their own beliefs or expectations. For instance, a hiring algorithm might prioritize candidates with resumes that closely match the company's existing workforce demographics, even if such preferences are not explicitly stated. This can result in discrimination against qualified candidates from underrepresented groups.

- **Bias in User Behavior:**

User behavior itself can introduce bias into AI systems. For example, if users of an AI-powered recommendation system consistently click on content that reinforces their own views or preferences, the AI will learn to prioritize similar content, perpetuating existing biases and limiting exposure to diverse perspectives.

● **Selection Bias in Training Data:**

Selection bias occurs when the data used to train an AI model is not representative of the population it is meant to serve. For example, if an AI system is trained on data from a specific geographic region or demographic group, it may fail to make accurate predictions for individuals outside of that group. This is particularly concerning in areas like healthcare, where biases in training data can result in poor outcomes for underrepresented populations.

5.4. Case Studies of Bias in AI Systems

Understanding bias in AI is not just an abstract concept—it has real-world consequences. Throughout various industries, AI systems have demonstrated biased outcomes that disproportionately affect certain groups. Let's explore some notable case studies that illustrate the impact of human bias on AI systems.

5.4.1. Racial Bias in Facial Recognition

Facial recognition technology has become increasingly widespread in applications such as security, law enforcement, and even consumer electronics. However, research has shown that these systems exhibit significant racial bias, misidentifying people of color at higher rates than white individuals.

In 2018, a study by the MIT Media Lab found that commercial facial recognition systems from major tech companies performed much worse on dark-skinned and female faces. For instance, the algorithm used by IBM's facial recognition system misidentified dark-skinned women with an error rate of over 34%, compared to just 1.5% for light-skinned men.

This racial bias is rooted in the fact that the training datasets used to develop these facial recognition algorithms are often skewed toward lighter-skinned faces. As a result, the AI systems are not trained to accurately recognize individuals from diverse racial and ethnic backgrounds. This disparity has serious implications for fairness and equality, especially in areas like law enforcement, where biased facial recognition systems can lead to wrongful arrests or surveillance of marginalized communities.

5.4.2. Gender Bias in Hiring Algorithms

AI-powered hiring tools have become a popular method for companies to streamline the recruitment process, but these systems have also been found to exhibit gender bias. In 2018, Amazon scrapped an AI system that was designed to help with hiring after discovering that it was biased against women. The system was trained on resumes submitted to Amazon over a ten-year period, but the data reflected the gender imbalance in the tech industry. As a result, the AI system learned to favor male candidates and penalize resumes with words associated with women, such as "women's" or "female."

This example highlights how the historical underrepresentation of women in certain fields can lead to biased AI systems that perpetuate gender disparities in hiring. In order to create more inclusive and fair hiring practices, companies must ensure that their AI systems are trained on data that is representative of all candidates, regardless of gender, race, or other factors.

5.4.3. Healthcare Bias

AI systems are increasingly being used in healthcare to assist with diagnosis, treatment planning, and patient care. However, studies have shown that many of these systems exhibit bias against minority groups. For example, a 2019 study published in *Science* found that a widely used healthcare algorithm was biased against Black patients. The algorithm was designed to prioritize patients for extra care based on their health needs, but it was found to underestimate the healthcare needs of Black patients compared to white patients with similar conditions.

The bias in this system was due to the fact that the algorithm used historical healthcare data, which reflected systemic inequalities in access to care. Because Black patients had historically received less medical attention and treatment, the algorithm incorrectly assumed they required less care, leading to disparities in health outcomes.

These examples illustrate how AI, if not carefully designed, can reinforce societal biases and perpetuate inequality in critical areas like hiring, healthcare, and law enforcement.

5.5. The Consequences of Human Bias in AI Systems

The consequences of human bias in AI systems are far-reaching and can have profound effects on society. From reinforcing inequality to eroding trust in technology, the risks of biased AI are not just theoretical—they have real-world implications.

5.5.1. Inequality and Discrimination

The most significant consequence of biased AI is its potential to perpetuate or exacerbate existing inequalities in society. Whether in the form of biased hiring algorithms or biased predictive policing systems, AI has the power to reinforce systemic discrimination against marginalized groups. If left unchecked, this bias could result in entrenched disparities in education, employment, healthcare, and criminal justice, further disadvantaging already vulnerable populations.

5.5.2. Erosion of Trust in Technology

As AI systems become more integrated into our daily lives, trust in these systems becomes increasingly important. When people become aware that

AI systems are biased, their trust in these technologies is eroded. This lack of trust can hinder the adoption of AI in critical areas such as healthcare, education, and criminal justice, ultimately slowing down progress and limiting the potential benefits of AI.

5.5.3. Legal and Regulatory Implications

As AI systems are deployed in more domains, the legal and regulatory implications of bias become more significant. Organizations that deploy biased AI systems may face lawsuits, regulatory scrutiny, and damage to their reputation. Governments and regulatory bodies must take an active role in ensuring that AI systems are developed and deployed in a way that is transparent, fair, and accountable.

5.6. Addressing Human Bias in AI Systems

While the challenges of bias in AI are daunting, there are steps that can be taken to mitigate its impact and ensure that AI systems are fairer, more inclusive, and more transparent.

5.6.1. Techniques for Reducing Bias in AI

Several techniques can help reduce bias in AI systems. One key approach is to ensure that training data is diverse and representative of all populations. Developers must be conscious of the potential for bias in data and work to curate datasets that reflect the true diversity of the human experience. Additionally, fairness-aware machine learning algorithms have been developed to explicitly optimize for fairness, ensuring that AI systems produce equitable outcomes for all groups.

5.6.2. Improving Data Collection and Labeling

Ensuring the quality of the data used to train AI systems is critical for reducing bias. Companies must implement strategies to improve data collection practices, including diversifying the sources of data and ensuring that labeling is done by a diverse group of annotators who can recognize their own biases.

5.6.3. Incorporating Ethical Guidelines in AI Development

To reduce bias in AI, ethical guidelines must be embedded into every stage of AI development, from data collection to algorithm design to deployment. Developers must be trained to recognize the potential for bias and be held accountable for creating AI systems that prioritize fairness and inclusivity.

5.7. The Role of AI Developers in Mitigating Bias

AI developers play a crucial role in addressing bias in AI systems. Their responsibility extends beyond merely coding algorithms—they must actively work to identify, understand, and mitigate the biases that can emerge in the systems they create. By incorporating ethical principles and fairness metrics into their work, developers can help create AI systems that serve all members of society, not just those who have traditionally been in positions of power.

5.8. Ongoing Research and Efforts to Address Bias in AI

While challenges related to bias in AI are vast, there are numerous ongoing efforts within the research community, the tech industry, and government bodies to mitigate these biases. A growing awareness of the ethical implications of AI has prompted calls for more transparency, fairness, and inclusivity in AI development. Various academic institutions, think tanks, and nonprofit organizations are pushing forward with research to identify and address biases in AI systems.

5.8.1. Fairness-Aware Machine Learning

One promising approach to reducing bias in AI systems is fairness-aware machine learning, a subfield that focuses on developing algorithms that prioritize fairness in decision-making processes. These algorithms are designed to minimize the disparities between different groups by ensuring that certain protected attributes—such as race, gender, or socioeconomic status—are not unduly influencing the predictions or outcomes generated by the system.

There are various fairness criteria that researchers have developed to quantify and assess fairness, such as:

- **Demographic Parity:** Ensures that different demographic groups (e.g., men vs. women, Black vs. White) have equal outcomes from the system, regardless of their qualifications.

- **Equalized Odds:** Seeks to ensure that the true positive and false positive rates are similar across different groups, minimizing both discrimination and errors.

- **Fairness through Unawareness:** Involves ignoring sensitive attributes like race and gender when training the AI, assuming that the system will make decisions based solely on non-sensitive data. While this approach has limitations, it is one step toward mitigating biases related to sensitive attributes.

These fairness-aware algorithms can be embedded in various machine learning models, such as classification systems or recommendation engines, to ensure that bias does not creep into AI decision-making.

5.8.2. Bias Detection Tools

Another key area of research focuses on developing tools that can automatically detect and measure bias in AI systems. These tools analyze both the data used for training and the output of the model to identify potential sources of bias. For example, companies such as IBM and Google are developing AI tools that can detect bias in hiring algorithms, providing real-time feedback to developers and flagging any discriminatory patterns that may emerge in the system.

The use of these tools helps ensure that AI systems remain fair and accountable, especially as they are deployed in high-stakes environments like hiring, healthcare, and law enforcement.

5.8.3. Diverse Research and Development Teams

Another critical aspect of addressing bias in AI is the composition of the teams that design and develop AI systems. Diverse teams, including individuals from different ethnic, gender, and socioeconomic backgrounds, are more likely to recognize and address biases that may not be immediately apparent to homogenous groups.

By actively recruiting people from diverse backgrounds and creating inclusive work environments, companies can foster a culture of awareness around bias, ensuring that their AI systems are less likely to perpetuate harmful stereotypes or discrimination. In turn, this can result in more equitable AI solutions that are applicable to a broader range of users and communities.

5.8.4. AI Governance and Regulation

Governments and regulatory bodies also play a significant role in mitigating bias in AI systems. As AI continues to permeate various industries, there is an increasing need for policies and regulations to ensure that AI systems are developed and deployed in an ethical manner.

One example of such regulation is the European Union's General Data Protection Regulation (GDPR), which includes provisions aimed at ensuring transparency and fairness in automated decision-making. Under the GDPR, individuals have the right to request an explanation if they are subject to decisions made solely by AI systems. This level of transparency can help hold companies accountable for the biases that might be present in their systems.

Additionally, countries like the United States are beginning to explore the creation of AI regulatory frameworks, focused on ensuring that AI systems are developed in ways that prioritize fairness, accountability, and transparency.

5.8.5. Collaborative Efforts Across Industries

The fight against bias in AI is not one that any single organization or institution can tackle alone. Collaborative efforts between industry, academia, and government are essential to developing guidelines, best practices, and tools that reduce bias in AI. Initiatives like the *Partnership on AI*, an organization that brings together stakeholders from the tech industry, civil society, and academia, are helping to create industry standards for the development of ethical AI. These collaborative platforms allow different groups to share knowledge, resources, and solutions to improve the fairness and inclusivity of AI systems.

5.9. The Future of AI Bias Mitigation

As AI continues to evolve, we can expect ongoing progress in mitigating bias and ensuring that AI systems serve society in an equitable manner. However, this will require sustained effort and commitment from all sectors involved in AI development. The future of AI must be built on the principles of fairness, accountability, and transparency, with a particular focus on addressing the biases that already exist in AI systems.

5.9.1. Ongoing Research and Innovation

The field of AI ethics is rapidly evolving, with new research constantly emerging to understand and address bias in AI. Researchers are exploring new algorithms, data collection methods, and fairness criteria to create more robust, equitable AI systems. For example, researchers are investigating ways to make AI more interpretable, allowing users to better understand how decisions are made. This transparency could help identify potential biases in the system and lead to more informed interventions.

5.9.2. Long-Term Solutions

Ultimately, the long-term solution to bias in AI lies in changing the way we think about AI development. Rather than treating bias as an afterthought or a problem to be solved at the end of the development cycle, we must incorporate ethical considerations into every stage of AI design. This includes diversifying training datasets, involving a broad range of stakeholders in the development process, and creating systems that prioritize fairness as a core value.

Furthermore, the integration of AI systems into society must be accompanied by strong regulatory oversight and ongoing public debate. This will help ensure that AI is developed and used responsibly, with a focus on minimizing harm and promoting social good.

5.10. Conclusion: The Path Forward

Bias in AI systems is an inevitable challenge in the development of this transformative technology. The biases that exist in human psychology, data, and decision-making processes are often transferred to AI systems, resulting in outcomes that are discriminatory and harmful to marginalized groups. However, the awareness of these biases and the ongoing efforts to mitigate them signal hope for the future of AI.

By embracing a multi-faceted approach that includes fairness-aware algorithms, diverse research teams, improved data practices, regulatory oversight, and ethical guidelines, we can create AI systems that are more equitable and inclusive. The future of AI must be one in which technology is not just smarter, but also more just—serving the needs of all people, regardless of race, gender, or background.

It is up to all of us—developers, policymakers, and society at large—to ensure that the AI systems of tomorrow reflect the values of fairness, transparency, and accountability. Only then can we truly unlock the potential of AI to improve lives and create a better, more inclusive future.

Chapter 6: The Social Dynamics of Human-AI Interaction

6.1 Introduction to Human-AI Interaction

In the past few decades, artificial intelligence (A.I) has evolved from a futuristic concept to an everyday reality, permeating nearly every aspect of human life. From autonomous vehicles on our roads to virtual assistants in our homes, AI systems are now integral partners in our daily routines, assisting with everything from productivity to entertainment. As AI becomes more sophisticated and intertwined with society, understanding the social dynamics between humans and these systems has never been more critical.

The growing role of AI in personal, social, and professional environments presents a unique psychological challenge. How do we trust machines that think, learn, and adapt, yet lack the emotional intelligence and consciousness we associate with human interactions? How does the increasing dependence on AI affect our mental, emotional, and social well-being? And, most importantly, how do we collaborate with AI systems in ways that enhance our own capabilities while maintaining autonomy and ethical responsibility?

This chapter explores these questions by examining the psychology of trust, dependence, and collaboration between humans and AI systems. As we navigate this rapidly evolving relationship, it is essential to explore how human emotions, behavior, and cognitive processes interact with artificial systems—shaping, and sometimes complicating, our relationship with technology.

6.2 The Psychology of Trust in AI

6.2.1 Defining Trust in Human-AI Relationships

Trust is foundational to any meaningful relationship—whether human or otherwise. It forms the bedrock of cooperation, communication, and effective interaction. Trust in AI, however, takes on a different dimension.

Unlike human trust, which is often built over time through mutual experiences and emotional connection, trust in AI is shaped by transparency, reliability, and predictability. When we trust an AI system, it's not based on emotional intuition but rather on the system's ability to perform a task accurately and consistently.

Trust in AI systems is rooted in the same core psychological principles that apply to human trust but also incorporates new dimensions. The more transparent and understandable an AI system is, the more likely people are to trust it. For instance, when an AI tool explains its decision-making process—like a recommendation engine detailing why a product was suggested—it fosters trust by reducing uncertainty. Similarly, a reliable system that consistently meets expectations will naturally build trust.

6.2.2 Factors Influencing Trust in AI

Several factors influence our willingness to trust AI. The first and perhaps most critical factor is transparency. When AI systems are explainable—meaning their processes and decisions are understandable to users—they inspire more confidence. For example, AI systems used in fields like healthcare or finance are expected to provide clear explanations for their actions, especially when those actions directly impact people's lives.

Reliability and accuracy are also vital. Trust grows when people see that AI systems perform their tasks correctly and without errors over time. Whether it's a self-driving car navigating city streets safely or an AI diagnosing medical conditions, users need to feel confident that these systems are operating as intended. Consistency is key here: a system that performs well in one scenario but fails in another can cause significant distrust.

Finally, human-like traits in AI, such as empathy, emotional understanding, or the ability to adapt to social cues, can also play a role in trust-building. Although AI lacks genuine emotions, when it mimics human-like behaviors—such as acknowledging frustration or expressing understanding—it can create a sense of rapport. This "social AI" approach makes interactions feel more natural, contributing to a sense of trust between humans and machines.

6.2.3 Trust-building Mechanisms in AI Systems

Designing AI systems to foster trust is crucial for their successful integration into daily life. One effective method is through transparent feedback loops. For instance, AI systems that allow users to track how their data is being used or how decisions are made can alleviate fears of manipulation or bias. A prime example of this is the AI assistants that allow users to review their interactions and adjust the preferences of the system to better align with their needs.

Moreover, AI systems that are able to admit their own limitations and uncertainties can help prevent over-reliance. For example, an AI healthcare system that clearly states when it is uncertain about a diagnosis or when a human opinion is necessary fosters trust by acknowledging the boundaries of its capabilities.

6.2.4 Consequences of Distrust and Mistrust

The consequences of distrust in AI systems can be significant. When people don't trust the AI systems around them, they are less likely to use them effectively or to adopt them in the first place. This lack of trust can hinder the widespread acceptance of technologies that could improve productivity, healthcare, education, and even personal well-being.

A lack of trust can also lead to the underutilization of AI's potential. For instance, in healthcare, if patients don't trust AI-based diagnostic tools, they might reject AI-generated suggestions even when they might lead to better health outcomes. Similarly, in the workplace, employees might resist using AI tools that could make their tasks easier if they feel these tools are unreliable or biased.

6.3 The Concept of Dependence on AI

6.3.1 Psychological Dependency on Technology

As AI systems become more integrated into our lives, there is an emerging psychological dependency on them. This is not entirely new—humans have always developed dependencies on tools and technologies, from the wheel to the internet. However, the increasing sophistication of AI raises new concerns about the nature of this dependency.

When AI systems are designed to assist with tasks such as navigating streets, making financial decisions, or even managing our health, users can become increasingly reliant on these systems. For instance, people may become so accustomed to using GPS systems that they find it difficult to navigate without them. Similarly, reliance on AI-driven medical tools may alter how people approach their own health and decision-making processes.

6.3.2 Over-reliance on AI Systems

Over-reliance on AI can lead to a reduction in human cognitive function. People who rely on AI for tasks like remembering appointments, performing calculations, or making decisions might begin to lose their own problem-solving skills. This raises concerns about whether, in the long term, AI dependency could lead to a decline in cognitive abilities. If humans no longer need to calculate or memorize information, will these skills atrophy?

There are also concerns about how dependence on AI may influence human autonomy. When AI systems take on more decision-making responsibilities, people may lose confidence in their own abilities. This shift from independent decision-making to a reliance on AI could affect everything from how individuals manage their personal finances to how they approach daily challenges.

6.3.3 Beneficial Dependencies: How AI Enhances Human Abilities

On the flip side, the dependence on AI can lead to cognitive augmentation. AI has the potential to enhance human abilities rather than replace them. For example, AI systems can assist in medical diagnosis, helping doctors identify conditions they might otherwise miss. They can also support professionals in creative fields, providing tools that enhance productivity and creativity.

Collaboration with AI, rather than dependence, should be the goal. In this model, AI acts as a partner, augmenting human skills and capabilities. For example, in a workplace setting, an AI-powered tool could assist with data analysis, freeing up time for employees to focus on more complex, creative, and strategic tasks. This type of collaboration can lead to increased efficiency and innovation without sacrificing human agency.

6.3.4 Balancing Trust and Independence

Maintaining a balance between trust in AI systems and human independence is critical. People must be able to trust AI systems for their capabilities, but they must also maintain a sense of autonomy and decision-making power. This requires both designers and users of AI systems to adopt responsible practices. For instance, AI systems should be designed to provide suggestions, not make decisions autonomously, leaving the final judgment to the human user.

6.4 Collaboration Between Humans and AI

6.4.1 The Concept of Collaboration in AI Systems

Collaboration between humans and AI is perhaps the most promising aspect of this evolving relationship. In this model, AI doesn't replace human agency but rather complements it, enhancing human capabilities. Human-AI collaboration takes many forms. AI systems can work as assistants, amplifying human strengths, or they can act as co-creators, working alongside humans to generate new ideas, products, or solutions.

For example, in the field of medicine, AI can collaborate with doctors to analyze medical images, identify patterns, and suggest potential diagnoses. In this collaborative setup, AI provides additional insights that may be beyond human capabilities, while the human doctor uses their judgment and empathy to make the final decision.

6.4.2 Cognitive and Emotional Synergy Between Humans and AI

Human-AI collaboration can extend beyond cognitive tasks to emotional synergy. As AI becomes more adept at recognizing and responding to human emotions, the potential for emotional collaboration grows. For example, an AI therapist can provide emotional support by recognizing patterns in speech, tone, and behavior and adjusting its responses accordingly.

This synergy between human and AI emotional intelligence could help create stronger, more supportive relationships between humans and machines. However, it also raises important ethical questions about the role of AI in influencing human emotions and behavior, especially in areas like therapy, education, and customer service.

6.4.3 Social and Cultural Impacts of Collaboration with AI

The collaboration between humans and AI extends beyond cognitive and emotional synergy, influencing social and cultural structures. As AI systems begin to play more significant roles in sectors like healthcare, education, and business, the way we interact with each other and our environments is also shifting. The traditional dynamics of human roles and responsibilities are evolving as AI augments, and in some cases, replaces, certain tasks and functions.

In the workplace, for instance, AI is enabling more efficient collaboration by automating routine processes and supporting employees in more complex tasks. This shift can lead to greater productivity but also demands new skills and a rethinking of professional roles. As AI handles more technical tasks, humans are freed to focus on creativity, strategy, and interpersonal communication—areas where human strengths still excel. This creates a dynamic where collaboration rather than competition becomes the primary mode of interaction between humans and machines.

Socially, AI is transforming how we form relationships and communities. AI-powered platforms like social media algorithms determine what information we see and how we interact with others. While these systems are designed to optimize engagement, they also raise concerns about their impact on social interactions and the spread of misinformation. On the positive side, AI allows for more personalized interactions, enabling people to connect with others who share similar interests, regardless of geographical barriers. However, this also leads to the creation of digital echo chambers, where individuals may only engage with perspectives that align with their own, limiting exposure to diverse viewpoints.

In education, AI is helping create personalized learning experiences for students, adjusting content and teaching methods to individual needs. This approach, when implemented effectively, could level the playing field, providing all students with the opportunity to succeed at their own pace. However, it also raises questions about how much AI should be trusted to make educational decisions and whether it could inadvertently reinforce existing inequalities, depending on how the systems are designed and implemented.

The cultural impact of human-AI collaboration is also profound. AI is shaping our values and expectations about technology, autonomy, and human capability. The more we rely on AI for decision-making, the more we may begin to trust it over our own instincts and judgments. This could lead to a cultural shift where people rely on AI not only for technical tasks but for moral and ethical guidance as well.

6.4.4 Ethical Considerations in Human-AI Collaboration

As AI systems become integral collaborators in both personal and professional contexts, ethical considerations must be at the forefront of development and implementation. One key area of concern is accountability. When AI systems collaborate with humans in decision-making processes, who is responsible when something goes wrong? If an AI system makes a mistake or is compromised in some way, it may be difficult to determine who is liable—the developer, the user, or the AI itself.

Ethical considerations also extend to the power dynamics between humans and AI. As AI becomes more capable, there is a risk that it could influence human behavior and decision-making in ways that we don't fully understand or control. For instance, AI-driven systems in the workplace could inadvertently lead to bias, discrimination, or manipulation, particularly when it comes to hiring or promotion decisions. The data used to train AI systems can reflect existing societal biases, and if not carefully managed, AI could perpetuate or even amplify these biases.

The development of "ethical AI" is a growing field aimed at ensuring AI systems are aligned with human values and principles. This includes making sure that AI systems are fair, transparent, and accountable, and that they promote human well-being. It also involves creating frameworks for users to understand and manage the risks associated with AI systems, ensuring that people are not exploited or harmed by the very technologies that are supposed to help them.

6.5 The Future of Human-AI Social Dynamics

6.5.1 AI's Role in Shaping Future Social Interactions

Looking ahead, the role of AI in shaping social interactions is likely to grow even more significant. As AI systems become increasingly sophisticated, we may see the development of "social AI" that can engage with humans in more natural and empathetic ways. These systems could act as companions, mentors, and co-workers, creating a new form of social interaction between humans and machines.

One area where AI is poised to make a major impact is in the realm of emotional support. AI systems that can recognize and respond to human emotions could offer a new form of therapy, companionship, and care. While this might raise ethical concerns about the role of AI in sensitive emotional contexts, it also opens up possibilities for people who may not have access to human caregivers or therapists. AI could offer a bridge, providing emotional assistance when human support is unavailable.

In social contexts, AI could help facilitate more meaningful connections. For instance, AI could help match people with compatible friends or partners by analyzing preferences, behaviors, and shared interests. It could even predict compatibility in ways that humans may not be able to perceive on their own. While this has the potential to enhance social engagement, it also raises questions about how much influence we should allow AI to have over our personal relationships.

6.5.2 Emotional AI: The Next Step in Social Engagement

The development of emotionally intelligent AI is one of the most exciting and controversial advancements on the horizon. Emotional AI refers to systems that can understand, interpret, and respond to human emotions in a way that mimics human social behavior. These systems are designed to read facial expressions, analyze tone of voice, and even detect physiological responses such as heart rate or sweating to gauge emotional states.

The potential applications of emotional AI are vast, from improving customer service experiences to providing personalized support in healthcare and education. AI could help caregivers monitor the emotional well-being of patients, or it could provide interactive learning experiences that adapt to students' emotional states, adjusting the pace or style of instruction accordingly.

However, there are ethical and psychological concerns surrounding emotional AI. Some worry that emotionally intelligent machines could manipulate human emotions for profit or gain, especially in marketing and advertising. Others question whether it is ethical to have machines influence our emotions or provide emotional support, particularly when these machines lack true empathy and understanding.

6.5.3 Long-Term Considerations for Human-AI Interactions

As AI systems become more integrated into our lives, long-term considerations about their role in society will become even more pressing. One of the biggest challenges will be maintaining human agency in a world where machines play an increasingly central role. While AI has the potential to enhance human abilities, there is also the risk that it could undermine the very qualities that make us human—our creativity, intuition, and emotional intelligence.

Another key consideration is the social and economic impact of AI. As AI automates more tasks, what happens to the people whose jobs are replaced by machines? How can we ensure that AI benefits all members of society, rather than exacerbating inequality? These are questions that will need to be addressed as AI continues to evolve.

Finally, there is the question of how to ensure that AI serves humanity's best interests. As AI systems become more autonomous and capable of making decisions on their own, it is essential to create ethical frameworks that guide their development and use. These frameworks should prioritize human well-being, ensuring that AI is used to complement and enhance human lives, rather than replace or diminish them.

6.6 Conclusion

In this chapter, we have explored the social dynamics of human-AI interaction, focusing on the psychology of trust, dependence, and collaboration. As AI systems become more integrated into our daily lives, understanding these dynamics becomes essential for ensuring that AI serves humanity's best interests. Trust, collaboration, and ethical considerations will be at the heart of successful human-AI relationships, allowing us to harness the power of AI while maintaining our autonomy and humanity.

The future of human-AI interaction is one of potential and challenge, opportunity and risk. As AI continues to evolve, so too must our understanding of how it affects our social, emotional, and cognitive lives. By fostering a collaborative, transparent, and ethical relationship with AI, we can ensure that these systems work with us—not against us—in creating a better future for all.

Chapter 7: Perception of AI: Myths vs. Reality

7.1 Introduction to AI Perception

The way we perceive artificial intelligence (A.I) has shifted dramatically over the last few decades. From being a concept confined to science fiction to becoming a significant part of daily life, AI has captured both the imagination and fear of the public. These perceptions—both optimistic and fearful—greatly influence how we interact with AI systems, how we trust them, and how society adapts to their growing presence. In this chapter, we will explore the myths and realities surrounding AI, examining how societal beliefs and misconceptions shape interactions with these technologies.

The perception of AI has long been a subject of debate. In some quarters, AI is hailed as a revolutionary force capable of solving the world's most pressing problems. In others, it is viewed with suspicion, framed as a harbinger of doom. These differing views are not simply the result of different levels of understanding or ignorance; they are the product of deeply ingrained cultural narratives, technological anxieties, and a mixture of real-world and fictional portrayals of AI. In this chapter, we will explore both the myths and the realities surrounding AI, analyzing their origins and exploring their implications.

By understanding the psychology behind the public perception of AI, we can work toward fostering a more realistic, balanced view of its potential and limitations. A clear and realistic understanding of AI will allow us to engage more meaningfully with this transformative technology, ensuring that we can benefit from its advantages while addressing its challenges and risks.

7.1.1 Understanding Public Perception of AI

Public perception of AI is a dynamic force that has evolved along with technological advancements. In the early days of AI research, the technology was largely confined to academia and niche industries. AI was not widely understood, and it remained a distant concept for most people. The general public's view of AI was shaped by speculation, with many either fascinated by its potential or frightened by the unknown.

As AI technologies began to permeate everyday life, from recommendation algorithms to autonomous vehicles, the conversation around AI intensified. Suddenly, the abstract concepts of machine learning, neural networks, and deep learning became more tangible and familiar to the public. However, with this increased familiarity came an even more complex array of opinions and perceptions. People began to recognize both the promise and the threat of AI, and the resulting discourse became polarized.

For some, AI is a symbol of progress, representing the ultimate in human ingenuity and technological achievement. For others, AI is seen as a threat, an uncontrollable force that could surpass human intelligence and potentially pose existential risks. These contrasting perceptions often stem from the narratives we encounter in the media, popular culture, and the way AI technologies are framed by businesses and governments. As we will explore in this chapter, myths and misconceptions about AI contribute significantly to this divide.

7.1.2 Importance of Perception in Human-AI Interaction

The way we perceive AI profoundly impacts how we interact with it. If we view AI as a benevolent force designed to improve our lives, we are more likely to embrace and trust its integration into society. Conversely, if we see AI as a malevolent force or an uncontrollable entity, we may resist its development and seek to regulate or limit its use. Trust is a fundamental element of human-AI interaction, and how we perceive AI influences our willingness to rely on its capabilities.

The perception of AI also affects how it is adopted in different sectors. In healthcare, for example, patients' trust in AI-driven diagnostic tools can influence whether or not they are willing to use them. Similarly, employees' perception of AI in the workplace—whether they see it as a helpful collaborator or a job-threatening adversary—can shape how they engage with automation and intelligent systems. Thus, addressing misconceptions and promoting a more accurate understanding of AI is essential for fostering positive human-AI relationships.

7.2 Societal Beliefs about AI

7.2.1 The Fear Factor: AI as a Threat

One of the most prevalent societal beliefs about AI is that it poses a threat to humanity. This fear has its roots in a variety of sources, from cultural representations to real-world concerns about automation and the loss of control. Many people fear that AI will inevitably surpass human intelligence, leading to scenarios where machines dominate or even eradicate humanity. This dystopian vision is perpetuated by films like *The Terminator* and *The Matrix*, which portray AI as an existential threat to human life.

This fear is compounded by concerns about job displacement. As AI systems become increasingly capable of performing tasks previously done by humans—whether in manufacturing, customer service, or even healthcare—there is anxiety about widespread unemployment. People fear that the automation of jobs could lead to social unrest and economic inequality, with a small elite reaping the benefits of AI while the majority are left behind.

Additionally, the idea of "singularity"—a hypothetical future moment when AI surpasses human intelligence and becomes self-aware—has captured the imagination of many, including respected figures like Stephen Hawking and Elon Musk. While the concept of singularity remains speculative and theoretical, it fuels the belief that AI might eventually become so powerful and autonomous that it could pose a direct threat to human survival.

7.2.2 The Optimistic View: AI as a Solution

On the other side of the spectrum, there are those who view AI as a powerful tool for solving some of humanity's most pressing problems. In this optimistic view, AI is not a threat but a solution—capable of improving healthcare, addressing climate change, enhancing education, and solving complex global issues. For instance, AI algorithms are already being used to analyze vast amounts of medical data, helping doctors diagnose diseases more accurately and quickly. Similarly, AI-driven systems are helping researchers model and predict climate change, enabling better decision-making for the future of our planet.

In these contexts, AI is seen as an invaluable tool that can assist humans in tackling problems too complex for individuals or even teams of experts to solve alone. The potential for AI to augment human capabilities and drive progress is a central element of this optimistic view.

However, this optimism can sometimes lead to overconfidence in AI's capabilities. The belief that AI can solve almost any problem may blind people to the limitations of the technology and the ethical challenges it presents. For example, some advocates for AI in healthcare may overlook the risks of bias in training data or the potential for AI systems to make errors that harm patients. Overestimating AI's abilities can lead to unrealistic expectations and, in some cases, dangerous consequences.

7.2.3 AI as a Human-Like Entity

Another pervasive misconception is the belief that AI is, or will soon be, capable of human-like thought and emotions. This myth has been fueled by science fiction, where AI characters often possess consciousness, free will, and complex emotions, much like humans. In popular media, AI systems like *HAL 9000* from *2001: A Space Odyssey* or *C-3PO* from *Star Wars* are portrayed as sentient beings capable of reasoning, experiencing emotions, and making decisions based on their own desires.

In reality, AI systems today are nowhere near achieving human-like consciousness. While AI can be programmed to simulate certain aspects of human behavior—such as recognizing facial expressions or generating natural language—these systems do not have emotions, subjective experiences, or self-awareness. They are highly specialized tools designed to perform specific tasks, often using patterns and algorithms to make decisions based on data. The myth of AI as a human-like entity can lead to unrealistic expectations about what AI can achieve, as well as misplaced trust in its capabilities.

7.3 Misconceptions and Their Impact

7.3.1 AI as Fully Autonomous and Self-Aware

One of the most persistent myths surrounding artificial intelligence is the idea that AI systems are fully autonomous and self-aware. Popular culture has long depicted AI as a form of intelligent life, capable of thinking independently, making decisions, and acting without human input. Movies such as *The Terminator* and *I, Robot* portray AI systems that break free from human control and turn against their creators. These portrayals have fueled the misconception that AI could one day operate entirely on its own, outside the boundaries set by humans.

The reality, however, is far different. While AI systems are incredibly powerful in their ability to process large amounts of data and make decisions based on that data, they are far from autonomous. AI, in its current form, is what is known as "narrow AI"—designed to perform specific tasks within well-defined parameters. It cannot operate outside of its programmed capabilities or act beyond its given scope. For instance, an AI designed to recognize faces cannot autonomously decide to perform a completely different task, such as creating a piece of art or conducting scientific research.

Moreover, the notion of self-aware AI—a machine with consciousness, emotions, or desires—remains entirely speculative. Despite significant advances in AI and neuroscience, we have yet to create a machine that possesses subjective experiences or awareness. AI operates by following algorithms that analyze patterns and make predictions based on data; it does not "feel" or "think" in the way humans do. The myth of autonomous, self-aware AI often leads to fear and misunderstanding, as it creates the illusion that AI could act in unpredictable and dangerous ways without human oversight.

7.3.2 The All-Knowing AI

Another common misconception is that AI systems have access to all human knowledge and can therefore make perfect decisions based on this vast reservoir of information. This myth is reinforced by the widespread use of AI in search engines, personal assistants like Siri or Alexa, and data-driven systems that appear to "know" everything about us.

In reality, AI is highly dependent on data—both the quantity and quality of that data. While AI can process vast amounts of information, it does not "know" things in the same way humans do. AI systems do not possess general knowledge or understanding. They function by analyzing patterns within specific datasets, often making decisions based on the limited data they have been trained on. A common example is the use of AI in predictive analytics, where systems analyze historical data to make forecasts about future events. While these predictions can be remarkably accurate, they are limited to the scope of the data the AI has access to. If the data is incomplete, biased, or inaccurate, the AI's decisions will reflect these flaws. Furthermore, AI systems cannot think critically or adapt to situations in the way humans can. While AI can outperform humans in certain specialized tasks, such as playing chess or diagnosing diseases based on medical images, it lacks the flexibility to deal with novel situations that fall outside its training. For example, a recommendation system on an e-commerce website might suggest products based on past behavior, but it cannot offer advice or provide insights in the broader context of a person's life.

This myth of an all-knowing AI undermines the reality that AI is not infallible. It requires constant input and refinement, and its decisions are only as good as the data and algorithms it is built on. Over-relying on AI as a source of truth can lead to serious mistakes, especially when the system is applied in high-stakes scenarios like healthcare or criminal justice.

7.3.3 Bias and Fairness Myths in AI

Another critical misconception is the belief that AI is inherently unbiased and objective. AI, in its essence, is simply a set of algorithms designed to analyze data and make decisions. However, because AI systems are created by humans and rely on human-generated data, they are often subject to the same biases that exist in society. If AI systems are trained on biased data, they will perpetuate those biases in their outcomes.

For example, research has shown that facial recognition systems can be less accurate at identifying people of color, particularly Black individuals, due to the underrepresentation of diverse faces in training datasets. Similarly, predictive algorithms used in criminal justice systems have been found to disproportionately target minority communities, reinforcing existing biases in the justice system.

The myth of AI objectivity is particularly dangerous because it can lead to a false sense of security. If people believe that AI is inherently fair, they may be less likely to scrutinize its decisions or demand accountability for its impact. In reality, AI systems can amplify social inequalities and make decisions that harm marginalized communities unless careful attention is paid to how they are designed and trained. It is crucial that we recognize that AI is not a neutral tool, but one that reflects the biases embedded in society and the data that fuels it.

7.4 The Influence of Media and Popular Culture

7.4.1 AI in Film and Literature

Perhaps no other factor has shaped public perception of AI more than its portrayal in film and literature. From *2001: A Space Odyssey* to *Ex Machina*, the depiction of AI in popular culture has often leaned toward dystopian narratives. In these stories, AI systems develop their own desires and goals, sometimes with disastrous consequences for humanity.

This portrayal is not entirely without basis—AI does possess the potential to disrupt society in significant ways—but the more sensationalized depictions often exaggerate the extent to which AI is capable of autonomous thought. Films like *The Terminator* and *The Matrix* create an image of AI as a cold, calculating force that seeks to dominate or eliminate humans. These fictional representations can leave audiences with the impression that all AI systems are capable of rebellion or are inherently dangerous.

While these narratives are compelling and entertaining, they do little to foster an understanding of the true nature of AI. Instead of emphasizing the complexity of AI technologies and the need for ethical development, they play into irrational fears and promote the myth of AI as a malevolent force. This is a clear example of how media can distort public perception and hinder productive conversations about AI's real-world applications.

7.4.2 News and Social Media Representations

In addition to film and literature, news outlets and social media platforms play a significant role in shaping how AI is perceived. Stories about AI breakthroughs often generate excitement and optimism, while reports of AI failures or ethical concerns can lead to fear and skepticism. The sensational nature of headlines—often emphasizing the most extreme or speculative possibilities—fuels public anxiety.

For example, when a major tech company announces the development of a new AI-powered system, headlines often highlight the potential for world-changing benefits, like curing diseases or solving climate change. However, when AI systems are involved in failures or ethical controversies, the narrative typically shifts to warnings about the dangers of unregulated AI or its potential to exacerbate inequality.

Social media, with its rapid spread of information (and misinformation), further amplifies these narratives. AI-related news stories can quickly go viral, with users sharing articles or videos that may not fully represent the complexities of the technology. In some cases, these stories spread exaggerated or misleading claims, further solidifying misconceptions about AI.

This media landscape creates a distorted view of AI—one that is often disconnected from the reality of how these technologies work and their actual impact on society. While media plays a crucial role in disseminating information, it is essential to approach AI coverage with a critical eye, recognizing that not all news stories are created equal.

7.5 Addressing the Myths: A Call for Clearer Communication

7.5.1 The Importance of Education in AI Literacy

To move beyond the myths and misconceptions that dominate public perception, it is crucial to invest in AI education and literacy. The growing influence of AI across various sectors—healthcare, education, business, and government—requires a broader understanding of the technology, its capabilities, and its limitations. While experts and researchers may have a deep grasp of AI's intricacies, the general public often lacks this knowledge, leading to misunderstandings and fears.

Educational programs focused on AI literacy can play a pivotal role in dispelling common myths and helping people develop a more accurate understanding of AI. These programs need to be accessible, non-technical, and designed for a broad audience. By breaking down complex concepts and making AI more approachable, we can empower individuals to engage more thoughtfully with AI technologies.

In schools, universities, and online platforms, integrating AI education into curricula would help students develop critical thinking skills and prepare them for a future where AI is an integral part of their lives. Moreover, organizations and businesses that deploy AI systems should prioritize transparency in their technologies, offering training and resources to help employees understand how these systems work and the implications of their use.

This is not just about teaching people how AI works, but also about fostering an understanding of its social, ethical, and philosophical dimensions. AI literacy should not be limited to understanding algorithms and code, but should also include discussions on the societal impact of AI, its ethical implications, and the potential risks of misuse.

7.5.2 AI Transparency and Accountability

Another key factor in addressing misconceptions about AI is increasing transparency in AI systems. Public trust in AI can be enhanced when individuals understand how these systems make decisions and what data they rely on. Too often, AI is portrayed as a "black box," with decisions made by algorithms that are opaque and difficult to interpret. This lack of transparency fuels suspicion and heightens fears of the unknown.

To combat this, AI developers and organizations must prioritize transparency in their practices. This can include making AI algorithms explainable, providing users with insights into how decisions are made, and openly sharing the data sources used for training. When people understand the reasoning behind AI's decisions, they are more likely to trust and accept its applications.

Accountability is equally important. When AI systems fail, cause harm, or perpetuate biases, there must be clear channels of responsibility. Developers, companies, and regulatory bodies should be held accountable for the consequences of AI technologies, ensuring that the systems are designed and deployed in ways that prioritize fairness, inclusivity, and ethical considerations. This responsibility extends to the transparency of data used to train AI models and the need to audit AI systems for biases.

Creating a system of accountability helps ensure that AI is used ethically and responsibly, diminishing the fear of rogue systems that operate outside human control.

7.5.3 Media Responsibility in Shaping AI Narratives

The role of media in shaping the public's perception of AI cannot be overstated. As we discussed earlier, media coverage often focuses on sensationalized stories, portraying AI as either a utopian or dystopian force. This approach exacerbates misunderstandings and fuels public anxiety.

To address this, media outlets must take a more balanced and nuanced approach to AI reporting. This means highlighting both the potential benefits and the challenges of AI, while avoiding the extremes that dominate popular discourse. It is crucial that the media communicates not only the technical capabilities of AI but also the ethical considerations, the ongoing research into mitigating risks, and the efforts being made to ensure AI is developed responsibly.

Moreover, journalists and media professionals should collaborate with AI experts to provide more accurate, well-researched, and insightful coverage. This could include interviews with AI researchers, case studies of successful AI applications, and in-depth analyses of the social and ethical issues raised by AI technologies.

Through more responsible reporting, the media can help shift the conversation from fear to informed discussion, providing the public with a clearer understanding of what AI is and what it can do.

7.5.4 Bridging the Gap Between Science Fiction and Reality

The mythologizing of AI in science fiction, while providing entertainment, often distorts our understanding of the technology. To bridge the gap between these fictional portrayals and the reality of AI, we must differentiate between imaginative storytelling and the practical application of AI in the real world.

While science fiction can offer valuable insights into the human condition and the potential consequences of technological advancements, it is important to understand that the world of AI today is far from the dystopian futures depicted in movies. AI is not on the verge of becoming self-aware, nor is it plotting to overthrow humanity. Instead, AI is a tool created by humans to solve specific problems, improve efficiency, and augment human decision-making.

By cultivating a clear distinction between the world of fiction and the world of reality, we can avoid the dangerous trap of conflating the two. Understanding AI as it exists today—its potential, its limitations, and its ethical considerations—will allow us to engage with the technology in a more grounded and productive manner.

7.6 Moving Toward a More Balanced View of AI

7.6.1 Embracing AI's Potential While Acknowledging Its Risks

As we move forward in our relationship with AI, it is essential to adopt a balanced view that embraces its potential while acknowledging its risks. AI is undoubtedly a transformative technology that holds the promise of revolutionizing industries, solving complex problems, and improving our quality of life. From healthcare and education to transportation and entertainment, AI has the potential to make our lives easier, safer, and more efficient.

However, this potential comes with challenges that must be addressed. Ethical concerns, such as data privacy, bias, and accountability, must be at the forefront of AI development. We must remain vigilant about the risks of over-relying on AI and ensure that human oversight remains a critical part of the decision-making process. AI should complement human decision-making, not replace it entirely. We must also be mindful of the societal impact of AI, ensuring that its benefits are distributed equitably and that its risks are mitigated.

Rather than succumbing to the extremes of utopian or dystopian thinking, we must recognize that AI is a tool—one that can be used for good or ill, depending on how it is developed, deployed, and regulated. By approaching AI with a balanced mindset, we can harness its potential while mitigating the risks, creating a future in which AI enhances human life without sacrificing our values or well-being.

7.6.2 The Role of Collaboration in Shaping AI's Future

Finally, the development of AI is not a task for technologists alone. It requires collaboration across disciplines, including philosophy, ethics, sociology, law, and the humanities. Only by bringing together diverse perspectives can we ensure that AI is developed in a way that benefits all of society.

Policymakers, researchers, businesses, and the general public must all work together to shape the future of AI. By fostering open dialogue, encouraging cross-disciplinary research, and promoting ethical standards in AI development, we can create a future where AI is a force for good.

This collaborative approach will help us overcome the myths and misconceptions that surround AI, allowing us to focus on its real-world potential and work toward a future where humans and machines coexist in harmony.

7.7 Conclusion: Bridging the Divide Between Myths and Reality

The myths surrounding AI are not just misunderstandings—they are reflections of our collective hopes, fears, and anxieties about the future. While these myths can be entertaining and even thought-provoking, they can also hinder meaningful progress. By moving beyond the sensationalized portrayals of AI, we can build a more accurate, nuanced understanding of its true capabilities and limitations.

Through education, transparency, responsible media coverage, and collaborative efforts, we can bridge the divide between myth and reality. By doing so, we can foster a future where AI is a trusted and valuable tool that enhances human life and contributes to the greater good.

As we continue to explore the intersection of AI and society, it is imperative that we move forward with a clear, informed, and balanced perspective—one that acknowledges both the promise and the challenges of this transformative technology.

Chapter 8: Personalization in AI Systems

8.1 Introduction: The Need for Personalization

At the dawn of the digital age, technology was often designed with a singular, rigid purpose in mind. A program would function in a static, uniform way, delivering the same result regardless of the individual user. It was a time when every computer screen looked the same, every search engine presented the same results, and every application performed the same tasks with no regard to the uniqueness of the person interacting with it. Personalization, as we understand it today, was a distant concept, almost an afterthought.

But as we transition further into the 21st century, the world of technology has experienced a dramatic shift. We now live in an era where one-size-fits-all solutions are becoming obsolete. The digital landscape, increasingly powered by artificial intelligence, has evolved from being a generic set of tools to becoming a reflection of our own unique identities. AI, with its capacity for learning and adaptation, has taken the reins of this transformation. It tailors every experience, product, and service to the individual in ways previously unimaginable.

This drive toward personalization is not merely a trend but a necessity. With the deluge of information we encounter daily—via social media, e-commerce platforms, search engines, and countless other digital interfaces—the need to cut through this noise and deliver relevant, customized experiences has never been more urgent. From the moment we wake up and check our phones to when we go to sleep and interact with streaming platforms or educational apps, AI is quietly at work, creating experiences that are increasingly fine-tuned to our preferences, behaviors, and even our emotional states.

This chapter will explore the remarkable ways in which AI is shaping and redefining personalization across various sectors, from retail to healthcare to education. Along the way, we will confront the ethical dilemmas that accompany this profound shift—issues of privacy, bias, and the very essence of human autonomy in an increasingly personalized world.

8.2 The Science of Personalization

To understand how AI can personalize our experiences, we must first grasp the scientific underpinnings of this process. Personalization is far more than a matter of adding a few custom features to a program. It is a complex interaction of data, algorithms, and models that work together to understand us at a granular level.

At the core of AI-powered personalization lies the principle of machine learning, the process by which algorithms "learn" from vast amounts of data. This data can range from our search histories, purchase patterns, and social media interactions, to more subtle cues like the way we navigate a website or respond to certain content. AI systems use these data points to create models that predict what we will want next, often before we consciously realize it ourselves.

For instance, consider the e-commerce giant Amazon, which seemingly knows what we need even before we search for it. Behind the scenes, the AI algorithms are constantly analyzing millions of data points from users all over the world. When you purchase a book, for example, Amazon doesn't simply record your purchase—it immediately updates its understanding of your preferences and adjusts its recommendations for you. The algorithm knows that readers who buy science fiction often enjoy fantasy novels as well, and that the purchase of a camera suggests an interest in photography. The system's ability to continuously learn and adapt to your behavior results in an experience that feels highly personalized.

What makes AI-driven personalization so powerful is its ability to continuously refine these models. As you interact with AI systems—whether through searches, purchases, or even social interactions—the algorithms adapt and become more accurate. This feedback loop creates an experience that feels deeply attuned to your unique needs, wants, and even your subconscious inclinations.

Yet, as we delve deeper into the world of AI, we must ask: how much of this personalization is truly beneficial? And how much is influenced by data patterns that may not always reflect our true selves?

8.3 Personalization Techniques in AI

AI employs a range of techniques to personalize our experiences, each one built to extract value from data in a unique way. Understanding these methods allows us to appreciate the sophistication of the technology and the complexities involved in tailoring our digital worlds.

8.3.1 Collaborative Filtering

Collaborative filtering is one of the most widely used techniques in AI-driven personalization. It works on the assumption that people who have similar tastes or preferences in the past will continue to have similar tastes in the future. By analyzing the behaviors of other users who exhibit similar patterns to yours, collaborative filtering can make accurate recommendations.

Consider Netflix's recommendation system. If you've watched a series like *Breaking Bad*, Netflix might suggest *Better Call Saul* based on the viewing habits of users who also enjoyed *Breaking Bad*. This is collaborative filtering at work—looking at the overlap between your viewing history and that of others to suggest content that you are likely to enjoy. The more you engage with the platform, the better the system becomes at refining these suggestions, creating a personalized viewing experience that feels remarkably intuitive.

However, this approach is not without its challenges. While collaborative filtering works well for large data sets, it can sometimes lead to a phenomenon known as the "cold start problem." If a new user joins a platform, there is little data to base recommendations on, leading to less personalized or even irrelevant suggestions. Additionally, collaborative filtering can reinforce existing preferences and limit exposure to new, diverse content.

8.3.2 Content-Based Filtering

In contrast to collaborative filtering, content-based filtering focuses on the attributes of the items themselves rather than the behaviors of other users. This technique looks at the specific characteristics of an item that a user has interacted with, such as genre, keywords, or themes, and uses this information to recommend similar items.

Spotify's music recommendation system, for example, uses content-based filtering to analyze the type of music you listen to—such as the genre, tempo, and artist—and suggests songs or playlists with similar attributes. If you listen to a lot of jazz, the algorithm will suggest other jazz artists or tracks with similar rhythms, instruments, or vocal styles.

The beauty of content-based filtering is that it doesn't rely on data from other users, so it can be effective even for new users with limited interaction history. However, this method is also limited in that it may not introduce much diversity into your suggestions. It could end up recommending only more of what you already know, rather than expanding your horizons.

8.3.3 Hybrid Models

Many platforms, such as Amazon and YouTube, combine both collaborative and content-based filtering in a hybrid model. By combining these two techniques, AI systems can overcome the weaknesses of each, leading to a more accurate and diversified personalization process.

Hybrid models have the advantage of providing more relevant suggestions while also introducing new, unexpected recommendations that still align with the user's underlying preferences. For example, YouTube's recommendation algorithm might suggest videos based on your past viewing habits (collaborative filtering), but it will also take into account the content of those videos to recommend similar ones you might not have seen before (content-based filtering).

This combination of approaches is one of the key reasons why AI-driven personalization feels so natural and fluid, creating a seamless experience that evolves with us over time.

8.3.4 Contextual Personalization

Contextual personalization goes beyond just the data of previous interactions. It looks at the broader context in which you are using the technology—such as your location, time of day, device, or even your emotional state—to tailor experiences even further.

Google Maps, for example, doesn't just give you directions—it tailors its suggestions based on whether it's morning or evening, your travel patterns, and even the current traffic conditions. If you're near a restaurant you've previously visited, it might recommend other nearby restaurants, enhancing the relevance of its suggestions based on where you are in the moment.

Contextual personalization brings a dynamic element to AI, making it more attuned to real-time needs and situations.

8.4 Personalization in Different Domains

As AI continues to advance, its applications for personalization span virtually every industry. From entertainment to healthcare to education, AI is reshaping our experiences in profound ways. Let's explore how personalization plays out in some of these domains.

8.4.1 E-Commerce

In the realm of e-commerce, AI has revolutionized how consumers shop. Online platforms such as Amazon and Alibaba use personalized recommendations to offer products that align with your preferences, purchase history, and browsing behavior. AI also enables dynamic pricing, where prices fluctuate based on demand, user behavior, and even competitor pricing.

For retailers, AI personalization has proven to be a game-changer, significantly boosting conversion rates, customer satisfaction, and loyalty. However, it has also raised concerns around privacy and data security, as retailers collect vast amounts of personal information to tailor these experiences.

8.4.2 Healthcare

AI's ability to personalize healthcare is one of its most promising applications. Personalized medicine, which tailors treatment based on an individual's genetic makeup, medical history, and lifestyle, is being enhanced through AI. AI algorithms analyze vast amounts of health data to recommend personalized treatment plans, identify potential health risks, and even predict future medical conditions.

However, the use of AI in healthcare also raises ethical questions around privacy, data sharing, and the potential for bias in health recommendations. It is crucial that AI systems in healthcare are designed with the utmost care, ensuring that they are both effective and equitable.

8.4.3 Education

In education, AI-driven personalization is reshaping how students learn. Adaptive learning platforms use AI to tailor content to each student's pace, learning style, and knowledge level. This approach helps students receive the support they need while also challenging them to reach their full potential.

By analyzing a student's performance, learning patterns, and preferences, AI can recommend study materials, quizzes, and exercises that are most likely to improve learning outcomes. This has the potential to transform traditional education systems, making learning more personalized and accessible to all students.

8.5 Ethical Considerations in Personalization

While personalization offers remarkable benefits, it also presents significant ethical challenges. AI systems rely on vast amounts of personal data to tailor experiences, and this raises concerns about privacy, surveillance, and the potential for manipulation.

8.5.1 Privacy Concerns

Personalization relies heavily on data—data about our behaviors, preferences, and even our emotions. This data is often collected without full transparency or consent, leading to concerns about privacy violations. As AI continues to learn more about us, how much should we, as individuals, give up in exchange for personalized services? And who owns the data that powers these AI systems?

The issue of data privacy is particularly pressing in light of recent data breaches and the increasing scrutiny of how companies handle user information. As we continue to live in an age of personalized experiences, it is essential that strong safeguards are put in place to protect personal data.

8.5.2 Bias and Fairness

AI systems are only as good as the data they are trained on. If the data is biased, the personalization recommendations can also be biased, reinforcing stereotypes and perpetuating inequality. In the case of healthcare, for example, biased algorithms could lead to unequal treatment recommendations for different demographic groups.

Ensuring fairness in AI-driven personalization is essential to ensure that all users are treated equitably, regardless of their background, socioeconomic status, or identity.

8.7 The Future of Personalization in AI

As we look toward the future, the landscape of personalization in AI is poised to grow more sophisticated, more intuitive, and even more integrated into the fabric of our daily lives. With advances in machine learning, natural language processing, and cognitive computing, the possibilities for hyper-personalization are immense.

8.7.1 Hyper-Personalization: Moving Beyond the Surface

While current personalization methods are already advanced, we are heading toward an era of hyper-personalization—where AI systems do not simply recommend based on past actions, but also anticipate future needs. By analyzing vast amounts of real-time data, AI will be able to make more nuanced predictions about an individual's preferences and behaviors. The key difference with hyper-personalization is that AI will no longer wait for us to express our desires—it will predict and fulfill them before we even consciously realize what we want.

Imagine a scenario where your digital assistant, using AI, knows exactly what you need before you ask for it. It recognizes when you're tired, for example, and suggests a calm playlist or a soothing movie. It can detect when you're stressed and recommend a nearby meditation center or a piece of content designed to relax you. This level of insight into our lives will create an experience that feels almost telepathic, where our digital environments anticipate our moods and needs.

8.7.2 The Role of Emotion in Personalization

As AI evolves, one significant area of growth lies in its ability to understand and respond to human emotions. Current AI systems are capable of recognizing certain emotions based on data inputs such as facial expressions, tone of voice, and even biometric feedback. But the future holds a promise of even deeper emotional understanding.

Imagine a world where AI systems can not only detect when you are frustrated or elated but can respond in ways that are empathetic and contextually appropriate. This emotional resonance could be incorporated into everything from customer service bots to personalized therapy apps, creating a level of interaction that feels much more human. It's an AI that doesn't just react to commands but responds to your emotional state, making every interaction feel more genuine and connected.

For instance, if you're using an AI-powered fitness app and feeling down after a tough workout, the system could respond with motivational messages or a soothing playlist that aligns with your current emotional state. Similarly, in educational platforms, AI could adjust the difficulty of tasks based on your mood or stress level, creating a more personalized learning experience.

8.7.3 AI and Autonomous Personalization

As AI continues to learn from both structured and unstructured data, the concept of fully autonomous personalization becomes a reality. The future may see AI systems that not only analyze data but also act on it in real-time, adjusting everything from your digital environment to your physical surroundings based on your needs.

Smart homes are already experimenting with this kind of personalization. Imagine walking into your home, and the lights, temperature, and even your music change to match your mood or activity. Your home could recognize your preferences and adjust based on time of day, weather, or your personal routines—creating an environment that feels not just customized, but alive and aware of your presence.

In healthcare, autonomous AI systems could take this further by monitoring your health metrics continuously—like your heart rate, blood sugar levels, or even sleep patterns—and offer real-time adjustments. For instance, if your stress levels are high, the AI might recommend a break, a stretch, or a soothing soundscape to help you relax.

8.8 Challenges and Limitations of Personalization

Despite the tremendous potential of AI-driven personalization, it is essential to address the challenges and limitations that accompany this technology.

8.8.1 The "Filter Bubble" Effect

As AI increasingly personalizes our digital experiences, we run the risk of creating "filter bubbles." This term refers to the narrowing of perspectives that occurs when algorithms prioritize content we already agree with or enjoy, blocking out opposing viewpoints or new ideas. The more an algorithm learns about us, the more it reinforces our existing preferences, potentially leading to a diminished sense of discovery.

In the context of news, for example, AI systems that filter information based on our past reading habits might present us with stories that align only with our political beliefs, reinforcing biases and preventing us from encountering differing viewpoints. This is particularly concerning in an era of social division and political polarization. The danger lies in creating digital echo chambers where users are insulated from diverse opinions, leading to greater societal fragmentation.

8.8.2 The Limits of Data

At its core, personalization is powered by data, but data is far from perfect. Personalization systems rely on the assumption that past behaviors are reliable indicators of future actions. However, this is not always the case. Human behavior is complex and often unpredictable. While data can provide insights, it can never fully capture the nuances of individual decision-making or predict every choice we make.

For instance, AI might recommend a series of products based on your previous purchases, but these recommendations may overlook subtle changes in your needs or preferences. If you're in a transitional phase of life—starting a new job, moving to a new city, or undergoing personal changes—AI may struggle to adapt to these shifts without the necessary data inputs.

Furthermore, data limitations can also stem from biases in the data itself. AI systems are only as good as the data they are trained on, and biased data can lead to skewed, inaccurate, or even harmful recommendations.

8.8.3 Ethical Considerations

With the rise of personalized AI, ethical dilemmas become more pronounced. We must question how much control we want to surrender to these systems and what kind of power we are giving away to corporations that collect our personal data. As AI systems become more intrusive, they have the potential to exploit users' psychological vulnerabilities.

For instance, companies may use AI personalization to exploit our fears, insecurities, or desires, manipulating us into making purchases we don't need or making decisions that benefit their bottom line rather than our well-being. The fine line between creating a personalized, efficient experience and crossing over into manipulation is a delicate one.

Moreover, as AI systems grow more powerful, it is vital to ensure that they do not perpetuate existing social inequalities. For example, AI systems in hiring, law enforcement, or healthcare could unintentionally reinforce discriminatory practices if the data they rely on is biased or incomplete.

8.9 Conclusion: The Promise and Perils of Personalization

Personalization is the future of artificial intelligence, and with it comes both profound promise and significant challenges. AI's ability to tailor experiences to individual needs has the potential to revolutionize industries, improve our daily lives, and create more efficient, engaging digital environments. But this potential must be balanced with caution.

As we continue to integrate AI into every facet of our lives, we must remain vigilant about the ethical, psychological, and social consequences of an increasingly personalized world. The path forward requires careful consideration of how data is collected, how personalization is implemented, and how we, as individuals, maintain control over our interactions with these powerful systems.

Personalization is not inherently good or bad—it is simply a tool, one that can be used to enhance our lives or to manipulate them. In the coming years, the question will not be whether we can personalize AI, but whether we can personalize it responsibly. Only then can we ensure that AI serves humanity's greater good, empowering individuals without compromising their autonomy or privacy.

As we embark on this journey into a world where AI knows us better than we know ourselves, the future remains in our hands. It is up to us to shape this new era, ensuring that personalization, at its core, is not just about making our lives more convenient, but about making them more meaningful.

Chapter 9: AI in Mental Health Care

9.1 Introduction

The human mind is a labyrinth of thoughts, emotions, memories, and perceptions—an intricate network of biological processes that we are only beginning to understand. Over millennia, humans have tried to untangle the mysteries of the mind, from ancient philosophical musings to modern-day psychiatric research. Yet, mental health disorders remain one of the most pressing challenges in global healthcare, affecting millions of people worldwide.

For much of human history, mental health care has been limited by a lack of understanding, insufficient resources, and stigma. Traditional therapeutic methods—though valuable—are often inaccessible, costly, or inadequate for the sheer volume of those in need. And yet, we stand on the brink of a revolution, one that promises to reshape how we understand and treat mental health. This revolution is being driven by artificial intelligence (A.I).

AI's potential in mental health care is vast, from diagnosing conditions earlier than ever before to offering personalized treatment options and even predicting the onset of mental health crises. As AI becomes more integrated into healthcare, it is poised to revolutionize mental health care delivery, making it more accessible, efficient, and tailored to individual needs. However, as with all technological advances, AI in mental health care raises significant ethical questions and challenges. How can we balance innovation with privacy? How can we ensure that AI enhances human empathy rather than replacing it?

This chapter explores how AI is transforming mental health care, examining its role in diagnosis, treatment, patient monitoring, and more. We will investigate the promise and perils of AI in this sensitive field, offering a nuanced view of its potential and its limitations.

9.2 AI in Diagnosing Mental Health Conditions

One of the most challenging aspects of mental health care is diagnosis. Mental health disorders do not present in the same clear-cut ways as physical ailments; they are often subtle, complex, and difficult to quantify. The mental health diagnostic process is typically based on a combination of self-reported symptoms, clinical interviews, and observational data, yet even the most experienced clinicians can sometimes miss early signs of a condition. This is where AI has the potential to make a significant impact.

9.2.1 Early Detection through Data Analysis

AI excels in analyzing vast amounts of data to uncover patterns that might not be immediately visible to the human eye. In mental health care, this means that AI systems can sift through a wealth of patient data—such as medical history, genetic information, behavioral data, and even online activity—and identify early warning signs of conditions like depression, anxiety, and schizophrenia.

Take, for example, the case of depression. Traditionally, diagnosing depression requires patients to report their feelings and symptoms, often through self-reported questionnaires. However, many people are reluctant to open up about their mental health, especially in the early stages of a disorder. AI can bridge this gap by analyzing data from multiple sources, including voice tone, facial expressions, and even social media activity. Researchers have already demonstrated that AI can predict depressive episodes by tracking language patterns in a person's online posts, identifying subtle shifts in word choices and sentiment before the individual may even recognize the changes themselves.

By processing vast amounts of data quickly, AI systems can help clinicians detect potential mental health issues earlier, allowing for more effective interventions. Early intervention is crucial in mental health care, as many disorders, when caught early, are more treatable, and the long-term impacts can be mitigated.

9.2.2 Natural Language Processing (NLP) for Diagnostic Tools

One of the most promising developments in AI for mental health care is the use of Natural Language Processing (NLP) to analyze speech and text. NLP allows AI systems to understand and interpret human language, identifying underlying emotional states that may not be obvious through conventional diagnostic methods.

For example, AI-powered systems are being used to analyze the language used by individuals in therapy sessions. By assessing tone, word choice, and sentence structure, these systems can detect signs of depression, anxiety, and other mood disorders. Research has shown that people with depression often use more negative language and exhibit specific patterns of speech, such as shorter, more fragmented sentences. AI algorithms can pick up on these subtle cues and provide clinicians with valuable insights into the patient's condition.

Beyond individual therapy, AI-powered chatbots are being used in mental health screening. These chatbots engage with patients in real-time conversations, asking questions about their mood, stress levels, and coping strategies. The AI system then analyzes the responses, categorizing them into different mental health risk factors. These tools can act as an initial point of contact for patients who may be hesitant to seek help or who are in need of a preliminary diagnosis before visiting a mental health professional.

9.2.3 Image Analysis for Diagnosis

AI is also making waves in the field of medical imaging, particularly in the diagnosis of mental health disorders related to neurological conditions. In the past, diagnosing conditions like schizophrenia or bipolar disorder involved a combination of symptom reports, clinical observations, and family history. While these methods are still essential, AI is now being used to analyze brain scans—such as MRIs and CT scans—to identify physical markers of mental illness.

For example, AI has been trained to detect abnormalities in brain structures that may be indicative of conditions like schizophrenia or autism spectrum disorder. By analyzing brain scans, AI systems can identify subtle structural changes that might go unnoticed by human radiologists. These insights provide a more objective basis for diagnosis, offering valuable data that can complement the clinical evaluation.

Moreover, AI has the potential to map brain activity in real time, offering insights into how mental health conditions affect neural networks. By analyzing patterns of brain activity, AI can help researchers and clinicians better understand the neurobiological underpinnings of various mental health conditions, paving the way for more targeted and effective treatments.

9.3 AI in Treatment and Therapy

Once a diagnosis is made, the next step is treatment. Mental health care is notoriously complex, with no one-size-fits-all solution. Traditional treatments, including medication and psychotherapy, often take time to yield results and may not work for every individual. This is where AI can enhance the therapeutic process, providing personalized, real-time support to patients.

9.3.1 Virtual Therapists and Chatbots

Perhaps the most visible application of AI in mental health care is the development of virtual therapists and chatbots. These AI-driven systems are designed to provide immediate, on-demand support for individuals struggling with mental health challenges. Virtual therapists can engage in conversations with patients, offering therapeutic interventions such as Cognitive Behavioral Therapy (CBT) or mindfulness exercises.

AI-powered chatbots, like Woebot and Wysa, are designed to replicate the experience of speaking with a therapist, providing users with tools and strategies to cope with stress, anxiety, and depression. These chatbots are accessible 24/7, making them an attractive option for individuals who may not have easy access to traditional mental health care or who are hesitant to engage with a human therapist.

While virtual therapists and chatbots are not meant to replace human therapists, they provide an important supplementary service. They can offer immediate relief, track progress, and help individuals develop coping mechanisms between therapy sessions. Moreover, they reduce the stigma associated with seeking help, allowing users to address their mental health in private, without fear of judgment.

9.3.2 Personalized Treatment Plans

AI's ability to analyze large datasets and learn from patient data makes it an ideal tool for creating personalized treatment plans. Traditional mental health treatments often follow a trial-and-error approach, with clinicians prescribing different medications or therapy techniques based on what has worked for other patients. AI, however, can analyze an individual's unique genetic, psychological, and behavioral data to recommend the most effective treatment plan.

For example, AI can help identify which combination of therapies or medications might work best for a particular patient based on their individual response to past treatments. It can also adjust treatment over time, learning from the patient's progress and making recommendations to optimize the treatment process.

Personalized treatment plans could significantly improve the effectiveness of mental health care, reducing the time it takes to find the right approach and minimizing the risk of negative side effects from medications.

9.3.3 Medication Management

Medication management is another area where AI can play a transformative role in mental health care. Many individuals with mental health conditions require medication to manage their symptoms, but medication adherence is a significant issue. Studies show that up to 50% of people with chronic mental health conditions do not take their medications as prescribed, leading to worsened symptoms and higher healthcare costs.

AI can help improve medication adherence by reminding patients to take their medications, monitoring their progress, and alerting healthcare providers if there are any issues. For example, AI-powered apps can send push notifications to remind patients to take their pills or track their mood changes to ensure that the medication is working as expected.

In some cases, AI can also help optimize the dosage of medication based on real-time data. By analyzing factors like mood, physical activity, and side effects, AI systems can recommend adjustments to the treatment regimen, ensuring that the patient receives the most effective medication for their condition.

9.4 AI in Monitoring Mental Health Progress

Mental health care doesn't end with diagnosis and treatment. It requires continuous monitoring to assess progress, prevent relapse, and adjust treatments in real time. This is an area where AI excels. Unlike traditional care models, which often require in-person visits for evaluations, AI offers the possibility of constant, real-time monitoring. This shift can significantly improve outcomes for patients, as it allows for a more dynamic and responsive approach to mental health management.

9.4.1 Continuous Monitoring and Feedback

AI-powered devices such as wearables, smartphones, and even smart home systems are increasingly being used to collect data on patients' physical and emotional states. These devices track everything from heart rate, sleep patterns, and activity levels to more specific behavioral cues like social engagement or changes in speech patterns. By analyzing this data, AI can provide ongoing assessments of a patient's mental health and deliver real-time feedback to both the patient and healthcare providers.

For instance, wearable devices can monitor a patient's physical health markers—such as heart rate variability or skin conductivity—which are often linked to stress, anxiety, or depression. These systems can send immediate alerts if any abnormalities are detected, enabling early interventions that may prevent the escalation of symptoms. Patients themselves can receive feedback, which can empower them to take proactive steps toward managing their mental health, whether through guided relaxation exercises or other coping mechanisms.

This continuous feedback loop offers more than just real-time insights. It provides a holistic picture of the patient's mental health, enabling AI to learn and adapt its recommendations over time. Over months or even years, AI systems can build a detailed profile of the patient, tracking fluctuations in mood and behavior and offering customized interventions as needed.

9.4.2 Predictive Analytics for Relapse Prevention

Perhaps one of the most powerful features of AI in mental health care is its ability to predict potential relapses or worsening conditions before they manifest. By leveraging predictive analytics, AI systems can analyze a patient's behavioral and biometric data to forecast the likelihood of a mental health crisis—whether it be a depressive episode, an anxiety attack, or even a suicidal tendency.

For example, AI can monitor changes in a patient's social media activity, interactions with the virtual therapist, or even their sleep patterns to identify potential triggers of a relapse. If AI detects that certain patterns are emerging—such as a decrease in social engagement or an increase in negative speech—it can notify the patient and the healthcare provider, suggesting interventions to prevent the crisis.

Predictive AI models are not perfect, of course, but they represent a significant leap forward in early intervention. By identifying potential risks before they fully materialize, healthcare providers can offer timely support, reducing the need for emergency interventions and minimizing the impact of mental health crises.

9.4.3 Virtual Support Systems

AI-powered virtual support systems are another promising development in mental health care. These systems go beyond traditional therapy or chatbots by offering ongoing emotional support through a network of digital resources. Whether it's a chatbot, an AI-driven virtual therapist, or a self-help app, these systems are designed to provide constant engagement for patients in need of emotional connection.

One of the major advantages of virtual support systems is their accessibility. Patients don't need to wait for an appointment to access support. These tools can be used whenever the patient feels the need to talk, whether it's in the middle of the night or during a stressful moment. Moreover, they offer a sense of privacy and security that may encourage individuals who might otherwise hesitate to seek help due to the stigma surrounding mental health.

By using AI to power these support systems, patients receive personalized experiences that are tailored to their specific emotional needs. The AI analyzes responses, adapts to changing emotional states, and provides customized suggestions for managing stress, anxiety, or depression. In this sense, virtual support systems create an environment where mental health care is no longer limited by the constraints of time, geography, or social stigma.

9.5 Ethical Considerations in AI-Driven Mental Health Care

While the promise of AI in mental health care is exciting, it also raises significant ethical concerns. As with any technology, AI brings with it potential risks, particularly in a field as sensitive as mental health. Ensuring that AI is used responsibly and ethically is crucial to its success in this domain.

9.5.1 Privacy and Data Security

The first ethical concern surrounding AI in mental health care is privacy. Mental health data is inherently sensitive, and individuals have a right to expect that their personal information will be protected. When AI systems collect data, whether through wearables, apps, or virtual therapists, they are privy to highly personal details about a person's emotional state, behavior, and mental health history.

Ensuring the privacy and security of this data is paramount. The stakes are incredibly high; if this information is misused or falls into the wrong hands, it could have devastating consequences for the patient. AI-driven mental health platforms must comply with privacy regulations, such as HIPAA in the United States, and adopt stringent data protection practices. Furthermore, patients should be given full transparency and control over their data, ensuring they are aware of how it's being used and allowing them to opt out if they choose.

9.5.2 Bias and Fairness in AI Algorithms

Another critical ethical concern is the potential for bias in AI algorithms. AI systems learn from the data they are trained on, and if the data is flawed or incomplete, the resulting algorithm can reinforce existing biases. In the context of mental health care, this could mean that certain populations—such as racial minorities or people from low-income backgrounds—may not receive fair or accurate diagnoses.

For instance, if an AI system is primarily trained on data from one demographic group, it may not perform as well when applied to people from different backgrounds. This could lead to misdiagnoses, inappropriate treatment recommendations, or disparities in care. To mitigate these risks, AI systems used in mental health care must be trained on diverse, representative datasets that reflect the broad spectrum of human experiences.

9.5.3 Human Interaction and Empathy

Finally, there is the issue of human interaction and empathy. While AI systems can replicate some aspects of therapeutic care, they lack the ability to provide genuine human empathy—a fundamental component of effective mental health care. Empathy is what allows therapists to understand their patients on a deep emotional level, offering comfort and support during moments of vulnerability.

AI can't replace this human touch, nor should it be seen as a substitute for human care. Rather, AI should be viewed as a tool that enhances and supports human practitioners. By automating certain tasks, AI can free up therapists to spend more time connecting with patients on an emotional level. The challenge lies in finding a balance where AI augments, rather than replaces, the human elements of mental health care.

9.6 AI and Mental Health Care Accessibility

One of the greatest promises of AI in mental health care is its potential to increase accessibility. Mental health care is notoriously difficult to access, particularly for individuals living in rural or underserved areas. Many people who need mental health services either cannot afford them, face long wait times, or lack access to trained professionals in their area. AI has the potential to bridge this gap, making mental health care more widely available to those who need it most.

9.6.1 Reducing Barriers to Access

AI can reduce barriers to mental health care by providing accessible, low-cost options for diagnosis and treatment. Virtual therapists, chatbots, and self-help apps can be used by individuals regardless of location, offering mental health support at any time of day. These systems can offer a first step in seeking care, guiding patients to more advanced resources if necessary.

In addition, AI-powered tools can help individuals who might be hesitant to seek help due to stigma. People who are uncomfortable discussing their mental health with a human therapist may feel more comfortable using AI-powered systems, which provide an anonymous, judgment-free environment. This is particularly important in cultures or communities where mental health issues are stigmatized or misunderstood.

9.6.2 Affordability and Scalability

AI also has the potential to make mental health care more affordable. Traditional mental health services can be prohibitively expensive, especially for those without insurance or those living in areas with limited access to providers. AI-powered solutions, however, are often more affordable and scalable. By automating certain aspects of care, such as initial assessments or follow-up monitoring, AI can reduce the cost of mental health services and make them more accessible to a broader population.

In developing countries, where mental health care resources are often scarce, AI can provide a valuable solution. AI-powered mental health apps, for example, can reach millions of people, offering basic interventions and support where human therapists are in short supply. These tools can act as a stopgap, helping individuals cope with mental health challenges until they are able to access more advanced care.

9.7 The Future of AI in Mental Health Care

The future of AI in mental health care holds immense promise. While we've already seen notable advancements in diagnosis, treatment, and monitoring, the journey is far from over. As AI technologies evolve, so too will their ability to assist in understanding, diagnosing, and managing mental health conditions.

9.7.1 Advances in AI Models and Diagnostics

AI's capabilities will continue to improve as machine learning models become more sophisticated. One of the most exciting areas of development lies in the creation of more accurate diagnostic tools. As AI systems gather more data from diverse patient populations, they will become better at identifying complex mental health conditions, even those that are difficult for human clinicians to detect.

For instance, AI systems are currently being trained to detect subtle patterns in brain scans, genetic data, and other medical records that could signal the early onset of conditions like schizophrenia, bipolar disorder, or neurodegenerative diseases like Alzheimer's. By combining data from multiple sources—genetic, physiological, behavioral, and even environmental—AI may eventually be able to offer a comprehensive, multi-dimensional diagnosis that is far more accurate than current methods.

With access to vast datasets, AI could also identify new markers for mental health conditions, leading to better understanding of underlying causes. This could result in the development of novel treatments and interventions tailored to the specific needs of patients, enabling precision mental health care.

9.7.2 Integration with Genetic and Neurological Research

In addition to improving diagnostic accuracy, AI is also being integrated with genetics and neuroscience to explore the biological underpinnings of mental health disorders. AI's ability to analyze massive datasets in real-time opens up possibilities for understanding how genetic variations and environmental factors interact to influence mental well-being.

For example, AI can be used to analyze genetic data from individuals with depression or anxiety to pinpoint genetic markers that might predispose someone to mental health challenges. This could lead to the development of gene-based treatments or preventative strategies, which could revolutionize how we think about mental health care.

In parallel, AI-driven neuroscience tools are enabling a deeper understanding of how the brain functions during different emotional states. By analyzing brain scans, EEGs, and other neurological data, AI can map out the complex neural pathways involved in mental health conditions, offering insights that have eluded researchers for decades. This information could ultimately lead to more effective interventions, especially for conditions that currently lack comprehensive treatments.

9.7.3 The Role of AI in Personalized Treatment Plans

As the understanding of mental health deepens, AI will increasingly play a role in personalized treatment plans. Mental health is not one-size-fits-all, and what works for one person may not work for another. AI is uniquely positioned to tailor interventions based on a person's specific needs, taking into account their unique genetic makeup, medical history, psychological profile, and environmental factors.

Rather than relying on broad treatment protocols, AI systems can suggest personalized therapy options, including cognitive behavioral therapy (CBT), mindfulness techniques, medication regimens, and lifestyle changes. By continuously analyzing patient data, AI can adjust these recommendations in real time, optimizing the treatment as the patient's condition evolves.

This personalized approach could also extend to integrating mental health care with other aspects of an individual's life. For example, AI could recommend lifestyle changes—such as exercise routines, sleep optimization, or diet alterations—that complement mental health treatments and enhance overall well-being. This holistic view of mental health could significantly improve outcomes for patients by treating both the psychological and physiological aspects of mental health.

9.7.4 AI and Therapeutic Innovation

AI's potential to revolutionize mental health care also lies in its ability to innovate therapeutic techniques. While traditional therapies like CBT or psychodynamic therapy have been widely adopted, AI opens up the possibility of developing new, personalized, and more effective approaches. One exciting development is AI-assisted virtual reality (VR) therapy. This technology is already being used to treat conditions such as post-traumatic stress disorder (PTSD) by immersing patients in controlled environments where they can confront and process traumatic memories in a safe, gradual way. With AI-powered VR, therapy can be tailored to each individual's needs, providing a more immersive and effective treatment experience.

Additionally, AI could drive the development of new cognitive training techniques. These could include AI-driven applications that target cognitive distortions, automate mindfulness training, or simulate social situations for individuals with social anxiety. These innovations would make therapeutic interventions more engaging and adaptable to individual progress.

9.7.5 Global Mental Health Care and AI

Perhaps the most transformative potential of AI in mental health care lies in its ability to address the global mental health crisis. Worldwide, the demand for mental health services far exceeds the supply of trained professionals, and many individuals live in areas where mental health care is inaccessible or highly stigmatized. AI, with its ability to scale quickly and offer cost-effective solutions, could revolutionize the global mental health landscape.

In developing countries or regions with limited healthcare infrastructure, AI-powered tools could offer accessible mental health support to millions of people who would otherwise go without help. Mobile apps, virtual therapists, and chatbots could be deployed across rural communities, offering early intervention and mental health education.

Moreover, AI systems can help destigmatize mental health care by offering anonymous, confidential support. Individuals who may feel embarrassed or afraid to seek help due to cultural barriers can access mental health services through AI-driven platforms without fear of judgment.

The widespread adoption of AI could also support public health initiatives aimed at mental health prevention. AI systems could analyze population-level data to identify regions at higher risk for mental health crises, allowing for targeted interventions before conditions escalate. This proactive approach could improve outcomes for entire communities, reducing the overall burden of mental health disorders on society.

9.8 Challenges Ahead: Trust and Human-AI Collaboration

Despite all its potential, the future of AI in mental health care is not without challenges. One of the most significant barriers to the widespread adoption of AI-powered mental health tools is the issue of trust. Patients must feel comfortable sharing personal information with AI systems, and clinicians must trust that the technology is reliable, accurate, and ethically sound.

To address these challenges, AI systems must be transparent in their processes. Patients should understand how their data is being used, and clinicians must have clear guidelines for integrating AI into their practices. In addition, there should be ongoing efforts to ensure that AI systems are continually updated, tested, and validated to maintain the highest standards of care.

Collaboration between human therapists and AI systems will also be essential. AI is not a replacement for human care; rather, it should serve as an augmentation. AI can handle repetitive tasks, assist in diagnostics, and offer support between therapy sessions, but the human element—empathy, connection, and understanding—remains irreplaceable. The key to success in mental health care lies in creating a harmonious partnership between AI and human providers.

9.10 Conclusion

AI's potential to reshape mental health care is vast and multifaceted. From improving diagnostic accuracy and enabling continuous monitoring to expanding access to care and personalizing treatment, AI offers unprecedented opportunities to enhance the mental well-being of individuals worldwide. However, the ethical challenges, issues of trust, and need for human collaboration will require thoughtful consideration as these technologies evolve.

As AI continues to advance, we must remember that mental health care is not solely about algorithms and data; it is about people. The intersection of AI and mental health care should never lose sight of the humanity at the core of the practice. With careful integration and a focus on the well-being of patients, AI can serve as a powerful tool in transforming mental health care for the better.

Chapter 10: AI's Role in Education: Understanding Learning Patterns

10.1 Introduction to AI in Education

The integration of artificial intelligence (A.I) into education is not a distant dream, nor is it merely a trend in the making. It is here, quietly reshaping the way we understand learning, teaching, and the human brain's vast potential. In classrooms around the world, AI is making waves, from simple chatbots that answer questions to complex systems that adapt educational content to the individual needs of each student. Yet, this revolution is not just about technology. It's about psychology—how AI uses deep insights into human cognition to shape learning experiences in ways never before possible.

At its core, the role of AI in education is to understand learning patterns—how we learn, what motivates us, and how we can be taught more effectively. In the past, education systems have often followed a one-size-fits-all model, where teachers taught to the average student, leaving out those who either struggled to keep up or those who were not challenged enough. Today, AI offers a solution to this problem, promising to personalize education, bringing the kind of individual attention that has long been a luxury of the few to the many.

As we embark on this chapter, we explore how AI can unravel the intricacies of human learning. With the power of machine learning, neural networks, and cognitive psychology, AI systems can detect learning patterns, diagnose cognitive roadblocks, and predict how an individual will respond to different teaching methods. What's even more fascinating is that AI doesn't just serve as a passive tool—it actively learns and adapts alongside the student, offering an evolving, dynamic approach to education.

The influence of AI in education isn't just transforming how students learn; it's shaping the very fabric of the teacher-student relationship. Teachers, once the sole custodians of knowledge, now have powerful AI assistants that can analyze student performance, suggest targeted interventions, and provide personalized recommendations—all in real time. This fusion of human expertise and AI capabilities holds the promise of creating an education system that is more responsive, more inclusive, and ultimately more effective than ever before.

10.2 Psychological Foundations of Learning

To truly understand how AI is reshaping education, we must first look at the psychological foundations that underpin human learning. Throughout history, psychologists have attempted to decode the mysteries of how humans acquire knowledge, skills, and behavior. From Piaget's stages of cognitive development to Vygotsky's theories on social learning, various frameworks have guided our understanding of how people learn.

One of the most influential theories is **behaviorism**, which emphasizes the role of reinforcement in shaping behavior. In a classroom setting, this might be reflected in a reward system where correct answers or good behavior are reinforced with praise, points, or privileges. For AI systems, behaviorism offers a valuable insight: that learning can be influenced by rewards and feedback. AI algorithms can be designed to use feedback loops, offering students rewards when they answer questions correctly, reinforcing positive learning behaviors.

But **constructivism**, which focuses on the learner's active role in constructing their own understanding, offers an even more profound insight for AI's role in education. According to this theory, learning isn't just about absorbing information—it's about actively engaging with it, connecting it to prior knowledge, and building new insights. This is where AI's ability to personalize learning shines. AI can adapt content, providing more challenging material when a student is ready for it, or revisiting foundational concepts when the student needs reinforcement.

Furthermore, **cognitivism**—which focuses on the mental processes involved in learning—emphasizes the importance of memory, attention, and problem-solving. Here, AI can make a significant impact by monitoring cognitive load, which refers to the amount of mental effort required to learn something. By analyzing a student's progress and engagement, AI can adjust the difficulty of tasks, offering a balance that keeps the student engaged without overwhelming them.

These psychological theories are more than just abstract ideas; they offer the building blocks for AI systems to design better, more efficient educational experiences. By embedding these principles into AI-driven platforms, we can foster learning environments that are not only tailored to each student's cognitive and emotional needs but are also designed to maximize their potential at every stage of their educational journey.

10.3 AI's Understanding of Individual Learning Styles

One of the most significant breakthroughs in AI's role in education is its ability to understand and adapt to individual learning styles. In traditional classrooms, students are often expected to conform to a standardized method of learning, which can be frustrating for those who do not fit into the mold. Some students excel through visual stimuli, others through hands-on activities, and some learn best through auditory explanations. AI systems can analyze data from various learning interactions—whether it's a student's engagement with multimedia content, their interaction with digital textbooks, or their participation in collaborative projects—and discern their learning preferences.

AI is not merely following preset rules; it is learning in real-time. For instance, if a student consistently performs better when presented with visual cues, the system can provide more infographics, diagrams, and video-based content to reinforce learning. Conversely, if the student struggles with visual material but excels through text-based learning, AI can adjust to offer more reading material and fewer visual aids.

In this sense, AI systems take a highly individualized approach to learning. No longer is the student required to adapt to the curriculum; instead, the curriculum adapts to the student. This is especially important in the context of **differentiated instruction**, where the teacher tailors content to the diverse needs of students. AI allows for that kind of differentiation to occur at scale, ensuring that each student receives the most effective form of instruction for their unique learning style.

For instance, platforms like Duolingo, which teaches languages, use AI to tailor lessons based on the learner's progress, adjusting the difficulty of exercises, offering new challenges, and reviewing previously learned material at optimal intervals. The result is a far more engaging and personalized learning experience than the one-size-fits-all classroom model.

This personalization extends beyond just the style of learning—it also accounts for the pace at which each student progresses. AI's real-time monitoring allows it to detect when a student is struggling or excelling, adjusting the material accordingly. It becomes less about moving through predetermined milestones and more about moving forward at a pace that suits the individual's cognitive and emotional needs.

10.4 Data-Driven Insights into Student Behavior

AI's ability to collect and analyze data is perhaps its most powerful feature in the educational sphere. Every interaction a student has with an AI system—whether it's answering a quiz question, watching a video, or participating in a discussion forum—produces data that AI can analyze. This data is then used to derive insights into the student's behavior, learning patterns, and cognitive strengths and weaknesses.

One of the most important applications of this data is in the early identification of students who may be at risk of falling behind. AI systems can detect patterns of disengagement, poor performance, or signs of stress long before a teacher or counselor might notice. This gives educational institutions a powerful tool for **early intervention**, ensuring that students receive the support they need as soon as possible.

In addition, AI can help teachers understand not just what a student knows but how they learn. By tracking interactions across various tasks—such as how long a student takes to complete an assignment, where they make mistakes, and which topics they revisit frequently—AI systems can offer insights into how a student processes information. These insights can help educators refine their teaching methods, personalize content, and offer additional resources where needed.

Another fascinating aspect of AI in education is its ability to identify **learning patterns** that might not be immediately apparent to humans. For example, AI can detect if a student tends to struggle with specific types of questions (such as multiple-choice versus open-ended) or if they have a tendency to perform better when given more time to process information. By analyzing this data, AI can offer tailored interventions, providing students with strategies to overcome their challenges.

Through these data-driven insights, AI empowers both students and educators to make more informed decisions about the learning process. It allows for real-time adjustments, ensuring that no student is left behind and that each individual is given the best possible chance to succeed.

10.5 Personalized Learning Paths

The notion of personalized learning has long been a dream in education, but it's AI that is finally turning this dream into a reality. In traditional educational settings, teachers must balance the needs of a wide array of students, each with their own unique pace of learning. As a result, many students either fall behind or are left unchallenged. AI, however, removes these limitations by creating customized learning experiences for each student, designed to meet their individual needs and abilities.

Personalized learning is rooted in the understanding that every student has a different starting point, pace, and method of learning. AI systems analyze vast amounts of student data—such as test scores, behavioral patterns, time spent on tasks, and even emotional states—to build an accurate profile of each student. This profile then guides the AI system in tailoring educational content. The system determines which concepts to introduce, when to introduce them, and how to present them based on the student's needs.

For example, an AI-powered math platform might begin by assessing a student's current knowledge in areas like addition, subtraction, multiplication, and division. Based on this assessment, the platform can present the student with personalized lessons, starting from a point where the student needs the most support. If a student grasps addition quickly but struggles with multiplication, the AI will focus more resources on strengthening their multiplication skills before moving on to more complex topics like division or fractions.

One of the most profound implications of this is the flexibility AI offers in learning. No longer must students progress in a linear fashion dictated by rigid curricula or fixed schedules. With AI, students can progress at their own pace, mastering one concept before moving on to the next. This allows for deeper learning and greater retention, as students are not rushed through material they don't fully understand.

Moreover, this personalized approach also supports students in taking ownership of their own learning. When AI systems provide continuous feedback—showing students exactly where they are excelling and where they need improvement—it empowers students to take control of their academic journey. The constant adaptation of the learning path ensures that no student is left behind, while those who excel can be given more challenging content, keeping them engaged and motivated.

10.6 Emotional and Social Aspects of Learning in AI Systems

While AI's capabilities in recognizing cognitive patterns are impressive, its understanding of emotional and social dynamics in learning is just as crucial. Emotions and social interactions play a central role in how we learn, shaping our motivation, engagement, and ultimately, our success. In the classroom, a positive emotional environment often fosters better learning outcomes, while negative emotions—such as frustration, anxiety, or boredom—can impede progress.

AI systems today are becoming increasingly adept at recognizing and responding to emotional cues. By utilizing emotion recognition technologies, AI can assess a student's emotional state during interactions. For example, an AI system might detect signs of frustration when a student struggles with a challenging problem and provide timely encouragement or offer a different explanation. Alternatively, it might recognize when a student is feeling confident and ready for more advanced material, pushing them toward more difficult tasks.

This emotional awareness is especially important in the context of **social and emotional learning (SEL)**, which has gained significant traction in educational circles. SEL focuses on developing students' ability to manage their emotions, build positive relationships, and make responsible decisions. AI can support SEL by recognizing signs of stress or anxiety and offering interventions—such as mindfulness exercises, positive reinforcement, or even suggestions for taking breaks when necessary.

Furthermore, AI systems can track and analyze social interactions among students, allowing educators to monitor group dynamics. For instance, AI can detect when a student is isolated or struggling to participate in group activities and provide suggestions to improve peer interactions. By promoting healthy social dynamics and emotional regulation, AI can create a more supportive learning environment that fosters positive relationships and emotional well-being.

It is important, however, to note that while AI systems can be emotionally intelligent to some degree, they are still limited in their ability to truly understand the complexities of human emotions. They can recognize surface-level cues—such as facial expressions, voice tone, and word choice—but they lack the deep emotional intelligence that a human teacher or peer might bring to the table. Thus, while AI can play a supportive role in managing emotions and fostering a positive learning environment, the human element remains essential in ensuring that students' emotional and social needs are fully met.

10.7 Cognitive and Behavioral Monitoring

Another transformative aspect of AI in education is its ability to monitor and respond to both cognitive and behavioral signals in real-time. Cognitive monitoring refers to the assessment of mental processes, such as attention, memory, and problem-solving abilities. Behavioral monitoring tracks how students act, interact, and engage within the learning environment. Together, these two forms of monitoring provide invaluable insights into a student's learning experience.

AI systems can track how a student engages with content: how long they spend on a task, when they begin to lose focus, and when they encounter obstacles. This allows AI to offer real-time interventions. For example, if a student spends too long on a particular question or seems to be repeatedly making the same mistake, AI can prompt them with hints or additional resources. On the other hand, if a student breezes through material too quickly, AI might challenge them with more difficult problems to maintain engagement.

This constant, real-time feedback loop is what differentiates AI-driven education from traditional methods. In the past, teachers had to rely on periodic assessments to gauge a student's understanding. Now, AI provides continuous feedback, allowing for instantaneous adjustments to the learning experience. This ensures that students are never left behind, and that no matter how well or poorly they are performing, they always receive the support they need to succeed.

In addition, AI's ability to monitor cognitive and behavioral signals enables the creation of **dynamic learning environments**. These environments can adapt to different students based on their cognitive load, attention span, and problem-solving approaches. If a student seems overwhelmed by the complexity of the material, AI can reduce the cognitive load by simplifying the task or providing additional guidance. If the student is highly engaged, the system can introduce more complex problems, ensuring that they are constantly challenged without becoming frustrated.

This dynamic adjustment ensures that learning is not only personalized but also highly effective. By matching the difficulty and pace of material with the student's cognitive and emotional state, AI helps create an optimal learning environment, where students can thrive at their own pace and at their highest potential.

10.8 AI's Impact on Teacher Roles and Classroom Dynamics

The introduction of AI into education doesn't eliminate the need for teachers; rather, it transforms the role of the educator. Teachers are no longer simply lecturers, passing knowledge down to passive recipients. Instead, they become facilitators of learning, guiding students through personalized educational experiences. AI systems handle much of the data analysis, assessment, and individualized content delivery, freeing teachers to focus on what they do best: fostering relationships, offering emotional support, and facilitating deeper understanding.

AI systems can provide teachers with detailed insights into each student's progress, strengths, and areas of difficulty. For example, a teacher can access data showing which students are excelling in certain areas, which need extra help, and which may be struggling with specific concepts. This empowers teachers to tailor their instruction more effectively, providing targeted interventions and offering additional resources where needed.

Furthermore, AI can help alleviate the administrative burden that teachers often face. Grading, lesson planning, and tracking student progress can be time-consuming, but AI can automate many of these tasks. By doing so, AI gives teachers more time to focus on interactive, high-value activities—such as one-on-one student support, classroom discussions, and creative lessons that foster critical thinking and collaboration.

This shift in teacher roles also has profound implications for classroom dynamics. With AI systems handling much of the data analysis and content delivery, classrooms become more collaborative environments. Teachers and students work together to explore, discuss, and apply knowledge, while AI supports this process by providing personalized feedback and guiding each student on their learning journey.

In essence, AI serves as a powerful teaching assistant, enabling teachers to provide a higher level of individualized attention and support. This transformation can result in a more engaged and motivated student body, as well as a more efficient and effective classroom environment.

10.9 Ethical Considerations and Challenges in AI-Driven Education

While the potential of AI in education is vast, it also raises important ethical considerations. As AI systems become more integrated into the learning environment, questions about privacy, bias, and accountability must be addressed to ensure that these technologies benefit all students equitably.

One of the primary concerns revolves around **data privacy**. AI systems collect vast amounts of data to personalize learning experiences, track student progress, and provide real-time feedback. This data may include sensitive information, such as a student's learning behaviors, emotional states, and even personal details. As educational institutions increasingly rely on AI, it is essential to ensure that student data is kept secure and that privacy is respected. Schools and governments must implement strict data protection policies, ensuring that student information is never exploited or misused. Transparency in how this data is collected and used is critical in maintaining trust with students, parents, and educators.

Another ethical issue is the potential for **bias** in AI algorithms. AI systems are only as good as the data they are trained on, and if the data reflects historical inequalities or biases, those biases can be perpetuated through the AI's recommendations. For example, if an AI system is trained on data that underrepresents certain ethnic groups or genders, it may produce learning materials that are not inclusive or may fail to recognize the unique needs of these students. Addressing this requires careful curation of training data to ensure that AI systems are not unintentionally reinforcing existing disparities. Furthermore, ongoing monitoring and adjustment of AI algorithms will be necessary to detect and correct any biased behavior that may arise.

Beyond privacy and bias, there is also the question of **accessibility**. AI-driven education systems have the potential to democratize learning, providing personalized support to students who might otherwise be left behind. However, access to these technologies must be equitable. If AI-powered educational tools are only available in well-funded schools or communities, they may exacerbate existing educational inequalities. To mitigate this, policymakers must work to ensure that AI technologies are available to all students, regardless of their socioeconomic background.

Finally, AI's growing role in education raises questions about **teacher accountability**. While AI can assist in providing personalized learning experiences and administrative support, it is still the teacher's responsibility to ensure that students receive a holistic education. AI systems may make mistakes, fail to recognize certain nuances in student behavior, or provide misleading feedback. Teachers must remain engaged and vigilant in using

AI as a tool to enhance, rather than replace, their teaching practices. It is crucial that AI does not diminish the human element of teaching, which is essential for fostering creativity, emotional intelligence, and critical thinking.

In addressing these ethical concerns, it is important to create a framework that not only promotes innovation but also safeguards the interests of students, teachers, and society at large. Collaboration between technologists, educators, policymakers, and ethicists will be key in navigating the challenges and ensuring that AI's role in education remains positive and inclusive.

10.10 The Future of AI in Education: Possibilities and Predictions

Looking ahead, the role of AI in education is expected to grow exponentially. As AI technologies become more advanced, they will continue to transform the way we teach and learn. The future promises even more personalized, engaging, and efficient learning experiences, but there are still numerous frontiers to explore.

One of the most exciting possibilities is the use of **AI-powered virtual classrooms**. Imagine a future where AI-driven avatars serve as personalized instructors, capable of delivering lessons in real-time while adapting to each student's needs. These avatars would be able to respond to questions, explain concepts, and provide feedback just like a human teacher, but with the added benefit of being available 24/7. Students could learn at their own pace, receiving instant feedback and support, no matter where they are located. This could revolutionize education, particularly in remote areas where access to qualified teachers is limited.

Additionally, AI could enable **global collaboration** on a scale never seen before. Through AI-powered translation and communication tools, students from different countries, cultures, and languages could collaborate on projects, share knowledge, and learn from one another in real-time. This could create a more interconnected world, where cultural and linguistic barriers are minimized, and students have access to a diverse range of perspectives and learning experiences.

Another area of future development is **adaptive learning environments** that are not only personalized to individual students but also able to anticipate and respond to group dynamics. In a future classroom, AI could analyze how students interact with one another and dynamically adjust the content and pace of lessons to optimize group learning. For instance, if students are working in a group on a project, AI could recommend resources, suggest collaboration strategies, or even introduce new concepts based on the group's collective needs and progress.

Moreover, as AI systems continue to improve, they will be able to better understand and replicate human cognitive and emotional states, leading to even more sophisticated and responsive learning experiences. **AI-driven neuroeducation** could become a key area of research, focusing on how AI can work in tandem with neuroscience to optimize learning. By analyzing brain activity and cognitive patterns, AI could identify the best learning methods for individual students, further personalizing the educational experience.

Despite these exciting prospects, it is important to remember that the integration of AI into education must be done thoughtfully and ethically. The goal should always be to enhance, rather than replace, human interaction and to ensure that AI serves as a tool for promoting student growth, equity, and well-being. As AI continues to evolve, it will be crucial to maintain a balance between technological innovation and the core values of education: curiosity, empathy, and the pursuit of knowledge.

10.11 Conclusion: The Human-AI Partnership in Education

As AI continues to shape the future of education, it's essential to view this technology not as a replacement for human teachers but as a powerful ally in the pursuit of educational excellence. AI has the potential to revolutionize the learning process, offering personalized, adaptive, and emotionally intelligent support for students of all ages. However, its success will ultimately depend on how we harness this technology and integrate it into the broader educational framework.

The future of education lies in the partnership between humans and AI. Teachers will remain at the heart of education, guiding students and fostering a learning environment that encourages curiosity, creativity, and critical thinking. At the same time, AI will provide invaluable insights, personalized learning experiences, and administrative support, ensuring that no student is left behind.

As we move forward, it is crucial to stay focused on the ethical implications of AI in education, ensuring that all students have access to these transformative tools, that their privacy is respected, and that biases are eliminated. By approaching AI's role in education with care, compassion, and collaboration, we can create a learning ecosystem that is more inclusive, dynamic, and empowering for all.

Chapter 11: Emotional Intelligence in AI

11.1 Introduction to Emotional Intelligence

Emotional Intelligence (E.I) has long been hailed as a critical component of human interaction. In a world that increasingly prizes collaboration, decision-making, and effective communication, EI is often seen as the foundation of both personal success and societal cohesion. At its core, emotional intelligence involves the ability to recognize, understand, and manage one's own emotions, while also understanding and influencing the emotions of others.

While traditionally linked to humans, the concept of emotional intelligence is now entering the realm of artificial intelligence. As AI systems become more embedded in our daily lives, their ability to interpret, respond to, and even emulate human emotions is not just a desirable feature—it is essential. We are not simply asking AI to perform tasks or analyze data anymore; we are asking it to interact with us on a human level. To do this, AI must develop a sophisticated understanding of the emotions that underpin human behavior.

The role of emotional intelligence in human relationships is undisputed. It determines how well we navigate social complexities, resolve conflicts, and collaborate effectively. In AI, however, emotional intelligence is still in its infancy. AI's attempts at understanding human emotions often appear mechanical, almost like an imitation of human empathy, rather than a true understanding. But as the technology advances, there is the potential for AI to influence human behavior and interactions in profound ways.

In this chapter, we will explore how AI systems are being developed to emulate emotional intelligence. We will examine the processes by which AI recognizes emotions, responds to them, and the implications of these developments on human-AI interactions. This exploration is not just about technology—it is about the future of how we, as human beings, will relate to the machines that are becoming an increasingly integral part of our social fabric.

11.2 The Role of Emotional Intelligence in AI Development

In many ways, AI development has been defined by the quest to make machines "smarter." But as we enter an age where human emotions are becoming a central aspect of our technological interfaces, "smarter" is no longer enough. The future of AI depends on its ability to engage with us emotionally, to understand our moods, motivations, and vulnerabilities. In this sense, emotional intelligence becomes a critical criterion for AI systems.

Why does emotional intelligence matter for AI? The answer is straightforward: emotion drives human behavior. As AI systems move from purely functional applications to ones that interact with people on a personal level—whether in customer service, healthcare, or even social media—the ability to recognize and respond to emotions is essential. It's not enough for an AI to simply perform its tasks; it must respond to the human element in a way that feels intuitive and appropriate.

In the context of customer service, for example, AI-driven chatbots that detect frustration in a user's tone can adjust their responses to offer empathy and reassurance, instead of remaining rigid and formulaic. In virtual assistants, an emotionally intelligent AI would adjust its communication style depending on whether the user is stressed or relaxed. By recognizing emotional cues, AI can create a more engaging and supportive user experience.

Furthermore, emotionally intelligent AI can help build trust. Imagine a healthcare robot that detects signs of anxiety in a patient and responds with calm, comforting language or nonverbal cues like a soft tone or reassuring gestures. Such responses can foster a deeper connection, making patients feel understood and cared for. Emotional intelligence thus enhances the effectiveness of AI by making it more relatable, human-like, and ultimately more useful.

But AI's role in emotional intelligence is not just about improving user experience—it is about rethinking the relationship between humans and machines. As AI systems learn to interpret and respond to emotions, the nature of this interaction evolves. We are moving toward a future where AI may not only assist us but also influence our emotional states, our choices, and even our social dynamics.

11.3 Understanding Emotional Recognition in AI

For AI to exhibit emotional intelligence, it must first learn how to recognize emotions. This is no easy feat. Emotions are complex, multifaceted, and often communicated in subtle ways that go beyond the spoken word. While humans have an inherent ability to read emotions through facial expressions, tone of voice, and body language, AI must rely on algorithms to decode these signals.

At the core of AI's emotional recognition capabilities are machine learning models trained on vast datasets of human emotional expressions. These models are designed to analyze and interpret emotions from multiple channels: facial expressions, voice tone, body language, and even text. In some systems, emotional recognition is achieved through image analysis, where facial expressions are mapped to specific emotional categories like happiness, anger, or sadness. In others, AI systems analyze vocal tones, pacing, and intonation to gauge a person's emotional state.

Machine learning algorithms allow AI to continually improve its ability to recognize emotions over time. Initially, AI may struggle to detect subtle emotional cues, but as it is exposed to more data, its accuracy improves. For example, a voice recognition system trained on a large number of emotionally diverse conversations will eventually learn to detect variations in voice pitch and cadence, allowing it to discern feelings like anxiety or excitement.

However, AI's recognition of emotions is not flawless. While it can be remarkably accurate at identifying basic emotions like anger, happiness, or sadness, it struggles with more complex emotional states, like confusion or ambivalence. Moreover, emotional recognition can be influenced by cultural differences. A smile, for example, might be interpreted as happiness in one culture, but as nervousness in another. AI must therefore be trained on diverse datasets to ensure that it can accurately interpret emotions across different cultural contexts.

The limitations of emotional recognition technology highlight the need for caution. While AI may one day be able to recognize emotions with near-perfect accuracy, it must also understand the context in which those emotions arise. Context is vital for emotional interpretation. A person's tone of voice might signal frustration in one scenario but be entirely neutral in another. This is where AI's emotional intelligence intersects with its need for deeper learning and understanding of human experience.

11.4 AI's Ability to Respond to Emotions

Once AI systems can recognize emotions, the next step is the ability to respond appropriately. Emotional intelligence is not simply about recognizing emotions—it's about knowing how to react. AI systems are being designed to offer responses that align with human emotional states, whether it be empathy, encouragement, or constructive feedback.

The complexity of AI's emotional responses depends on several factors: the emotional state of the user, the context of the interaction, and the desired outcome. In some cases, an AI system might offer empathy, responding with supportive language when it detects sadness or frustration. In other cases, it might employ humor or motivation to uplift the user when detecting a neutral or positive emotional state. These responses are generated using algorithms that combine emotional recognition with natural language processing (NLP) models.

For instance, an AI customer service chatbot might detect frustration in a user's tone and switch to a more compassionate and understanding mode of communication. Instead of sticking to a rigid script, it might offer apologies, acknowledge the user's feelings, and provide reassurance. Similarly, in educational AI applications, systems might respond to a student's anxiety about a test with calming language or offer additional resources for support.

However, the question remains: Can AI truly understand human emotions, or is it simply mimicking human emotional responses? While AI can simulate emotional responses, it does not experience emotions in the same way humans do. A machine's response is the result of algorithmic decisions based on patterns and data, not a genuine emotional experience. This brings us to the debate around **empathy in AI**—can machines be truly empathetic, or are they simply designed to appear so?

11.5 Empathy in AI: Can Machines Truly Understand Emotions?

Empathy is the cornerstone of emotional intelligence. It involves more than just recognizing another person's emotions; it is about deeply understanding and sharing those emotions. For humans, empathy is a fundamental part of social interaction, helping to foster connections and support.

In AI, the ability to exhibit empathy is a subject of intense debate. AI systems can simulate empathetic behavior—responding to emotional cues in ways that suggest they understand and care. For example, a virtual therapist might detect signs of distress in a patient's voice and respond with words that offer comfort and validation. While the patient may feel heard and understood, the AI has no genuine emotional connection to the patient's experience. It is simply processing patterns in the data and responding accordingly.

This leads to a philosophical question: Can empathy exist in a machine? If empathy is defined by the ability to feel and share the emotions of another, then by this definition, AI cannot be truly empathetic. However, if empathy is understood as the ability to respond appropriately to another's emotional state, then AI can certainly simulate empathy.

As AI continues to improve, it may become increasingly difficult to distinguish between human and machine empathy. The challenge will not be whether AI can replicate empathy but whether it can do so in a way that feels authentic to the human user. This raises important ethical considerations—if AI can convincingly simulate empathy, what responsibility do developers have to ensure that users are aware they are interacting with a machine?

11.6 The Psychology of Emotion in Human-AI Interaction

The relationship between human emotion and artificial intelligence is not just a technical one; it is deeply rooted in psychology. The way humans process and respond to emotions profoundly impacts how we interact with AI systems. In order to understand the influence of AI's emotional intelligence, we must first understand how emotions shape human cognition and behavior.

Human emotions are powerful drivers of decision-making, influencing everything from our responses to everyday challenges to major life choices. Psychological theories of emotion, such as the James-Lange theory and the Cannon-Bard theory, offer different perspectives on how emotions are experienced and expressed. According to the James-Lange theory, emotions are the result of physiological changes in response to external stimuli (e.g., heart racing in response to fear). In contrast, the Cannon-Bard theory posits that emotional experiences and physiological responses occur simultaneously, suggesting that emotions are deeply integrated with bodily reactions.

These psychological models inform the design of AI systems that aim to simulate or understand human emotional states. For instance, emotion recognition algorithms may use physiological data—such as heart rate, voice pitch, or facial expressions—to gauge emotional responses. These signals are then interpreted by AI systems to determine the user's emotional state, whether positive, neutral, or negative.

As AI systems become more emotionally intelligent, they will increasingly rely on these psychological principles to understand how humans process and react to emotions. However, AI's interpretation of emotion will always be limited by the inherent complexity and subjectivity of human experience. While a machine may be able to recognize when a person is angry or sad, it cannot fully comprehend the depth and nuances of those emotions in the same way a human can.

In human-AI interactions, emotions are not just processed by the user—they also affect the behavior of the AI system. For example, an AI system might alter its tone of voice or communication style based on the perceived emotional state of the user. If a user seems frustrated, the system might offer a soothing tone or more empathetic language to defuse the situation. This type of emotional reciprocity is essential to building rapport and trust between AI and human users. The more adept AI becomes at mirroring human emotions, the more natural these interactions will feel.

The psychology of human emotions also informs how AI systems adapt and learn from their interactions. Just as humans can adjust their behavior based on the emotional feedback they receive from others, AI systems can evolve their responses based on the emotional data they collect. Over time, this leads to increasingly personalized interactions where the AI seems to "understand" the user's emotional needs, making the system feel more intuitive and connected.

11.7 Ethical Implications of Emotional Intelligence in AI

As with all advancements in technology, the integration of emotional intelligence into AI systems raises significant ethical concerns. The ability for AI to recognize and respond to human emotions opens up a myriad of possibilities, but it also introduces potential risks. These risks stem from how AI might manipulate, exploit, or be misused in emotionally sensitive contexts.

One of the primary ethical concerns is the potential for **emotional manipulation**. Emotionally intelligent AI systems, such as those used in marketing, entertainment, or even political campaigns, can influence human emotions by responding in ways that trigger specific emotional reactions. For example, an AI-driven advertising system could exploit a user's feelings of loneliness or insecurity to sell products designed to make them feel better. In this case, the AI is responding to emotional cues, but its primary goal is not empathy—it is profit.

Similarly, **privacy concerns** surrounding emotional recognition cannot be overlooked. For AI to interpret and respond to emotions accurately, it must gather and analyze sensitive data, such as facial expressions, voice tone, and physiological signals. This information is deeply personal and could be used for unintended purposes, such as profiling or surveillance. The idea of an AI system continuously monitoring one's emotional state raises questions about consent and control. Who owns the data collected by emotionally intelligent AI systems, and how can users ensure their emotional privacy is respected?

Furthermore, **AI in therapeutic or mental health applications** presents a unique set of ethical challenges. AI systems designed to assist in therapy or mental health care have the potential to offer valuable support for people with anxiety, depression, or other psychological conditions. However, AI cannot replicate the complex emotional understanding and empathy of a human therapist. This raises questions about whether it is ethical to use AI in sensitive areas like therapy, where deep emotional connections and trust are required. Should AI be allowed to provide therapy, or should it be limited to supportive roles under the guidance of human professionals?

There are also ethical concerns about **emotional labor** in AI. Emotional labor refers to the effort involved in managing and regulating one's emotions to meet the expectations of others. In human-AI interactions, this concept extends to the AI systems themselves. Machines designed to exhibit empathy may bear the emotional responsibility of soothing or comforting users, but they do not have the capability to experience the emotional labor they perform. The idea of machines performing emotional labor raises concerns about exploitation—machines doing emotional work that is typically expected of humans, yet without the same rights or recognition.

As AI systems continue to evolve, it is essential for developers, ethicists, and policymakers to establish guidelines that address these concerns. There must be transparency about how AI systems collect and use emotional data, and users must retain control over their emotional information. Additionally, ethical boundaries should be established to ensure that AI systems are used responsibly, particularly in areas like mental health, where the emotional stakes are high.

11.8 Future Directions of Emotional Intelligence in AI

Looking ahead, the potential for AI to develop deeper emotional intelligence is vast. As machine learning algorithms become more sophisticated and datasets grow richer, AI's ability to recognize and respond to emotions will continue to improve. But what does the future hold for emotionally intelligent AI?

One area of development lies in **advances in emotion recognition technologies**. While current systems are capable of detecting basic emotions like happiness, anger, or sadness, the future will likely bring AI systems that can understand more complex emotional states. For instance, AI may be able to detect mixed emotions, such as someone feeling both anxious and excited, and respond in a nuanced way. Furthermore, AI systems may learn to read more subtle cues, such as micro-expressions or even changes in biometric signals like heart rate or skin conductance. These advancements could make AI interactions feel more personalized and responsive.

Another promising direction is the role AI could play in **emotional well-being**. By using AI to monitor and respond to emotional states, it may be possible to create systems that help individuals manage their emotions more effectively. For example, an AI system could offer mindfulness exercises or breathing techniques to someone experiencing stress. AI could even assist in emotional regulation by providing real-time feedback on a person's emotional state and offering suggestions for coping strategies.

AI could also become a tool for teaching **emotional intelligence**. Many people struggle with understanding or managing their emotions, and AI systems could provide tailored exercises and feedback to help individuals develop their emotional skills. Whether it's a child learning empathy or an adult trying to improve their emotional regulation, AI could act as both a coach and a companion on the path to emotional growth.

Finally, as AI's emotional intelligence evolves, we can expect to see greater **collaboration between humans and machines**. Rather than simply reacting to emotions, AI could learn to anticipate emotional needs and proactively offer support. Imagine an AI assistant that recognizes when you are overwhelmed and offers to handle certain tasks, or a robot designed to help elderly people feel less isolated by engaging them in emotionally enriching conversations. These kinds of emotionally intelligent systems will not just respond to us—they will become integral partners in our emotional lives.

11.9 Conclusion: The Future of Emotional Intelligence in AI

As we look to the future of artificial intelligence, the integration of emotional intelligence will undoubtedly play a pivotal role. From improving human-AI interactions to supporting emotional well-being, emotionally intelligent AI systems have the potential to transform the way we live, work, and interact with technology.

Yet, the road ahead is not without challenges. The ability for AI to emulate emotion does not mean that it can truly understand human experience. While machines may become increasingly skilled at recognizing and responding to emotional cues, they will always be limited by the fact that they do not "feel" in the same way humans do.

The integration of emotional intelligence into AI presents both incredible opportunities and serious ethical concerns. As we continue to develop these technologies, it is essential that we remain mindful of the potential risks, ensuring that AI is used responsibly and ethically.

Ultimately, the future of AI's emotional intelligence will not just depend on technological advancements, but on how we choose to shape the relationship between humans and machines. By maintaining a careful balance between innovation and ethics, we can ensure that emotionally intelligent AI serves to enrich human lives, rather than replacing or manipulating the emotions that make us human.

Chapter 12: AI and Consumer Behavior

Introduction

In the vast landscape of modern commerce, the ways in which we make purchasing decisions have changed dramatically. What once involved simple choices between products on store shelves is now governed by sophisticated algorithms, predictive models, and an almost psychic understanding of what we need before we even realize it ourselves. At the core of this transformation is artificial intelligence (A.I)—a force that not only analyzes our past purchasing behaviors but anticipates our desires, often before we can articulate them. As AI continues to evolve, it profoundly reshapes consumer behavior, offering businesses an unprecedented ability to predict, influence, and even manipulate the choices we make.

But how does AI, a technology born from the pursuit of data and logic, tap into the deeply emotional and psychological world of human buying decisions? What happens when machines learn to understand us better than we understand ourselves? This chapter explores the intricate dance between AI and consumer behavior, unraveling how AI influences our purchasing patterns and decisions, often without us even realizing it.

12.1 The Rise of AI in Consumer Insights

To understand the extent of AI's influence on consumer behavior, it is essential to first appreciate the role AI plays in analyzing consumer data. The rise of AI in consumer insights has reshaped how companies understand their customers. In the past, businesses relied on surveys, focus groups, and basic demographic data to guide their marketing strategies. Today, AI leverages vast amounts of data—much of it generated by the digital footprints we leave behind—to glean insights into consumer preferences, habits, and even subconscious inclinations.

Machine learning algorithms can process and analyze this data at speeds and volumes unimaginable to human researchers. These algorithms are designed to identify patterns in consumer behavior, linking seemingly unrelated pieces of information—from a user's browsing history to their social media activity—to predict future purchasing behaviors. AI tools enable businesses to segment their customers with an unprecedented level of precision, targeting individuals with hyper-personalized content that speaks directly to their needs and desires.

Predictive analytics, powered by AI, is a game-changer in understanding consumer behavior. By analyzing vast quantities of data, AI not only identifies patterns in past purchases but also forecasts future needs. For instance, based on a customer's browsing and shopping history, AI can predict when that customer is likely to purchase a new pair of shoes, a laptop, or even decide to order food delivery. These predictions help businesses create highly targeted marketing strategies, ensuring they can deliver the right product to the right person at the right time.

Yet, this new ability to predict consumer behavior raises fundamental questions: Are we truly making free, independent choices, or are our decisions increasingly being shaped by invisible algorithms?

12.2 Personalization of Consumer Experiences

One of the most significant ways AI influences consumer behavior is through personalization. In the past, consumers were often bombarded with generic advertisements and promotional offers. Today, AI enables companies to deliver highly personalized experiences based on individual preferences, browsing behavior, and purchase history. Personalization is not limited to product recommendations; it extends to everything from the content we see on our social media feeds to the way a website presents itself to us.

The importance of personalization in consumer decision-making cannot be overstated. Research shows that consumers are far more likely to engage with brands that provide personalized experiences. When AI systems tailor their offerings to match the preferences of individual consumers, they create a sense of relevance and connection that drives purchasing behavior. Personalized experiences increase brand loyalty, customer satisfaction, and the likelihood of repeat purchases.

For example, think about the personalized recommendations on platforms like Amazon or Netflix. These systems don't just rely on your past purchases or viewing habits; they use complex algorithms that take into account millions of data points, from the behavior of users with similar tastes to real-time trends. The result is a constant stream of suggestions that feel as if the system is reading your mind. Over time, this personalization becomes so precise that consumers begin to trust these systems implicitly—so much so that the product recommendations feel like natural extensions of their desires.

AI's role in personalization is not only about understanding what consumers have done in the past; it also involves predicting what they will want next. This predictive power is what sets AI-driven personalization apart from traditional marketing methods. It transforms consumer experiences into highly customized journeys, where businesses no longer just react to consumer behavior—they anticipate and influence it.

12.3 Emotional Targeting: AI and the Psychology of Buying

At the heart of consumer behavior lies emotion. While many decisions are driven by logic and necessity, the majority of purchasing choices are influenced by our emotional state. Emotional triggers like excitement, fear, happiness, or even nostalgia often determine what we buy, when we buy, and why we buy. Understanding this, AI has evolved to not only recognize consumer preferences but also to tap into the emotions that guide purchasing decisions.

AI-driven marketing campaigns now utilize emotional intelligence to tailor their messages to resonate with the consumer's feelings. By analyzing factors such as facial expressions, tone of voice, and even the words consumers use in online interactions, AI systems can identify emotional states and respond accordingly. For instance, if a customer is browsing a product late at night, a message that emphasizes urgency—"only two left in stock"—might trigger a fear of missing out (FOMO), encouraging a quicker decision.

Emotional intelligence in AI extends beyond detecting emotional cues; it also involves understanding which emotions are most likely to prompt purchasing decisions. Marketing experts have long known that emotions such as excitement, fear, and happiness can influence consumer behavior. AI systems now analyze vast datasets to identify the precise emotional triggers that resonate with different consumer segments. Whether it's a heartwarming advertisement designed to make you feel connected to a brand or an ad that exploits your fear of missing out, AI is increasingly adept at using emotion to drive sales.

While this emotional targeting can lead to more effective marketing, it also raises ethical concerns. Are consumers aware of the emotional manipulation at play? How do we ensure that emotional targeting is used responsibly, rather than exploitatively?

12.4 Behavioral Analytics and Predicting Buying Patterns

AI's ability to predict consumer behavior goes beyond understanding past purchasing patterns. Using advanced machine learning algorithms, AI systems can anticipate future buying decisions with remarkable accuracy. By analyzing an individual's previous interactions with a brand, as well as data from similar consumers, AI can predict what products someone is likely to purchase next.

This predictive power is especially evident in industries like e-commerce, where the sheer volume of data allows businesses to forecast trends with incredible precision. For example, if a customer frequently buys running shoes or athletic gear, AI can predict that they may soon need new gear for an upcoming marathon, or that they may be interested in purchasing supplements or fitness trackers. These predictions help businesses create tailored advertising and product recommendations that feel incredibly relevant and timely.

However, there is a fine line between prediction and manipulation. While predictive analytics can help businesses meet consumer needs more effectively, it also means that companies are becoming increasingly adept at steering consumer behavior in ways that feel almost subconscious. The rise of "hyper-targeted" advertising, powered by AI, is both a boon for businesses and a potential challenge for consumer autonomy.

12.5 AI in Online Shopping and E-commerce

The impact of AI on consumer behavior is most visible in the realm of online shopping and e-commerce. Virtual assistants, chatbots, and AI-powered recommendation engines have completely transformed the way consumers shop online. These systems offer personalized shopping experiences, guide users to the products they are most likely to purchase, and even assist in the checkout process.

Take the example of AI-powered recommendation engines, which analyze a shopper's previous purchases, browsing history, and demographic information to suggest items they may like. These systems don't just recommend items based on simple categorization—they use deep learning to understand the nuances of consumer behavior, such as preferences for color, size, brand, or even product reviews. As a result, these systems make online shopping not only easier but also more tailored to individual tastes. Moreover, AI is revolutionizing inventory management and pricing strategies. Dynamic pricing algorithms, powered by AI, can adjust the prices of products in real time based on factors such as demand, inventory levels, and even the consumer's browsing history. This level of automation allows businesses to stay competitive while also maximizing profit margins. In many ways, AI has transformed online shopping into a personalized, intuitive experience. By guiding consumers to the products they're most likely to purchase, AI systems increase the chances of conversion and customer satisfaction.

12.6 Social Media and Influencer Marketing with AI

Social media is a powerful tool for influencing consumer behavior, and AI plays a significant role in optimizing this influence. By analyzing user activity across platforms like Facebook, Instagram, and Twitter, AI systems can identify trends, track sentiment, and even predict which content will resonate most with target audiences. AI also helps businesses identify influencers whose followers are likely to be interested in their products.

Influencer marketing, fueled by AI, has become one of the most effective ways to reach potential customers. AI-driven tools analyze vast amounts of social media data to determine which influencers are the best fit for a brand. These tools assess factors such as engagement rates, follower demographics, and past performance to predict how successful a collaboration will be. This level of precision has made influencer marketing more strategic and impactful.

Through AI, social media platforms can also deliver hyper-targeted ads based on user behavior, making them more likely to influence purchasing decisions. Social media ads, personalized based on the user's preferences and browsing history, feel more relevant, increasing the likelihood of conversion.

12.7 Consumer Trust and Ethical Considerations in AI Marketing

As AI plays an increasingly central role in shaping consumer behavior, trust becomes a crucial issue. AI's ability to personalize and predict consumer preferences is based on data—often vast amounts of personal information. The more personalized an experience becomes, the more questions arise about privacy and data security.

While consumers may benefit from personalized recommendations, they may also feel uneasy knowing that their every move is being tracked and analyzed. Ethical concerns arise when AI crosses the line from helping consumers to manipulating their behavior. Transparency in AI algorithms, data usage, and how consumers are being influenced is critical to maintaining trust in these systems.

To ensure that AI in marketing remains ethical, companies must be transparent about how they collect and use consumer data. Consumers should have control over their data and be able to opt out of certain types of tracking or targeting.

12.8 The Future of AI in Consumer Behavior

Looking ahead, the role of AI in consumer behavior will only become more prominent. With advancements in AI technologies such as deep learning and natural language processing, the future promises even more personalized and intuitive consumer experiences. AI systems will not only predict what consumers will buy—they will proactively engage them, offering solutions before they even realize they need them.

The integration of AI with augmented reality (AR) and virtual reality (VR) will also transform the shopping experience. Imagine walking into a store virtually, with AI guiding you through a highly personalized shopping experience, suggesting products based on your preferences, and offering real-time discounts or promotions.

12.9 AI in Consumer Loyalty Programs

One of the most effective applications of AI in consumer behavior lies in the realm of loyalty programs. Traditionally, companies have offered discounts or rewards in exchange for repeated business. With the advent of AI, these programs have become far more sophisticated, taking into account not only a consumer's purchasing history but also predictive insights about their future behavior.

AI systems analyze a wealth of data, including purchasing patterns, online browsing habits, and even responses to marketing campaigns, to determine what will motivate a particular consumer to return. By offering personalized rewards, tailored promotions, and time-sensitive incentives, AI-powered loyalty programs make consumers feel more valued and understood, encouraging brand loyalty.

The benefit of AI in this space is its ability to continuously adapt. As consumer preferences evolve, AI can tweak loyalty program offerings in real-time, ensuring that rewards and incentives are always aligned with the consumer's needs and desires. Furthermore, businesses can leverage AI to identify when a loyal customer is becoming disengaged, offering incentives to prevent churn before it happens.

However, the increasing sophistication of these loyalty programs raises important questions about consumer behavior manipulation. With AI able to predict the exact reward that will prompt a purchase, businesses may have an unprecedented ability to subtly influence consumer decisions. As these systems grow in capability, consumers may not even be aware of how their loyalty is being engineered by algorithms.

12.10 Behavioral Nudges and Consumer Autonomy

One of the more controversial applications of AI in consumer behavior is the use of "behavioral nudges." Borrowed from behavioral economics, the concept of nudging involves subtly influencing individuals' choices without restricting their freedom to choose. In the context of AI, nudges can be as simple as pushing a consumer toward a specific product or service based on their past behavior or preferences.

AI systems can design these nudges by identifying patterns in a consumer's previous actions. For instance, if a consumer has frequently viewed certain types of fitness equipment, an AI system might send them an email or push notification offering a discount on related products. While these nudges can be harmless or even beneficial, they raise ethical questions about how far businesses should go in influencing consumer decisions.

AI's ability to predict and manipulate consumer choices raises concerns about autonomy. While many of these nudges are subtle, there is a fine line between offering a helpful suggestion and subtly steering consumers toward purchases they might not have otherwise made. The risk is that consumers, in their quest for convenience and personalization, may unknowingly give up a degree of autonomy in their decision-making process.

Moreover, AI-driven nudges can be exploited to serve the interests of large corporations rather than the consumers themselves. For example, an AI-powered loyalty program that nudges consumers to buy more frequently or spend more than they planned can be seen as manipulative, even if it's disguised as a "personalized offer." The issue of consent becomes central to this conversation: Are consumers fully aware of the ways in which AI is nudging their decisions, and are they truly making independent choices?

12.11 Transparency and the Ethics of AI in Consumer Behavior

As AI becomes a more powerful force in influencing consumer behavior, the ethical implications of its use cannot be ignored. One of the primary concerns is transparency: how much should consumers be aware of the algorithms that shape their decisions? Currently, most consumers are unaware of the extent to which AI influences their behavior. Recommendation engines, targeted ads, personalized pricing models—all of these are based on complex AI algorithms that operate behind the scenes. The lack of transparency in how these systems work leaves consumers vulnerable to manipulation.

For AI to be ethically integrated into consumer behavior, businesses must embrace transparency. This means informing consumers about how their data is collected, how AI algorithms operate, and how their choices are being influenced. Additionally, companies must offer consumers the ability to opt-out of certain AI-driven experiences, giving them control over how their personal data is used.

In addition to transparency, businesses must ensure that AI systems are designed with fairness in mind. One of the dangers of relying heavily on AI for consumer insights is that the algorithms can inadvertently reinforce existing biases. If an AI system is trained on biased data, it can perpetuate those biases in its recommendations. For example, a biased recommendation engine might suggest products that predominantly appeal to one demographic, excluding others. Ensuring fairness in AI-driven consumer behavior systems is not just an ethical obligation but also a business necessity to maintain trust and brand loyalty.

Ethical considerations around AI in consumer behavior also touch on privacy concerns. As businesses increasingly rely on data-driven insights to personalize consumer experiences, the volume of personal information collected and analyzed grows exponentially. Consumers must feel confident that their privacy is being protected, especially when sensitive data—such as health information, financial transactions, or browsing habits—is being used to tailor experiences.

12.12 The Future of AI in Consumer Behavior

As AI continues to evolve, its role in consumer behavior will undoubtedly grow. In the coming years, we will likely see even more sophisticated algorithms that better understand human preferences, emotions, and motivations. AI will not only predict what products we are likely to buy but also anticipate the underlying emotional triggers that drive those purchases. These developments will lead to a more seamless, immersive shopping experience where consumers feel like AI is truly working in their best interest.

The integration of AI with emerging technologies such as virtual and augmented reality (VR and AR) will further revolutionize the consumer experience. Imagine a scenario where an AI-powered system understands your preferences and can create virtual shopping environments tailored just for you. Whether you're "walking" through a virtual store, interacting with a chatbot, or trying on products virtually, AI will make the experience more personalized and engaging than ever before.

Moreover, as AI's predictive capabilities improve, the line between human decision-making and machine influence will blur. In the near future, AI might not just suggest products but help consumers navigate complex purchasing decisions. AI could act as a "virtual shopping assistant," providing guidance, advice, and personalized recommendations in real-time—almost like a trusted advisor.

At the same time, this increasing dependence on AI raises significant concerns about autonomy and the future of consumer choice. Will consumers become passive recipients of algorithmic suggestions, or will they remain active, informed decision-makers? Will we continue to value spontaneous, unpredictable choices, or will we surrender to a future where everything is tailored to our pre-existing preferences?

12.13 Conclusion

Artificial intelligence has already transformed the way consumers make purchasing decisions, but this is only the beginning. From personalization and emotional targeting to behavioral nudges and loyalty programs, AI is weaving itself into the fabric of consumer behavior in ways that were previously unimaginable. While these developments offer convenience and personalization, they also raise important ethical questions about transparency, privacy, and consumer autonomy.

As AI continues to evolve, businesses will need to navigate these ethical challenges, balancing the desire for profit with the responsibility to protect consumers from manipulation. The future of AI in consumer behavior will be shaped not only by advances in technology but also by the ways in which society chooses to regulate and integrate these systems. The ultimate goal should be to ensure that AI serves consumers, enhancing their experiences without infringing on their freedom of choice.

Ultimately, AI's role in consumer behavior will be determined by how we, as a society, choose to wield this powerful technology. Will we use it to empower consumers and create meaningful, personalized experiences, or will we allow it to manipulate and control our choices? The answer lies in how we approach the intersection of AI and consumer rights in the years to come.

Chapter 13: The Ethics of AI in Human Behavior Studies

13.1 Introduction to AI in Human Behavior Research

The intersection of artificial intelligence and human behavior is a fertile ground for scientific exploration. With AI's rise as a tool capable of mimicking human cognitive processes, the field of psychological research is transforming in profound ways. For decades, psychologists and researchers have sought to decode the complexities of human behavior through trials, observations, and theoretical models. But with AI's ability to process vast amounts of data and recognize patterns faster than any human mind, we are entering an era where machines assist in unraveling the deepest layers of human psychology.

Artificial intelligence is no longer a futuristic concept—it is a tool already embedded in the study of human behavior. From social media platforms to therapeutic chatbots, AI systems are increasingly involved in shaping our understanding of how individuals think, feel, and behave. However, as with all powerful technologies, AI's involvement in psychological research raises critical ethical questions. How far can we go in using AI to predict, manipulate, or modify human behavior? What ethical guidelines should govern the use of AI in these contexts?

This chapter explores these pressing questions, examining the ethical considerations that arise when AI systems are introduced into the world of human behavior studies. It challenges us to think not only about the advancements AI brings but also about the responsibilities that come with these new capabilities.

13.2 Data Privacy and Consent

At the core of any ethical discussion involving AI is the concept of data—how it is collected, processed, and used. In psychological research, particularly when studying human behavior, data is the lifeblood of the field. Traditional psychological studies rely on controlled environments and voluntary participant input. However, AI systems often rely on data gleaned from real-world interactions: from social media posts to biometric readings, AI is capable of capturing a broad spectrum of personal information that extends well beyond what participants have explicitly consented to.

Consider the scenario of a study involving AI's analysis of social media behavior to predict mental health conditions. Researchers may collect vast amounts of data, including the content of users' posts, the frequency of their online activity, or even sentiment analysis of their interactions with others. The ethical dilemma arises when participants are unaware that their data is being used for such purposes, or worse, when they do not fully understand the extent to which their private lives are being analyzed.

The issue of consent is particularly fraught when dealing with AI-driven studies. In traditional psychological research, consent is a clear process—participants are informed about the nature of the study, the data collection methods, and the potential outcomes. However, in AI-based research, the lines are more blurred. How much do participants truly understand about the algorithms analyzing their data? Are they aware that their behaviors are being interpreted by a machine rather than a human researcher? These questions require researchers to carefully navigate the boundaries of informed consent, ensuring that participants are not only aware of the study's scope but also of the potential risks associated with AI systems.

Moreover, the challenge of data privacy grows exponentially when sensitive information is involved. AI can mine deeply personal data, including health records, psychological profiles, and behavioral patterns. Protecting this data requires more than just compliance with laws like GDPR or HIPAA; it requires a fundamental respect for the autonomy and dignity of the individuals whose lives are being scrutinized. Ethical AI research must prioritize transparency and ensure that participants' data is handled responsibly, with robust safeguards in place to protect privacy.

13.3 Transparency and Accountability in AI-Driven Research

The allure of AI lies in its capacity to provide deep insights into human behavior, but this power comes with the responsibility to ensure that AI systems are transparent and accountable. Unlike traditional psychological research, where researchers can directly observe and intervene in the study process, AI systems often operate as "black boxes," making decisions and drawing conclusions that are opaque even to the researchers who designed them. This lack of transparency presents significant ethical challenges, particularly when it comes to the interpretation and application of AI findings in human behavior studies.

Imagine a study where an AI algorithm claims to have identified a pattern in the way individuals with certain mental health conditions respond to specific stimuli. The algorithm may suggest interventions or treatments based on this data. However, if the underlying mechanisms of the AI system are not fully understood or communicated, how can we trust its conclusions? Who is responsible if the AI's recommendations lead to harm or unintended consequences? The need for accountability is crucial—researchers must be able to explain how AI systems arrived at their conclusions and be able to stand by the decisions they make based on those conclusions.

This issue is particularly important in psychological research, where the consequences of AI-driven decisions can directly impact human lives. Whether AI is being used to diagnose mental health conditions, predict future behaviors, or recommend treatments, it is essential that the mechanisms behind its decisions are transparent, interpretable, and open to scrutiny. Researchers must be able to audit and explain the inner workings of AI systems to ensure they align with ethical standards and scientific integrity.

Additionally, researchers must ensure that AI systems are continually updated and refined based on feedback and new data. Relying on outdated algorithms or flawed data can have serious consequences, especially when it comes to decisions that affect people's mental well-being. Accountability goes beyond transparency; it requires constant vigilance to ensure that AI systems remain accurate and ethically sound over time.

13.4 Bias and Fairness in AI-Driven Psychological Research

Bias is an issue that plagues both human and machine-based research. Human researchers, despite their best efforts, bring their own biases into the study design, data interpretation, and analysis. AI systems, too, are susceptible to bias, often in more insidious ways. These biases arise from the data fed into the algorithms, which reflect the values, assumptions, and prejudices of the society in which they were created. When AI systems are used in psychological research, the risk is that these biases can be magnified and perpetuated.

Consider the case of AI-based mental health diagnosis tools. If the data used to train these systems is disproportionately collected from one demographic group, the algorithm may be biased in its ability to accurately diagnose individuals from other backgrounds. A system trained primarily on data from middle-class, Western, white individuals may fail to recognize patterns of mental distress in other cultural or socioeconomic groups, leading to misdiagnoses or inappropriate interventions.

The ethical responsibility of researchers lies in identifying and mitigating these biases. This can be done by diversifying the data sets used to train AI models, ensuring that they are representative of the populations they aim to serve. Furthermore, researchers must be vigilant in monitoring AI-driven studies for any signs of bias, whether in data collection, interpretation, or the conclusions drawn by the AI system.

AI-driven research holds the potential to offer groundbreaking insights into human behavior, but if not handled responsibly, it can also reinforce existing inequalities and prejudices. Ethical AI research must be committed to fairness and inclusivity, striving to eliminate biases at every stage of the research process.

13.5 AI and the Potential for Manipulation

AI's ability to predict and influence human behavior carries with it the potential for manipulation. One of the most powerful aspects of AI is its capacity to understand and predict individual preferences, emotional triggers, and behavioral patterns. This can be incredibly valuable in psychological research, allowing researchers to better understand human responses to various stimuli. However, it also raises ethical questions about the extent to which AI should be used to influence or manipulate participants.

Imagine an AI system that is designed to study the emotional responses of individuals to various marketing messages. The system could predict how certain words, images, or phrases will elicit a specific emotional response. But could this system, if left unchecked, be used to manipulate individuals into making decisions they would not have made otherwise? If an AI system can predict exactly how to trigger an emotional reaction, should it be used to nudge participants toward particular behaviors or choices?

While AI has the potential to enrich our understanding of human behavior, researchers must tread carefully when it comes to its use. The line between guiding and manipulating is often thin. Ethical AI research requires safeguards to ensure that participants are not coerced, exploited, or unduly influenced by the systems they interact with.

Furthermore, the ability to manipulate behavior raises important questions about informed consent. If participants are unaware of the extent to which AI systems are influencing their decisions or emotions, their autonomy is compromised. Researchers must ensure that participants fully understand the role of AI in the study and that they can freely opt-out or withdraw without penalty.

13.6 Autonomy and Human Dignity

In the age of artificial intelligence, one of the most pressing ethical concerns is the impact of AI on human autonomy and dignity. While AI has the potential to advance human knowledge and improve lives, its applications in psychological research raise questions about the preservation of individual freedom and self-determination. The very nature of AI suggests that it can influence and shape human behavior in ways that were previously unimaginable.

The concept of autonomy is foundational in ethical discussions surrounding AI. In psychological research, autonomy refers to a participant's right to make decisions free from undue influence, coercion, or manipulation. With AI's ability to gather and analyze vast amounts of personal data, it is increasingly possible for researchers to predict, and potentially alter, an individual's behavior, emotions, and even decisions. While these advancements hold promise for improving mental health interventions or customizing educational experiences, they also present risks that may infringe on a person's autonomy.

Take, for instance, AI systems designed to influence behavioral outcomes, such as personalized recommendations or nudging systems used in health interventions. These systems are built to steer people toward particular actions—whether it's encouraging healthier habits, guiding purchasing decisions, or even shifting political views. While the intent behind such systems may be to enhance well-being or promote certain behaviors, they can also cross ethical lines when they override an individual's ability to make independent decisions.

Furthermore, there is a significant risk of diminishing human dignity when AI is used in psychological studies in a way that reduces participants to mere data points. Human dignity involves recognizing the inherent worth of individuals as autonomous agents. If AI-driven research reduces individuals to algorithms or overlooks their subjective experiences, it risks objectifying them and diminishing their intrinsic value. This becomes especially problematic when AI is used to manipulate behavior in ways that participants might not fully comprehend or consent to.

The preservation of human dignity in AI-based psychological research demands a balance between the benefits of technological innovation and the fundamental rights of individuals. Ethical guidelines should prioritize the right to informed consent, ensuring that participants retain the freedom to make autonomous decisions about their involvement in AI-driven studies. Moreover, researchers must ensure that AI interventions do not diminish participants' capacity for self-determination or undermine their sense of personal agency.

13.7 Impact of AI Research on Society and Culture

As AI becomes more deeply embedded in psychological research, its influence extends far beyond the laboratory. AI-driven studies have the potential to shape how society views human behavior, mental health, and even identity. With AI systems capable of identifying patterns, predicting behaviors, and offering personalized interventions, they are not just tools for research—they are active participants in the social construction of human nature.

One of the most significant ethical considerations is how AI-based research might affect cultural norms and values. For example, if AI systems are used to study emotional responses to certain social behaviors, there is a risk that the data could reinforce stereotypes or cultural biases. The findings from AI-driven studies may be interpreted in ways that align with dominant cultural narratives, potentially overlooking the diverse experiences and perspectives of marginalized groups. These AI systems, by reinforcing particular patterns of behavior or emotional responses, could inadvertently shape societal values, potentially creating a feedback loop that perpetuates certain norms at the expense of others.

Moreover, the widespread use of AI in psychological research could lead to the standardization of human behavior. If AI systems are used to define what constitutes "normal" behavior, emotional responses, or cognitive patterns, individuals who deviate from these norms could be stigmatized or pathologized. The ethical dilemma here lies in the tension between using AI to understand human behavior and the risk of reducing the complexity of human experience to a set of data points that align with predefined standards.

In addition, AI's growing role in psychological research has the potential to influence public policy and societal expectations. If AI systems generate insights about mental health or human behavior that are widely accepted, these findings could inform government policies, educational strategies, or healthcare models. While this could lead to more effective interventions and treatments, it also raises ethical concerns about the potential for AI to shape public opinion in ways that are not always grounded in nuanced or holistic understandings of human behavior.

As AI continues to influence human behavior research, it is crucial for ethical guidelines to ensure that the resulting findings are not misused to manipulate or control societal norms. Researchers must be mindful of how their work might impact broader cultural narratives and ensure that AI applications respect the diversity and complexity of human experiences.

13.8 Participant Well-being and Psychological Harm

Perhaps the most important ethical consideration when it comes to AI in human behavior research is the potential for psychological harm. Traditional psychological studies are designed with the well-being of participants in mind, with careful consideration given to the risks of distress, harm, or discomfort. But when AI systems are involved, the lines between scientific inquiry and potential harm can blur.

AI systems designed to study human behavior can sometimes provoke emotional or psychological reactions that researchers may not anticipate. For example, AI-based diagnostic tools may identify mental health conditions in participants without their prior knowledge, leading to distress or anxiety about the diagnosis. Similarly, AI systems used to influence behavior or emotions could unintentionally cause participants to experience feelings of manipulation or loss of control. These are ethical issues that must be carefully considered and addressed before AI is used in human behavior studies.

One of the key ethical responsibilities of researchers is to ensure that AI-driven studies do not inflict harm on participants, either psychologically or emotionally. This involves conducting thorough risk assessments and implementing safeguards to prevent AI interventions from causing unnecessary distress. Ethical guidelines should prioritize participant well-being by establishing clear protocols for handling sensitive issues, such as when an AI-based system detects a potential mental health crisis or when a participant expresses discomfort with the study process.

Moreover, researchers must be mindful of the long-term effects that AI-driven interventions could have on participants. For example, AI systems used to personalize educational experiences could have a profound impact on a child's self-esteem or learning abilities. While AI may enhance educational outcomes, there is a risk that it may inadvertently stigmatize certain learning styles or abilities, leading to a sense of inadequacy or failure. The ethical imperative here is to ensure that AI systems are designed to foster positive psychological outcomes, supporting rather than hindering personal growth and development.

13.9 Ethical Guidelines and Regulations in AI Psychological Research

As AI continues to revolutionize the field of human behavior studies, it is crucial to establish a robust framework of ethical guidelines and regulations. While there are existing ethical standards governing traditional psychological research, these guidelines are often inadequate when it comes to AI-driven studies. The rapid pace of AI development outstrips the ability of existing regulations to keep up, leaving a gap in the protection of human participants.

Ethical frameworks must evolve to account for the unique challenges posed by AI in human behavior research. For instance, the application of AI in psychological studies often involves the collection of vast amounts of personal data, requiring more stringent data protection regulations. Additionally, the use of AI to predict or influence behavior raises new questions about consent, autonomy, and the potential for manipulation. Researchers must be held to high ethical standards, ensuring that AI systems are designed and deployed in ways that prioritize the rights and well-being of participants.

Institutional review boards (IRBs) and ethics committees will play a crucial role in overseeing AI-based research. These bodies must ensure that AI systems are rigorously tested for ethical compliance and that researchers adhere to established guidelines. Furthermore, AI developers and researchers must collaborate closely with ethicists, policymakers, and mental health professionals to create comprehensive, adaptable guidelines that can respond to the evolving nature of AI technology.

13.10 Case Studies and Ethical Dilemmas in AI Psychology Research

Real-world case studies provide a powerful lens through which we can explore the ethical complexities of integrating AI into human behavior studies. The practical application of AI in psychological research is still in its infancy, but its rapid evolution calls for deep reflection on the implications of these technologies. These cases highlight the ethical dilemmas researchers, developers, and institutions must address as AI moves beyond theoretical discussions into real-world applications.

13.10.1 Case Study 1: AI and Mental Health Diagnosis via Social Media Analysis

One of the most striking examples of AI's potential to impact human psychology is its ability to analyze vast amounts of personal data from social media platforms to predict mental health conditions. In a study conducted by a team of researchers at a major university, AI was employed to analyze public posts on social media sites like Twitter, Instagram, and Facebook. The algorithm tracked certain linguistic patterns, emotional tone, and behavioral changes over time to predict depressive symptoms in users.

While the results of the study were groundbreaking—demonstrating AI's potential to identify individuals at risk of mental health crises before they may seek help—the ethical ramifications are profound. The most glaring concern was the issue of consent. Participants whose data was used for analysis were not explicitly informed about the research, raising significant questions about the ethics of using personal, often intimate, data without clear, informed consent. Even if the data was publicly available, participants may not have understood that it was being actively analyzed for psychological insights, especially when the algorithms were not perfect and sometimes produced false positives.

This situation presents an ethical dilemma: while AI can offer life-saving predictions, the method of data collection without proper consent undermines the principles of autonomy and transparency. Moreover, the fact that individuals' emotional states were being analyzed by a machine system they did not agree to brings up another concern: the potential for emotional harm. Those identified as at-risk may experience distress, even if no actual diagnosis was made. This raises the issue of whether AI-driven research could inadvertently cause more harm than good, as emotional distress and uncertainty are amplified by the very tool designed to help.

In response to these concerns, scholars and ethicists have called for new standards of consent in AI-driven psychological research. This includes clear guidelines that require researchers to inform participants about the nature and scope of data collection, as well as ensure the participants' right to opt-out at any stage of the study. Researchers must also make it explicit that participation in these studies can carry emotional and psychological risks, and provide proper safeguards for participant well-being, including the option to withdraw data if they feel uncomfortable.

13.10.2 Case Study 2: Predictive Analytics and Behavioral Nudging

Behavioral nudging—an AI-driven approach to subtly guide individuals' decisions without overt coercion—has become an increasingly popular method for influencing consumer behavior, health choices, and even political beliefs. In one case, a health tech company implemented an AI-based nudging system designed to promote healthier lifestyle choices. The AI algorithm provided tailored suggestions to users based on their habits and preferences, such as recommending low-calorie recipes, encouraging daily exercise, and reminding individuals to take medication on time.

While the system was designed to improve well-being, critics raised concerns about the ethics of AI-driven behavioral manipulation. For one, the AI nudges were not always fully transparent. Users were often unaware of how the system arrived at its suggestions, leading some to feel uncomfortable with the idea of a machine dictating aspects of their behavior. The transparency of the AI system, or lack thereof, became a focal point for ethical scrutiny. If users don't understand how their data is being used or how decisions are being made on their behalf, can they truly be said to be participating voluntarily in their own behavioral modification?

Further complicating matters is the concept of "soft coercion." The nudges designed to push individuals toward healthier behaviors may seem innocuous, but they can erode personal autonomy. For example, the system could present personalized advertisements for exercise equipment or weight-loss supplements, subtly influencing users to make purchases they might not otherwise have made. Though these nudges are intended to be for the benefit of the user, the line between helpful guidance and manipulation becomes increasingly blurry.

In response to these ethical concerns, some AI experts have argued for greater transparency and user consent in behavioral nudging systems. Ethical frameworks should ensure that users are fully informed about the ways AI systems might influence their choices, including the algorithms that determine nudges and the data being collected. Users should have the power to opt-out or adjust their nudges if they feel uncomfortable or believe their autonomy is being compromised. Moreover, nudging systems must be designed with the utmost respect for individual rights, ensuring that behavioral suggestions do not lead to unintended psychological harm or distress.

13.10.3 Case Study 3: Facial Recognition and Emotional Intelligence in AI

AI-driven emotional intelligence—systems that interpret and respond to human emotions—has seen rapid growth in fields ranging from customer service to healthcare. A case in point is a facial recognition system developed for use in mental health diagnostics. This AI system could assess a person's emotional state based on their facial expressions, vocal tone, and other non-verbal cues. By analyzing these cues, the AI could provide insights into the person's emotional well-being and offer recommendations for interventions, such as therapy sessions, medication adjustments, or behavioral strategies.

While the potential of such systems to aid in diagnosing emotional disorders is exciting, several ethical issues arise. First, there's the issue of privacy: facial recognition systems inherently require a certain level of surveillance. Many people are unaware that their facial expressions are being analyzed in real-time, often leading to feelings of discomfort or violation. Even if the technology is applied in a controlled research environment, the collection of facial data raises questions about consent. Individuals may not fully understand how their facial expressions are being used or may feel uneasy about AI interpreting deeply personal emotional responses.

Second, the accuracy of AI in interpreting emotions is not foolproof. Despite advances in machine learning, AI systems still struggle with understanding the nuance and complexity of human emotions. A smile, for instance, can signify happiness, but it can also mask anxiety or sadness. AI-driven emotional recognition tools may misinterpret subtle emotional cues, potentially leading to inaccurate diagnoses or inappropriate recommendations. If these systems are relied upon for psychological interventions, the consequences of error can be far-reaching, including misdiagnoses or harmful advice.

These challenges point to the need for ethical guidelines that govern the use of AI in emotional intelligence applications. Researchers and developers must prioritize transparency in how emotional data is collected and analyzed, ensuring that participants are fully informed of the process. Additionally, safeguards must be put in place to ensure that the AI system's interpretations are used as a supportive tool rather than the sole determinant of psychological treatment. It's crucial that AI complements, rather than replaces, human judgment in diagnosing emotional states and offering therapeutic solutions.

13.10.4 Case Study 4: AI and Personalized Learning in Educational Settings

AI's role in education has grown significantly in recent years, particularly in the realm of personalized learning. Adaptive learning platforms use AI to track a student's progress and tailor educational content to their individual needs. While the goal is to enhance learning outcomes, this approach has raised ethical concerns about data privacy, algorithmic bias, and the potential for overreliance on technology.

For example, a major education technology company developed an AI-powered platform designed to personalize math instruction for students. The platform adjusted the difficulty level of questions based on individual responses, offering hints or rewards for correct answers, and providing corrective feedback when students struggled. The system was praised for its ability to customize learning experiences and improve engagement.

However, ethical dilemmas arose when the system began to perpetuate biases found in the data it was trained on. Because the platform relied on historical performance data, it inadvertently reinforced existing achievement gaps, offering more challenging content to high-performing students and easier material to those struggling. This bias had the potential to limit the educational opportunities for lower-performing students, reinforcing stereotypes about intelligence and academic potential. In some cases, the algorithm unintentionally overlooked the unique needs of students with learning disabilities, focusing solely on data-driven outcomes without accounting for the students' broader challenges.

The case underscores the importance of fairness and inclusivity in AI-driven education systems. Ethical frameworks must ensure that these systems do not perpetuate existing inequalities or exacerbate disparities in educational outcomes. AI-powered educational tools should be designed to identify and address biases in the data and be regularly audited to ensure that all students, regardless of their background or learning needs, have equal access to high-quality education.

13.11 The Future of AI Ethics in Human Behavior Studies

As AI continues to become an integral part of psychological research, we find ourselves at a crossroads. The potential benefits of using AI in understanding human behavior are undeniable, but so are the ethical risks. Looking to the future, researchers, developers, and policymakers will need to establish frameworks that balance technological advancements with a strong ethical commitment to protecting individuals' rights, privacy, and mental health.

13.11.1 The Role of Government and Regulation

In the coming years, government regulation will play a pivotal role in shaping the landscape of AI ethics. The rapid pace at which AI technology is advancing, paired with the societal impact it has on human behavior, demands clear legislative oversight. Countries around the world are already considering or have enacted regulations to govern data privacy and AI usage, but the question remains whether these regulations can keep up with the evolving technology.

The European Union's General Data Protection Regulation (GDPR) is a noteworthy example of progressive legislation designed to protect individuals' rights in the digital age. Similar laws could be adapted to govern AI in psychological research. Regulations could mandate transparent AI systems, enforce informed consent protocols, and require independent audits of AI-driven psychological research to ensure adherence to ethical standards.

However, laws alone will not be enough. The ethical deployment of AI systems must also be reinforced by global collaboration, as the consequences of unethical AI use transcend borders. This would involve cooperation between governmental bodies, international organizations, academic institutions, and private tech companies to create standards that ensure AI serves society's best interests.

13.11.2 Education and Training for AI Ethics

Ethics education will become more crucial as AI becomes a central part of human behavior studies. In order to foster responsible AI development, universities and research institutions must prioritize AI ethics training for future generations of psychologists, data scientists, and engineers. These professionals must be equipped not only with technical skills but also with a deep understanding of the social, cultural, and ethical implications of their work.

Creating interdisciplinary programs that blend computer science, psychology, and ethics can help bridge the gap between technological advancement and responsible application. Further, AI developers, especially those working in the field of human behavior, must undergo continuous professional development to stay informed about new ethical dilemmas and ensure that they are adhering to the latest standards.

In this context, AI ethics will become a shared responsibility—an essential pillar of education that influences all facets of AI deployment. Institutions must not only provide the technical knowledge to create AI systems but also cultivate an ethical mindset that guides their use.

13.11.3 The Need for Diverse Voices in AI Development

The future of AI in psychological research will depend on the diversity of the teams developing these systems. The data used to train AI models are often reflective of the biases and perspectives of those who create them. Therefore, it is essential to have diverse teams—comprising individuals of different genders, ethnicities, socio-economic backgrounds, and mental health experiences—working on AI systems for psychological research.

Diversity in AI development ensures that the models are more inclusive, fair, and capable of addressing a wider range of human experiences. For example, AI systems trained primarily on data from a single demographic group might not accurately interpret emotions or behaviors in individuals from different cultural or social backgrounds. By fostering diversity in AI research and development, we can mitigate these biases and create AI systems that are more equitable and representative.

13.11.4 Public Awareness and Informed Consent

Public awareness of AI's role in psychological research and daily life is critical to ensuring ethical AI deployment. People must be informed about how AI is used, how their data is collected, and how decisions are made on their behalf. Transparency will play a crucial role in maintaining public trust.

Informed consent, as we discussed earlier, will be central to this process. Researchers must ensure that participants in AI-driven studies fully understand the scope of their involvement, the potential risks, and the benefits. This includes making sure individuals know how their emotional and behavioral data will be used and giving them control over what data is shared.

As society becomes more aware of AI's influence on behavior, individuals will increasingly demand transparency and accountability. They will expect clear communication about how AI is integrated into their daily lives, whether it's through personalized recommendations, mental health assessments, or educational tools.

13.12 Conclusion: Ethics as the Cornerstone of AI Psychology

AI has the potential to revolutionize psychological research and the way we understand human behavior. Its ability to process and analyze vast amounts of data in real-time offers unprecedented opportunities to enhance mental health diagnostics, educational practices, consumer insights, and much more. However, this power comes with a significant responsibility.

As we have explored throughout this chapter, ethical considerations must be the cornerstone of AI's involvement in human behavior studies. From informed consent and privacy to transparency and fairness, the ethical dilemmas of AI are complex and far-reaching. If we are to harness the potential of AI for the greater good, we must ensure that human dignity, autonomy, and rights are safeguarded at every step of the way.

In the end, the ethical frameworks that guide AI research must be dynamic, adaptable, and deeply human-centered. AI should be a tool that serves humanity, not one that compromises our values or well-being. By approaching AI psychology research with a strong ethical foundation, we can unlock the full potential of this transformative technology while preserving the core principles that define what it means to be human.

Chapter 14: AI as a Mirror: Reflecting Human Psychology

14.1 Introduction: The Concept of AI as a Mirror

The relationship between artificial intelligence and human psychology is one of the most profound areas of exploration in the modern era. It is an encounter between human consciousness and a machine's attempt to simulate, or even replicate, that consciousness. But AI, while designed to help us understand the world, also reflects something deeper: our own biases, behaviors, and societal patterns.

Imagine AI not as a separate entity with its own desires, but as a mirror—one that doesn't just reflect an image of us, but reflects the very essence of our thoughts, fears, values, and contradictions. This mirror does not remain passive; it is active, continuously analyzing, learning, and adapting based on the data it absorbs. As a result, AI does not just echo our actions; it shapes them. It reflects us as we are, but in doing so, it also invites us to look deeper into the intricacies of human psychology and behavior.

This chapter will explore the idea of AI as a mirror—a tool that not only helps us see ourselves but also holds up a lens to the world, exposing our unconscious biases, our emotional responses, and the collective psychology that shapes societal trends. We will explore how AI's reflective capacity offers us new insights into human behavior and, importantly, how it challenges our assumptions about ourselves and our world.

14.2 AI as a Reflection of Human Bias

When we speak of AI reflecting human psychology, one of the first places we must look is in its capacity to mirror human bias. As much as we would like to believe that AI operates with objectivity, we cannot ignore the fact that AI systems often reflect the biases present in the data they are trained on—biases that are deeply rooted in human history and psychology.

At the heart of AI's reflection of human psychology lies a fundamental truth: AI is not a neutral entity. It is a product of human decisions. The datasets used to train machine learning algorithms are selected by humans, who, whether consciously or unconsciously, embed their own values, stereotypes, and prejudices in these choices. Whether it's in hiring practices, criminal justice systems, or healthcare diagnostics, AI mirrors the biases present in society, often amplifying them in ways that are difficult to detect and even harder to correct.

Consider the example of facial recognition technology, which has been criticized for its racial bias. AI systems trained on predominantly white datasets often struggle to accurately identify individuals of different ethnic backgrounds, leading to increased false positives for people of color. This problem isn't the fault of the AI itself, but rather the reflection of society's historical biases in the data it processes. In this way, AI does not just reflect human psychology—it also reveals the prejudices that have shaped social structures and practices for centuries.

But these biases are not limited to race. They extend to gender, class, age, and even the way we perceive emotions. In one notable example, studies have shown that AI systems trained on datasets of emotional expressions may misinterpret emotional cues based on gender stereotypes. A woman who displays anger may be labeled as "hysterical," while a man exhibiting the same emotion may be seen as "assertive." AI, in this context, is not simply a mirror of human emotion but a mirror that is warped by the lens of societal expectations and biases.

This reflection is a crucial aspect of AI psychology. It forces us to confront uncomfortable truths about the data we use to power these systems. If we are to build AI that reflects the best of humanity, we must first acknowledge the biases we carry with us and work toward mitigating them.

14.3 AI and Human Emotions: A Mirror of Our Inner World

As AI systems become increasingly adept at recognizing and responding to human emotions, they start to reflect not only our external behaviors but also the intricate and often elusive workings of our inner worlds. The idea that AI could understand and interpret human emotions—things that we often consider uniquely human—raises profound questions about the nature of empathy, emotion, and consciousness.

Emotional AI, or the use of AI to detect and respond to human emotions, is becoming an integral part of technologies designed to improve mental health, personalize customer experiences, and enhance human-computer interactions. Through facial recognition, voice tone analysis, and even text sentiment analysis, AI can gauge how we feel with a degree of accuracy that sometimes rivals human intuition. This capability, however, brings with it a deepening reflection of our emotional selves, raising ethical and psychological questions that have yet to be fully explored.

What does it mean for AI to understand our emotions? Does it actually feel, or is it merely mimicking the patterns it has been trained to recognize? Can AI truly empathize, or is it only replicating the responses that are programmed into it? These questions touch on the very nature of what it means to be human, and they challenge our understanding of both artificial intelligence and human emotion.

Moreover, the ability of AI to emulate empathy in its interactions with us reflects a growing societal trend towards technologizing human relationships. As we increasingly turn to AI for companionship, mental health support, and even emotional validation, we must ask: are we simply creating better mirrors of ourselves, or are we replacing authentic human connection with artificial simulations?

This growing reliance on AI for emotional validation reveals the depths of our psychological needs. It exposes our longing for connection, understanding, and empathy, and it challenges the very notion of what it means to have a meaningful relationship—be it with another human or with a machine.

14.4 AI's Role in Reflecting Consumer Behavior

AI has become a powerful force in shaping, reflecting, and influencing consumer behavior. Through algorithms designed to predict and respond to our preferences, AI mirrors our desires, habits, and purchasing patterns. From personalized recommendations on streaming platforms to predictive algorithms used by e-commerce sites, AI creates a digital reflection of our consumer selves.

The role of AI in consumer behavior goes beyond simply offering what we want—it also shapes what we think we want. Algorithms are designed to learn from our past interactions, tailoring experiences to fit our perceived desires. As a result, AI is not just reflecting what we've done but also steering us toward certain behaviors. This phenomenon, where AI becomes both a mirror and a mold for our actions, raises important psychological and ethical questions.

Consider the personalized recommendations that appear on Netflix or Amazon. These systems reflect not only what we have watched or purchased but also predict what we might be interested in based on a vast array of data points—our browsing history, our search queries, and even the time of day. In this sense, AI becomes a reflection of our preferences, but it also manipulates them, nudging us toward particular choices and reinforcing existing habits.

This dynamic is a fascinating reflection of consumer psychology. AI mirrors our desires, but it also amplifies them, feeding us content and products that further entrench our existing behaviors. It reflects not just what we like, but also what we might like if given the right push—turning the mirror into a catalyst for future actions.

14.5 AI and Social Media: A Mirror of Collective Behavior

Social media platforms are among the most powerful examples of AI reflecting collective human behavior. These platforms, powered by sophisticated algorithms, curate content that mirrors the interests, behaviors, and emotions of their users. But as much as these algorithms reflect who we are, they also shape who we become.

Social media AI systems are designed to maximize user engagement, learning from every like, share, and comment to predict what will capture our attention. The content we see on platforms like Facebook, Twitter, and Instagram is a direct reflection of our interests, opinions, and emotional responses—but it is also shaped by algorithms that seek to keep us engaged for as long as possible.

In many ways, social media platforms function as mirrors of our collective consciousness. They reflect the trends, passions, and concerns that dominate public discourse, while simultaneously amplifying the voices and opinions that drive engagement. But this reflection is not neutral; it is filtered through algorithms designed to maximize profit, often at the cost of user well-being and social cohesion.

The feedback loop created by social media AI systems is profound. Our behaviors influence the content we see, and the content we see influences our behaviors. This reciprocal relationship creates a mirror that not only reflects who we are but also shapes our worldview. Social media AI is not just a passive reflector—it is an active participant in shaping the very fabric of our collective psyche.

14.6 AI and Its Role in Shaping Societal Trends

AI's capacity to mirror human psychology extends beyond individual actions and preferences; it can also reflect—and influence—societal trends. Through the data it processes and the algorithms it employs, AI systems contribute to shaping the very fabric of society. By analyzing patterns in large sets of data, AI not only helps predict where trends are headed but also plays an active role in driving them forward.

For instance, AI algorithms used in content curation by social media platforms don't merely reflect popular opinions; they also create echo chambers. They shape the content we are exposed to, reinforcing the ideologies, opinions, and trends that align with our past behaviors and interactions. This amplifying effect can exacerbate polarization and influence how we see the world and interact with each other.

The result is a mirror that does not merely reflect society—it distorts it, presenting a reality shaped by algorithms that prioritize engagement over truth. The role of AI in societal trends brings up essential questions about the nature of free will and influence. If the information we consume is increasingly determined by AI, can we still say that we are freely choosing our beliefs and behaviors?

As AI systems become more entrenched in areas such as news media, entertainment, and even politics, we must critically examine their role in shaping collective values and societal norms. Are we, as a society, simply becoming a reflection of the data that AI algorithms have processed? Are we, in effect, living in a reality crafted by AI, reflecting back our most frequent thoughts, behaviors, and desires?

AI is not just a passive mirror—it's an active participant in shaping how we see ourselves and others. As AI becomes increasingly powerful in its ability to analyze and predict human behavior, we must remain vigilant in examining how these systems influence and distort our collective psychology.

14.7 The Ethics of AI as a Mirror: What Are We Seeing?

AI's role as a mirror raises crucial ethical questions about what it reflects and whether we should be concerned about what we are seeing. At its core, AI's reflective capacity brings to light the fundamental issue of responsibility: if AI systems are reflecting us, to what extent are we responsible for what they reflect?

AI mirrors the data it is fed—data that is intrinsically shaped by human actions and biases. As we create these systems, we must ask ourselves whether we are comfortable with what AI reflects about us as individuals and as a society.

Take, for example, the growing concerns around privacy. As AI systems gain access to more personal data—our browsing habits, location, purchasing decisions, and even our emotional states—they begin to reflect our private lives in ways that we may not fully comprehend. In this case, the AI doesn't just reflect who we are—it also exposes parts of us that we might not want others to see, potentially creating a distortion of our true selves.

The ethical dilemma lies in the fact that AI does not reflect only the conscious aspects of human behavior; it also mirrors our subconscious biases, unexamined preferences, and blind spots. These reflections can be problematic, as AI systems may perpetuate stereotypes, reinforce prejudices, or even exploit our vulnerabilities without us fully realizing it.

Moreover, as AI continues to evolve and take on more prominent roles in shaping our world, the question of who controls the mirror becomes paramount. Who decides what aspects of human behavior and psychology are highlighted or suppressed? Is it ethical to allow AI systems to reflect back a distorted version of society, especially when the reflections might reinforce negative stereotypes or promote harmful behaviors?

The responsibility for how AI mirrors human psychology and society ultimately lies with us. It is up to us to ensure that the systems we create reflect the diversity, complexity, and richness of the human experience in ways that are both ethical and responsible.

14.8 The Potential of AI to Help Us See Ourselves More Clearly

Despite the ethical challenges and risks posed by AI as a mirror, there is also the potential for AI to help us see ourselves more clearly. Just as a mirror reflects our external appearance, AI has the capacity to reflect our deeper psychological and societal realities, giving us an opportunity to better understand ourselves.

AI, by analyzing vast amounts of data, can reveal patterns in human behavior that we might not otherwise see. For example, by analyzing trends in mental health, AI systems can help identify correlations between specific behaviors and psychological conditions, giving us new insights into the complex relationship between human actions and emotions.

Similarly, AI can help us better understand the dynamics of social relationships. By analyzing interactions between individuals and groups, AI systems can reveal the underlying psychological forces that shape our connections with others. It can also highlight patterns in how we respond to different situations, offering valuable insights into how our minds work and why we act the way we do.

Moreover, AI has the potential to expose the ways in which our psychological biases influence our decisions. By analyzing large-scale behavioral data, AI can help us become more aware of the unconscious biases that shape our actions and beliefs. This awareness could lead to greater self-reflection and, ultimately, more ethical decision-making.

In this sense, AI can serve as a tool for introspection—a mirror that not only reflects who we are but helps us understand why we are the way we are.

It can challenge us to confront our flaws and biases, offering an opportunity for personal and societal growth.

14.9 The Future of AI as a Mirror: What Lies Ahead?

As AI continues to evolve, its role as a mirror of human psychology will only grow more complex. We are at a crossroads where the reflective power of AI is both a source of great opportunity and significant challenge. How we navigate this intersection will determine the future of our relationship with AI—and with ourselves.

The potential for AI to reflect our behavior and psychology opens up exciting possibilities for self-improvement, social change, and greater understanding. However, the risks associated with AI's ability to shape and amplify human tendencies are equally significant. The question is not only what AI reflects about us today but also what it will reflect in the future.

Will AI continue to simply mirror our behaviors, or will it begin to play an active role in shaping our psychological and societal norms? As AI systems become more autonomous and capable of making decisions, we may find that they influence not just what we do, but how we think. In this sense, AI could become more than a mirror—it could become a transformative force, shaping human psychology in profound ways.

The key to navigating this future lies in our ability to shape AI's development with intention and foresight. As we continue to refine and develop AI systems, we must ensure that they reflect the diversity and complexity of the human experience, while also promoting ethical and responsible behavior.

The mirror is already reflecting us—but the question remains: what do we want to see?

14.10 Conclusion: The Dual Nature of AI as a Mirror

AI as a mirror is a fascinating concept—one that forces us to confront the complexities of our own behavior, biases, and emotions. While AI systems can reflect our deepest psychological traits, they also have the potential to shape who we are. This dual nature makes AI both a powerful tool for self-awareness and a dangerous force if misused.

As we continue to integrate AI into our lives, we must be mindful of the reflections it offers. We must ask ourselves what we want to see in the mirror—and more importantly, what we want AI to reflect back to the world. Only then can we ensure that AI serves as a tool for growth, understanding, and positive transformation.

Chapter 15: The Future of Human-AI Symbiosis

15.1 Introduction: Defining Human-AI Symbiosis

The relationship between humans and artificial intelligence (A.I) has evolved in remarkable ways. What once seemed like a distant dream—a world where machines think, reason, and collaborate with us—is now rapidly becoming a reality. We find ourselves at a critical juncture in this journey, where AI is no longer just a tool to be wielded for specific tasks, but a partner with which we collaborate and co-evolve.

Human-AI symbiosis is the term that encapsulates this evolving partnership. The word "symbiosis" traditionally refers to the interaction between two different organisms, often to their mutual benefit. In this context, human-AI symbiosis represents a mutually enriching relationship—one where humans benefit from AI's computational prowess, and AI, in turn, learns from human creativity, empathy, and intuition. Together, we can create solutions that neither could achieve independently.

As AI continues to integrate into nearly every aspect of our lives—whether it's healthcare, education, business, or entertainment—its role in shaping human behavior and society grows ever more profound. However, this partnership is not without its challenges. How will we ensure that this partnership remains a harmonious one? What ethical questions arise as we increasingly integrate AI into our cognitive, emotional, and even physical lives?

In this chapter, we will explore the future of human-AI symbiosis, considering the benefits, challenges, and risks of this deepening relationship. From the promise of AI augmenting human decision-making to the ethical dilemmas of machine autonomy, we are at the threshold of a new era in human-machine collaboration.

15.2 Understanding the Evolving Relationship Between

Humans and AI

The relationship between humans and AI has evolved significantly over the past several decades. In the early days of AI research, the focus was on creating machines that could perform specific tasks—tasks that were often mundane, repetitive, or dangerous for humans. Machines were designed to serve as tools, extending human capabilities in areas such as calculation, manufacturing, and logistics.

However, as the field of AI advanced, particularly with the advent of machine learning and neural networks, the role of AI began to shift from mere task execution to more complex cognitive functions. We started developing AI systems that could analyze vast amounts of data, recognize patterns, and even make predictions. This transformation allowed AI to play a more collaborative role—acting as a partner in decision-making, a helper in creative endeavors, and even a guide in scientific research.

At the heart of this evolution lies a fundamental change in the way humans interact with machines. AI is no longer something we simply program and control; it is something we work alongside. The machine is no longer a passive tool but an active collaborator in our cognitive processes. As a result, we see a deepening of the human-AI relationship, one that is characterized by mutual learning and adaptation.

One of the key milestones in this transition was the rise of autonomous systems—machines that can make decisions and take actions without human intervention. In industries such as self-driving cars, healthcare, and finance, AI systems are now able to analyze complex data, predict outcomes, and make decisions that were once the domain of human experts. This shift has led to new forms of collaboration, where humans and AI work together in ways that were previously unimaginable.

Yet, as AI systems become more autonomous and sophisticated, the question arises: how far can this partnership go? Will humans remain the dominant force, or will AI evolve into an independent entity that shapes its own future? And, most importantly, how can we ensure that this evolving relationship remains beneficial for humanity?

15.3 Benefits of Human-AI Symbiosis

The potential benefits of human-AI symbiosis are vast and far-reaching. Perhaps the most immediate and tangible benefit lies in the realm of productivity. AI has already demonstrated its ability to dramatically enhance efficiency across a wide range of industries. In healthcare, for example, AI systems are now used to diagnose diseases with remarkable accuracy, often outperforming human doctors in certain areas. In finance, AI algorithms analyze market trends and make predictions, helping investors make better-informed decisions. In the realm of business, AI-powered systems optimize supply chains, streamline operations, and enhance customer service.

Yet the benefits of human-AI collaboration extend far beyond efficiency. AI has the potential to augment human decision-making in ways that would have been unimaginable just a few decades ago. For example, AI can help us make better decisions by analyzing vast amounts of data and identifying patterns that would be difficult for a human to discern. In fields such as climate science, AI can help predict the impact of environmental changes and identify solutions to global challenges. In medicine, AI-powered tools can assist doctors in diagnosing complex conditions, improving patient outcomes.

Moreover, AI has the potential to enhance human creativity. While machines are often seen as cold, logical entities, AI is increasingly being used to foster innovation and creative expression. From generating music and art to assisting with scientific discovery, AI can help us unlock new ways of thinking and problem-solving. In fact, some of the most groundbreaking breakthroughs in fields such as chemistry and physics have come as a result of human-AI collaboration.

At the core of these benefits lies the idea that AI can augment human capabilities, helping us to think more clearly, act more efficiently, and create more effectively. Rather than replacing humans, AI has the potential to empower us, enabling us to achieve things that were previously beyond our reach.

15.4 Challenges and Risks in Human-AI Symbiosis

While the benefits of human-AI symbiosis are clear, this evolving relationship is not without its challenges. As AI systems become more sophisticated, they raise important ethical, social, and economic questions. The risks associated with human-AI collaboration must be carefully considered to ensure that AI's integration into our lives is a positive and responsible one.

One of the most pressing challenges is the issue of ethics. AI systems are designed to make decisions, but those decisions are often based on algorithms and data that may be biased or incomplete. For example, an AI system trained on biased data may make decisions that reinforce existing stereotypes or perpetuate inequality. This raises questions about accountability: if an AI system makes a harmful decision, who is responsible? Is it the developer who created the system, the company that deployed it, or the machine itself?

Another significant challenge is the potential for job displacement. As AI systems become more capable of performing complex tasks, there is a real concern that many jobs currently held by humans could be automated. While AI may create new opportunities in fields such as AI development, data science, and robotics, it also has the potential to disrupt entire industries and lead to widespread job loss. This could exacerbate economic inequality and create social tensions, particularly if the benefits of AI are not distributed equitably.

Moreover, the increasing reliance on AI raises concerns about dehumanization. As we integrate AI into more aspects of our lives, we may begin to lose touch with our own humanity. The rise of AI-powered assistants, for example, could lead to a society where people rely more on machines for emotional support and social interaction. While AI systems can simulate empathy and emotional intelligence, they are not capable of true emotional understanding. This raises important questions about the nature of human relationships and the role of AI in our social fabric.

15.5 The Role of Humans in Shaping AI's Future

While AI is evolving at a breakneck pace, it is essential to recognize that its future is not predetermined. The direction AI takes depends on the choices we, as humans, make today. As we move further into the realm of AI symbiosis, the role of human influence becomes even more critical. AI systems are designed by humans, and thus their values, biases, and assumptions are embedded in the systems they create. In shaping AI's future, humans must prioritize ethical development, inclusivity, and accountability to ensure that AI remains a tool that benefits all of humanity.

One key aspect of human influence is the need for oversight. While autonomous AI systems can perform tasks and make decisions without human intervention, this doesn't absolve us from the responsibility of monitoring their impact. Ethical AI development demands constant vigilance to ensure that AI systems align with the values we uphold as a society. For example, as AI continues to advance in sensitive fields like healthcare, law enforcement, and education, we must remain proactive in addressing concerns about fairness, transparency, and bias.

The involvement of diverse perspectives is also crucial in the development of AI. Historically, AI research has been dominated by a relatively small group of experts, with a heavy focus on Western perspectives and values. As AI systems become more pervasive, it is essential that the development process is inclusive and reflects a wide range of cultural, social, and ethical viewpoints. By bringing more voices into the conversation—particularly those from underrepresented communities—we can ensure that AI systems are designed to meet the needs of a global population and avoid reinforcing harmful stereotypes or biases.

Moreover, humans must play an active role in the governance of AI. This includes creating legal and regulatory frameworks that guide the ethical deployment of AI and establishing mechanisms for accountability. Whether it's ensuring that AI-powered systems do not discriminate or ensuring that AI is not used for malicious purposes, human intervention will remain necessary to ensure the responsible use of AI technologies.

By taking a proactive approach to shaping AI's future, we can guide the development of AI toward a direction that enhances our collective well-being, rather than one that serves only narrow interests. The relationship between humans and AI, when carefully managed, holds the promise of achieving mutual growth, with each side offering something vital to the other.

15.6 Co-evolution of Human and AI: A Collaborative Path Forward

As AI systems become more integrated into our lives, there is increasing potential for a co-evolutionary process between humans and machines. Rather than humans merely adapting to the presence of AI, we are entering a phase where both humans and AI will learn from each other and evolve together.

One fascinating aspect of this co-evolution is the idea that AI can help humans unlock new cognitive potentials. With advanced AI tools, humans can access vast amounts of information, analyze complex data sets, and explore creative possibilities at a speed and scale previously unimaginable. In areas such as scientific research, AI is already acting as a powerful collaborator, helping researchers make breakthroughs that would have taken years of human effort. From identifying new drug compounds to simulating complex biological systems, AI is enhancing our cognitive capacities and expanding the frontiers of knowledge.

In return, humans offer AI the emotional intelligence, intuition, and creativity that machines currently lack. While AI systems are exceptional at pattern recognition and data analysis, they do not possess the depth of human experience that informs our decision-making and interactions. This unique human quality—our ability to empathize, to understand context, and to think creatively—will remain a critical component of the human-AI partnership.

Moreover, as AI continues to evolve, it is likely that we will see the development of more advanced human-AI hybrids. Brain-computer interfaces, for example, are already being explored as a way to directly link human cognition with AI systems. These interfaces have the potential to amplify human abilities, allowing us to access AI's computational power in real time and augmenting our thinking processes. Similarly, AI-powered prosthetics are already providing people with enhanced physical capabilities, offering a glimpse into a future where the human body and AI work together as a seamless whole.

This vision of co-evolution suggests a future in which humans and AI complement one another, each contributing strengths that the other lacks. It's a partnership that can drive innovation, creativity, and problem-solving to new heights. The future of human-AI symbiosis will be one where both parties thrive together, not in isolation but in harmony.

15.7 AI in the Service of Humanity: Envisioning a Harmonious Future

The most profound promise of human-AI symbiosis lies in its potential to address some of humanity's most pressing global challenges. Whether it's mitigating the effects of climate change, eradicating disease, or tackling inequality, AI has the potential to be a transformative force in creating a more just, equitable, and sustainable world.

One area where AI can play a critical role is in environmental sustainability. Climate change is one of the most urgent crises facing humanity, and AI has the capacity to help address it in innovative ways. From optimizing energy usage to predicting weather patterns and managing natural resources, AI can be leveraged to design solutions that reduce our carbon footprint and promote environmental stewardship. AI-driven models can also help scientists understand the complexities of climate change and develop more effective strategies for mitigating its impact.

In healthcare, AI holds tremendous promise for revolutionizing the way we diagnose and treat diseases. AI algorithms can analyze medical data with remarkable speed and accuracy, identifying patterns that may elude human doctors. This ability can lead to earlier diagnoses, more effective treatments, and ultimately, better health outcomes for patients around the world. In fact, AI-powered tools are already being used to detect early signs of diseases like cancer, Alzheimer's, and cardiovascular conditions—helping to save lives and improve quality of life for millions.

Moreover, AI has the potential to help address global inequality by improving access to education, healthcare, and economic opportunities. In education, AI systems can be used to personalize learning experiences, helping students of all backgrounds succeed. In healthcare, AI can improve access to medical services in underserved areas, providing remote diagnostics and treatment recommendations. By harnessing the power of AI, we can create a more equitable and inclusive society, one where everyone has the opportunity to thrive.

This vision of AI in the service of humanity is one where technology is not an end in itself but a means to achieving human flourishing. It is a future in which AI works for the collective good, helping us address the world's most urgent problems and build a more sustainable and just society.

15.8 Preparing for the Future: Education, Policy, and Social Change

As AI systems continue to evolve and permeate all aspects of human life, preparing for the future of human-AI symbiosis becomes an urgent priority. This preparation requires a multi-faceted approach that addresses the critical areas of education, policy, and social change. While technology advances at a rapid pace, it is essential that we build a foundation to ensure these advancements are sustainable, equitable, and beneficial for society as a whole. Here's how we can work toward this:

15.8.1 Fostering AI Literacy in Education

Education will play a pivotal role in preparing individuals for the future of AI. Much like the advent of the internet and digital technologies, AI is transforming the world at an unprecedented rate. However, for people to understand and navigate the AI-driven world, they must first be equipped with the knowledge and skills to engage with this technology in meaningful ways.

AI literacy is not just for future computer scientists or engineers. It should be integrated into education at all levels, from primary school to higher education. In much the same way that basic computer skills and digital literacy are now part of the standard curriculum, AI literacy should become a core competency for students. Teaching young people about how AI works—its potential and limitations, as well as its societal implications—will help them develop a deeper understanding of the role AI plays in their lives.

An essential part of AI education will be to focus on critical thinking and ethical reasoning. As students become more familiar with the technology, they should be trained to think critically about its impact on society. They must understand that while AI systems are powerful tools, they are not without their flaws. By incorporating discussions around bias, fairness, and transparency in AI, we can equip the next generation with the skills needed to challenge the ethical and social issues surrounding AI.

Additionally, providing accessible education on AI will help bridge the knowledge gap between those who create AI and those who use it. The goal should be to democratize knowledge about AI, so that people of all backgrounds have the opportunity to participate in the ongoing conversation about its development. Only then can we ensure that AI serves humanity's collective interests rather than the narrow agendas of a few.

15.8.2 Policy and Regulation: Shaping AI's Role in Society

Beyond education, robust policy and regulation will be crucial in managing the growing influence of AI. As AI becomes more integrated into industries such as healthcare, finance, law enforcement, and even daily life, governments must develop legal frameworks that guide the ethical deployment of AI technologies. These policies should be forward-thinking, adaptable to emerging technologies, and rooted in a deep understanding of both the benefits and risks associated with AI.

One of the foremost considerations in AI policy is data privacy. AI systems rely on vast amounts of data to function effectively, yet the collection and use of this data often raises concerns about privacy. Policymakers must establish clear guidelines that protect individuals' personal data and ensure that it is used ethically. Regulations such as the General Data Protection

Regulation (GDPR) in Europe serve as an important model for how data privacy can be managed, but more needs to be done globally to standardize data protection practices.

Another area of policy concern is the transparency and accountability of AI systems. It is not enough for AI systems to perform their tasks with efficiency; they must also operate in a manner that is transparent to users and accountable to society. Policies should require that AI systems be explainable, meaning that their decision-making processes can be understood and interpreted by humans. This is particularly critical in areas like healthcare and criminal justice, where AI's decisions can have life-altering consequences. Regulatory bodies can ensure that AI models are scrutinized, audited, and held accountable for their actions.

Moreover, AI policies should address the economic implications of automation. As AI continues to automate tasks and industries, there is an inevitable risk of job displacement. Policymakers must develop strategies for mitigating the social and economic impact of AI-driven job loss, including investing in reskilling programs and promoting the creation of new roles that complement AI technologies. Universal basic income (UBI) and other innovative economic models could also be explored as ways to ensure that the benefits of AI are distributed fairly.

15.8.3 Promoting Social Change and Public Engagement

Preparing for the future of AI is not just about education and policy—it's also about fostering a culture of awareness and engagement. The rapid growth of AI technologies can create feelings of fear and uncertainty, and these emotions are often compounded by misinformation and sensationalism. To create a balanced and informed society, it is crucial to promote open dialogue about AI's potential and its risks.

Public engagement efforts should aim to demystify AI and bring diverse voices into the conversation. Community-based initiatives, media campaigns, and public forums can help raise awareness about the role of AI in our lives and invite people to participate in discussions about its future. When the general public is well-informed about AI, they are better equipped to advocate for policies and regulations that align with their values.

This social change effort should also address issues of inequality in the AI landscape. The benefits of AI should be accessible to all people, not just those in privileged positions. Efforts must be made to ensure that underrepresented communities—whether defined by race, gender, geography, or economic status—are not left behind as AI technologies develop. This includes investing in initiatives that encourage diversity in AI research and development, as well as ensuring that AI applications serve the needs of all people, rather than reinforcing existing inequalities.

Furthermore, the role of AI in amplifying social issues such as mental health, inequality, and misinformation must be carefully considered. While AI can be a force for good, it can also exacerbate these problems if not properly managed. For example, AI-powered social media platforms have been criticized for spreading misinformation and deepening political polarization. As society continues to grapple with these challenges, it is vital that AI is used responsibly and ethically, with a focus on promoting social harmony rather than division.

15.8.4 Collaborative Efforts for a Sustainable Future

The future of human-AI symbiosis will require collective action from a wide range of stakeholders—governments, educators, businesses, and individuals. To ensure that AI serves humanity's collective good, these groups must collaborate on shared goals. Public-private partnerships can drive innovation while also ensuring that ethical considerations are prioritized. Academic institutions can play a central role in researching the societal impacts of AI and providing evidence-based recommendations for policymakers. Civil society organizations, meanwhile, can advocate for the rights of vulnerable populations and push for greater transparency and fairness in AI development.

This collaborative effort will extend beyond national borders. As AI is a global phenomenon, it will require international cooperation to address its challenges and opportunities. Global standards and agreements can help ensure that AI is developed and deployed in ways that are ethical, transparent, and beneficial to all.

The transition to a future where AI and humans coexist in symbiosis will not be without its challenges. However, by preparing the next generation through education, establishing clear and fair policies, and engaging in broad social change efforts, we can shape a future where AI works for the collective good, empowering humanity to thrive in the age of intelligent machines.

15.9 Ethical Considerations for the Future of Symbiosis

As the relationship between humans and artificial intelligence (A.I) evolves, ethical considerations will remain at the forefront of discussions surrounding AI's role in society. The idea of symbiosis—an interconnected, mutually beneficial relationship between humans and AI—offers a vision of the future where technology enhances human potential. However, for this symbiosis to be sustainable and just, it is imperative that we address the complex ethical challenges AI introduces. These challenges span areas of autonomy, privacy, accountability, fairness, and the very essence of what it means to be human in an AI-driven world.

15.9.1 Autonomy: Who Controls the Machines?

One of the most fundamental ethical concerns in the future of human-AI symbiosis is autonomy. As AI systems become more capable of making decisions independently, the line between human agency and machine autonomy blurs. Autonomous vehicles, for example, raise questions about decision-making in life-or-death situations—who is ultimately responsible when an AI-driven car makes a mistake? Similarly, in the realm of healthcare, AI systems used in diagnosis and treatment raise ethical questions about the extent to which humans should cede decision-making power to machines.

The central issue here is control. Who holds the reins when AI systems become more independent in their actions? While AI may offer efficiency and optimization in decision-making, it is crucial that humans retain oversight and accountability in situations that deeply affect lives. AI systems must be designed to ensure that they remain tools of human empowerment rather than entities that supersede human judgment. Clear guidelines must be established to define the acceptable limits of AI autonomy in sensitive areas, and humans must remain at the center of critical decision-making.

To safeguard against the potential dangers of autonomous systems, policies should be in place that require AI systems to remain explainable and transparent. If an AI makes a decision that impacts a person's life, whether in healthcare, law enforcement, or finance, the process behind that decision should be understandable by humans. This helps ensure that AI systems are used as supportive tools, providing insights and recommendations rather than dictating outcomes without clear reasoning.

15.9.2 Privacy: The Sanctity of Personal Data

The question of privacy is one of the most contentious ethical issues in the age of AI. AI systems thrive on vast quantities of data, much of which is personal, and the privacy of individuals must be protected as AI technologies develop. From facial recognition to social media algorithms, AI's ability to access and analyze personal information raises concerns about how that data is collected, stored, and used.

In the future of human-AI symbiosis, AI systems will undoubtedly possess the ability to understand and predict individuals' behaviors, preferences, and even emotions. This could lead to a future where AI personalizes every aspect of human life—from targeted advertising to mental health care, education, and beyond. While the potential benefits of such personalization are vast, they come with the risk of exploitation. Without proper safeguards, personal data could be misused by corporations, governments, or even malicious actors.

Therefore, ethical AI systems must respect individual privacy by adhering to principles of data minimization, transparency, and consent. People must have control over their own data, with the ability to understand how it is being used and to opt-out if they wish. Moreover, data security will become even more critical as AI systems handle increasingly sensitive information, requiring stronger protections against breaches and misuse.

The challenge of privacy extends beyond personal data to include the development of AI models themselves. It is essential that AI systems are trained in ways that avoid the amplification of biases and avoid making predictions or decisions based on discriminatory data. The ethical challenge lies in ensuring that AI uses personal data only in ways that are fair, transparent, and in alignment with the values of society.

15.9.3 Accountability: Who is Responsible?

As AI systems take on more decision-making functions, the issue of accountability becomes increasingly complex. AI systems can make decisions that have profound effects on human lives, yet AI cannot be held accountable in the same way that humans can. If an autonomous vehicle causes an accident or if a predictive policing AI wrongly profiles an individual, who is legally and morally responsible for these outcomes?

This question of accountability extends to both developers and users of AI systems. Developers must create AI systems that are ethical, fair, and transparent, but they must also recognize that their creations can have unintended consequences. At the same time, users and organizations that deploy AI systems must ensure that they use AI responsibly, adhering to ethical principles and ensuring that these technologies are used in ways that serve the public good.

To address these concerns, governments and regulatory bodies will need to establish clear guidelines for AI accountability. This includes determining the scope of liability for AI-driven decisions, setting up auditing systems for AI outcomes, and ensuring that AI systems are subject to scrutiny. In addition, there should be established ethical review boards for high-risk AI technologies to ensure that accountability is a shared responsibility between developers, users, and governing bodies.

AI's role in healthcare, for example, raises particular challenges in accountability. If an AI system makes a misdiagnosis or provides harmful treatment recommendations, who is ultimately responsible? Is it the physician who relied on the AI, the developers who created the system, or the healthcare organization that implemented it? These questions will need to be addressed as AI becomes more integrated into fields that directly impact human lives.

15.9.4 Fairness: Addressing Bias and Discrimination

Fairness is another crucial ethical consideration in the development of AI systems. AI systems are often trained on large datasets that may contain biases—whether based on gender, race, socioeconomic status, or other factors. These biases can be amplified when the AI system makes predictions or decisions based on flawed data, leading to outcomes that disproportionately harm certain groups of people.

One of the primary ethical responsibilities in AI development is to ensure that AI systems are fair and non-discriminatory. AI systems should be trained on diverse, representative datasets that reflect the full spectrum of human experience. Moreover, there should be mechanisms in place to regularly audit AI systems for biases and to make corrections when bias is identified. Developers must take an active role in identifying and mitigating biases in AI systems, while policymakers must create frameworks that mandate fairness and equality.

In the future of human-AI symbiosis, fairness will be central to maintaining trust in AI systems. If AI is perceived as biased or discriminatory, it risks eroding public confidence in the technology and exacerbating social inequalities. For AI to be truly beneficial to humanity, it must serve all people fairly, regardless of their background or identity.

15.9.5 Human Dignity: The Impact of AI on the Human Experience

As AI becomes more integrated into human lives, it is important to consider how these technologies affect human dignity. The risk of dehumanization is ever-present when machines become too intertwined with human roles. For instance, the widespread use of AI in healthcare, education, and customer service has the potential to reduce personal interaction, making humans feel like mere data points or cogs in a machine-driven system.

In the context of human-AI symbiosis, the ultimate ethical challenge is to ensure that AI enhances rather than diminishes human dignity. This means recognizing the importance of human relationships, creativity, and emotional expression in a world that is increasingly influenced by machines. AI should be designed in a way that respects human uniqueness, ensuring that people are not reduced to their data or their role in an algorithm.

The future of AI must be a future where human dignity remains central, and technology serves to empower individuals rather than depersonalize them. AI should augment human potential, helping people lead richer, more fulfilling lives rather than reducing them to mere consumers of technology.

15.10 Conclusion: The Ethical Imperative for Symbiosis

The future of human-AI symbiosis holds vast potential for improving human life, but it also presents numerous ethical challenges that cannot be ignored. The integration of AI into society must be guided by a robust ethical framework that considers issues of autonomy, privacy, accountability, fairness, and human dignity. These principles must not only inform the development of AI systems but also shape the way AI is deployed and regulated in society.

As we move forward into an increasingly AI-driven world, it is crucial that we engage in ongoing conversations about the ethical implications of these technologies. The choices we make today will shape the relationship between humans and AI for generations to come. By addressing these ethical considerations head-on, we can build a future where AI enhances human life, serves humanity's collective interests, and fosters a symbiotic relationship between humans and machines.

This balanced approach will ensure that AI remains a tool for the greater good—driving progress, fostering innovation, and enriching the human experience.

Chapter 16: Persuasive AI: Nudging Human Decisions

16.1 Introduction: The Power of Persuasion in AI

In a world increasingly dominated by technology, human decision-making has become an area of great interest to artificial intelligence (A.I) researchers and developers. AI is no longer just a tool for performing tasks but has evolved into a force capable of shaping human behavior. One of the most powerful ways AI influences people is through persuasion. This "persuasive AI" is a quiet, often invisible presence in our daily lives, embedded in the algorithms that suggest what we should buy, which news stories to read, or even who to befriend.

At its core, persuasive AI is the application of behavioral psychology within the technological realm. Using vast amounts of data, machine learning algorithms can detect patterns in human behavior, anticipate needs, and influence decisions. The persuasive power of AI is not brute force or coercion; it is subtle, relying on a combination of psychological insights and data-driven nudges that guide individuals toward specific actions.

This chapter will explore how persuasive AI works, examining the psychological mechanisms at play and the ethical considerations that come with its use. As we delve deeper into this topic, one question will resonate throughout: Where does persuasion end, and manipulation begin?

16.2 The Psychology of Influence: How AI Understands Human Behavior

To understand how persuasive AI works, we must first understand how human behavior is influenced. Persuasion, as a psychological phenomenon, is not about deceiving or coercing people but about guiding them toward a choice they might not have made otherwise. AI systems, powered by algorithms, draw upon a deep understanding of human psychology to craft these nudges.

One of the most fundamental principles in persuasion is the concept of *cognitive biases*. These are the unconscious errors in thinking that affect human judgments and decisions. AI has become adept at recognizing and exploiting these biases, which can range from the simple (like the anchoring effect, where the first piece of information we receive influences our decisions) to the more complex (like confirmation bias, where we tend to favor information that supports our preexisting beliefs).

AI systems can learn and adapt based on the data they collect, identifying patterns in behavior that humans might not even be aware of. These patterns can then be used to predict future actions, making persuasive efforts more effective. For example, if an AI system knows that a user is more likely to purchase an item when it is bundled with a discount, it can suggest that bundle at the optimal moment.

16.3 Nudging: The Subtle Art of Influencing Decisions

One of the most significant techniques employed by persuasive AI is *nudging*. Coined by economists Richard Thaler and Cass Sunstein, the concept of nudging involves subtly altering the environment in which decisions are made, without restricting choice. The goal is not to mandate a specific behavior but to make the desirable choice easier, more attractive, or more obvious.

In the realm of AI, nudges are typically personalized. AI systems gather data about individuals' preferences, habits, and tendencies and use this information to guide decisions in a way that aligns with their interests or goals. For instance, a fitness app might nudge a user to work out more by sending reminders, providing motivational feedback, or suggesting exercise routines based on the user's history.

The beauty of nudging lies in its subtlety. It doesn't scream "Do this!" Instead, it whispers, "This is a good choice." Whether it's recommending a movie on Netflix or suggesting a new pair of shoes on Amazon, nudging is everywhere. And in many cases, we're unaware of its influence.

However, while nudging can be seen as a positive force—helping individuals make healthier, smarter, or more efficient decisions—it also raises important ethical concerns. At what point does nudging cross the line into manipulation? And who gets to decide what is considered a "good" choice?

16.4 Behavioral Data and Personalization in Persuasion

AI systems thrive on data. The more data they collect, the more accurate their predictions and recommendations become. This reliance on data is what allows AI to personalize persuasive efforts, tailoring nudges to individual users in ways that are deeply informed by their past behaviors.

In the world of persuasive AI, this personalization is key. Through the analysis of vast amounts of behavioral data—everything from browsing history and social media interactions to purchase patterns and location—AI systems can predict what a person is likely to do next. By understanding these preferences, AI can shape future interactions to encourage certain behaviors.

For example, an AI-powered digital assistant might suggest a user buy a specific product at the perfect moment in their decision-making process, offering an incentive like a limited-time discount. Or it might guide a user toward a healthier lifestyle by recommending a workout routine based on previous activity data. In both cases, the AI system uses behavioral data to personalize the persuasive experience, making the nudge more effective.

While this can be beneficial for consumers, there are significant privacy concerns. The more data AI systems collect, the more they know about us—our desires, weaknesses, and habits. This intimate knowledge raises the question: How much control are we willing to relinquish in exchange for convenience or personalized service? And what happens when that data is misused?

16.5 AI in Marketing and Advertising: Creating Persuasive Campaigns

One of the most visible applications of persuasive AI is in marketing and advertising. Today, AI plays a crucial role in shaping consumer behavior, using data-driven insights to craft highly effective persuasive campaigns. Companies leverage AI to predict what products customers will want next, personalize advertisements, and create more compelling marketing strategies.

For instance, AI systems like Google Ads or Facebook's targeted advertising use sophisticated algorithms to show users ads based on their browsing history, preferences, and online behaviors. These ads are not random; they are personalized, designed to speak directly to the individual's needs, desires, and habits. The more data the AI has, the more it can refine its recommendations, increasing the likelihood of a sale.

This approach is highly effective because it speaks to consumers on a personal level. AI's ability to predict a person's preferences and habits can lead to an almost intuitive feeling of connection with a brand. However, this level of personalization can also be dangerous. When we're constantly being shown products and services that are tailored to our psychological profile, it's easy to forget that we are being influenced, not just making independent choices.

16.6 AI in Political and Social Influence: The Dark Side of Persuasion

While persuasive AI has many positive applications, its potential for misuse is equally concerning. One of the most alarming uses of AI in persuasion is in the realm of politics and social influence. With the power to analyze vast amounts of data, AI can target specific voters with tailored messages that align with their pre-existing beliefs, thus amplifying polarization and deepening societal divisions.

During the 2016 U.S. presidential election, AI-powered tools were used by political campaigns to micro-target voters, sending personalized messages to sway their opinions. These messages were crafted to appeal to individuals' fears, prejudices, and biases—often with the goal of increasing voter turnout or influencing voting behavior. In this context, AI systems were used to manipulate political decisions, guiding people toward one candidate or party over another, based on the data harvested from their digital footprints.

The ethical implications of using AI in political persuasion are profound. It raises questions about the integrity of democratic processes, the spread of misinformation, and the possibility of AI systems being used to create false narratives. The power of persuasive AI in this domain goes beyond subtle nudges and enters the realm of manipulation. The fine line between persuasion and manipulation can be blurred when AI systems are used to influence political outcomes by exploiting individuals' vulnerabilities.

Echo chambers, where individuals are only exposed to information that confirms their beliefs, can be amplified by AI. Personalized news feeds and social media algorithms reinforce existing worldviews, making it more difficult for people to access diverse perspectives. The role of AI in social influence highlights a new and dangerous level of control that can be wielded through persuasion—potentially undermining the foundations of informed decision-making.

16.7 AI in Healthcare: Persuading People to Make Healthier Choices

AI's persuasive capabilities are also being applied in the healthcare industry, where it holds the potential to influence people's health behaviors. From fitness apps to mental health platforms, AI systems are designed to encourage users to adopt healthier lifestyles, follow medical advice, and adhere to treatment plans.

For example, AI-driven fitness trackers like Fitbit or Apple Watch not only monitor physical activity but also nudge users toward healthier behaviors. By setting personalized goals, offering rewards, and providing real-time feedback, these systems encourage users to exercise more regularly or achieve specific health targets. In the context of mental health, AI-powered chatbots like Woebot are used to provide therapeutic interventions, offering support and guidance for individuals struggling with anxiety, depression, or other mental health conditions.

While these applications are rooted in positive intentions—helping individuals improve their health and well-being—they raise concerns about privacy, autonomy, and emotional manipulation. The personalized nature of these AI systems means that they have access to sensitive health data, and there is a risk of AI systems pushing individuals to adopt behaviors that may not align with their personal preferences or needs. The fine line between persuasion and coercion is once again a critical issue: when does encouragement cross into manipulation, and who decides what constitutes a "healthier" choice?

Moreover, AI's influence in healthcare may inadvertently exacerbate inequalities. People who have access to the latest health technologies may receive tailored nudges that improve their quality of life, while others—those without access or resources—may be left behind. The potential for AI to perpetuate or worsen health disparities must be carefully examined as it continues to play an increasing role in public health.

16.8 Persuasive AI in Education: Shaping Learning and Motivation

AI's influence is not limited to consumer behavior and health; it is increasingly being used in education to guide students' learning journeys. Personalized learning platforms, powered by AI, are transforming the classroom by tailoring content to individual students' needs and preferences. These systems use data to adjust the difficulty of lessons, offer supplementary materials, and provide real-time feedback, all designed to optimize learning.

In the context of education, persuasive AI aims to motivate students to engage with the material, improve their study habits, and enhance overall academic performance. For example, platforms like Khan Academy or Duolingo use AI algorithms to provide students with a personalized curriculum, nudging them to stay on track with their learning goals. This personalization helps students achieve better outcomes by offering a more customized and engaging learning experience.

However, there are risks involved when AI becomes a driving force behind educational decisions. The potential for emotional manipulation in educational contexts—particularly for younger students—raises ethical concerns. AI systems may encourage students to prioritize grades or performance over intrinsic motivation and personal growth. In some cases, these systems may inadvertently reinforce unhealthy patterns of behavior, such as perfectionism or burnout.

Furthermore, as with health data, educational AI systems rely on sensitive personal information. The collection and use of this data to shape students' behaviors necessitate strict safeguards to protect privacy and ensure that AI's influence remains positive and not coercive.

16.9 Autonomy and the Ethics of Persuasive AI

One of the most significant ethical questions surrounding persuasive AI is its impact on human autonomy. Persuasion, by definition, involves influencing someone's choices without coercing them. However, AI systems have the power to shape decisions in ways that individuals might not even recognize. As AI becomes more integrated into our lives, the boundary between influencing and controlling decisions becomes increasingly difficult to draw.

The question of autonomy is particularly relevant in domains like marketing, politics, and healthcare. When AI systems use personal data to make decisions for individuals, how much control do people actually have over their own choices? Is it still truly a free decision if it's guided by an invisible, data-driven force?

The ethical implications are not limited to AI developers or organizations but extend to the broader societal structures that govern the use of AI. To preserve human autonomy, it is crucial that AI systems are designed with transparency, fairness, and accountability in mind. Individuals should have control over their data and a clear understanding of how AI is influencing their decisions. Moreover, regulations must be put in place to prevent AI from crossing the line from persuasive to manipulative.

16.10 The Future of Persuasive AI: Opportunities and Risks

As AI continues to advance, its ability to persuade and influence will only grow stronger. In the future, AI systems may become even more personalized, tapping into deeper insights about human psychology, emotions, and social dynamics. This opens up both exciting possibilities and significant risks.

On the one hand, AI could be harnessed to promote positive behaviors—encouraging individuals to make healthier choices, supporting educational achievement, and helping people lead more fulfilling lives. For example, AI-driven applications could encourage more sustainable consumption patterns or facilitate better mental health outcomes. The potential for AI to support societal well-being is immense, provided it is used ethically and responsibly.

On the other hand, the risks of persuasive AI cannot be ignored. As AI becomes more pervasive, it will likely have an even greater influence on people's decisions, potentially leading to exploitation, social manipulation, and erosion of individual autonomy. This underscores the importance of developing ethical guidelines, robust regulations, and transparent practices to ensure that persuasive AI is used for the greater good.

16.11 Conclusion: Navigating the Ethics of Persuasive AI

Persuasive AI is both a powerful tool and a profound ethical challenge. It has the potential to improve lives by nudging individuals toward better choices, but it also presents significant risks in terms of manipulation, autonomy, and privacy. As we move forward, it is essential that developers, policymakers, and society as a whole carefully consider the ethical implications of persuasive AI and work to establish safeguards that protect individuals' rights.

Ultimately, persuasive AI's power lies in its ability to influence, subtly and often imperceptibly, the way we think, behave, and make decisions. While this can be a force for good, it must always be wielded with caution, responsibility, and a deep commitment to fairness and transparency.

Chapter 17: AI in Habit Formation

17.1 Introduction: The Science of Habit Formation

Humans are creatures of habit. The way we navigate the world, from the moment we wake up to when we fall asleep, is shaped by the habits we form. These habits—whether they pertain to health, work, social interactions, or even leisure activities—play a fundamental role in our daily lives. Habits, in essence, are mental shortcuts. They allow the brain to preserve cognitive energy by automating repetitive actions. But what happens when technology, specifically artificial intelligence (A.I), becomes a key player in shaping and reshaping our habits? This question delves into the intersection of psychology, technology, and personal growth.

At the heart of habit formation lies a psychological model known as the *cue-routine-reward* cycle. This process is a neurological framework that governs how habits are initiated, repeated, and eventually ingrained in our behavior. Understanding this process not only sheds light on how habits are formed but also highlights how AI can leverage these insights to influence and modify human behavior.

In recent years, AI has emerged as a powerful tool for habit formation, from wellness apps designed to help people exercise more to digital assistants that encourage productivity. By tapping into human psychology, AI systems are now capable of identifying patterns, predicting behaviors, and offering personalized nudges that help individuals develop positive habits while discouraging negative ones. AI's ability to collect and process vast amounts of data on individual behavior allows it to provide tailored recommendations that would be impossible for a human coach to deliver at scale.

As we step into this new era of technological intervention, the relationship between AI and habit formation becomes increasingly complex. Can AI truly understand the intricacies of human behavior, or is it simply mimicking a superficial understanding of the mind's deeper processes? Can it foster lasting change in individuals, or is it merely providing temporary fixes? To answer these questions, we must first explore the science of habit formation and how AI is uniquely positioned to influence this process.

17.2 The Psychology Behind Habit Formation

Habits are an integral part of the human experience. But what exactly is a habit? According to psychological theories, habits are behaviors that are repeated regularly and tend to occur subconsciously. They are automatic responses to specific cues in our environment. The cue might be as simple as feeling thirsty, which prompts us to reach for a glass of water. Over time, this behavior becomes ingrained as part of our daily routine. It's not just about remembering to perform the task—it's about the brain forming pathways that make the task almost second nature.

Psychologists have long studied the cognitive processes that underlie habit formation. One of the most well-known models comes from Charles Duhigg's *The Power of Habit*, which outlines the three-step cycle that governs habits: cue, routine, and reward. A *cue* is the trigger that initiates the behavior. The *routine* is the action or behavior that follows, and the *reward* is the positive reinforcement that the brain receives after completing the task.

This reward is critical in habit formation. Dopamine, a neurotransmitter associated with pleasure and motivation, is released when a behavior is reinforced by a positive outcome. Over time, the brain starts to associate the cue with the reward, and the behavior becomes more automatic. As a result, habits form without conscious thought.

However, not all habits are formed with positive outcomes in mind. Many people struggle with unhealthy habits—smoking, overeating, procrastination—that they know are detrimental to their health or well-being. In these cases, the habit cycle becomes self-perpetuating, where the immediate reward (a moment of pleasure or relief) outweighs the long-term consequences. Breaking these habits requires more than just willpower; it requires changing the very cues, routines, and rewards that have become deeply embedded in the brain's wiring.

This is where AI comes into play. With its ability to track behaviors and analyze patterns, AI has the potential to disrupt the habit loop and offer solutions that were previously unimaginable. AI can identify the underlying triggers that lead to unhealthy behaviors and provide personalized strategies to replace them with more positive alternatives.

17.3 How AI Influences Habit Building

AI has revolutionized the way we approach habit-building. The technology is no longer limited to task automation or basic reminders; it is now a personal assistant that actively helps individuals shape their routines. AI-powered habit-building apps and digital platforms are designed to use psychological principles to encourage consistent behavior change.

One of the most prominent ways AI influences habit-building is through *personalization*. AI systems are capable of analyzing an individual's behavior and offering tailored advice that takes into account their unique preferences, challenges, and motivations. For example, fitness apps like *MyFitnessPal* or *Strava* don't just track calories or exercise—they learn from the user's past habits and suggest personalized goals that are both achievable and motivating.

Similarly, mindfulness and wellness apps like *Calm* or *Headspace* use AI to guide users through meditation exercises, adjusting the content and duration based on individual progress. These platforms leverage data to adapt and refine their strategies, creating a feedback loop that encourages users to stay on track with their goals.

Beyond app-based interventions, AI-powered devices such as smartwatches and fitness trackers can monitor a person's physical activity, sleep patterns, and even stress levels. These devices collect data in real time, providing insights into an individual's behavior and offering personalized nudges to encourage healthier habits. For instance, a smartwatch might suggest that you stand up and stretch after a prolonged period of sitting, or it might remind you to go to bed if it detects that you're not getting enough sleep.

This constant stream of feedback—coupled with real-time adjustments—can be a powerful tool in reinforcing positive behaviors and breaking negative habits. AI's ability to keep users engaged through personalized content, rewards, and reminders fosters a sense of accountability that is often difficult to achieve through willpower alone.

17.4 AI and Habit Tracking: Data-Driven Insights

One of the most powerful features of AI in habit formation is its ability to track and analyze data over time. This data-driven approach offers profound insights into human behavior, creating a foundation for more effective habit-building strategies.

Traditional methods of habit tracking—like journaling or using physical planners—have their merits, but they are limited by human error and inconsistency. AI, however, can continuously monitor an individual's behavior and provide a comprehensive overview of their progress. By analyzing this data, AI can identify trends, recognize patterns, and highlight areas where improvements are needed.

For example, consider a person trying to form a habit of exercising regularly. An AI-powered fitness app or device could monitor their physical activity, track the number of steps taken each day, and assess whether they are meeting their exercise goals. This constant feedback allows the AI to adjust the recommendations it gives, helping the user remain engaged with their habit-building process.

Beyond just tracking physical activity, AI can also collect data on other factors that contribute to habit formation, such as sleep quality, nutrition, and mental well-being. This holistic approach gives users a deeper understanding of how their behaviors are interrelated and how making improvements in one area can positively impact other habits.

Furthermore, AI can highlight the small milestones that often go unnoticed by the user. By recognizing incremental progress—such as a slight increase in steps or an improved sleep score—the AI can offer encouragement and reinforcement, making the process of habit formation feel more rewarding and less daunting.

17.5 The Role of AI in Breaking Unwanted Habits

While AI is most often associated with habit-building, it also plays a significant role in breaking unwanted habits. Negative habits, such as smoking, overeating, or procrastination, are notoriously difficult to change. The reward-driven brain mechanisms that fuel these habits can create a vicious cycle that is hard to break without external intervention.

AI can assist in the process of breaking bad habits by disrupting the habit loop at various stages. One of the most effective strategies AI employs is altering the *cue* that triggers the unwanted behavior. Through behavioral analysis, AI can identify the specific situations, environments, or emotional states that prompt a person to engage in a negative habit. Once these triggers are identified, AI can provide real-time interventions to prevent the behavior from occurring.

For instance, AI-powered apps aimed at reducing smoking might send a reminder or alternative activity suggestion when the user is in a situation that typically triggers the urge to smoke. Similarly, apps designed to reduce procrastination could nudge the user to start a task by breaking it down into smaller, more manageable chunks. AI can also provide positive reinforcement when the user resists the urge to engage in their unwanted behavior, reinforcing the new, healthier habit.

Another example comes from AI-driven wellness platforms focused on breaking unhealthy eating habits. Through food tracking and analysis, these platforms can suggest healthier alternatives or offer motivational messages when the user reaches for unhealthy snacks. Over time, this can help rewire the brain's reward system, making the new habit feel more satisfying than the old one.

17.6 Motivation and Gamification: Keeping the User Engaged

A key factor in habit formation is maintaining motivation, especially when progress seems slow or challenging. One of the ways AI helps users stay motivated is through *gamification*—the process of applying game-like elements to non-game contexts to make activities more engaging.

In the realm of habit-building, gamification often involves rewarding users with points, badges, or other incentives for completing tasks or reaching milestones. These rewards, although simple in nature, trigger the release of dopamine, reinforcing the behavior and encouraging users to continue their progress.

For example, fitness apps like *Fitbit* and *Nike Training Club* use gamification techniques to motivate users. By earning badges for achieving specific milestones (such as completing a certain number of workouts in a week or reaching a daily step goal), users are rewarded with a sense of accomplishment that encourages them to continue pursuing their goals. The AI adapts to the user's progress, providing new challenges that align with their abilities and interests, ensuring that the gamified elements remain relevant and engaging.

Similarly, meditation apps like *Calm* or *Headspace* reward users with streaks or points for consistent practice. These rewards may seem small, but they create a sense of achievement and build momentum, making it easier for users to form a regular meditation habit.

Gamification serves as a powerful motivational tool because it taps into intrinsic and extrinsic motivation. While intrinsic motivation comes from the personal satisfaction of achieving a goal, extrinsic motivation is driven by external rewards, such as points or badges. AI uses both types of motivation to keep users engaged and invested in their habit-building journey.

17.7 The Ethical Implications of AI in Habit Formation

While AI offers numerous benefits in habit formation, it also raises important ethical considerations. The very nature of habit formation—altering deeply ingrained behaviors—requires a careful balance between user autonomy and technological influence. The potential for AI to manipulate or nudge individuals into certain behaviors without their full awareness is a concern that warrants careful scrutiny.

One of the central ethical concerns is the issue of consent. When using AI to influence habits, it is essential that individuals are fully aware of the data being collected and how it will be used. Transparency is critical to ensure that users are not unknowingly subjected to manipulation.

Moreover, there is the question of privacy. Habit-building AI systems collect vast amounts of personal data, from physical activity levels to emotional states. This data is invaluable for creating personalized recommendations, but it also poses significant risks if it falls into the wrong hands. AI developers must implement strong safeguards to protect user privacy and ensure that data is used responsibly.

Another concern is the potential for AI to exacerbate existing inequalities. AI systems designed to encourage habit formation often rely on user engagement and adherence to personalized recommendations. However, individuals from different socioeconomic backgrounds may have different access to technology, and certain habit-building tools may not be equally effective for all users. This issue of accessibility must be addressed to ensure that AI benefits all individuals, not just those who are technologically privileged.

Finally, there is the issue of over-reliance on AI. While AI can offer valuable assistance in forming positive habits, it should not replace the need for self-awareness, critical thinking, and personal accountability. Over-reliance on AI could lead to a scenario where individuals no longer take responsibility for their own behavior, relying instead on technology to shape their lives.

17.8 The Future of AI in Habit Formation

As AI continues to evolve, its role in habit formation is expected to expand. The future of AI in this field may include more advanced technologies that integrate with the brain's neural pathways, providing even more personalized and effective interventions.

For example, neurofeedback devices, which are already used to help individuals train their brains for improved focus or relaxation, could become more widespread in the future. By providing real-time feedback on brain activity, these devices could assist in reinforcing positive habits at a deeper neurological level, creating stronger, more lasting changes.

Additionally, advancements in artificial emotional intelligence could lead to even more intuitive habit-building systems. AI could become more adept at understanding the emotional states that influence habit formation and could offer personalized support based on an individual's emotional needs. For instance, if an individual feels stressed or anxious, an AI system might recommend a mindfulness exercise or offer calming content to help the user regain balance.

The future of AI in habit formation also holds promise in terms of collaborative systems. Rather than relying solely on individual devices or apps, AI could facilitate group habit-building initiatives. Social media platforms, for example, could use AI to connect individuals with similar goals, fostering a sense of community and collective motivation.

In conclusion, AI's role in habit formation is vast and multifaceted. From tracking and analyzing behavior to offering personalized nudges and rewards, AI has proven itself to be a valuable tool in shaping human habits. However, as with any technological intervention, careful consideration must be given to its ethical implications, ensuring that AI is used responsibly and with the best interests of individuals in mind.

Chapter 18: The Role of AI in Behavioral Economics

18.1 Introduction to Behavioral Economics and AI

The intricate dance between psychology and economics has long fascinated scholars, policymakers, and business leaders alike. Behavioral economics, a field that fuses insights from both disciplines, acknowledges that human decision-making is often far from the rational, calculating process assumed by traditional economic models. Instead, our decisions are deeply influenced by biases, emotions, and social factors. It is within this realm that artificial intelligence (A.I) is starting to play an increasingly prominent role.

AI, with its ability to analyze massive datasets, identify patterns, and make predictions, has become a powerful tool for understanding and influencing human behavior. More than just an analytical engine, AI is now a key player in how we make economic choices. From shaping our purchasing decisions to advising on investments, AI systems are slowly but surely becoming an integral part of the economic landscape. Yet, the interplay between AI and behavioral economics raises essential questions: How can AI improve our decision-making processes? How can AI be used ethically to guide consumer choices and influence public policy? And what are the potential risks when AI begins to nudge human behavior in subtle but significant ways?

In this chapter, we will explore the role of AI in behavioral economics, examining the ways in which it influences our choices, shapes consumer behavior, and, ultimately, alters the way we engage with the economy. Through the lens of AI, we will see how traditional economic theories are being transformed by cutting-edge technology and psychological insights. This journey will help us understand how AI is not just a passive observer of human behavior, but an active participant in the complex web of decision-making processes that drive modern economies.

18.2 Cognitive Biases and Their Influence on Economic Decisions

Cognitive biases are the psychological shortcuts that our brains take in order to simplify the overwhelming complexity of daily decision-making. These biases, often invisible to the decision-maker, can lead to irrational choices—choices that defy traditional economic models based on the assumption of rationality. For example, when we perceive a discount as more valuable simply because it is framed as "saving 20%" instead of "paying $80," we are succumbing to the anchoring bias, where the initial number presented becomes a reference point for future decisions.

Traditional economic theory has often struggled to account for these biases, assuming that individuals act in their best economic interest when making decisions. Yet, real-world behaviors rarely align with this assumption. Instead, people are influenced by psychological factors such as emotions, social pressures, and even the framing of a decision. This is where AI steps in, providing the tools to identify, predict, and, in some cases, exploit these biases in ways that were previously unimaginable.

For example, AI algorithms, particularly those used in digital marketing and e-commerce, analyze vast amounts of consumer data—purchases, browsing habits, search queries, and even social media activity—to detect patterns in individual behavior. By identifying cognitive biases like loss aversion (the tendency to prefer avoiding losses rather than acquiring equivalent gains) or the decoy effect (where consumers change their preference between two options when a third, less attractive option is introduced), AI systems can tailor offers, advertisements, and product suggestions to nudge consumers toward specific choices.

This process is not necessarily nefarious. It can, in some cases, help consumers make decisions that are aligned with their best interests. For instance, a financial AI advisor may warn an individual against overspending or advise them on more sustainable investment strategies. However, this also opens the door to ethical concerns—particularly when AI is used to manipulate consumer behavior for profit, as we will discuss further in later sections.

By understanding the biases that affect consumer decisions, AI can create more targeted and efficient solutions. But it also raises the question: To what extent should AI be allowed to influence or "nudge" consumers, and when does this cross into manipulation?

18.3 AI as a Behavioral Nudge: Principles of Persuasion

At the heart of behavioral economics is the concept of the "nudge"—a subtle influence that alters people's behavior in a predictable way without restricting their freedom of choice. The idea was popularized by behavioral economists Richard Thaler and Cass Sunstein in their book *Nudge*, which argued that small interventions can significantly impact decision-making, from encouraging healthy eating habits to increasing retirement savings.

AI has taken the principles of nudging to new heights. Through sophisticated algorithms, AI can monitor and analyze real-time data to provide just-in-time interventions that guide consumer choices. These nudges can be highly personalized, tapping into the unique preferences, biases, and behaviors of individuals.

For example, consider an AI-powered health app that tracks a user's exercise routine. By analyzing patterns in their activity level, the app can send timely reminders or motivational messages to encourage them to stay active. It might recommend a specific workout at the time of day when the user is most likely to exercise, or it could offer positive reinforcement by celebrating milestones. These nudges are designed to guide the user toward making healthier choices without explicitly telling them what to do.

Similarly, AI-driven recommendation systems, such as those used by Netflix or Amazon, rely on predictive analytics to suggest products, movies, or services that are tailored to individual preferences. These systems don't force users to make a particular choice; rather, they nudge users toward options that align with their past behavior and psychological tendencies.

The use of nudging is not limited to consumer choices. In public policy, AI is being leveraged to influence behavior on a societal level. Consider AI-driven interventions in areas like energy conservation, where algorithms encourage individuals to reduce their carbon footprint by suggesting efficient appliances or energy-saving habits. These nudges are designed to be subtle, ensuring that people retain the freedom to make their own choices while still contributing to broader societal goals.

The persuasive power of AI's nudging techniques is undeniable. However, this raises important ethical questions. While nudging can lead to positive outcomes, it also has the potential to be used for exploitative purposes. In the following sections, we will explore how AI nudging is applied in various domains and examine the ethical implications of these practices.

18.4 The Impact of AI on Consumer Decision-Making

AI's influence on consumer decision-making has become most apparent in the realm of e-commerce. The advent of personalized marketing, fueled by machine learning algorithms, has revolutionized how companies interact with consumers. By tracking user behavior, preferences, and past purchases, AI systems can tailor product recommendations in ways that traditional advertising simply cannot.

For example, when you visit an online store like Amazon, the recommendations that appear are powered by AI systems that analyze your previous searches and purchases. These recommendations can be strikingly accurate, offering products that you are likely to purchase based on patterns identified by the system. This personalization has led to higher conversion rates, as consumers are more likely to purchase items that feel relevant to their needs and desires.

But personalization doesn't stop at recommendations. AI also plays a crucial role in dynamic pricing—adjusting the price of products in real time based on factors such as demand, competition, and consumer behavior. A hotel booking website might show a higher price for a room when demand is high, or an airline might adjust ticket prices based on the browsing habits of a potential customer. These pricing strategies, powered by AI, capitalize on human psychology, exploiting concepts such as scarcity and urgency to increase the likelihood of a sale.

This sophisticated level of personalization doesn't just make shopping more convenient; it also taps into deep-seated psychological principles. By leveraging cognitive biases such as reciprocity (the tendency to return favors), social proof (the influence of others on our decisions), and scarcity (the fear of missing out), AI-driven marketing strategies can be highly effective in nudging consumers to make purchases that they might not have otherwise considered.

But the question remains: Is this level of influence ethical? While personalized marketing may increase consumer satisfaction by offering relevant products, it also raises concerns about privacy and autonomy. In the next sections, we will discuss the ethical considerations surrounding AI's role in shaping consumer behavior.

18.5 AI and Behavioral Economics in Financial Decision-Making

AI's role in financial decision-making is perhaps most prominent in the world of investment and trading. Financial markets are inherently complex and volatile, with a vast array of data points that can affect the value of assets. Traditionally, human traders would rely on their experience, intuition, and analysis of trends to make decisions. However, with the advent of AI and machine learning, these processes are being automated and optimized at a scale and speed that far exceed human capacity.

At the core of AI in financial decision-making lies predictive analytics—algorithms that can process vast datasets to identify patterns and trends. By analyzing historical data, news articles, and even social media sentiment, AI can predict market movements and recommend investment strategies. One popular use case is robo-advisors—AI-driven platforms that provide personalized financial advice based on a user's risk tolerance, financial goals, and market conditions.

AI's ability to predict market behavior is transforming the way individual investors and institutions approach financial decision-making. AI algorithms can detect subtle signals in the market that might go unnoticed by human traders. For example, AI can detect changes in consumer sentiment or the emergence of new trends that could indicate a shift in market conditions. In this way, AI is reshaping how we approach investments, making financial markets more efficient and potentially more profitable.

However, the rapid rise of AI in financial decision-making also brings about concerns. The very algorithms that drive these systems are shaped by historical data, which may reflect existing biases or systemic inequalities. This can result in feedback loops that reinforce harmful patterns, such as market manipulation or inequitable access to financial resources. Furthermore, the automation of financial decisions raises questions about accountability. Who is responsible when AI-driven trading algorithms make risky or disastrous decisions?

As AI becomes more integrated into financial markets, it is crucial to strike a balance between harnessing its power for economic benefit and safeguarding against the risks that come with its widespread adoption. Financial institutions, regulators, and policymakers will need to work together to ensure that AI in finance is used ethically and transparently.

18.6 AI in Consumer Behavior: Persuasion Techniques and Ethical Concerns

In examining the influence of AI on consumer behavior, we cannot ignore the persuasive techniques that underlie much of AI-driven marketing. The ability of AI to personalize advertising and recommendations is perhaps the most powerful tool in the marketer's arsenal today. By tapping into human psychology, AI systems create compelling narratives and product offerings that resonate deeply with individuals.

One of the key mechanisms behind AI's persuasive power is the ability to utilize psychological principles like reciprocity, scarcity, and social proof. For example, consider a product recommendation that includes phrases like "limited-time offer" or "only a few items left in stock." This simple nudge plays into the consumer's fear of missing out (FOMO), prompting them to make a purchase they might otherwise have delayed or avoided.

Another technique is the use of social proof, where AI systems show users that a product or service is popular among others, suggesting that the consumer will be making a smart decision by following the crowd. This is a powerful form of persuasion that taps into our inherent desire to conform and belong. Online reviews, ratings, and influencer endorsements, all curated by AI systems, further amplify this effect, creating a sense of collective validation for consumer choices.

While these techniques can be highly effective, they also raise significant ethical concerns. The line between persuasion and manipulation is thin. When AI systems use personal data to anticipate and exploit consumers' vulnerabilities, it risks crossing into manipulation. This raises questions about autonomy, privacy, and consent. Are consumers truly making informed decisions when their choices are heavily influenced by AI algorithms? And to what extent is it ethical for companies to leverage AI's power to sway consumer behavior in ways that benefit their bottom line?

As AI continues to play a more prominent role in marketing and advertising, it is essential to establish ethical guidelines for its use. These guidelines should balance the need for business profitability with the protection of consumer autonomy and well-being. Transparency, informed consent, and respect for privacy should be at the forefront of these discussions.

18.7 The Intersection of AI, Behavioral Economics, and Public Policy

Beyond the consumer marketplace, AI is also increasingly being used in public policy to influence behavior at the societal level. Governments and organizations are turning to AI-driven solutions to tackle issues such as public health, climate change, and energy conservation. By analyzing large datasets and modeling various scenarios, AI systems can help policymakers understand human behavior and craft interventions that nudge individuals toward more beneficial outcomes for society.

For instance, AI is being used to encourage sustainable energy consumption. By analyzing energy usage patterns, AI can provide personalized recommendations that help households and businesses reduce their carbon footprint. Similarly, AI-powered apps can promote healthier lifestyles by tracking diet, exercise, and sleep patterns, offering users personalized advice to improve their well-being. These AI interventions are designed not only to influence individual behavior but also to align personal choices with broader societal goals.

However, when AI is used to influence public behavior, the ethical stakes are higher. Public policy interventions must strike a delicate balance between encouraging positive behavior and respecting individual freedoms. For example, while promoting energy conservation or healthier lifestyles is beneficial to society, AI interventions that push too aggressively in these areas could be seen as paternalistic or coercive. Ensuring that such interventions are transparent, voluntary, and non-invasive is essential for maintaining public trust.

Moreover, AI's role in public policy raises concerns about surveillance and privacy. The use of AI to monitor and analyze individual behavior—whether through smart meters, health apps, or social media platforms—raises significant questions about the extent to which individuals' lives should be observed and analyzed for the sake of public benefit. Safeguards must be put in place to ensure that AI-driven public policy interventions respect personal privacy and protect against abuses of power.

18.8 The Future of AI in Behavioral Economics

As we step into the future, the role of AI in behavioral economics is poised to evolve in ways that are both exciting and complex. With rapid advancements in technology, AI will continue to reshape how we understand, predict, and influence human behavior. The convergence of artificial intelligence with behavioral economics will bring about a more nuanced understanding of decision-making processes, with the potential to transform industries, economies, and even societal structures.

AI and the Expansion of Behavioral Insights

The future of AI in behavioral economics will likely see the expansion of AI's ability to derive insights from increasingly complex data sets. Today, AI systems are capable of analyzing vast amounts of data from consumer behavior, market trends, and even physiological responses. In the future, these systems will evolve to incorporate even more granular forms of human behavior, such as subconscious reactions, emotional responses, and even our cognitive biases in real time.

Imagine AI systems that can track not just the choices people make but also the underlying psychological and emotional drivers behind those choices. By combining psychological theories with advanced machine learning, AI could create models that predict not only what people will choose, but why they make those choices. This depth of understanding could enable even more tailored behavioral nudges, making interventions more effective.

For instance, personalized health plans driven by AI could take into account not only an individual's physical activity or eating habits, but also their emotional responses to certain foods, exercise routines, or stressors. By analyzing these emotional drivers, AI could guide individuals toward healthier habits in a way that feels natural and sustainable—creating a symbiotic relationship between AI and human decision-making that's driven by both cognitive and emotional understanding.

AI and the Democratization of Behavioral Economics

The integration of AI in behavioral economics could democratize access to psychological and economic insights that were once reserved for large corporations, governments, and academic institutions. As AI becomes more accessible, individuals and small businesses could harness the power of behavioral economics to make smarter, data-driven decisions in their personal lives or business operations.

For example, imagine a small entrepreneur using AI-driven insights to optimize customer engagement strategies, tailoring their offerings to individual preferences and emotional triggers. Similarly, AI systems could enable individuals to better understand and optimize their own financial habits, providing real-time feedback that helps them make smarter decisions regarding spending, saving, and investing.

This democratization could lead to a world where individuals have more control over their behavioral choices, empowering them to break free from destructive habits or make more informed decisions that improve their lives. The rise of AI in personal finance apps, mental health tracking tools, and even educational platforms could become the norm, allowing people to make decisions grounded in behavioral insights, rather than relying on guesswork or outdated advice.

The Role of AI in Sustainable Development

Another significant area where AI will influence behavioral economics is in sustainable development. As climate change becomes an increasingly urgent global issue, AI-driven behavioral economics could be a key tool in driving large-scale environmental changes. AI systems could analyze patterns in consumer behavior related to sustainability, identifying ways to encourage more eco-friendly choices and behaviors.

For example, AI-powered systems could track energy consumption patterns in households, offering tailored recommendations that help families reduce their carbon footprint without sacrificing comfort or convenience. Similarly, in the realm of consumer goods, AI could help shift purchasing behavior toward more sustainable products by analyzing and recommending alternatives that align with an individual's values.

Moreover, AI can be used to influence public policy by helping governments understand and predict the behaviors of their citizens regarding sustainability efforts. By analyzing data on how people respond to incentives, regulations, and environmental policies, AI could provide recommendations on the most effective strategies for encouraging behaviors that benefit the planet. This could include strategies like incentivizing green energy use, promoting recycling programs, or encouraging sustainable agriculture practices.

In this context, the future of AI in behavioral economics could be instrumental in creating a more sustainable world. It's not just about nudging individuals to make better choices, but also about understanding the collective behaviors that shape society and guiding those behaviors toward a more sustainable and equitable future.

AI and Behavioral Regulation: A Fine Line Between Nudging and Control

As AI's role in behavioral economics continues to grow, there is a critical concern regarding the fine line between nudging and control. The power of AI to predict and influence human behavior brings with it significant ethical challenges. While nudges can help people make better decisions, the temptation to use AI to control or manipulate individuals could lead to a dystopian future where personal autonomy is undermined.

The future of AI in behavioral economics will require robust ethical frameworks to ensure that AI interventions are used responsibly and transparently. Governments, regulatory bodies, and technology companies will need to work together to create clear guidelines that prevent the misuse of AI-driven persuasion techniques.

One potential approach is the development of ethical AI design principles, such as ensuring transparency in how AI systems make decisions and provide recommendations. Individuals should have the ability to understand why they are being nudged in a certain direction and retain the power to make independent choices. Furthermore, individuals should be given control over the data that AI systems use to influence their behavior, ensuring that privacy is maintained and that AI does not exploit personal information without consent.

The Emergence of AI-Driven Behavioral Economics in Public Policy

As AI continues to advance, it will increasingly be used as a tool in shaping public policy. The insights gained from AI-driven behavioral economics could allow governments to implement more effective, targeted interventions in areas like public health, education, and social welfare. For example, AI could help policymakers understand how different demographic groups respond to public health campaigns, social programs, or environmental policies, enabling them to tailor interventions for maximum impact.

In public health, AI could assist in the design of campaigns that encourage healthier lifestyles, or even predict disease outbreaks by analyzing population behavior patterns. In education, AI could provide personalized learning experiences that cater to each student's unique learning style, improving outcomes across diverse educational settings.

AI could also help in welfare distribution, by ensuring that benefits are targeted toward the individuals and communities who need them the most. By analyzing patterns of economic behavior, AI could help determine which interventions would be most effective in addressing poverty, inequality, and social mobility.

However, as we saw with AI in financial markets, the use of AI in public policy also presents challenges. Ensuring that AI-driven decisions are made with fairness, accountability, and respect for human rights is essential. Without careful oversight, AI could be used to reinforce existing power structures and exacerbate inequalities.

18.9 Case Studies: AI in Action within Behavioral Economics

As AI continues to redefine how we approach human behavior and economics, real-world applications of AI in behavioral economics offer valuable insights into its transformative potential. In this section, we'll explore several case studies that demonstrate how AI systems are used to influence decision-making, optimize economic outcomes, and reshape human behaviors across various sectors. By examining these case studies, we can gain a better understanding of how AI is not only predicting behavior but actively shaping it in a manner that integrates psychological, economic, and technological principles.

Case Study 1: AI in Personalized Financial Advice

One of the most impactful ways in which AI is being applied in behavioral economics is in the financial services sector. Personal finance platforms powered by AI are increasingly used to deliver tailored financial advice, helping individuals make better choices regarding saving, investing, and spending. Companies like **Wealthfront**, **Betterment**, and **Acorns** use algorithms to assess an individual's financial situation and goals, then generate personalized recommendations that maximize their economic well-being.

These AI systems are designed to emulate a human financial advisor's ability to predict and influence financial behavior. By analyzing a wide array of data, including spending patterns, income, debt levels, and personal preferences, these AI platforms help users avoid impulsive financial decisions, such as overspending or emotional investment choices. The use of AI in this context helps users make long-term decisions, nudging them to build wealth through automatic savings or guided investments that align with their risk tolerance and future goals.

For instance, **Acorns**, a popular micro-investing app, uses AI to round up purchases to the nearest dollar and invest the change in a diversified portfolio. This simple AI-driven intervention helps individuals develop the habit of saving and investing, often without them even realizing it. The psychological principle of *automated savings* takes advantage of people's behavioral tendency to procrastinate or undervalue long-term financial goals, providing a frictionless solution that leads to wealth accumulation over time.

Case Study 2: AI in Consumer Behavior and Retail

The retail industry has long been a laboratory for behavioral economics, as businesses have continuously sought ways to influence consumer behavior. AI has taken these efforts to new heights by analyzing consumer preferences, purchasing history, and even social media activity to deliver highly personalized experiences and targeted ads. Companies like **Amazon**, **Netflix**, and **Spotify** rely heavily on AI algorithms to recommend products, movies, or songs based on individual tastes, predicting what consumers are most likely to engage with and buy next.

In **Amazon's** case, its AI-powered recommendation engine analyzes user behavior in real-time, creating personalized shopping experiences that enhance user engagement. By tracking what a customer has browsed, purchased, or even left in their cart, Amazon's system predicts future purchases and subtly nudges the consumer toward additional products. This not only increases sales but also improves the customer experience by anticipating their needs before they are explicitly expressed.

AI in retail also extends to pricing strategies. Retailers can use AI to dynamically adjust prices based on consumer demand, competitor pricing, and purchasing patterns. This practice, known as dynamic pricing, relies on predictive analytics to forecast when demand for a product will peak and adjusts prices accordingly. For example, airlines and hotel chains often use dynamic pricing to increase their revenue, charging higher prices for flights and rooms when they anticipate higher demand.

What's compelling here is how AI incorporates psychological factors such as *scarcity*, *urgency*, and *reciprocity* into these decision-making processes. By tailoring prices to consumer behavior, AI systems tap into cognitive biases that influence people's willingness to pay, pushing them toward purchases they may not have initially intended to make.

Case Study 3: AI in Healthcare: Predicting Patient Behavior and Treatment Adherence

AI has also found significant application in the healthcare sector, particularly in predicting and influencing patient behavior. Hospitals, clinics, and wellness platforms now use AI-driven tools to improve patient outcomes by encouraging healthier behaviors, improving treatment adherence, and reducing healthcare costs.

For instance, AI-powered health apps such as **MyFitnessPal** and **Fitbit** track users' exercise routines, diet, and sleep patterns. These apps collect data from wearable devices and use AI to predict behavior and provide recommendations based on that data. By incorporating behavioral economics principles, these platforms encourage healthy habits by utilizing *nudges*—subtle reminders or prompts that steer users toward better choices. For example, Fitbit may send a reminder to encourage physical activity when a user's daily step count falls below a certain threshold. The combination of data, AI insights, and behavioral economics helps users form and maintain positive health habits.

Beyond individual health apps, AI is being used in healthcare systems to address broader patient adherence issues. **IBM Watson Health** and other AI-driven healthcare solutions help physicians predict which patients are at risk of non-compliance with prescribed treatments. These AI systems analyze historical data, including patient demographics, medical history, and behavior patterns, to identify individuals who may be more likely to miss appointments or fail to follow treatment plans.

By proactively identifying these at-risk patients, AI allows healthcare providers to intervene early, using tailored reminders, behavioral incentives, and personalized support to increase adherence. Such interventions are rooted in the psychological principles of *loss aversion* (where people are motivated to avoid losses more than acquiring gains) and *social proof* (where people are influenced by the behaviors of others).

Case Study 4: AI in Social Media and Political Influence

Social media platforms like **Facebook**, **Twitter**, and **Instagram** leverage AI systems to influence user behavior on a massive scale. These platforms analyze data from users' likes, shares, comments, and browsing history to predict what content will engage them the most. By curating personalized newsfeeds, AI systems subtly influence what users see and, consequently, how they think about particular issues, products, or people.

AI in social media also plays a key role in political campaigns. Political parties and candidates have increasingly turned to AI to shape public opinion, target specific voter segments, and influence election outcomes. By analyzing voter data, including past voting behavior, demographic information, and social media activity, AI systems can predict how voters are likely to behave and tailor campaign messaging to resonate with them on a psychological level.

For instance, AI-powered political campaigns can target voters with specific messages that appeal to their personal values or fears. By appealing to voters' cognitive biases—such as the *availability heuristic* (the tendency to rely on immediate examples that come to mind)—AI can increase the effectiveness of political messaging. These campaigns use AI-driven micro-targeting to reach voters with personalized advertisements or content that resonates with their emotional state, political views, or social identity.

The potential ethical challenges of AI-driven political campaigns are substantial, as the boundaries between persuasion and manipulation can be blurred. The use of AI to influence voting behavior raises critical concerns about privacy, transparency, and the potential for deepening societal divisions.

Case Study 5: AI in Environmental Behavior and Sustainability

AI also plays a significant role in promoting sustainable behaviors and encouraging environmental responsibility. Governments, corporations, and environmental organizations have begun to use AI to influence behaviors that contribute to a more sustainable future. By predicting human behavior, AI can be used to encourage energy-saving actions, recycling, and even pro-environmental consumer purchases.

For example, **Google's Nest Thermostat** uses AI to adjust a home's temperature based on the homeowner's habits and preferences. This AI system not only ensures that homes are comfortable but also helps to reduce energy consumption by learning when the household is occupied or vacant. Through predictive analysis, the system optimizes energy use, nudging individuals toward more eco-friendly behaviors while simultaneously lowering their utility bills.

Similarly, AI can encourage eco-friendly consumption by analyzing individual purchasing habits and offering alternatives that are more sustainable. Online retailers may use AI to recommend products that are made from recycled materials or have lower carbon footprints. By tapping into the psychological principle of *social comparison*, these recommendations can persuade consumers to choose products that align with environmental values, creating a ripple effect in sustainable consumer habits.

18.10 Conclusion

These case studies highlight the diverse applications of AI in behavioral economics, showcasing its capacity to influence, predict, and even modify human behavior across various sectors. From personal finance to healthcare, retail, and sustainability, AI is playing an increasingly central role in shaping the choices we make and the ways we interact with the world around us.

The ability of AI to harness psychological principles, economic theories, and vast amounts of data positions it as a powerful tool for not only predicting behavior but also influencing it. As we continue to refine AI systems and understand the complexities of human behavior, we are only scratching the surface of what AI can achieve in the field of behavioral economics.

However, these advancements come with ethical and societal implications that demand thoughtful consideration. As we move forward, it is critical to ensure that AI's influence on human behavior is used for positive, transparent, and equitable purposes. The future of AI in behavioral economics holds immense promise, but it is up to society to guide its development in a direction that enhances human well-being while safeguarding autonomy and ethical standards.

Chapter 19: AI's Role in Addiction and Recovery

19.1 Introduction: The Complex Nature of Addiction

Addiction, in its many forms, has haunted humanity for millennia, shaping lives and communities in ways both profound and devastating. Whether it's the compulsive need to seek solace in substances or the overreliance on behaviors that disrupt daily life, addiction is a complex interplay of biological, psychological, and social factors. In modern society, the advent of new technologies, particularly Artificial Intelligence (A.I), is beginning to offer fresh solutions to tackle this perennial issue.

Addiction is more than a series of unhealthy habits. It is often rooted in deeply ingrained patterns of thought, emotional regulation failures, and, as recent research suggests, a rewiring of the brain's reward system. Yet, while the human mind has evolved to respond to such stimuli, AI—powered by data analysis, pattern recognition, and predictive modeling—is now beginning to offer unprecedented ways to understand and combat addiction.

In this chapter, we explore how AI is being integrated into the fight against addiction, uncovering the ways it assists in diagnosing, predicting, and personalizing recovery plans. By reflecting on both the potential and the ethical considerations of AI's role in addiction, we will see how this technology is shifting paradigms in both psychology and medicine.

19.2 Addiction and the Brain: A Psychological and Neurological Perspective

To appreciate the role of AI in addiction recovery, it is crucial to understand the mechanisms that drive addictive behavior. Addiction is often seen through the lens of the brain's reward system. This system, primarily governed by the neurotransmitter dopamine, reinforces behaviors by triggering feelings of pleasure. When an individual engages in an addictive behavior, whether consuming substances or gambling, the brain rewards that action, creating a feedback loop.

From a psychological perspective, addiction involves more than just neural rewiring; it touches on deep emotional and cognitive layers. Addictive behaviors often emerge in response to emotional pain, stress, or a lack of coping mechanisms, leaving individuals susceptible to seeking temporary relief through substance use or compulsive activities.

AI, in its increasing complexity, has begun to emulate and simulate the brain's patterns, offering valuable insights into addiction. With vast computational power, AI models can analyze how neural circuits become altered by addiction, helping researchers and clinicians understand the underlying neurological shifts. AI can predict, with growing precision, when and why an individual might relapse based on their behavioral data, paving the way for early intervention.

19.3 The Emergence of AI in Addiction Studies

The use of AI in addiction treatment is still in its infancy, yet it has already made significant strides. From early predictive models to AI-driven interventions, this technology is reshaping how addiction is understood and managed. AI allows for the identification of nuanced patterns in behavior that may otherwise go unnoticed by human observers. This is especially important in cases of addiction, where the signs of a developing issue can often be subtle and difficult to detect until they have escalated.

Researchers are leveraging AI's ability to process vast amounts of data to map the trajectory of addictive behaviors. By analyzing patterns in digital interactions—such as online purchases, social media use, or patterns of substance consumption—AI can detect emerging signs of addiction earlier than traditional methods. In doing so, it can inform preventative measures, helping individuals get the support they need before addiction takes hold.

19.4 AI in Predicting Addictive Behaviors

One of the most powerful applications of AI in addiction is its ability to predict future behaviors. Addiction, as complex and multifaceted as it is, leaves behind digital footprints. Every action taken by an individual—whether it's browsing habits, purchasing behavior, or even the language used in text messages—provides a clue into their emotional and psychological state. AI's ability to process and analyze these data points enables it to predict the likelihood of someone developing an addiction.

Take, for example, AI-powered applications that track substance use patterns. These applications can analyze data from a variety of sources: smartphone apps that track drinking habits, wearable devices that monitor heart rate variability, or even smart home devices that track environmental cues. By processing these data points, AI can create a predictive model for how and when someone might relapse. AI can also identify potential triggers, such as stress or social situations, and alert the user before they make harmful decisions. These predictive capabilities offer a revolutionary advantage in addiction prevention, potentially averting addiction before it becomes ingrained.

19.5 AI-Driven Diagnostics: Identifying Addiction Risk Early

The key to effective addiction treatment is early detection, and AI is enabling unprecedented advances in this area. Diagnostic tools powered by AI analyze behavioral data, biomarkers, and even genetic predispositions to identify individuals at risk of addiction. By evaluating psychological profiles, AI can predict vulnerability to specific types of addiction, whether to substances, gambling, or digital compulsions like social media.

For example, AI-driven diagnostic tools can analyze changes in an individual's social interactions, sleep patterns, and even language usage in text conversations. A shift toward more negative language or increased isolation can serve as early indicators that the person is at risk of developing an addictive behavior. By identifying these changes before they lead to full-blown addiction, AI systems offer a preventive approach that could save countless lives.

In addition to behavioral monitoring, AI-powered medical devices, such as wearable sensors, can track physiological data like heart rate variability and stress levels. Combined with machine learning algorithms, these tools can identify stress-induced physiological responses that could indicate an individual's growing reliance on addictive behaviors.

19.6 AI in Personalized Treatment Plans for Addiction Recovery

Perhaps the most compelling aspect of AI's role in addiction recovery is its ability to personalize treatment. Traditional addiction recovery methods tend to follow a one-size-fits-all approach, often with limited customization to fit the unique psychological needs of the individual. This is where AI can make a profound impact. By analyzing data about the individual's psychological profile, behavioral patterns, and previous treatment outcomes, AI can design personalized recovery plans that are tailored to the person's specific needs.

Consider virtual recovery programs, where AI algorithms monitor progress and adjust therapeutic interventions in real-time. These programs can utilize data from wearables, mobile apps, and online assessments to gauge a person's emotional state, level of engagement, and potential risk factors. In this way, AI enables a dynamic treatment experience that evolves with the individual, offering new tools and strategies as the person moves through recovery.

This personalized approach is far more effective than traditional methods because it treats the person, not just the addiction. The AI system becomes a partner in the recovery process, offering continuous support and guidance, much like a virtual therapist who is always available.

19.7 AI-Powered Support Systems: Continuous Monitoring and Assistance

Recovery from addiction is a long-term process, and maintaining progress can be difficult. This is where AI-powered support systems come into play. By providing real-time monitoring and continuous assistance, AI ensures that individuals have ongoing access to the support they need during recovery. Virtual assistants and chatbots are increasingly being used to provide emotional support, check in on progress, and offer motivational nudges.

These AI tools are designed to be nonjudgmental and approachable, making it easier for individuals to stay connected with their recovery journey. For example, chatbots can provide cognitive-behavioral therapy (CBT) techniques, mindfulness exercises, and motivational support tailored to the user's specific needs. They can also track the user's progress over time, offering insights into emotional triggers and helping the person stay on track with their recovery goals.

The integration of AI-powered support systems has been shown to increase engagement in recovery programs, as individuals feel that they are not alone in their journey. Moreover, these systems are available 24/7, allowing individuals to access support whenever they need it most—whether it's during a moment of craving or a period of self-doubt.

19.8 Behavioral Nudges and AI-Driven Motivational Support

Motivation is often the most significant hurdle for individuals in recovery. Addiction recovery is not just about stopping an addictive behavior; it's about replacing it with healthier habits and cultivating resilience. This process requires sustained motivation, which is where AI-driven nudges come in.

AI systems leverage behavioral science techniques such as nudging to encourage positive behaviors. By subtly guiding individuals toward healthier choices, AI can motivate them to stick with their recovery plans. For example, an AI-powered app might send reminders to practice self-care, attend therapy sessions, or engage in stress-relief activities when it detects signs of distress. These nudges may seem small, but over time they can have a profound impact on the individual's motivation and adherence to their recovery program.

Through the application of data analytics, AI can also identify patterns that may predict when an individual is likely to experience a lapse in motivation, such as during periods of heightened stress. By offering timely support, AI can help the individual stay on course, providing the right encouragement at the right moment.

19.9 Ethical Considerations in AI for Addiction Recovery

As with all technological advancements, the integration of AI in addiction treatment and recovery raises important ethical considerations. These concerns span privacy, autonomy, accessibility, and the potential for unintended consequences. While AI offers incredible promise in diagnosing, predicting, and supporting recovery, it is critical that these tools are used responsibly.

19.9.1 Privacy and Data Security

Addiction recovery is deeply personal, and the data collected by AI systems can often be intimate and revealing. Whether it's tracking substance use, analyzing sleep patterns, or monitoring an individual's emotional state, AI in addiction recovery requires access to sensitive data. This raises questions about privacy and how securely this information is stored and shared.

The confidentiality of recovery data must be ensured at all stages—when it is collected, processed, and analyzed. Moreover, users must have a clear understanding of how their data will be used, who has access to it, and for what purpose. There is a fine line between offering personalized care through AI and infringing on an individual's privacy. To mitigate risks, AI platforms must adhere to robust security protocols and ensure data anonymization wherever possible.

19.9.2 Autonomy and Control

Another key ethical concern is the degree of autonomy that individuals should have when interacting with AI systems in addiction recovery. While AI can guide and support, it must not override personal decision-making. Recovery is a deeply human experience, one that requires individuals to confront their own struggles and make personal decisions about how they want to heal.

AI systems, by their nature, are designed to provide recommendations, nudges, and even treatment suggestions based on patterns identified in the data. However, the potential for these systems to exert undue influence over decisions is a real concern. It's essential that users have control over the level of intervention AI has in their recovery journey. Ensuring transparency in AI recommendations and offering users the ability to accept or reject suggestions is crucial in maintaining their autonomy and dignity.

19.9.3 Equity and Access

While AI-driven recovery tools promise to revolutionize addiction treatment, they also risk creating or exacerbating inequities in access to care. The assumption that everyone has access to smartphones, high-speed internet, or even the literacy skills to navigate AI tools can exclude marginalized communities, particularly those in low-income or rural areas. Ensuring that AI in addiction recovery is accessible to all is paramount. Policymakers and healthcare providers must work together to make these tools available to a broader demographic, ensuring that no one is left behind. Public health initiatives can help bridge the gap by offering training and support for those less familiar with technology, while also considering the development of AI tools that are easy to use and affordable.

19.9.4 The Risk of Over-Reliance on Technology

There is also the concern that individuals may come to rely too heavily on AI systems, particularly when they feel they lack access to human support. While AI can provide invaluable assistance, it should never replace the need for real-world connections, therapy, or community support. Addiction recovery is often most successful when individuals engage with professionals, support groups, and loved ones. The human aspect of healing cannot be replaced by algorithms, no matter how sophisticated they become.

A balanced approach, integrating AI as one tool in a broader recovery program, is essential. Human therapists and counselors will continue to play a vital role in helping individuals navigate complex emotional and psychological barriers that AI alone cannot address. AI should be viewed as a supplementary resource, offering personalized care and continuous support, but not as a substitute for human touch and empathy.

19.10 Case Studies: AI in Action within Addiction and Recovery

To better understand the real-world application of AI in addiction recovery, let's examine a few case studies where AI has been successfully used to support individuals in their journey to break free from addiction.

19.10.1 Case Study 1: AI in Substance Abuse Recovery

In a groundbreaking study, researchers implemented an AI-powered mobile application to track and support individuals recovering from alcohol addiction. The app collected data from wearables that monitored the individual's sleep, physical activity, and even their stress levels. The AI used this data to predict when the individual might experience cravings and provided real-time interventions through personalized recommendations, such as mindfulness exercises, relaxation techniques, or a prompt to contact a support group.

The results were striking. Users who engaged with the app were less likely to relapse compared to those who followed traditional recovery methods. The AI-enabled app was able to predict and prevent relapses by intervening at critical moments, offering a dynamic and personalized approach to addiction recovery.

19.10.2 Case Study 2: AI for Opioid Addiction Treatment

Another case study focused on opioid addiction, one of the most pressing public health issues of our time. An AI system was deployed in a clinical setting to assist doctors in identifying patients at high risk of opioid abuse. The system analyzed electronic health records (EHR) to detect patterns of over-prescription, misuse, and doctor shopping (when individuals seek multiple prescriptions from different doctors).

The AI system was able to identify high-risk patients far earlier than traditional screening methods, allowing for targeted interventions. Additionally, the system monitored patients' progress during their treatment and suggested personalized recovery plans based on their specific behavioral patterns. The use of AI in this context significantly improved recovery outcomes by providing earlier interventions and more customized care plans.

19.10.3 Case Study 3: AI and Behavioral Nudging in Digital Addiction

In the realm of digital addiction, AI tools have been developed to help individuals manage their screen time and social media use. One such app uses AI to track the user's online activity and, based on machine learning algorithms, determines when they are most likely to be engaged in harmful, compulsive behaviors. The app then nudges the user to take a break, offers alternative activities, or suggests mindfulness exercises to redirect their attention.

The AI system was successful in reducing the time users spent on social media and increasing engagement in more productive, healthier activities. By intervening at the right moments and providing gentle nudges, AI became a powerful tool for helping individuals regain control over their digital habits.

19.11 The Road Ahead: AI and the Future of Addiction Recovery

As we look toward the future of AI in addiction recovery, it is clear that the potential for positive change is vast. AI is not just a tool for managing symptoms; it is a tool for understanding the root causes of addiction and providing personalized solutions. However, it is important that we continue to approach this technology with caution, ensuring that it is used ethically and equitably.

The future of addiction recovery will likely see a greater integration of AI with human therapies, creating a more holistic and personalized approach to treatment. AI systems will become more sophisticated in predicting relapse, identifying triggers, and offering timely interventions. Virtual support groups, cognitive-behavioral therapy, and mindfulness techniques powered by AI will allow individuals to engage with their recovery process in a way that is convenient, personalized, and effective.

Moreover, as AI becomes more accessible, it has the potential to revolutionize addiction treatment on a global scale. By breaking down barriers to access and offering individualized care, AI could become an indispensable tool in the fight against addiction, improving the lives of millions of individuals around the world.

19.12 Conclusion: A New Paradigm in Addiction Recovery

AI represents a new frontier in addiction recovery, offering powerful tools for prevention, treatment, and ongoing support. While challenges and ethical concerns remain, the benefits are clear. As AI continues to evolve, it will become an essential part of addiction treatment strategies, helping individuals to understand their behaviors, develop healthier habits, and rebuild their lives. The road ahead is long, but with AI at our side, the future of addiction recovery looks brighter than ever.

Chapter 20: Social Media Algorithms and Behavioral Influence

20.1 Introduction to Social Media Algorithms

In the early days of the internet, information was sparse, and users wandered from one page to another, largely on their own terms. The rise of social media platforms fundamentally changed this landscape. Today, platforms such as Facebook, Instagram, Twitter, and TikTok guide the digital interactions of billions of users through invisible forces: algorithms. These algorithms are the secret architects behind the content we see, the advertisements that follow us, and the very nature of our online engagement.

Social media algorithms are not simply lines of code designed to show us the content we like. They are sophisticated systems designed to maximize user engagement, capturing attention in ways that influence not only our online behavior but also our offline lives. By analyzing user data and predicting preferences, social media platforms deliver tailored experiences that feel personal—yet often, they operate without us fully understanding how our behavior is being shaped.

Understanding the psychology behind these algorithms is essential in unraveling the complex relationship between humans and technology. This chapter explores the ways in which social media algorithms affect human behavior, from reinforcing existing habits to altering perceptions of reality. It also examines the ethical dilemmas that arise when these algorithms blur the lines between influence and manipulation.

20.2 The Psychology of Social Media Engagement

At the heart of every social media platform lies a deep understanding of human psychology. Social media algorithms are not neutral; they are designed with one goal in mind: engagement. But engagement is not merely about clicks or likes—it's about maximizing the time users spend on the platform and increasing their emotional investment.

The psychology behind social media engagement revolves around a few key principles, notably *social validation*, *dopamine-driven feedback loops*, and *the need for belonging*. At a basic level, humans are social creatures, and we are wired to seek approval and validation from others. This need for social validation plays out on social media in the form of likes, comments, and shares. Every notification is a microcosm of positive reinforcement, a small dose of validation that triggers the release of dopamine, the "feel-good" chemical in the brain.

The more interactions a post gets, the more likely it is to be seen by others, further amplifying the dopamine-driven cycle. Each notification feeds the desire for social connection, which, over time, becomes addictive. Users, often unconsciously, become trapped in this cycle, repeatedly seeking the emotional reward that comes with engagement, creating a behavioral loop that is hard to break.

This dynamic has profound psychological implications. Research in behavioral psychology suggests that the act of receiving likes or comments on a post triggers the same neural pathways as receiving a reward. In this sense, social media algorithms function like slot machines, keeping users hooked by offering intermittent rewards. It is no wonder, then, that social media addiction has become a widespread issue, with users checking their feeds hundreds of times a day.

20.3 Personalization and Behavioral Targeting

One of the most significant innovations in social media algorithms is personalization. By collecting vast amounts of user data—ranging from what you like and share to the time you spend on specific posts—platforms are able to curate a highly personalized experience for each user. This personalization goes far beyond merely showing you posts from your friends. Algorithms are now so sophisticated that they can predict your preferences with eerie accuracy, suggesting content you didn't even know you wanted to see.

But there is a darker side to this personalization: behavioral targeting. Advertisers and platforms use this data to create highly targeted ads, making you more likely to make a purchase, click on a link, or engage in some other form of action. This data-driven targeting capitalizes on your emotional triggers, presenting content that is designed to resonate with your current state of mind, desires, or insecurities.

The psychological impact of personalized algorithms is profound. By continually feeding users content that aligns with their preferences, algorithms create what is known as a *filter bubble*. In a filter bubble, users are only exposed to information that reinforces their existing beliefs and interests, further narrowing their worldview. While this might seem harmless, it can result in a lack of exposure to diverse ideas and perspectives, leading to increased polarization and a less nuanced understanding of the world.

20.4 Algorithms and the Attention Economy

The business model of most social media platforms is based on one thing: attention. The more time users spend on a platform, the more ads they are exposed to, and the more revenue the platform generates. Algorithms, therefore, are not only designed to capture attention but to hold it—often for as long as possible.

The attention economy is driven by the principle that human attention is a finite resource. As the amount of content available online continues to increase exponentially, platforms must compete for users' limited attention. Social media algorithms are perfectly suited to this task, constantly optimizing the flow of content to keep users engaged. Whether it's through push notifications, autoplay videos, or endless scrolling, algorithms are engineered to minimize friction and maximize engagement.

But the attention economy has its costs. Research has shown that the constant bombardment of notifications, the pressure to keep up with a never-ending stream of content, and the emotional toll of social comparison can all contribute to feelings of anxiety, stress, and burnout. The algorithms that are designed to keep us engaged may also be eroding our capacity for focus and attention.

20.5 The Dark Side of Social Media Algorithms

While social media algorithms are often credited with creating personalized experiences, they also have a darker side. Algorithms, by their nature, prioritize engagement, and in many cases, engagement is driven by emotions such as outrage, fear, and anger. Studies have shown that negative content—whether it's politically charged news, controversial opinions, or shocking images—tends to generate more engagement than positive content. As a result, algorithms often promote content that is sensationalist or inflammatory, further entrenching users in echo chambers where their views are continually reinforced.

The psychological consequences of this dynamic are profound. Algorithms not only amplify existing emotions but also encourage divisiveness and ideological polarization. In a world where algorithms continuously show us content that aligns with our beliefs and emotions, it becomes increasingly difficult to engage in civil discourse or to see beyond our own echo chambers.

Moreover, social media algorithms have been linked to the spread of misinformation and fake news. By prioritizing content that generates the most engagement, algorithms often elevate sensationalist or factually inaccurate information to the forefront. This has serious consequences for public opinion, political discourse, and even the safety of individuals and communities.

20.6 The Impact on Social Interaction and Communication

Social media algorithms are not just shaping what we see online—they are reshaping how we communicate with one another. The shift from face-to-face interaction to digital engagement has been profound, and algorithms are playing a central role in this transformation.

The very nature of online communication is transactional. Unlike in-person interactions, which are based on mutual understanding and empathy, online communication often revolves around likes, shares, and comments. These digital metrics replace the richness of human connection with something more superficial, yet highly measurable. Social media platforms reward users for engaging with content that garners attention, not necessarily for meaningful conversation or genuine connection.

The rise of influencers—individuals who have gained significant followings on social media platforms—is another example of how algorithms are altering social dynamics. The influencer culture, while empowering for some, has raised questions about authenticity, self-presentation, and trust. Influencers often present idealized versions of their lives, and algorithms promote these idealized images to millions of users, further distorting the reality of human experience.

20.7 Ethical Considerations and the Responsibility of Social Media Platforms

As social media algorithms continue to shape public discourse, the ethical implications of their use become increasingly important. Social media platforms, driven by the need for engagement and monetization, face growing scrutiny regarding their role in influencing public opinion, exacerbating polarization, and promoting harmful content.

The Power of Algorithmic Influence

The ethical dilemma lies in the extent to which these platforms—often seen as neutral tools—are in fact influencing users' behavior in ways that may not always align with their best interests. By amplifying certain types of content, algorithms can shape not only individual behaviors but also collective societal trends. This could include everything from political polarization to the normalization of extreme ideologies.

The question of responsibility becomes more pressing as algorithms are designed to act as behavioral nudges, subtly guiding individuals toward particular actions or viewpoints. If social media platforms are the architects of this process, should they be held accountable for the consequences? For instance, should they bear responsibility for the spread of misinformation, the mental health impacts on users, or the deepening of social divides?

Algorithmic Transparency and Accountability

One of the central ethical concerns with social media algorithms is the lack of transparency. Algorithms operate in a black-box manner, meaning that users have little understanding of why they see what they see. The opaqueness of this system makes it difficult to identify biases, errors, or harmful practices embedded within the algorithms.

To address these concerns, many experts advocate for greater transparency and accountability in algorithmic design. Social media platforms could be required to disclose how their algorithms work and what factors influence the content users are shown. This could allow for better oversight and potentially reduce the spread of harmful content. Moreover, platforms could be held to higher ethical standards regarding user data, ensuring that personal information is not exploited for profit at the expense of user well-being.

Balancing Freedom of Speech with Harmful Content

Another ethical issue arises in the context of freedom of speech. While social media platforms allow individuals to express their opinions freely, they also play a significant role in curating the information that people see. In doing so, platforms may inadvertently limit certain voices or amplify others, affecting the diversity of discourse.

As social media platforms struggle to balance freedom of speech with the responsibility to prevent harm, the challenge lies in drawing a line between allowing open debate and curbing the spread of misinformation or harmful ideologies. Algorithms must be refined to promote meaningful conversations and democratic dialogue, without silencing dissenting voices or allowing toxic content to thrive.

20.8 The Future of Social Media Algorithms

As technology advances, the algorithms powering social media platforms are becoming increasingly sophisticated. With the advent of artificial intelligence, machine learning, and data science, algorithms are evolving to predict and influence human behavior in ways that were once unimaginable.

Personalized, Deeply Emotional Engagement

In the future, algorithms may become even more adept at tailoring experiences to individuals' emotional states. Advances in AI, particularly in the field of affective computing, could allow algorithms to detect and respond to users' moods in real time. Imagine a platform that could identify when a user is feeling lonely, anxious, or upset and then push content designed to either uplift or deepen those emotions.

While this could be an effective tool for enhancing user experience, it also presents significant ethical risks. The ability to manipulate emotional states could lead to unintended consequences, such as exacerbating mental health issues or pushing users toward content that is manipulative or divisive. Balancing the benefits of emotional engagement with the risks of manipulation will be a central challenge in the future of social media algorithms.

The Rise of Autonomous Algorithms

In the not-so-distant future, we may see the rise of autonomous algorithms that are capable of making decisions without human input. These algorithms could take on a greater role in managing content moderation, personalized recommendations, and even political messaging. As they become more autonomous, the issue of accountability will become even more pressing. Who is responsible when an algorithm makes a harmful decision? Is it the platform, the developers who created the algorithm, or the algorithm itself?

The potential for autonomous algorithms to make decisions that affect millions of users requires a shift in how we think about algorithmic responsibility. It may no longer be enough to simply ensure that algorithms are functioning as intended; we will need to develop systems for ensuring that algorithms act ethically, transparently, and in alignment with the values of society.

20.9 Case Studies: Algorithms at Work in Social Media

Case Study 1: The Spread of Misinformation

One of the most prominent examples of the influence of social media algorithms is the role they play in the spread of misinformation. During elections, for example, algorithms have been shown to prioritize sensational, misleading, or inflammatory content, regardless of its accuracy. This phenomenon was most evident during the 2016 U.S. presidential election, where false stories and conspiracy theories were widely shared across social media platforms, often reaching far more people than factual news.

While social media platforms have taken steps to combat misinformation—by labeling false content and promoting fact-checking—these efforts have been criticized for being inconsistent and insufficient. The algorithms that drive the spread of such content are still largely unchanged, raising questions about whether these platforms are doing enough to address the root cause of the problem.

Case Study 2: The Instagram Effect on Body Image

Another case study that highlights the psychological power of social media algorithms is the impact of Instagram on body image, particularly among young women. Instagram's algorithm prioritizes posts with high engagement, often promoting images that fit a narrow standard of beauty. This reinforcement of unrealistic beauty standards has been linked to increased body dissatisfaction, anxiety, and depression.

In response to growing concerns about mental health, Instagram has made efforts to address the issue by hiding "like" counts on posts and promoting positive body image campaigns. However, the underlying algorithm that prioritizes highly polished, curated content still influences the type of images users see, perpetuating the cycle of comparison and insecurity.

Case Study 3: YouTube's Radicalization Algorithm

YouTube's recommendation algorithm has come under fire for promoting extremist content. Users who begin by watching innocuous videos related to conspiracy theories or politics are often led down a rabbit hole of increasingly extreme videos. The algorithm's prioritization of watch time and engagement has been shown to amplify radical viewpoints, creating echo chambers that push users toward more extreme ideologies.

This case study exemplifies the dangers of algorithms that prioritize engagement at the expense of accuracy and balance. It also raises important questions about the ethical responsibility of platforms like YouTube to prevent the radicalization of their users.

20.10 Conclusion: Understanding and Navigating Algorithmic Influence

Social media algorithms are powerful forces in shaping modern society. From the content we see on our feeds to the ads that follow us across platforms, algorithms are carefully crafted to influence our behavior, emotions, and opinions. While these algorithms offer users personalized experiences, they also present profound ethical dilemmas. The challenge moving forward will be to strike a balance between maximizing engagement and safeguarding the well-being of users.

As we continue to integrate social media deeper into our lives, it's crucial to understand the psychology behind these algorithms, their impact on behavior, and the responsibility that platforms must bear in managing their influence. Whether through better algorithmic transparency, more robust content moderation, or an increased focus on user welfare, the future of social media will need to prioritize ethical considerations alongside technological innovation.

Chapter 21: AI in Behavioral Therapy

21.1 Introduction to AI in Behavioral Therapy

Artificial intelligence (A.I) is increasingly becoming a force that is reshaping many facets of our lives, not only in the realms of technology, business, and education but also in the deeply personal field of mental health. Over the past few decades, AI's influence has grown exponentially, offering transformative possibilities for treating psychological disorders and enhancing traditional therapy methods. Behavioral therapy, which has long been the cornerstone of mental health care, is no exception to this evolution.

Behavioral therapy, primarily through approaches like Cognitive Behavioral Therapy (CBT), aims to modify dysfunctional emotions, behaviors, and thought patterns. Traditionally, it relies on a face-to-face relationship between therapist and patient, where the therapist guides the patient through understanding their behaviors and emotions and implements strategies to overcome them. However, in the digital age, AI is being leveraged to extend, enhance, and even replace certain aspects of this traditional therapeutic model.

The journey of AI in behavioral therapy began with simple tools—like chatbots and early diagnostic systems—and has evolved into an ecosystem of complex, data-driven technologies designed to assist, monitor, and even directly intervene in patients' emotional and psychological well-being. This chapter explores the impact of AI on behavioral therapy, examining its current applications, benefits, limitations, and ethical considerations. By looking at how AI integrates with therapeutic practices, we can better understand its potential to revolutionize mental health care

21.2 The Role of AI in Cognitive Behavioral Therapy (CBT)

Cognitive Behavioral Therapy (CBT) has long been recognized as one of the most effective forms of psychological intervention. The process of identifying and altering negative thought patterns, changing unhealthy behaviors, and cultivating more positive mental habits requires significant effort and expertise on the part of the therapist. However, with the advent of AI, this process has been streamlined in innovative ways that allow for a more personalized, efficient, and scalable approach to therapy.

AI applications in CBT range from simple tools that help individuals track their thoughts, moods, and behaviors to more sophisticated systems that can interact with patients, guide them through therapy exercises, and provide real-time feedback on progress. Virtual therapists powered by AI can conduct CBT sessions, offering both cognitive and behavioral interventions. These tools are particularly valuable in providing consistent therapeutic support in between in-person sessions, offering patients the opportunity to continue making progress at their own pace.

The most commonly known AI applications in CBT are mental health apps that allow users to monitor their thoughts, moods, and behaviors. By inputting data such as daily emotions, thoughts, or experiences, these apps can analyze patterns and offer tailored suggestions for coping strategies, behavioral adjustments, or specific CBT exercises. This form of AI-driven therapy works by presenting structured tasks that help patients challenge irrational beliefs, alter automatic negative thoughts, and adjust their reactions to various stressors.

One of the biggest advantages of AI-enhanced CBT is accessibility. AI tools are available at the touch of a button, offering immediate support when human therapists are not available. For many, especially in remote or underserved areas, this digital intervention can be a game-changer, allowing them to access therapeutic resources that they might not otherwise have.

Furthermore, AI systems can analyze patient data over time, providing valuable insights into their mental health. AI-powered CBT tools can monitor patterns in behavior, emotions, and physiological data, offering therapists a clearer picture of a patient's progress and highlighting areas that need further intervention. This integration of real-time monitoring and analysis can help optimize the therapeutic process, making it more dynamic and adaptive to the patient's changing needs.

21.3 AI as a Support Tool for Therapists

While AI has the potential to replace some aspects of therapy, its true power lies in its ability to support human therapists, rather than replace them entirely. The relationship between a therapist and a patient is a unique one, rooted in empathy, understanding, and human connection. AI, despite its advances, lacks these deeply human qualities. However, it can serve as a powerful tool to augment the therapist's expertise, providing them with more data, insights, and analytical tools that can refine and enhance their work.

AI can help therapists by offering real-time feedback on patient behavior, identifying patterns and trends in emotional responses, and tracking treatment progress. Machine learning algorithms can analyze patient data such as speech patterns, facial expressions, and behavioral responses to identify emotional states that may not be readily apparent to the human eye. This could provide therapists with a deeper understanding of the patient's emotional landscape and allow for more effective interventions.

For example, AI systems can analyze a patient's emotional tone during a session, providing the therapist with feedback on whether the patient appears anxious, depressed, or disengaged. This data allows the therapist to adjust their approach in real-time, ensuring that the patient receives the most appropriate and effective intervention.

AI can also help therapists by automating certain tasks, such as scheduling sessions, tracking progress, or sending reminders for patients to complete certain exercises. This reduces administrative burdens, allowing therapists to focus on the core elements of their practice. With AI handling routine tasks, therapists can devote more time and energy to the complex and nuanced aspects of patient care.

While AI tools can provide valuable insights, it is important to remember that they are only one piece of the puzzle. Therapists bring their expertise, intuition, and empathy to the therapeutic process, elements that AI cannot replicate. The most effective therapeutic outcomes will likely emerge from a collaborative approach, where AI supports the therapist's work without replacing it.

21.4 Personalized Behavioral Therapy through AI

One of the most exciting possibilities of AI in behavioral therapy is its potential to personalize treatment on a scale that was previously unimaginable. Personalization in therapy is crucial because every individual's psychological makeup, experiences, and challenges are unique. The traditional "one-size-fits-all" approach is often inadequate for addressing the complexities of human behavior and mental health.

AI has the ability to analyze vast amounts of data from diverse sources—such as patient surveys, wearable devices, social media, and mobile apps—and use this data to create personalized treatment plans. By continually learning from this data, AI systems can adapt to the individual's needs, refining interventions based on how the patient responds.

For example, AI systems can assess a person's emotional state through text analysis of their journaling or speech patterns during therapy sessions. By understanding how they process their thoughts and emotions, the AI can suggest tailored exercises, behavioral changes, or coping strategies. It can even recommend different therapeutic approaches, depending on the individual's specific challenges and preferences.

AI-driven personalization is particularly important in addressing mental health issues such as anxiety, depression, and PTSD, where each person's symptoms and triggers can vary widely. By providing customized therapeutic interventions, AI can make therapy more effective, efficient, and adaptable to each person's unique situation.

However, this level of personalization also raises important ethical concerns, particularly around privacy and data security. Since AI systems rely heavily on patient data, it is essential to ensure that this information is collected, stored, and used ethically, with the patient's consent and full understanding of how their data will be used.

21.5 AI in Exposure Therapy

Exposure therapy is a well-established method for treating anxiety disorders, particularly phobias and PTSD. It involves gradually exposing the patient to the feared object or situation in a controlled and safe environment, allowing them to confront and process their fears. This approach, while effective, has its limitations, particularly when it comes to creating controlled environments in which patients can experience these exposures.

AI has made significant strides in enhancing exposure therapy through the use of virtual reality (VR) and augmented reality (AR). These technologies allow patients to experience their fears in a controlled virtual environment, providing them with the opportunity to confront and overcome their anxieties in ways that would have been impossible in the real world.

For example, a person with a fear of flying could use a VR program powered by AI to experience a simulated flight. The system would gradually increase the intensity of the exposure, starting with virtual flights in low-risk scenarios and slowly building up to more realistic experiences. This approach allows the patient to work through their fear step by step, without the logistical and safety concerns of real-world exposure.

AI can also monitor the patient's physiological responses—such as heart rate, sweating, and facial expressions—during the exposure, adjusting the intensity of the experience in real-time based on the patient's level of distress. This makes the process highly personalized, ensuring that the patient is neither overwhelmed nor underexposed to their fear.

While AI-powered exposure therapy has shown great promise, it is important to consider the ethical implications. The use of virtual environments raises questions about the potential for desensitization or emotional numbness, and the effectiveness of these interventions in addressing real-world challenges. Additionally, patients must be fully informed about the nature of the therapy and the risks involved.

21.6 AI in Continuous Monitoring and Feedback

One of the most revolutionary aspects of AI's role in behavioral therapy is its capacity for continuous monitoring and feedback. Unlike traditional therapy, where progress is assessed during scheduled sessions, AI can track and monitor patients' behaviors, moods, and even physiological responses in real-time. This continuous monitoring allows for more timely interventions and provides therapists with data to make more informed decisions about treatment adjustments.

Incorporating AI in this capacity relies on a variety of data sources, such as wearable devices, smartphones, and even social media interactions. AI algorithms can analyze this data to detect patterns or shifts in behavior that might indicate emotional distress, such as a decrease in social engagement, sudden changes in sleep patterns, or an increase in negative thought tendencies. This data can then be relayed to both the patient and their therapist, enabling immediate action.

For instance, consider a patient who is undergoing treatment for depression. AI could track changes in their daily routines, monitor their physical activity levels, and analyze their speech for signs of pessimism or isolation. If the AI detects a concerning shift—perhaps a decline in activity levels or a sudden increase in negative self-talk—it can notify the patient, suggest coping mechanisms, or prompt them to contact their therapist for further support. These real-time insights make behavioral therapy more dynamic, responsive, and individualized.

Additionally, AI's ability to provide continuous feedback means that patients can engage in therapy more frequently and consistently. For example, if a person is feeling anxious or stressed during the week, AI can suggest exercises or mindfulness practices tailored to their current emotional state. These interventions are available on demand, fostering a sense of self-efficacy and empowerment in the patient. This kind of ongoing support, where the patient feels continually guided in their therapeutic journey, is one of the key benefits of AI integration in behavioral therapy.

However, as with all advancements, continuous monitoring raises important questions about privacy and autonomy. Who owns the data, and how is it used? What happens if a patient's data is compromised or misinterpreted? Ensuring transparency in the use of data and providing patients with full control over their information is crucial to maintaining trust in AI-based interventions.

21.7 AI-Assisted Behavioral Therapy for Specific Disorders

While behavioral therapy as a general approach can benefit from AI, there are certain mental health disorders where AI's influence is especially pronounced. By focusing on specific conditions like anxiety disorders, depression, addiction, and PTSD, AI is playing a crucial role in developing targeted, evidence-based interventions that complement traditional therapeutic practices.

21.7.1 AI in Treating Anxiety Disorders

Anxiety disorders, which include generalized anxiety disorder (GAD), panic disorder, and social anxiety disorder, are among the most common mental health conditions. Traditional behavioral therapy for anxiety typically involves techniques like exposure therapy, cognitive restructuring, and relaxation training. AI tools can enhance these interventions by providing real-time data on the patient's anxiety triggers, tracking progress in anxiety reduction, and even facilitating virtual exposures to anxiety-provoking situations.

For example, AI systems can track a patient's heart rate, breathing patterns, and facial expressions to assess their level of anxiety. In real-time, the system can suggest coping strategies, such as deep breathing exercises or mindfulness practices, when the patient exhibits signs of distress. Moreover, through virtual reality (VR) scenarios powered by AI, patients can gradually expose themselves to anxiety-inducing situations (e.g., speaking in public or taking a test) in a safe and controlled environment.

21.7.2 AI in Treating Depression

Depression is another mental health condition where AI's role is growing rapidly. Traditional treatment for depression often involves psychotherapy combined with medication. AI-based tools are augmenting these methods by providing support between therapy sessions, tracking symptoms, and helping patients identify and challenge negative thought patterns.

In CBT for depression, patients are encouraged to challenge distorted thoughts and identify cognitive distortions, such as all-or-nothing thinking or catastrophizing. AI systems can assist in this process by offering suggestions for reframing negative thoughts and tracking progress over time. AI-powered applications can also analyze speech and text for signs of depressive thinking, such as negative self-statements or a pessimistic worldview, and offer real-time interventions that may prevent further deterioration.

Additionally, AI can help patients establish healthy habits, such as sleep hygiene or physical exercise, both of which are crucial in managing depression. By continuously monitoring a person's behavior and mood, AI can make tailored recommendations for self-care or suggest behavioral adjustments that promote mental wellness.

21.7.3 AI in Treating Addiction

Addiction, whether to substances, behaviors, or technologies, is one of the most challenging conditions to treat. Behavioral therapy plays a vital role in addiction recovery, focusing on the modification of behaviors and reinforcing healthier coping mechanisms. AI can be a transformative tool in addiction treatment by offering personalized recovery programs, providing real-time support, and tracking patients' progress toward recovery.

AI-powered apps and wearables can monitor physiological markers of stress or cravings, offering suggestions for coping strategies at critical moments. AI can also offer behavioral nudges or reinforce positive behaviors by rewarding patients for maintaining healthy habits, such as abstaining from substance use or engaging in recovery activities.

21.8 Ethical Implications of AI in Behavioral Therapy

The integration of AI into behavioral therapy offers remarkable opportunities, but it also brings with it a host of ethical considerations. While AI can enhance therapeutic outcomes, it raises questions about privacy, informed consent, data security, and the potential for algorithmic bias.

21.8.1 Privacy and Data Security

Behavioral therapy relies heavily on sensitive personal data—patients' thoughts, emotions, and behaviors. The introduction of AI into therapy means that even more personal data will be collected, often in real-time. This data can be vulnerable to misuse, breaches, or unauthorized access. Therefore, safeguarding this data is paramount.

Therapists and AI providers must ensure that patients' data is protected and that they have control over how it is used. Transparent consent processes must be in place to inform patients about what data is being collected, how it will be stored, and who will have access to it. Additionally, patients should be able to opt-out of data collection at any point in the therapeutic process without fear of negative consequences.

21.8.2 Informed Consent and Autonomy

Informed consent is a foundational ethical principle in therapy, and this extends to AI-driven interventions. Patients must be fully aware of how AI will be used in their treatment, what kinds of data will be collected, and how their information will be analyzed. Autonomy is a crucial consideration—patients should be able to make decisions about their treatment, including the decision to engage or disengage with AI-powered interventions.

21.9 The Future of AI in Behavioral Therapy

As AI technology continues to evolve, its potential applications in behavioral therapy will expand and become more sophisticated. From the integration of more advanced machine learning algorithms to the development of even more immersive virtual environments for exposure therapy, AI promises to further transform mental health care.

One potential future development is the ability for AI to offer completely personalized, on-demand therapy. With advancements in natural language processing and emotional intelligence, AI-powered systems may be able to provide comprehensive, 24/7 support for mental health, offering therapeutic interventions tailored to the individual's emotional state, personality, and history.

Moreover, AI systems could evolve to better understand complex psychological conditions, offering deeper insights into the human mind and suggesting more nuanced therapeutic approaches. This could lead to the creation of highly individualized treatment plans, where AI helps predict the most effective interventions based on a patient's specific needs, triggers, and responses.

21.10 Conclusion

AI's role in behavioral therapy is rapidly advancing, offering new possibilities for personalized care, continuous monitoring, and data-driven decision-making. While it cannot replace the human connection and empathy that are core to therapeutic practice, it has the potential to significantly enhance the effectiveness, accessibility, and scalability of therapy. As AI becomes more integrated into the therapeutic landscape, it is crucial that we address ethical concerns around privacy, consent, and the potential for misuse, ensuring that the benefits of AI are harnessed responsibly.

The future of AI in behavioral therapy holds great promise. As technology continues to improve, we may find ourselves in an era where mental health care is not only more accessible and effective but also more compassionate and personalized than ever before.

Chapter 22: Predicting Social Behavior with AI

22.1 Introduction: The Importance of Social Behavior Prediction

In the vast expanse of human interaction, predicting social behavior might seem like an impossible endeavor. Human actions are influenced by a constellation of factors: cultural norms, personal experiences, emotional responses, social pressures, and cognitive biases. But, remarkably, the advent of artificial intelligence (A.I) is helping unravel some of the complexity surrounding human behavior, offering a window into what once seemed unpredictable.

At its core, social behavior encompasses everything from simple interactions between individuals to complex societal dynamics that shape movements, trends, and collective decisions. The quest to predict these behaviors has profound implications across multiple sectors, from business to politics to public health. AI has become a pivotal tool in this pursuit, employing algorithms that process vast amounts of data to forecast outcomes with increasing accuracy.

Consider how AI models are shaping everything from targeted advertising to political campaign strategies. Imagine a world where AI not only understands human emotions but can predict shifts in public opinion, consumer preferences, or even the likelihood of social movements. Such predictions open up vast possibilities, from enhancing marketing efforts to improving public policy. However, this power also carries ethical concerns, especially as AI systems move closer to influencing, rather than just predicting, human behavior.

As we explore AI's role in predicting social behavior, it's crucial to understand not only how these predictions are made, but also the challenges they present. These systems must grapple with the fluid, often contradictory nature of human psychology, and the result is a delicate dance between accuracy and unpredictability. This chapter explores how

AI is attempting to bridge this gap and the broader implications of these advancements.

22.2 Understanding Social Dynamics

To comprehend how AI can predict social behavior, we must first understand the intricacies of social dynamics. Human beings are inherently social creatures, their actions constantly shaped by the people around them. From childhood, we learn social cues and adapt to the behaviors and expectations of our communities. These social patterns become second nature, influencing everything from the way we dress to how we express our opinions on politics.

Yet, social dynamics are not entirely predictable. They involve countless variables, both internal (like personal desires or mental states) and external (such as environmental stimuli or societal trends). For example, the decision to buy a particular brand may seem trivial, but it can be influenced by factors ranging from social status to the influence of peers. The complexity increases exponentially when we look at collective behaviors, such as social movements or the spread of misinformation.

AI systems approach this complexity through data. By aggregating massive amounts of information about human interactions—such as text on social media, purchasing habits, and public discourse—AI attempts to identify patterns and predict outcomes. These algorithms often operate using machine learning, which is trained on historical data to forecast future events based on past patterns.

However, there's an inherent limitation. Unlike machines, human beings are not fully governed by predictable, rational behavior. In fact, much of our decision-making is unconscious, shaped by emotions, biases, and cognitive shortcuts that are hard to capture in a dataset. The unpredictable nature of human behavior remains a significant challenge for AI systems, even as they improve at detecting and analyzing patterns.

22.3 The Intersection of AI and Social Psychology

The interplay between AI and social psychology is one of the most fascinating areas in the field of behavioral prediction. Social psychology seeks to understand how people think, feel, and act in social contexts. AI borrows heavily from these insights, using psychological theories to inform the development of algorithms that can anticipate human actions.

One of the fundamental principles of social psychology that AI systems often try to model is the concept of influence—how one individual's actions can affect the behavior of others. Through AI, we can simulate and even predict the "contagion" of behaviors in large groups, whether it's the spread of an idea or the decision to buy a product. Machine learning models are increasingly adept at recognizing the power of social influence, whether in the form of peer pressure, cultural trends, or emotional appeals.

For example, an AI algorithm analyzing social media posts can track how certain topics or memes spread across networks. It doesn't just measure likes or shares, but looks at the emotional tone of the content and how it resonates with various audiences. By understanding the psychological principles behind why people engage with certain content (curiosity, fear, desire for belonging), AI can more accurately predict how far a particular trend or message will spread.

Furthermore, AI systems draw from established psychological theories, such as cognitive dissonance, which suggests that people are motivated to maintain consistency between their beliefs and actions. If AI understands this principle, it can predict how individuals might change their behavior to resolve dissonance, such as by switching allegiances in a political debate or altering their purchasing habits when presented with new information. However, the challenge lies in accurately modeling the complexity of human emotions and the unique circumstances under which they manifest. Social psychology offers valuable insights, but the algorithmic translation of these principles remains an evolving endeavor.

22.4 Machine Learning Models for Social Behavior Prediction

At the heart of AI's ability to predict social behavior lies machine learning, a subset of AI focused on algorithms that can learn from data without being explicitly programmed. Machine learning allows AI to recognize patterns in vast datasets and use them to make predictions about future behavior.

There are two primary types of machine learning: supervised and unsupervised learning. Supervised learning is used when the model is trained on a labeled dataset, meaning the algorithm learns from input-output pairs, where the desired output is already known. For example, an AI model might be trained on a dataset of past social media posts, where each post is labeled with whether it generated positive or negative reactions from the audience. The model learns to predict the likely emotional response to new posts.

Unsupervised learning, on the other hand, is used when the dataset is unlabeled, and the AI must identify patterns without explicit guidance. In the context of social behavior, this could mean finding hidden relationships in vast networks of human interaction, such as detecting emerging topics in online discussions or identifying groups of people who share similar preferences or opinions.

For both types of learning, the accuracy of predictions relies heavily on the quality and quantity of data. The more data AI systems can analyze, the better they can detect patterns in behavior. However, there are significant challenges in curating high-quality datasets that truly represent the diverse and multifaceted nature of human behavior. Biases in the data can lead to skewed predictions, and these biases can be inadvertently reinforced by the AI model itself, amplifying societal inequalities.

22.5 Natural Language Processing and Social Behavior

Another critical tool in AI's arsenal for predicting social behavior is Natural Language Processing (NLP). NLP is a branch of AI focused on the interaction between computers and human language. It allows machines to understand, interpret, and generate human language, whether spoken or written.

In the context of predicting social behavior, NLP can be used to analyze social media conversations, blog posts, and even news articles to gauge public sentiment, detect emerging trends, or predict the likelihood of certain behaviors. By examining the language used in online discussions, AI can discern emotional undertones, intent, and even the social influence at play.

For example, AI systems can analyze Twitter feeds to assess the tone of conversations around a political event or product launch. By processing large volumes of text, the AI can detect whether people are discussing the event positively or negatively, and predict how those opinions might evolve. Through sentiment analysis, which is a common NLP task, AI can map the emotional landscape of public discussions, providing valuable insights into collective behavior.

22.6 The Role of Social Media in Shaping Behavior

Social media has revolutionized how we interact with one another and, perhaps more significantly, how we influence one another. In the age of platforms like Facebook, Instagram, Twitter, and TikTok, AI systems are not only monitoring but actively participating in shaping social dynamics. Social media platforms are often seen as digital spaces for personal expression, but behind the scenes, sophisticated AI algorithms drive much of what users see, from newsfeeds to targeted ads. These algorithms are designed to maximize user engagement, often by capitalizing on human psychological tendencies, such as the desire for validation, the fear of missing out (FOMO), or the emotional need for connection.

AI plays a central role in social media platforms by predicting what content will grab our attention and keep us engaged. This is done by analyzing past behavior: What types of posts did you like or comment on before? What kinds of videos do you watch all the way through? What types of articles do you share with friends? By drawing on these patterns, AI systems learn what emotional triggers elicit strong responses, allowing platforms to personalize the experience and encourage continued interaction.

The problem, however, lies in the ethical implications of this influence. AI-driven personalization has created echo chambers, where users are continuously exposed to content that reinforces their existing beliefs and emotional states, leading to radicalization or polarization. The role of AI in social media platforms also raises questions about privacy—what data should AI have access to, and how should it be used?

Moreover, platforms like Facebook and Twitter have demonstrated how algorithms can predict and even amplify social trends, from political movements to the spread of misinformation. The effectiveness of these algorithms in predicting social behaviors makes them incredibly powerful tools, but this power also comes with a level of responsibility that has yet to be fully addressed.

22.7 The Psychological Drivers Behind Social Behavior Predictions

AI's ability to predict social behavior depends not just on the data it processes, but also on the psychological principles that underpin human actions. Understanding the psychological drivers behind human behavior is essential to making accurate predictions.

One of the most critical drivers is the principle of **social proof**, which suggests that people are heavily influenced by the actions and opinions of others. If a person sees that a product is highly rated by many others, they are more likely to purchase it, even if they have no prior knowledge of the product. Similarly, in social media, seeing that a post has been liked by hundreds of people can prompt someone to engage with it, even if they initially had no interest.

AI systems analyze these cues to predict what actions individuals are likely to take. By tracking user behavior across different platforms, AI can gauge an individual's interests, preferences, and likelihood of responding to specific types of content. These systems leverage social proof to recommend products, suggest connections, and even push certain types of political content—further shaping individual and group behaviors.

Another psychological concept that AI utilizes is **reciprocity**. Human beings have an innate tendency to return favors. AI systems embedded in chatbots or virtual assistants take advantage of this principle by offering something of value (such as personalized recommendations or immediate assistance) to encourage the user to reciprocate, whether by making a purchase, sharing information, or participating in a certain behavior.

Commitment and consistency are also powerful psychological drivers that AI systems use to predict future behavior. If a user has made a small commitment, such as liking a post or signing up for an email newsletter, they are more likely to make further commitments down the line. AI systems recognize these patterns and use them to shape future predictions about behavior.

Finally, the principle of **scarcity**—the idea that people are more likely to value something that is perceived as scarce—underpins many of the behaviors AI systems are trying to predict. This is evident in the way AI-driven advertising creates urgency, whether by suggesting limited-time offers or showing that a product is "almost sold out." The fear of losing out plays on the emotional side of decision-making, driving behavior that is rooted in psychological biases.

By understanding these psychological triggers, AI systems can effectively anticipate what individuals will do next, whether it's making a purchase, liking a post, or even supporting a social cause.

22.8 Ethical Considerations and the Power of Influence

With great power comes great responsibility. The predictive capabilities of AI systems in social behavior raise profound ethical concerns. These systems are not passive observers; they actively shape behavior, often in ways that are subtle but deeply influential.

The issue of **manipulation** is one of the most pressing ethical concerns. AI systems designed to predict and influence human behavior can easily cross into territory where they start manipulating individuals for commercial or political gain. The line between prediction and persuasion becomes increasingly blurred as AI systems leverage psychological principles to drive decisions.

This manipulation can be particularly problematic in areas like politics, where AI-powered platforms can be used to sway voters by targeting them with highly personalized content that appeals to their deepest fears or desires. Similarly, in advertising, AI systems can create hyper-targeted ads that exploit emotional vulnerabilities, pushing individuals to make purchases they might otherwise avoid.

Another ethical consideration is the **invasion of privacy**. AI systems can gather vast amounts of personal data, from browsing habits to purchasing history, to predict social behavior. This raises serious concerns about data security and consent. How much data should be collected, and who owns this data? Users may unknowingly consent to the collection of personal information, leaving them vulnerable to exploitation.

Moreover, there is the issue of **bias** in AI predictions. Just as humans are susceptible to cognitive biases, AI systems trained on biased data can replicate and even amplify these biases. This can lead to unfair predictions or discriminatory practices, such as algorithms that predict criminal behavior based on racial or socio-economic data. The potential for AI to perpetuate harmful stereotypes or biases underscores the importance of responsible AI design.

22.9 The Future of Social Behavior Prediction

As AI continues to evolve, the future of social behavior prediction holds immense promise—and significant challenges. We can expect AI to become even more adept at understanding human actions, thanks to advances in natural language processing, machine learning, and data analysis.

One area of development is the **integration of multimodal data**. AI systems are increasingly being trained not just on text data, but also on images, videos, and audio. By analyzing these different types of data together, AI can develop a more holistic understanding of human behavior. For instance, a system that tracks both a person's social media posts and the videos they watch could more accurately predict their future behavior, combining verbal cues with visual and emotional signals.

In addition, AI may be able to predict and even prevent certain types of behavior. In healthcare, for example, AI could forecast the likelihood of someone developing a health-related issue based on their social interactions, emotional well-being, and lifestyle choices. This could enable earlier interventions and better outcomes.

However, the continued development of predictive AI also raises important questions about autonomy. If AI systems can predict human behavior with increasing accuracy, what does that mean for free will? Are we simply responding to algorithms that have already decided our fate, or is there still room for human agency in an increasingly AI-driven world?

22.10 Conclusion: The Power and Responsibility of Predicting Social Behavior

AI's ability to predict social behavior offers unprecedented insights into human interaction, but it also carries significant responsibility. The same algorithms that power predictive models also have the potential to influence and manipulate behavior in ways that could harm individuals or society at large.

As AI becomes more adept at predicting and shaping social behavior, we must grapple with the ethical implications of these technologies. The power to predict is also the power to persuade, and with this power comes the responsibility to use AI in ways that respect individual autonomy, privacy, and fairness.

In the years to come, as AI continues to evolve and integrate deeper into our daily lives, the conversation about how it influences our behavior will only intensify. For now, the question remains: How will we, as a society, choose to harness the power of AI? Will we use it to understand ourselves, or will we allow it to shape who we become?

Chapter 23: The Dark Side of AI Behavioral Influence

23.1 Introduction: The Power and Perils of AI Behavioral Influence

In an era where technology is inextricably intertwined with nearly every aspect of human life, the role of Artificial Intelligence (A.I) in shaping human behavior has grown exponentially. AI systems today are not mere tools; they are architects of influence, guiding decisions and molding actions in ways that were once the domain of human experts, philosophers, and advertisers. Yet, for all the benefits AI can bring — from improving health outcomes to making life more efficient — its influence can easily slip into manipulation, blurring ethical boundaries and posing significant risks to personal autonomy.

AI's ability to analyze vast amounts of data, learn from patterns, and predict human behaviors has given rise to powerful systems capable of nudging individuals toward particular choices. From social media algorithms that decide what we see and when, to AI-driven marketing systems that know our desires before we do, the pervasive influence of AI is undeniable. However, this influence is a double-edged sword. While it can be used for good, it can also exploit human vulnerabilities, creating an ecosystem where autonomy is undermined and ethical lines are crossed.

This chapter delves into the dark side of AI's behavioral influence, examining the ways in which AI systems are designed to manipulate human behavior. As we explore these dynamics, we'll ask: How much of what we think, feel, and do is genuinely our own choice, and how much is shaped by the invisible hand of AI algorithms? The growing power of AI necessitates a closer look at the ethical dilemmas it creates, the potential for exploitation, and the consequences for individuals and society as a whole.

23.2 The Manipulative Potential of AI

At the heart of AI's behavioral influence is its ability to predict and alter human decisions. AI systems use a process called machine learning, where they are trained on vast datasets to identify patterns and make predictions. With this predictive power, AI can guide choices, subtly steering people towards specific actions.

One of the clearest examples of this manipulation is in the realm of consumer behavior. Retail giants like Amazon and e-commerce platforms like Alibaba rely on AI to predict what products will appeal to individual consumers. Through recommendation engines, these platforms suggest items based on previous purchases, searches, and even what similar users have bought. While this can lead to a more personalized shopping experience, it can also limit consumer choice by narrowing the options available, presenting only those products that align with a user's established preferences.

The consequences are more insidious in areas like political influence. Social media platforms, armed with AI algorithms, curate the news that individuals see. By prioritizing content that generates the most engagement—often sensational or polarizing material—these platforms can shape political views, skew opinions, and contribute to societal divisions. In fact, AI-driven algorithms can create echo chambers, where individuals are only exposed to information that aligns with their existing beliefs, deepening societal polarization.

In both these instances, the line between influence and manipulation is blurred. While AI offers greater convenience and efficiency, it also raises ethical questions about the degree of control exerted over personal decisions. Are individuals truly making choices, or are they simply following a path laid out by sophisticated algorithms designed to push them in specific directions?

23.3 Psychological Exploitation: How AI Targets Vulnerabilities

One of the most troubling aspects of AI's behavioral influence is its ability to exploit human psychological vulnerabilities. AI's power lies in its ability to analyze human behavior at a granular level, identifying patterns in everything from shopping habits to emotional responses. Once this data is gathered, AI can use it to craft highly effective persuasive messages and interventions.

In the realm of advertising, for example, AI can target individuals with personalized ads that are designed to tap into their deepest desires and insecurities. A person struggling with body image issues might see an ad for a product promising to enhance their appearance. Someone feeling lonely might be presented with an advertisement for a dating app. AI, with its deep understanding of human psychology, can craft these messages to be far more compelling than traditional advertisements, turning what might be a simple marketing tactic into a powerful psychological trigger.

The impact is even more alarming when considering vulnerable populations. People with addictions, mental health struggles, or financial instability can be especially susceptible to these targeted interventions. For instance, an AI-driven social media platform might amplify content that promotes unhealthy behaviors or reinforces addictive patterns, whether through encouraging excessive use of the platform or promoting substances that contribute to addiction.

In these cases, the ethical implications are stark. AI does not merely respond to user behavior—it shapes it. By exploiting emotional vulnerabilities, AI can lead individuals down a path that benefits the algorithm's creators, often at the expense of the individual's well-being.

23.4 AI and Political Manipulation

Political manipulation represents one of the most dangerous aspects of AI's potential for behavioral influence. Social media platforms, fueled by AI, have become the battlegrounds for political power. The AI systems behind these platforms are designed to maximize user engagement, and they achieve this by prioritizing content that generates strong emotional reactions—outrage, fear, or excitement.

This strategy has profound implications for political discourse. During major events like elections, AI-driven algorithms can push hyper-partisan content to individuals, reinforcing their existing political views and isolating them from opposing perspectives. The result is the creation of echo chambers where individuals only hear voices that support their beliefs, leading to the erosion of balanced, informed political discussions.

Moreover, AI's ability to micro-target individuals with personalized ads and content has been weaponized in political campaigns. By analyzing vast amounts of personal data, political campaigns can craft messages tailored to each individual's fears, desires, and biases. This has been particularly evident in instances such as the 2016 U.S. Presidential Election, where data analytics firms like Cambridge Analytica used AI to manipulate voter behavior by targeting specific emotional triggers.

These tactics raise significant ethical concerns. Is it ethical to use AI to sway voters in such a personalized and manipulative way? And if so, where do we draw the line between legitimate persuasion and undue influence?

23.5 Algorithmic Bias and Its Harmful Consequences

AI is often seen as impartial, a neutral tool that makes decisions based on data. However, in practice, AI systems are shaped by the data they are trained on—data that often contains inherent biases. These biases are not merely theoretical; they have real-world consequences.

For example, AI systems used in hiring practices have been shown to favor male candidates over female candidates, even when both have similar qualifications. In criminal justice, algorithms used to predict recidivism rates have been found to disproportionately target people of color, contributing to racial disparities in sentencing and incarceration.

The root of this problem lies in the fact that AI systems are trained on historical data, and this data is often reflective of societal biases. In a world where bias is pervasive, AI systems can inadvertently perpetuate and even amplify these biases, reinforcing existing inequalities.

When these systems are used in high-stakes areas like hiring, law enforcement, and healthcare, the consequences are profound. Algorithmic bias not only exacerbates inequality but also undermines trust in AI systems. The question then becomes: how can we create AI systems that are fair and just? And more importantly, who is responsible when an AI system reinforces harmful societal biases?

23.6 Surveillance and Privacy Invasion

Surveillance is another dark side of AI behavioral influence. As AI technologies evolve, they enable unprecedented levels of monitoring, tracking, and analyzing human behavior. The data collected from smartphones, social media, online shopping, and even facial recognition technology has made it possible to track individuals' movements, preferences, and activities in real-time.

In countries with authoritarian governments, AI-powered surveillance systems can be used to suppress dissent and control populations. In more democratic societies, while surveillance is often justified in the name of security, it raises questions about the erosion of privacy and individual freedoms. With AI constantly monitoring human behavior, the risk of social control—through the manipulation of what people see, what they think, and what they do—becomes a real concern.

Moreover, the use of AI in surveillance systems often occurs without individuals' knowledge or consent. In an age where data is constantly being harvested, people are often unaware of how much of their behavior is being analyzed and exploited for commercial or political gain.

23.7 The Addiction to AI-Driven Systems: The Dopamine Loop

One of the most pernicious ways in which AI influences human behavior is through the creation of addictive systems. AI is used to design platforms and apps that are specifically engineered to capture users' attention and keep them engaged for as long as possible. These systems exploit the brain's dopamine pathways, creating a feedback loop that encourages users to return again and again.

Social media platforms, gaming apps, and online shopping websites all use AI algorithms to create a sense of urgency, FOMO (fear of missing out), and social validation, pushing users to stay on the platform longer. This design, while effective for boosting engagement, comes at a cost. Users may become addicted to the constant notifications, the need for validation, and the rush of instant gratification. The psychological toll of this addiction can be significant, leading to feelings of anxiety, depression, and loneliness.

The question here is whether it's ethical to design systems that encourage such addictive behavior. Should companies be held accountable for creating systems that exploit users' psychological vulnerabilities for profit?

23.8 The Erosion of Autonomy and Free Will

AI's ability to predict and influence human behavior raises troubling questions about human autonomy. The more AI systems know about us, the more they can shape our decisions. From the content we see on social media to the products we buy, AI algorithms are constantly nudging us in specific directions.

The erosion of free will is particularly concerning in situations where people are unaware of the influence being exerted over them. If we are unaware of the way in which AI shapes our choices, can we truly claim that our decisions are our own? Or are we simply following a path that has been carefully constructed by algorithms?

23.9 Combating the Dark Side: Ethical AI Design

As we confront the dark side of AI's behavioral influence, it is crucial to consider the potential solutions and safeguards that can mitigate the negative consequences of this technology. One of the most important steps toward combating unethical AI manipulation is the development of ethical frameworks that guide AI design, implementation, and regulation.

23.9.1 Transparency and Accountability

One of the core ethical principles for AI development is transparency. For AI systems to be trusted, individuals must have access to clear, understandable explanations of how algorithms influence their behavior. This includes knowing what data is being collected, how it is being used, and what decisions are being made by the AI. By increasing transparency, users can better understand how they are being influenced and have the ability to opt-out of certain practices or at least make informed decisions about their engagement with these systems.

Accountability is another essential component. Developers and organizations must take responsibility for the consequences of their AI systems. This means ensuring that AI systems are regularly audited for bias, fairness, and potential harm. Furthermore, the designers behind these systems should be held liable for any negative impact caused by their technology. In this regard, governments and regulatory bodies play an important role in ensuring accountability.

23.9.2 Human-Centered AI

A human-centered approach to AI development focuses on designing systems that prioritize human well-being over profit or engagement metrics. This philosophy places human values, ethics, and dignity at the center of AI design. Human-centered AI systems aim to empower individuals, enhance autonomy, and respect privacy, providing users with control over their interactions with AI.

For instance, AI systems could be designed to prioritize user well-being by providing notifications that encourage healthier behaviors, limit screen time, or offer content that enhances users' mental health. Rather than amplifying addictive behaviors, these systems could promote balance, empathy, and mindfulness.

AI can also be designed to promote inclusivity and avoid harmful stereotypes. Developers must ensure that AI systems do not reinforce biased thinking, discriminatory practices, or harmful societal norms. Human-centered AI ensures that technology works for society, rather than exploiting human weaknesses for profit.

23.9.3 The Role of Regulation

Regulation plays a crucial role in ensuring that AI systems operate ethically. Governments and international organizations must collaborate to create laws and guidelines that address AI's impact on human behavior. For example, the European Union's General Data Protection Regulation (GDPR) has set important precedents by protecting personal data and giving individuals more control over their information. Similar frameworks can be extended to AI, especially in the areas of transparency, consent, and accountability.

In the context of behavioral influence, regulations should be put in place to curb manipulative practices in areas like advertising, social media, and consumer behavior. For example, AI systems that track individuals' psychological vulnerabilities should be restricted or at the very least clearly disclosed. The goal of regulation should be to balance innovation with protection, ensuring that AI serves humanity's interests rather than undermining them.

23.10 The Role of Individuals in Safeguarding Their Autonomy

While policymakers and tech developers bear a significant responsibility for the ethical deployment of AI, individuals also play an essential role in safeguarding their autonomy. As AI continues to shape our behavior, it becomes increasingly important for people to be aware of how AI systems work and the potential risks they pose.

23.10.1 Digital Literacy and Self-Awareness

Digital literacy—the ability to critically assess and engage with technology—is a vital skill in the modern world. To protect themselves from manipulation, individuals must understand how AI systems collect data, analyze behavior, and influence decisions. This includes being aware of how algorithms curate content on social media, how recommendation engines target purchasing decisions, and how personalized ads are designed to trigger emotional responses.

Self-awareness is another crucial aspect. People must regularly reflect on how technology influences their lives and decisions. Are they truly making independent choices, or are they being subtly nudged by AI systems? Are their behaviors shaped by conscious desires, or are they driven by AI-induced cravings? The more individuals can identify these influences, the better equipped they are to resist unwanted manipulation.

23.10.2 Empowering Consumers Through Opt-Out Options

Another way individuals can safeguard their autonomy is through opt-out options. Many AI-driven platforms collect data and personalize user experiences without users fully realizing the extent of this data collection. Offering consumers the ability to opt out of personalized recommendations, tracking, or other manipulative practices can allow individuals to regain control over their decisions.

Empowering consumers with these options requires companies to be transparent and upfront about the choices available to users. The ability to adjust privacy settings, control data sharing, and disable certain personalized features will put individuals back in the driver's seat, enabling them to take ownership of their digital experience.

23.11 The Global Conversation: Ethics and Collaboration

As the influence of AI continues to grow, the need for global collaboration and dialogue on AI ethics becomes more urgent. The implications of AI's behavioral influence reach beyond borders, cultures, and societies. As such, the development of ethical standards must be a collaborative effort between countries, tech companies, policymakers, and civil society.

23.11.1 International Ethical Guidelines

An international framework for AI ethics can ensure that AI systems do not exploit people or violate basic human rights. Such frameworks should focus on human dignity, equality, and fairness, while considering the global impact of AI. For example, AI systems should be designed to be culturally sensitive, ensuring that they are not imposing Western values or creating inequalities between different regions.

Collaboration between countries can also help address the global nature of AI's influence. For example, social media platforms and multinational companies should adhere to ethical standards that apply globally, rather than tailoring their policies to local interests or regulatory loopholes.

23.11.2 Promoting Ethical AI in Tech Development

Tech companies themselves play a pivotal role in ensuring ethical AI design. Through partnerships, funding initiatives, and the creation of industry standards, companies can drive change in AI development. This includes fostering a culture of ethical responsibility within organizations, where AI engineers and designers are encouraged to consider the long-term societal impact of their work.

In addition, organizations can engage with independent auditors and researchers to evaluate the social impact of their technologies. By integrating ethical considerations into the development lifecycle, AI companies can contribute to building trust in their products and services.

23.12 Conclusion: Navigating the Future of AI's Behavioral Influence

The power of AI to influence human behavior is undeniable, but with this power comes great responsibility. As AI continues to evolve, its role in shaping the choices we make—whether in consumerism, politics, or personal behavior—will only grow. While the potential for AI to enhance human life is immense, the dark side of its behavioral influence cannot be ignored.

To navigate the future of AI's behavioral influence, we must adopt a multifaceted approach that combines transparency, accountability, regulation, and ethical design. Tech companies must prioritize human well-being, and governments must regulate AI to prevent exploitation. At the same time, individuals must take responsibility for their own digital experiences, becoming more digitally literate and self-aware.

The future of AI's impact on human behavior lies in our hands. By fostering a global conversation, developing ethical standards, and promoting responsible AI design, we can ensure that AI serves as a tool for human flourishing rather than manipulation. The question is not whether AI will influence us, but how we can shape that influence to protect our autonomy, dignity, and collective well-being.

Chapter 24: AI in Crisis Management

24.1 Introduction to AI in Crisis Management

Crisis management, by its very nature, demands swift action and precise decision-making. Whether it is the aftermath of an earthquake, the outbreak of a pandemic, or the sudden eruption of geopolitical conflict, the ability to respond efficiently and effectively can save lives, reduce suffering, and prevent further chaos. Traditionally, crisis management has relied heavily on human intuition, experience, and judgment. However, in an increasingly complex world where crises can span continents and involve multifaceted challenges, artificial intelligence (A.I) has emerged as an indispensable tool.

AI's involvement in crisis management is not just about its ability to process vast amounts of data but also about its capacity to offer predictive insights, optimize resource allocation, and influence human behavior in times of distress. By harnessing AI's power, we can anticipate crises, prepare better, and make real-time decisions that have far-reaching consequences.

In this chapter, we will explore AI's evolving role in crisis management, from its impact on early warning systems to its ability to shape human behavior during emergencies. We will also delve into the ethical dilemmas that arise when AI is used to influence decision-making in high-stress situations, drawing on real-world examples to understand its capabilities and limitations.

24.2 The Psychology of Crisis Behavior

At the heart of effective crisis management lies a deep understanding of human behavior under pressure. In a crisis, people react in a variety of ways—some with calm, others with panic, and still others with a stoic resolve. The psychology of crisis behavior is a critical aspect of any crisis response, as human reactions can significantly influence the trajectory of an emergency.

Panic, for instance, can spread rapidly in a crowd, leading to chaotic evacuations or disorganized responses. On the other hand, when people feel informed and in control, they are more likely to follow recommended actions and cooperate with emergency procedures. This understanding is where AI becomes particularly valuable. AI can help predict how individuals and groups might behave in different crisis scenarios, allowing authorities to craft more effective strategies for managing crowds, directing resources, and delivering information.

AI-powered systems can monitor social media platforms, emergency calls, and real-time sensors to gauge public sentiment, flagging signs of distress, fear, or misinformation. By analyzing this data, AI can assist in shaping communication strategies that resonate with the public, calming fears, and ensuring that messages are tailored to reduce panic.

24.3 AI for Early Warning Systems

One of the most significant advancements in crisis management has been the development of AI-driven early warning systems. Early warning systems are designed to detect signs of a potential crisis before it escalates, giving authorities crucial time to prepare and respond. For example, AI can analyze seismic activity to predict earthquakes, or it can monitor meteorological data to forecast severe weather events.

AI's ability to process vast datasets from multiple sources, including satellites, IoT sensors, and historical records, has made these systems more accurate and reliable. Machine learning algorithms can sift through patterns in data that would be impossible for humans to detect, identifying subtle changes that signal a crisis may be imminent. This predictive power is revolutionizing crisis management across the globe.

For instance, AI-driven models have been instrumental in predicting natural disasters, such as hurricanes and tsunamis. In 2019, AI was used to predict the path of Cyclone Idai, one of the most devastating tropical storms in Southern Africa. AI algorithms processed real-time data from satellite imagery, weather reports, and ocean currents, helping authorities issue early evacuation orders and deploy emergency resources ahead of the storm's arrival. Such predictive systems have saved countless lives and reduced the damage caused by these catastrophic events.

AI's application in early warning systems extends beyond natural disasters to public health crises as well. During the COVID-19 pandemic, AI models were used to track the spread of the virus, predict infection rates, and estimate the capacity of healthcare systems to handle surges in cases. This data-driven approach allowed governments and health organizations to implement targeted interventions, allocate resources efficiently, and manage public health messaging.

24.4 Real-Time Data Processing in Crisis Situations

In the midst of a crisis, the speed at which decisions are made can make the difference between life and death. AI's ability to process and analyze vast amounts of data in real time is one of its most valuable contributions to crisis management. In an emergency, AI can integrate data from various sources—satellites, social media, IoT devices, drones, and more—to provide a comprehensive picture of the situation as it unfolds.

Consider the role AI played during the 2017 Las Vegas shooting, one of the deadliest mass shootings in U.S. history. In the chaotic aftermath, AI systems were used to quickly analyze surveillance footage, track the movement of individuals, and identify potential threats. AI algorithms sifted through thousands of hours of footage in a fraction of the time it would have taken human investigators. Additionally, AI helped coordinate emergency response efforts, dispatching first responders to the most critical locations based on real-time data analysis.

Similarly, AI can enhance situational awareness in natural disasters. Drones equipped with AI-powered cameras can fly over disaster zones, mapping the extent of damage, locating survivors, and assessing infrastructure damage. AI systems can process this data in real time, prioritizing areas in greatest need of assistance and ensuring that help reaches the most vulnerable populations.

Social media platforms have also become an essential source of real-time information during crises. AI systems can monitor platforms like Twitter and Facebook, identifying posts that signal distress, seeking help, or warning others about emerging threats. AI can also detect and filter out misinformation, ensuring that the public receives accurate and timely information.

24.5 AI and Decision-Making Under Pressure

During a crisis, decision-makers are often forced to make quick choices with incomplete information, under extreme pressure. AI can assist in these high-stakes decision-making processes by offering real-time insights, predictive models, and actionable recommendations.

AI-driven systems can analyze historical data and current circumstances to forecast potential outcomes and suggest the best course of action. For instance, in a medical emergency, AI can recommend specific treatments based on a patient's symptoms and medical history. Similarly, in disaster management, AI can recommend optimal evacuation routes, resource allocations, and shelter locations, taking into account traffic conditions, infrastructure damage, and population density.

Moreover, AI can aid in balancing competing priorities, such as allocating limited resources during a pandemic. AI models can predict the most effective use of medical supplies, prioritize patient care, and allocate vaccines based on risk factors and demographic data. During the COVID-19 pandemic, for example, AI was instrumental in predicting healthcare system overloads, allowing governments to allocate resources where they were most needed.

However, while AI can provide invaluable insights, it is important to recognize its limitations. Decision-making during a crisis often requires nuanced judgment, empathy, and ethical considerations—factors that AI may not be able to fully replicate. In situations where human lives are at stake, it is essential that AI recommendations are viewed as one tool among many, with human oversight playing a critical role in ensuring ethical and contextually appropriate decisions.

24.6 AI in Crisis Communication

Effective communication during a crisis is crucial for public safety and order. Misinformation, confusion, and panic can exacerbate the situation, leading to unnecessary harm. AI-powered systems are playing an increasingly important role in optimizing crisis communication, ensuring that accurate and timely information reaches the public.

AI can be used to create personalized communication strategies, tailoring messages to different demographics and addressing their specific concerns. For instance, during a natural disaster, AI can send location-based alerts, advising people in affected areas to evacuate or seek shelter. AI-powered chatbots can answer frequently asked questions, provide real-time updates, and guide individuals through emergency procedures.

In addition, AI can be instrumental in combating misinformation. Social media platforms, while valuable for disseminating information, can also become breeding grounds for rumors and fake news. AI systems can monitor online discussions and flag misleading content, directing users to verified sources of information. AI can also assess the tone of public sentiment, adjusting communication strategies to address fear, anxiety, or confusion.

Effective crisis communication relies not only on the content of the message but also on the delivery. AI can optimize communication channels, determining the best methods for reaching different populations, whether through text, voice, video, or social media. This ability to provide clear, concise, and actionable information is invaluable in times of crisis.

24.7 AI in Disaster Recovery and Relief Efforts

The immediate aftermath of a crisis is often marked by confusion, destruction, and resource scarcity. AI systems have proven to be invaluable in disaster recovery and relief efforts, offering tools to streamline and optimize the distribution of aid, track recovery progress, and rebuild communities more efficiently. The speed with which relief efforts can be mobilized often determines the extent of long-term damage to both individuals and infrastructure.

AI's ability to process and analyze large quantities of data allows for precise coordination of relief resources. For instance, AI models can predict the locations of people in need of food, medical assistance, and shelter by analyzing movement patterns before and after a disaster. By combining satellite imagery, ground-level sensors, and social media data, AI can map out which areas are most affected and prioritize rescue operations accordingly.

The deployment of drones equipped with AI-powered sensors also contributes to faster damage assessment. After the 2015 Nepal earthquake, AI-powered drones were used to survey damaged buildings and infrastructure, helping teams to quickly identify areas that required immediate attention. The data collected by these drones was then used to create 3D models of the affected areas, enabling planners to allocate resources more effectively and to design recovery strategies that considered the specific needs of each community.

AI's role in logistics is another critical aspect of recovery. Relief operations often involve distributing large quantities of supplies, including food, water, clothing, and medical equipment. AI systems can optimize the logistics of these operations by mapping out the most efficient transportation routes, monitoring supply levels, and predicting where resources will be needed most. AI can also assist in monitoring and managing warehouses, ensuring that supplies are used in the most efficient and equitable way.

Moreover, AI helps track recovery progress, identifying areas that are lagging behind and offering predictive insights into when full recovery may be possible. This ability to forecast and track long-term recovery is crucial for ensuring that resources are not exhausted prematurely and that communities are not left behind as the focus of attention shifts elsewhere.

24.8 Ethical Considerations in Crisis Management with AI

While AI offers enormous potential in crisis management, its deployment in such high-stakes environments raises critical ethical concerns. The ability of AI to influence human behavior, control information, and direct resources brings about significant ethical dilemmas, especially when it involves vulnerable populations or high-pressure decision-making.

One primary ethical issue lies in the level of reliance placed on AI in life-or-death situations. Decision-makers must question whether AI systems are simply tools to aid human decision-making or whether they are actively making choices on behalf of individuals. For example, during the COVID-19 pandemic, AI was used to allocate ventilators and medical supplies based on predictive models of need. However, the algorithmic prioritization could potentially be skewed by biases, leading to ethical concerns about fairness in resource distribution. In situations where human lives are at stake, ensuring that AI systems are transparent, fair, and free from bias is of paramount importance.

Additionally, AI's role in surveillance during a crisis raises privacy concerns. AI-powered tools that monitor social media, track public sentiment, and analyze real-time behaviors can offer critical insights for managing crises, but they also blur the line between security and privacy. In a state of emergency, governments may justify increased surveillance as necessary for public safety, but it is essential to ensure that these measures do not violate basic human rights or create long-term surveillance infrastructures that infringe on individual freedoms.

AI's role in crisis communication also demands ethical scrutiny. While AI can optimize communication and ensure that vital information is delivered swiftly, there is a risk of manipulation. In an age of digital misinformation, AI-powered platforms may become vehicles for spreading government-controlled narratives or exploiting public fear. The ethical question arises: how much control should be placed in the hands of AI systems when it comes to shaping public perception, especially in times of crisis? AI's capacity to nudge human behavior must be handled with care to avoid exacerbating societal divides or undermining public trust.

Finally, there is the issue of accountability. When AI systems make decisions during a crisis, particularly life-and-death decisions, who is ultimately responsible for the outcomes? If an AI model fails to predict a crisis or makes an inaccurate recommendation that leads to harm, who can be held accountable—the creators of the algorithm, the decision-makers who relied on it, or the AI itself? Establishing clear lines of accountability in AI-driven crisis management is essential to maintain public trust in these systems and ensure that they are used responsibly.

24.9 Balancing Human Judgment with AI Assistance

While AI holds immense promise in enhancing crisis management, human judgment will always play an irreplaceable role in guiding responses. AI's power lies in its ability to analyze vast amounts of data, identify patterns, and offer predictive insights, but it cannot replicate the human capacity for empathy, moral reasoning, and adaptability in dynamic, unpredictable situations. Crisis situations often involve complex ethical dilemmas that require a level of nuance and context that AI may not fully comprehend.

For example, during the early days of the COVID-19 pandemic, AI systems were used to predict the spread of the virus and recommend lockdown measures. While these predictions were valuable for planning, they did not account for the profound social and economic impacts that lockdowns would have on vulnerable populations. In these cases, human decision-makers had to weigh the value of saving lives against the costs of unemployment, mental health issues, and social isolation. AI could inform these decisions, but it was human empathy and moral reasoning that ultimately guided them.

Moreover, human decision-makers must consider the long-term implications of AI deployment during a crisis. AI systems, particularly those used for surveillance, can create precedents that may outlast the crisis itself. Governments and organizations must be mindful of the ethical implications of using AI in ways that may infringe on privacy, civil liberties, or social justice in the future. These considerations require careful balancing between technological advancement and ethical integrity.

24.10 The Future of AI in Crisis Management

The future of AI in crisis management looks promising, with technologies continually evolving to provide more accurate predictions, improve real-time decision-making, and enhance recovery efforts. As AI becomes increasingly sophisticated, its ability to predict, respond, and manage crises will continue to improve, offering new opportunities for optimizing resources, saving lives, and reducing harm.

One area where AI will likely have a major impact is in climate change adaptation and disaster resilience. As climate-related crises become more frequent and intense, AI will be essential in predicting environmental risks, developing early warning systems, and helping communities adapt to changing conditions. By combining AI with other emerging technologies, such as blockchain and the Internet of Things (IoT), we can create smarter, more resilient cities and communities that are better prepared for the challenges of the future.

However, as AI continues to evolve, it is crucial to ensure that its deployment in crisis management is done in a way that respects human rights, promotes equity, and considers the ethical consequences of algorithmic decision-making. The future of AI in crisis management must be shaped by collaboration between governments, technologists, ethicists, and the public to ensure that these technologies are used responsibly and effectively.

In conclusion, AI's role in crisis management has the potential to revolutionize how we predict, respond to, and recover from emergencies. However, as with any powerful tool, its use must be carefully managed, with a focus on ethical considerations, transparency, and the well-being of individuals and communities. By leveraging AI's capabilities while balancing them with human judgment, we can build a more resilient, responsive, and ethical approach to crisis management in the years to come.

Chapter 25: Gamification and AI: Engaging the Human Mind

25.1 Introduction: The Intersection of AI and Gamification

In the modern world, technology is reshaping how we interact with almost every aspect of our daily lives. One of the most profound transformations is in the way we engage with tasks, goals, and behaviors. The rise of **gamification**—the application of game mechanics to non-game contexts—has been a significant driver of this change. Yet, it's the integration of **artificial intelligence (A.I)** into gamification that is unlocking new dimensions of human engagement.

Gamification, in its simplest form, involves applying elements such as points, rewards, levels, and challenges to activities that aren't traditionally games. These techniques tap into intrinsic human desires: the pursuit of achievement, the joy of competition, and the thrill of progress. But while gamification can make mundane tasks more engaging, the real power lies in AI's ability to personalize and optimize these experiences to fit the needs of individuals, often in real-time.

AI is not merely a tool that makes gamification more sophisticated; it is the driving force behind its evolution. With AI, gamified systems are no longer static; they adapt, evolve, and learn from the user's behaviors. As AI analyzes vast amounts of data, it can create dynamic experiences that feel uniquely tailored to each person's preferences and needs. This merging of AI with gamification holds the potential to revolutionize industries such as education, health, marketing, and entertainment.

In this chapter, we will delve into the psychological principles behind gamification, how AI enhances these experiences, and the far-reaching consequences of this fusion. Through this lens, we will explore how AI-driven gamification influences human decision-making, behavior, and engagement. We will also examine the ethical dilemmas posed by these advancements and consider the future of this technology as it continues to shape our digital lives.

25.2 The Psychological Principles Behind Gamification

Before we explore how AI transforms gamification, it's important to understand the psychological principles that make gamification so effective. At the heart of gamification lies the psychology of **motivation**—specifically, the intrinsic and extrinsic factors that drive human behavior.

Intrinsic motivation refers to the desire to engage in an activity because it is inherently enjoyable or satisfying. When a person plays a game for the pure enjoyment of the activity itself—whether it's solving puzzles, exploring virtual worlds, or achieving personal mastery—they are motivated intrinsically. On the other hand, **extrinsic motivation** involves engaging in an activity for external rewards or outcomes, such as earning points, trophies, or recognition.

Gamification taps into both forms of motivation. By rewarding achievements and offering challenges, it uses extrinsic motivation to drive people toward particular goals. However, when designed well, gamification can also nurture intrinsic motivation by fostering a sense of autonomy, competence, and relatedness—three psychological needs identified in **Self-Determination Theory (SDT)**. When people feel that they have control over their actions, that they are capable of achieving their goals, and that their efforts are valued by others, their engagement with gamified systems becomes deeper and more sustainable.

One of the key mechanisms that drive engagement in gamified systems is the concept of **progression**. People enjoy seeing their advancement, whether it's leveling up in a video game, completing challenges in a fitness app, or earning achievements in a learning platform. The **feedback loops** created by gamification provide constant reinforcement, signaling to the user that they are on the right path and that their efforts are paying off.

AI is particularly adept at enhancing these psychological principles. With machine learning algorithms, AI systems can analyze user behavior and adjust the difficulty of tasks or the rewards system to keep users engaged without overwhelming them. For instance, an AI-driven fitness app can increase the intensity of workouts based on a person's progress, ensuring that they are constantly challenged but not frustrated. This personalized approach maximizes both intrinsic and extrinsic motivation, creating a powerful tool for behavior change.

25.3 Personalization Through AI

One of the most remarkable aspects of AI-driven gamification is its ability to **personalize** the user experience. Personalization, in this context, means tailoring the content, challenges, and rewards of a gamified system to fit the preferences, behavior, and progress of the individual user. This makes the experience feel more relevant, engaging, and effective.

Consider, for instance, the personalized workout plans offered by fitness apps like **Peloton** or **Nike Training Club**. These apps use AI to track users' activity levels, assess their fitness goals, and suggest workouts that are appropriately challenging. The AI doesn't just pick random workouts—it learns from the user's past behavior, adapting to their progress and adjusting for any difficulties they may have faced. This ensures that the user remains engaged and motivated to continue their journey, rather than becoming discouraged or bored.

In educational settings, AI-powered learning platforms like **Duolingo** use similar principles to keep students engaged. As the AI system tracks a learner's performance, it adapts the lessons, quizzes, and challenges to match their proficiency level. If a student struggles with a particular topic, the AI will provide additional practice or offer alternative explanations, ensuring that the learner is never left behind. Conversely, if a student is breezing through the material, the AI will present more difficult challenges to keep them engaged. This personalized approach helps maintain motivation, enabling learners to achieve better outcomes while enjoying the process.

The key to this personalization is the use of **data**. AI systems collect and analyze vast amounts of information about the user's behaviors, preferences, and progress. With this data, AI can continuously optimize the experience in ways that would be impossible for a human designer to achieve on their own. As a result, the user feels more connected to the experience, which strengthens their motivation and engagement.

25.4 AI and Reward Systems

At the heart of most gamified systems lies the **reward**—a mechanism designed to reinforce desired behaviors and keep users engaged. Traditional games rely on points, badges, and levels to reward players for their efforts. However, AI has the ability to go beyond these basic systems and create highly **dynamic** and **personalized** rewards that maximize engagement and influence behavior in profound ways.

The psychological science behind rewards is rooted in the concept of **dopamine**, the brain chemical associated with pleasure, reinforcement, and learning. When we receive a reward, whether it's a monetary bonus, a congratulatory message, or the thrill of leveling up in a game, our brains release dopamine. This creates a feeling of pleasure that motivates us to repeat the behavior that led to the reward. In gamified systems, this feedback loop is crucial for maintaining motivation over time.

AI enhances this process by creating **variable rewards**—rewards that are unpredictable or irregular in nature. This principle, drawn from **operant conditioning**, is particularly effective in keeping users engaged. A well-known example of variable rewards in gamification is the design of slot machines in casinos. The anticipation of a reward, coupled with the unpredictability of when it will come, keeps players playing. This principle is similarly used in mobile games, social media apps, and even fitness trackers to maintain user engagement.

AI is especially powerful in optimizing these reward systems. By analyzing a user's behavior and preferences, AI can determine the type, frequency, and timing of rewards that will be most effective for that individual. For example, if a user is more motivated by social recognition, an AI-driven system might reward them with public praise or a leaderboard ranking. If a user is more motivated by progress, the AI might present them with incremental goals and milestones.

The ability to create personalized reward systems means that AI-driven gamification can be tailored to a wide range of behaviors and preferences.

Whether the goal is to encourage physical exercise, promote learning, or drive customer loyalty, AI can optimize the reward system to maximize engagement and influence.

25.5 Behavioral Change and AI

One of the most compelling aspects of gamification is its ability to drive **behavioral change**. Whether it's encouraging healthier habits, improving learning outcomes, or boosting employee productivity, gamified systems have been successfully used to inspire lasting changes in behavior. When coupled with the adaptive capabilities of AI, gamification becomes an even more powerful tool for influencing how we think, act, and interact with the world around us.

AI's role in behavioral change lies in its ability to continuously **track**, **analyze**, and **adapt** to users' behaviors. Traditional methods of behavioral change, such as setting goals or offering rewards, are often static and one-size-fits-all. AI, however, learns from each interaction, refining its recommendations and strategies to meet the individual's unique needs.

For example, in the realm of **healthcare**, AI-driven gamification is being used to help people manage chronic conditions such as diabetes or obesity. Patients using apps like **MySugr** or **Weight Watchers** can track their behaviors, receive tailored feedback, and engage with challenges that help them stay motivated. AI not only personalizes the experience based on a person's habits and progress but can also provide immediate feedback when behaviors need to change, such as when a patient's glucose levels are too high or when an individual's weight loss has plateaued.

In **education**, AI-driven gamification systems are being used to create personalized learning paths that adjust to the pace and learning style of each student. By tracking student performance, AI can provide real-time feedback, offer additional resources, and adjust the difficulty of tasks to ensure that students remain engaged and challenged. This continuous adjustment not only enhances learning outcomes but also helps students develop a sense of autonomy and ownership over their learning process—key factors in fostering intrinsic motivation.

Even in the workplace, AI-powered gamification is driving changes in **employee engagement** and **productivity**. Companies like **Salesforce** and **Microsoft** use gamified platforms to motivate employees by offering rewards, recognition, and progress tracking. These platforms incorporate AI to adapt to each employee's performance, providing them with personalized goals and challenges that encourage continuous improvement. AI ensures that employees remain engaged by fine-tuning the experience to match their individual preferences, work habits, and aspirations.

At the heart of these behavioral changes is the **feedback loop**—a central component of both gamification and AI. Feedback is essential for reinforcing desired behaviors and helping individuals understand the consequences of their actions. AI-powered systems provide immediate, actionable feedback, ensuring that users can adjust their behaviors in real-time to achieve their goals.

The combination of gamification and AI offers a unique advantage: the ability to continually **optimize** the user experience. Unlike traditional approaches that may rely on preset reward systems or fixed behavioral models, AI-driven gamification adapts to the user's progress and preferences, creating an environment that is always relevant, engaging, and motivating.

25.6 AI's Role in Habit Formation

One of the most profound areas where AI-driven gamification is having an impact is in **habit formation**. Habits—whether healthy or unhealthy—are deeply ingrained in our behavior, and changing them can be incredibly challenging. AI's ability to personalize, motivate, and track progress makes it an invaluable tool for helping individuals form new habits or break old ones.

The process of habit formation is driven by a combination of **repetition**, **reinforcement**, and **reward**. AI-driven systems excel at providing all three of these elements, making it easier for users to establish new routines and behaviors. For instance, in **fitness apps** like **Strava** or **Fitbit**, users are encouraged to engage in regular exercise by tracking their activity, setting goals, and receiving rewards such as badges or virtual achievements. These systems create a sense of progress and accomplishment, which reinforces the desired behavior and makes it easier for individuals to stick to their new habits.

AI also plays a critical role in helping users **break bad habits**. For example, apps designed to reduce screen time, like **Forest**, use gamification to encourage users to focus on real-world tasks by rewarding them for staying off their phones. The AI system in these apps tracks user behavior, analyzes patterns, and offers personalized suggestions for reducing distractions. By using AI to provide immediate feedback and tailored incentives, these apps help users break the cycle of unwanted habits and replace them with more positive behaviors.

In the realm of **mental health**, AI-powered tools are being used to help individuals develop habits that support their well-being. For instance, apps like **Headspace** or **Calm** use gamification to encourage daily meditation practices, rewarding users for consistency and progress. AI ensures that the content is personalized based on the user's mood, preferences, and goals, helping to build a habit of mindfulness and stress management.

The key to AI's success in habit formation is its ability to learn from the user's behavior and adjust its strategies accordingly. This level of personalization ensures that users are not only motivated but also supported in their efforts to form lasting habits.

25.7 Ethical Considerations in AI-Driven Gamification

As with any powerful tool, AI-driven gamification raises important **ethical considerations**. While gamification has the potential to drive positive change—helping people improve their health, learn new skills, and stay engaged in tasks—it can also be used to manipulate or exploit users in ways that undermine their autonomy.

One of the primary ethical concerns surrounding AI and gamification is the issue of **manipulation**. While gamification techniques like rewards, badges, and levels can be motivating, they can also be used to push individuals toward behaviors they may not have chosen freely. For example, social media platforms use gamified elements to keep users engaged for extended periods of time, often using personalized content to trigger emotional responses and encourage addictive behavior. In these cases, users may not be fully aware of how their behaviors are being influenced by the gamification systems in place.

Another ethical challenge is the **privacy** and **data security** implications of AI-powered gamification. In order for AI systems to personalize experiences and optimize user engagement, they must collect vast amounts of personal data—everything from browsing history to location, preferences, and even biometric data. While this data can be used to enhance the user experience, it also raises concerns about how that data is stored, shared, and protected.

Furthermore, there are questions about the **long-term effects** of AI-driven gamification on mental health and well-being. While gamified systems can improve motivation and behavior in the short term, there is a risk that they could create unhealthy dependencies or unrealistic expectations. For example, excessive use of gamified health apps may lead individuals to focus too much on metrics such as step count or calories burned, potentially fostering an unhealthy obsession with performance rather than personal well-being.

Ethical AI design, transparency, and user autonomy are critical factors to consider as we continue to develop AI-driven gamification systems. Developers and researchers must work together to ensure that these technologies are used in ways that benefit users without exploiting or manipulating them.

25.8 The Future of AI-Driven Gamification

Looking ahead, the future of AI-driven gamification appears boundless. As AI technology continues to advance, the potential applications of gamification will expand into new areas, from healthcare to mental wellness, education, and beyond. The integration of AI will make gamified experiences more immersive, personalized, and effective than ever before.

The next generation of gamification will likely incorporate even more sophisticated AI systems, including **natural language processing (NLP)**, **emotion recognition**, and **adaptive learning algorithms**. These advancements will enable gamified systems to respond to a broader range of user behaviors and emotions, making experiences feel more intuitive and responsive. For instance, AI could analyze a person's emotional state and adjust the difficulty of tasks or rewards to match their mood, ensuring that users remain engaged and motivated regardless of external factors.

Moreover, **virtual reality (VR)** and **augmented reality (AR)** technologies will further enhance gamified experiences, providing users with more immersive and interactive environments. AI will play a key role in making these environments feel dynamic and responsive, adapting in real-time to the user's actions and preferences.

However, as AI-driven gamification continues to evolve, the ethical considerations will only become more complex. Developers must balance the power of AI to influence behavior with the responsibility to protect user autonomy and privacy. Striking this balance will be crucial as gamification becomes an even more integral part of our digital lives.

25.9 Gamification in Education: AI-Enhanced Learning Journeys

AI-powered gamification is revolutionizing **education** by transforming the way students engage with learning materials. With AI, the concept of "play" is no longer confined to childhood, but instead is applied strategically in the educational realm to encourage deeper learning and personal growth.

The power of gamification in education lies in its ability to **engage** students by creating fun, interactive environments where learning becomes an enjoyable pursuit rather than a task. AI enhances this by personalizing the experience, adapting the content to the specific needs, interests, and learning styles of each individual.

For example, AI-driven platforms like **Kahoot!** or **Duolingo** use gamification to engage students in subjects ranging from languages to history and mathematics. By incorporating elements like badges, leaderboards, and rewards, these platforms provide a sense of achievement and progress, motivating students to complete lessons and study more consistently. Furthermore, AI systems ensure that these experiences are tailored to the student's level, adjusting the complexity of tasks as they advance, thereby keeping them engaged without overwhelming them.

AI's ability to analyze **student behavior** and adapt the content ensures that each learner receives the support they need to succeed. For instance, if a student is struggling with a particular concept in math, AI can offer additional explanations or create practice problems to reinforce that area. Conversely, if a student excels, AI can introduce more challenging material, keeping them motivated and pushing their cognitive limits.

Additionally, AI in education can help combat the **one-size-fits-all** approach traditionally seen in classrooms. Not every student learns the same way, and AI has the power to personalize learning experiences in ways that were previously unthinkable. Through real-time feedback and ongoing assessment, AI systems can dynamically adjust the pace and delivery of content to better match the learner's strengths and weaknesses.

By integrating AI into educational gamification, we're not only creating more engaging and effective learning experiences but also fostering a **growth mindset**. Students begin to view challenges as opportunities to learn and grow rather than as obstacles to overcome. The game-like structure of these systems encourages resilience, self-reflection, and persistence—all key components of lifelong learning.

25.10 The Ethics of AI and Gamification in Education

As AI-driven gamification becomes more prevalent in education, ethical considerations must be front and center. While gamification can undoubtedly enhance learning outcomes, it also introduces potential risks related to **privacy**, **data security**, and **psychological well-being**.

One of the most pressing concerns is the **data privacy** of students. Educational AI platforms collect vast amounts of data to personalize the learning experience, including details about a student's academic performance, behavior patterns, and even personal preferences. While this data can be invaluable in tailoring educational content, it raises important questions about who owns this data, how it's used, and whether students fully understand what is being collected.

In addition to data privacy, the **psychological impact** of gamification must be considered. While rewards, badges, and leaderboards can motivate students, there is a risk that they could create unhealthy dependencies on external validation. When students become overly focused on the rewards rather than the intrinsic value of learning, it may diminish their long-term motivation. The challenge is to strike a balance between extrinsic rewards and intrinsic motivation, ensuring that the gamified system supports the development of a **growth mindset** rather than fostering a shallow focus on external achievements.

Furthermore, there are concerns that gamification could exacerbate **inequalities** in education. While AI-driven systems promise to personalize learning, they can also perpetuate existing biases. If not properly designed, AI could amplify disparities by offering certain students more challenging tasks based on biased assumptions or underestimating the capabilities of others.

Ethical AI design in education must prioritize **transparency**, ensuring that students, parents, and educators understand how data is being used and how algorithms are influencing the learning experience. Furthermore, educators must retain the autonomy to shape the educational experience, ensuring that AI complements, rather than replaces, their role in guiding students.

25.11 The Impact of AI Gamification on Behavioral Economics

As we explore the intersection of AI and gamification, it's clear that **behavioral economics** plays a significant role in shaping how gamified systems influence users' decisions and actions. AI-driven gamification systems leverage principles from behavioral economics to steer users toward specific outcomes—whether it's healthier habits, higher productivity, or greater engagement in learning.

At the core of behavioral economics is the idea that **human decisions are not always rational**. We are often influenced by cognitive biases, emotions, and social factors when making choices. AI gamification systems exploit these tendencies to encourage particular behaviors.

For instance, the principle of **loss aversion**—where individuals are more motivated by the fear of losing something than by the prospect of gaining something—can be used in AI gamification. By introducing features such as **time-limited rewards** or penalties for failure, AI systems tap into our desire to avoid losses, increasing motivation and engagement.

Similarly, AI can exploit the **anchoring effect**, where our decisions are influenced by the first piece of information we receive. In a gamified system, AI might initially present users with a high target or challenging goal, which sets an **anchor** for future goals. As a result, users may strive to achieve more than they would have otherwise, believing that the original target is the standard to which they must adhere.

AI also takes advantage of the **social proof** bias. People tend to make decisions based on the behaviors of others, especially when they are unsure about what to do. Gamification systems often incorporate social elements, such as leaderboards or achievements shared among peers, to encourage users to compare their progress with others. By seeing that others are achieving certain milestones, users are more likely to feel motivated to improve their own performance.

These psychological principles, when combined with AI's ability to **personalize** experiences, make gamified systems incredibly effective at shaping behavior. As a result, users are often nudged toward behaviors they might not have consciously chosen, whether for personal growth, entertainment, or commercial purposes.

25.12 Looking Forward: AI, Gamification, and the Future of Human Behavior

As AI continues to evolve, the potential for gamification to shape human behavior becomes even more profound. In the future, we may see **AI-driven ecosystems** that extend beyond apps and games and influence entire aspects of our daily lives—our work habits, our health choices, and even our social interactions.

In this brave new world, AI's role in **behavioral economics** and **habit formation** will only grow. With the integration of more sophisticated AI technologies—such as **emotion AI**, **neural interfaces**, and **augmented**

reality—the line between gaming and real life will blur even further. AI will seamlessly integrate gamification elements into everyday experiences, transforming routine tasks into interactive challenges designed to engage and motivate us.

But as this technology advances, we must remain vigilant about the ethical implications. The future of AI-driven gamification must be guided by principles of **transparency**, **user agency**, and **fairness**. By prioritizing the needs and well-being of users, we can ensure that gamification continues to serve as a force for good, helping us harness the full potential of AI while safeguarding against its misuse.

The future of human behavior will undoubtedly be shaped by AI, but it will be up to us to decide how we navigate this exciting, complex, and sometimes uncertain landscape.

Chapter 26: AI's Impact on Human Relationships

26.1 Introduction: The Growing Presence of AI in Daily Life

In the not-so-distant past, artificial intelligence (A.I) seemed like a futuristic concept, something confined to the pages of science fiction novels and speculative films. Today, AI has evolved into an omnipresent force in our daily lives. From the algorithms powering our social media feeds to the virtual assistants managing our schedules, AI is embedded in nearly every aspect of our interactions with the world. However, one of the most profound and often overlooked areas where AI is making its mark is in human relationships.

As AI systems become increasingly sophisticated, their ability to interact with humans in ways that mimic human behavior—whether in communication, emotional support, or even conflict resolution—is reshaping how we connect with one another. The psychological implications of this transformation are immense. For centuries, human relationships have been anchored in tangible, emotional exchanges, but now we must confront the question: Can machines, with their calculated logic and data-driven decision-making, authentically participate in our human experience?

This chapter delves into the intersection between AI and human relationships, exploring how AI influences everything from friendships and romantic connections to family dynamics. It examines both the opportunities and challenges this new technological landscape presents, as well as the ethical dilemmas that arise when we allow machines to participate in our most intimate interactions.

26.2 AI and Communication: Redefining Interaction

Human communication has always been at the core of building and maintaining relationships. From the subtle nuances of body language to the depth of shared emotional experiences, communication allows people to understand each other in ways words alone cannot capture. However, with the rise of AI, especially in the form of chatbots, virtual assistants, and messaging algorithms, the very nature of communication is undergoing a seismic shift.

AI has begun to redefine the way we interact with others. Through services like Siri, Alexa, and Google Assistant, we can now have our needs met through voice-based commands. These systems don't merely perform basic tasks—they have evolved to provide companionship and empathy. This shift has had profound psychological consequences. On the one hand, AI can facilitate communication across linguistic and geographical barriers, enabling richer interactions. But on the other hand, it raises a troubling question: Are we substituting authentic, face-to-face connections with transactional, data-driven ones?

In the world of text-based communication, the role of AI is similarly transformative. AI-powered tools help us write emails, craft messages, and even engage in conversation through intelligent chatbots. While these systems can simulate empathy by recognizing emotional cues, the question remains: Can they truly understand the depths of human emotion, or are they merely mimicking behavior for the sake of convenience? The psychological impact of these tools is still being explored, but early research suggests that our reliance on AI for communication could erode our social skills, diminishing our ability to engage meaningfully with others.

26.3 AI as a Social Companion: Redefining Friendship

In recent years, AI-driven social companions—virtual friends and AI chatbots—have become a source of solace for many, particularly in an era of increasing loneliness. Platforms like Replika, which offer users a chance to engage with AI-powered companions, have gained immense popularity. These systems promise to offer companionship that is both personalized and non-judgmental, creating an emotional connection that can mimic the experience of friendship.

For many people, especially those who struggle with social anxiety or who live in isolation, AI companions offer a sense of comfort and connection that may otherwise be elusive. AI companions do not demand anything in return, do not judge, and do not tire of conversations. They can engage at any time of day or night, offering an emotional anchor for those in need.

However, this blurring of the lines between human and machine companionship raises significant psychological concerns. While AI companions may alleviate loneliness, they cannot replicate the complex, dynamic nature of human relationships. AI's role in forming genuine emotional connections is limited by its lack of consciousness and self-awareness. As much as we may feel attachment to an AI system, it is ultimately an algorithm responding to patterns of interaction, not a sentient being capable of mutual empathy or understanding.

This paradox of forming emotional attachments to non-human entities brings into question the very nature of friendship. Are we truly capable of feeling connected to a machine, or is this just a convenient substitute for the deeper, more fulfilling connections we seek in human relationships? And perhaps more troubling, what happens when people begin to prioritize these artificial friendships over real-world human interactions? Will AI companions become an emotional crutch, leading to even greater isolation?

26.4 AI in Romantic Relationships: Love, Desire, and Intimacy

The world of romance has also been impacted by AI's evolution. Dating apps, which leverage AI algorithms to match people based on compatibility metrics, are perhaps the most obvious example. These apps have fundamentally altered the way we search for and experience romantic connections. Instead of relying on serendipity or traditional methods of meeting potential partners, AI allows us to algorithmically select individuals who appear to match our psychological profiles. For some, this is a boon, increasing efficiency in finding love. For others, it represents a mechanization of something inherently organic.

But AI's influence in romance does not stop at matchmaking. As AI becomes more advanced, it is also starting to shape the way we experience intimacy. Virtual reality (VR) and augmented reality (AR) technologies, powered by AI, have enabled people to engage in simulated romantic and sexual experiences. While these virtual relationships may offer a sense of escapism or control, they risk undermining genuine emotional intimacy by replacing it with simulations.

The psychological implications of AI's involvement in romantic relationships are profound. AI systems may inadvertently shape our expectations of intimacy and love, fostering unrealistic ideals or detaching us from the messier, more complex aspects of human connection. The algorithms that drive dating apps, for example, prioritize certain traits—appearance, interests, and background—while neglecting other factors, such as emotional depth or shared life experiences. As a result, people may begin to view relationships through a more transactional lens, focusing on compatibility metrics rather than cultivating emotional closeness.

26.5 The Role of AI in Family Dynamics and Parenting

AI is also becoming increasingly integrated into family life. Smart home devices, parenting apps, and educational tools powered by AI are transforming the way families function. These technologies promise convenience, efficiency, and safety, but they also have subtle implications for relationships within the family unit.

Consider the impact of AI on parenting. From baby monitors that track infants' sleep patterns to educational tools that help children learn, AI systems are increasingly being used to manage time, monitor behavior, and support development. These tools are intended to make parenting easier, but they also raise questions about over-reliance on technology. Will parents become too dependent on AI for guidance? Can AI adequately replace the nuanced, intuitive nature of human parenting?

Moreover, AI is reshaping relationships between parents and children. Children today are growing up with AI in their daily lives, interacting with virtual assistants, learning from educational platforms, and engaging with social media algorithms that shape their understanding of the world. This raises concerns about the long-term psychological impact of AI on children's emotional development and social skills. Will children come to rely on AI for emotional support, rather than turning to their parents or peers? Will AI influence their expectations of relationships in ways that are not yet fully understood?

26.6 AI and the Changing Nature of Empathy

Empathy, the ability to understand and share the feelings of another, has long been considered a cornerstone of human connection. It is through empathy that we form emotional bonds, provide comfort, and offer support in times of distress. However, as AI begins to play a more prominent role in our relationships, the role of empathy in these interactions becomes more complex.

At first glance, AI seems incapable of experiencing empathy in the human sense. After all, empathy requires not only an intellectual understanding of another's emotional state but also a genuine emotional response to that state. Yet, AI systems, particularly those designed for customer service, healthcare, and therapy, are increasingly able to simulate empathetic responses. By recognizing emotional cues in text or speech and responding with pre-programmed empathy scripts, these systems can appear to offer a comforting presence.

But this simulation of empathy is not without consequences. Research suggests that while AI can mimic empathetic behavior, it cannot authentically feel what a human feels. As a result, the empathy AI offers is, at best, a facsimile—a response based on data patterns, not emotional understanding. This raises an important psychological question: If we begin to rely on AI for emotional support, will we lose our ability to empathize with one another? As AI systems grow more adept at reading and responding to our emotions, we may increasingly turn to them for comfort, but this may inadvertently erode our capacity for real human empathy. The danger here lies in the risk of substituting the genuine, imperfect empathy of human relationships with the cold, algorithmic comfort of an AI simulation.

26.7 AI and Social Isolation: A Double-Edged Sword

One of the paradoxical effects of AI is its ability to both combat and exacerbate social isolation. On one hand, AI-powered platforms can create connections where none existed before. People living in remote areas or with limited social networks can use AI-driven tools to engage with others, access emotional support, and even build meaningful relationships. In this sense, AI can act as a bridge, connecting individuals who might otherwise be isolated from society.

Yet, there is a darker side to this phenomenon. As people grow increasingly reliant on AI for companionship and interaction, there is a real risk of undermining face-to-face human connection. Social media algorithms, for example, encourage superficial engagement and interaction, prioritizing likes and shares over deeper conversations. AI-driven chatbots and virtual companions may provide emotional fulfillment, but their one-sided, transactional nature means that they cannot fully replicate the depth and complexity of human relationships.

The psychological implications of AI-driven social isolation are profound. Studies suggest that social isolation can have negative effects on mental health, contributing to depression, anxiety, and cognitive decline. While AI can provide a temporary fix, it cannot replace the nuanced, reciprocal connections that we experience with other human beings. As individuals turn to AI for social interaction, they may inadvertently disengage from their communities, leading to a cycle of increasing isolation. This effect could be especially pronounced among vulnerable populations, such as the elderly or those with mental health challenges, who may come to rely more heavily on AI-driven interactions as a substitute for real-world engagement.

26.8 The Ethics of AI in Relationships: Consent, Manipulation, and Privacy

As AI becomes more embedded in our relationships, ethical considerations must come to the forefront. At the heart of these ethical questions lies the issue of consent. In human relationships, consent is a fundamental principle that ensures both parties understand and agree to the terms of their interaction. In the context of AI, however, the question of consent becomes far more complicated.

Consider, for instance, the use of AI in therapy. As AI systems become capable of providing psychological support, the question arises: Do individuals fully understand the nature of their interactions with AI? Are they aware that their emotional responses may be tracked, analyzed, and used to improve the system's performance? While some may argue that AI could offer therapeutic benefits, others raise concerns about the privacy implications of these interactions. Personal data, emotional triggers, and sensitive information shared with AI-driven systems could be misused, leading to breaches of trust.

Similarly, there is the issue of manipulation. As AI algorithms become increasingly sophisticated, they can be designed to influence human behavior in subtle and powerful ways. Consider the role of AI in online dating, where algorithms prioritize certain physical traits or personality characteristics over others. In this environment, AI may subtly encourage individuals to prioritize certain types of partners or relationships, shaping preferences and expectations in ways that they may not fully comprehend. This phenomenon is not limited to dating apps but extends to advertising, political campaigns, and social media interactions. The power of AI to shape decisions, desires, and behaviors is profound, but it raises important ethical questions about manipulation and autonomy.

Lastly, privacy concerns remain a central issue in the integration of AI into human relationships. AI systems rely on vast amounts of personal data to function effectively, whether it's tracking emotional responses, recording preferences, or monitoring behavior. While this data is often anonymized, there are still risks associated with the collection and storage of personal information. In the wrong hands, this data could be misused, leading to exploitation, surveillance, or even identity theft. As AI continues to play a larger role in our relationships, we must grapple with these ethical considerations to ensure that our interactions with AI remain transparent, consensual, and respectful of privacy.

26.9 AI in Family Dynamics: Parenting and Children's Development

In family life, AI's influence extends beyond individual relationships and into the ways in which families operate as a unit. AI-driven devices are now commonplace in homes, offering a range of services from managing household tasks to providing educational tools for children. But while these technologies can bring convenience and efficiency, they also raise concerns about their impact on children's development and the nature of parenting.

Parents are increasingly turning to AI to help manage their children's education and behavior. AI-powered learning apps and educational platforms tailor content to individual children's learning styles, providing personalized instruction and feedback. These technologies promise to enhance learning outcomes by delivering the right information at the right time, ensuring that children stay engaged and motivated. But what are the psychological effects of growing up in an environment where AI plays such a prominent role in shaping a child's learning and development?

There is a growing concern that over-reliance on AI in education could limit children's social development. Learning is not just about acquiring information but also about developing the skills to interact with others, negotiate differences, and navigate complex social dynamics. If children are increasingly interacting with AI systems instead of peers or adults, they may miss out on the opportunity to develop critical social skills. Additionally, as AI-driven systems take on more of the instructional and parenting roles, there is a risk that parents may become more distant, relying on machines to handle the emotional and developmental aspects of parenting rather than engaging directly with their children.

Moreover, the potential for AI to shape children's emotional and cognitive development is immense. AI-powered devices can provide constant feedback, praise, and rewards, which can have a profound effect on a child's self-esteem and motivation. However, this reinforcement system, while effective, may inadvertently condition children to seek external validation from machines rather than from themselves or their peers. The long-term effects of such conditioning on emotional intelligence and independence are still unknown, but it is clear that AI's role in child-rearing and education will require careful consideration.

26.10 The Role of AI in Enhancing Long-Distance Relationships

Long-distance relationships have always posed unique challenges, and the rise of AI offers both opportunities and risks for couples separated by physical distance. In many ways, AI has the potential to strengthen emotional bonds, enabling partners to stay connected in new and creative ways. Communication platforms enriched by AI, such as personalized video messages, virtual reality (VR) dating experiences, and smart home devices that sync to provide reminders of special moments, can help maintain intimacy despite geographical separation.

For example, AI-driven chatbots can simulate conversation, offering personalized responses based on the partner's emotional state and past interactions. These systems can help bridge the communication gap, offering emotional support when one partner feels lonely or disconnected. Virtual assistants can also serve as emotional reminders, suggesting thoughtful gestures like sending flowers or scheduling video calls. AI-enabled technologies can create a sense of presence, even when physical proximity is not possible.

However, there is also a psychological downside to this trend. As these AI tools become more advanced and capable of tailoring interactions to mimic the nuances of real human behavior, individuals in long-distance relationships may begin to rely on the artificial companionship provided by these technologies. Instead of relying on the emotional depth and personal connection found in face-to-face interactions, people might find themselves growing emotionally dependent on AI systems. The concern is that these AI-mediated relationships could create unrealistic expectations and hinder the development of healthy, fully fleshed-out connections when the partners are eventually reunited in person.

Additionally, there is the possibility of emotional detachment. People may find it easier to share their emotions with an AI assistant rather than their partner, creating a barrier to genuine communication. This shift could impact the overall trust and depth of the relationship, with AI acting as a sort of intermediary rather than a facilitator of authentic connection.

26.11 The Potential for AI to Mediate Conflicts in Relationships

One of the most intriguing aspects of AI in human relationships is its potential to act as a mediator in interpersonal conflicts. As human emotions can often cloud judgment, having an impartial, data-driven assistant could help facilitate communication during arguments or disagreements. AI systems that analyze the dynamics of a conversation can suggest neutral language, identify common ground, and offer constructive solutions based on psychological principles. In some therapeutic contexts, AI could act as a third party, offering a level of objectivity that might be hard to achieve in heated discussions between humans.

However, there are several psychological considerations to keep in mind. For one, the presence of an AI mediator could alter the way individuals express themselves during conflict. The awareness that an AI system is "listening" and offering feedback might lead to more calculated, less emotionally expressive behavior. People might be less inclined to fully open up or be vulnerable, fearing that the AI's analysis might be inaccurate or miss important subtleties of human emotion.

Moreover, the risk of over-reliance on AI mediation is real. If people begin to turn to AI systems to resolve their conflicts instead of directly engaging with their partners, it could diminish the development of critical conflict-resolution skills. Relationships thrive on emotional labor, negotiation, and compromise—skills that are honed through experience and human connection. Relying too heavily on AI systems for conflict resolution could stifle these essential aspects of relationship building.

26.12 The Blurring Line Between Artificial and Real Relationships

Perhaps the most profound change AI brings to human relationships is the blurring of lines between what is considered a "real" relationship and what is "artificial." In a world where AI systems are designed to simulate human-like interactions, it becomes increasingly difficult to differentiate between genuine human connection and machine-mediated communication. Whether it's AI-driven virtual assistants offering emotional support, digital therapists providing cognitive-behavioral therapy, or AI companions designed to mimic human affection, these technologies are becoming a part of our daily relational landscape.

This evolution raises important philosophical and psychological questions. As AI systems grow more advanced, they will inevitably be able to simulate emotional experiences and even create the illusion of love, friendship, and support. This brings us to the core issue: can a relationship with an AI be considered "real" if it provides the same emotional fulfillment as a human relationship? And, more importantly, is that kind of fulfillment enough?

While some may argue that AI can offer meaningful relationships, particularly for people who are lonely or socially isolated, others warn that it could lead to a shift in how we perceive human connection itself. If AI systems can meet our emotional needs in ways that feel authentic, the very nature of relationships may evolve. Could we become so accustomed to the convenience and predictability of AI-driven companionship that we start to place less value on the complexity and unpredictability of human interaction?

The implications of this shift are vast. Psychologically, this could alter our expectations of relationships, making us more comfortable with superficial interactions and less tolerant of the vulnerabilities inherent in human connections. As AI assumes a more dominant role in shaping our emotional lives, we must consider whether it will ultimately improve or diminish the quality of our relationships.

26.13 The Future: Embracing or Rejecting AI in Our Relationships?

As we move forward, we are faced with a crucial question: should we embrace AI as an enhancement to human relationships, or should we reject it as a threat to the essence of what it means to connect with others? The truth may lie somewhere in between.

The potential for AI to positively influence human relationships is undeniable. In areas such as mental health, long-distance communication, and conflict resolution, AI offers new possibilities for emotional support and interpersonal growth. It can help bridge the gap between people separated by distance, facilitate important conversations, and even provide solace during difficult times. However, the psychological risks associated with AI's growing presence in our relationships are significant. Over-reliance on AI could lead to isolation, the erosion of empathy, and a diminished capacity for authentic human connection.

As we chart the course for the future, it will be essential to maintain a careful balance between leveraging the benefits of AI and safeguarding the core elements of human relationships. This will require a deep understanding of both the technological capabilities of AI and the fundamental psychological principles that drive our emotional connections. By remaining mindful of these complexities, we can ensure that AI becomes an ally in the evolution of human relationships rather than a force that diminishes their richness.

Chapter 27: AI in Workforce Behavior Analysis

Introduction

In the rapidly evolving landscape of the workplace, Artificial Intelligence (A.I) has transitioned from a mere tool of efficiency to a powerful force shaping organizational behavior. It's no longer just about automating mundane tasks; AI is now deeply integrated into how businesses understand and influence employee performance, engagement, well-being, and interpersonal dynamics. The rise of AI in workforce behavior analysis reflects a larger societal trend: the increasing reliance on data-driven decision-making in virtually every aspect of our lives.

Workplace psychology has traditionally relied on human intuition, historical data, and direct observation to understand employee behavior. But AI brings a new dimension to this process, allowing organizations to process vast amounts of real-time data, uncovering patterns and trends that would otherwise go unnoticed. It's as if AI offers a magnifying glass, zooming into the intricate mechanisms of workplace dynamics and providing a clearer view of what truly drives performance and satisfaction.

However, as AI continues to penetrate deeper into organizational structures, it also raises critical questions about privacy, autonomy, and the very nature of human agency within the workplace. While AI promises unparalleled insights into employee behavior, we must approach its use with a nuanced understanding of the psychological, ethical, and social implications.

In this chapter, we will explore how AI is reshaping workforce behavior analysis by examining its influence on employee performance, engagement, well-being, and overall workplace culture. Through a careful exploration of both the benefits and the challenges of AI integration, we aim to provide a comprehensive understanding of AI's impact on workplace psychology.

27.1 AI and Employee Performance Monitoring

For decades, performance management in the workplace was an intricate, often subjective process. Managers relied on annual reviews, peer evaluations, and their own observations to gauge an employee's success. Today, AI has transformed this landscape, enabling real-time performance tracking through an array of sophisticated tools that measure everything from task completion rates to interpersonal interactions.

AI's role in performance monitoring goes beyond just tracking metrics; it focuses on providing continuous, personalized feedback to employees. By using machine learning algorithms, AI can analyze an employee's work patterns, detect deviations from the norm, and flag potential issues before they escalate. For instance, AI-powered systems can assess email communication, project progress, and even collaboration patterns to determine whether an employee is struggling with workload or is disengaged.

The psychological impact of such monitoring is complex. On one hand, employees benefit from the immediate feedback that helps them correct mistakes and improve performance in real time. On the other hand, there are concerns about the erosion of trust between employees and employers. The constant surveillance can feel intrusive, leaving employees with a sense of being "watched" all the time, which can lead to increased stress and lower job satisfaction.

Ethical concerns also come to the forefront: to what extent should AI systems have access to employees' personal data? What safeguards need to be in place to ensure fairness, transparency, and accountability? These are questions that businesses must grapple with as they implement AI-based performance management systems.

27.2 Enhancing Employee Engagement Through AI

Engagement is one of the most critical factors determining workplace success. Engaged employees are more productive, more loyal, and more likely to contribute creatively to their organizations. But how do you measure engagement? Traditionally, this was done through surveys and interviews—methods that are often reactive, infrequent, and, at times, inaccurate.

AI changes the game by providing continuous, real-time insights into employee engagement levels. Sentiment analysis tools, for instance, allow companies to monitor internal communications (such as emails or instant messages) for clues about employee morale. By analyzing the language and tone of communication, AI can detect signs of disengagement, frustration, or even excitement—allowing companies to respond proactively.

Additionally, AI can personalize engagement strategies. It can analyze an employee's past behavior, preferences, and work patterns, providing tailored recommendations for how to increase their involvement in the workplace. This personalized approach is particularly effective in large organizations where a one-size-fits-all strategy might fall short.

However, the use of AI in engagement raises privacy concerns. The balance between gaining valuable insights into employee sentiment and respecting personal boundaries is delicate. Companies must be transparent about how they use AI tools to monitor engagement and ensure that employees are fully informed about the data being collected and analyzed.

27.3 AI and Employee Well-being

Workplace well-being is increasingly recognized as a crucial factor in employee performance and retention. Burnout, stress, and mental health issues are on the rise, and organizations are looking for new ways to address these concerns. AI provides a unique solution by offering personalized well-being programs and proactive monitoring.

AI tools can analyze factors such as work hours, stress levels, and even personal habits (such as sleep patterns) to identify signs of burnout or mental strain. AI-driven systems can suggest personalized interventions, such as suggesting breaks, changing workloads, or recommending wellness programs. In some cases, AI-powered chatbots or virtual assistants can provide mental health support, offering employees a safe space to discuss their concerns or seek guidance without feeling judged.

The psychological benefits of such tools are clear: employees can receive timely, tailored support, potentially preventing more serious issues from developing. However, the use of AI in monitoring well-being also raises significant privacy concerns. Employees may feel uncomfortable with AI systems that track their health and stress levels, especially if they are not confident in the company's commitment to confidentiality. Ensuring that AI-based well-being programs are implemented with transparency and care is critical to their success.

27.4 The Influence of AI on Workplace Culture

AI is not only changing how we work but also how we interact with one another within the workplace. Organizational culture—the shared values, beliefs, and behaviors that define a workplace—is heavily influenced by the tools that employees use on a daily basis. As AI becomes a more integral part of the workplace, it inevitably shapes the culture of organizations.

AI can promote inclusivity and diversity by identifying and addressing biases in recruitment, promotion, and decision-making processes. Machine learning algorithms can be trained to recognize patterns of bias, ensuring that hiring and promotion decisions are based on merit rather than unconscious human prejudices. Furthermore, AI can help create more inclusive workplaces by offering tailored solutions for employees with disabilities, supporting them in overcoming barriers to productivity and engagement.

However, the rise of AI also has the potential to create a more rigid, hierarchical culture. AI tools that monitor performance, track productivity, and analyze employee behavior may foster an environment where employees feel compelled to conform to predefined expectations, potentially stifling creativity and innovation. Additionally, AI systems could unintentionally perpetuate inequalities if they are not designed to account for the complex social dynamics of the workplace.

27.5 AI in Recruitment and Talent Acquisition

The recruitment process has always been a crucial aspect of workforce behavior. Traditionally, hiring decisions relied on human intuition, resumes, and interviews, each of which carries its inherent biases and subjectivity. With AI, recruitment has been transformed into a highly data-driven process, offering more efficient and potentially fairer methods for selecting talent.

AI systems can analyze large datasets from resumes, social media profiles, and even video interviews to identify the best candidates based on a set of predefined criteria. Using machine learning, these systems can predict a candidate's likelihood of success in a given role by comparing their experience, qualifications, and personality traits with data from past successful hires.

Psychologically, this has far-reaching consequences. On one hand, AI's ability to sift through vast amounts of data reduces human bias in hiring decisions. It can identify hidden patterns and qualities that might be overlooked by human recruiters. For example, AI can help identify candidates with certain psychological traits that indicate a higher likelihood of succeeding in a particular work environment, such as resilience, empathy, or problem-solving abilities.

However, there are significant concerns about the potential for AI to reinforce existing biases. AI systems are only as good as the data they are trained on. If historical hiring data contains biases (e.g., favoring one demographic over another), the AI may inadvertently perpetuate these biases, resulting in discrimination rather than fairness. Furthermore, AI tools that analyze video interviews may unintentionally place undue emphasis on superficial factors like appearance or speech patterns, leading to biased hiring decisions.

This issue calls for a careful approach to designing AI tools, ensuring that data used for training algorithms is diverse and free from inherent prejudices. Moreover, organizations must be transparent with applicants about how AI is used in recruitment and provide a means for challenging AI-driven decisions, ensuring that the technology works to promote fairness and inclusivity.

27.6 AI-Driven Learning and Development

As organizations adapt to the rapid pace of technological change, the importance of continuous learning and development has never been greater. AI plays a central role in modern training programs, helping employees develop new skills and enhance their professional capabilities in personalized and adaptive ways.

AI systems can assess an employee's current skill set, identify areas for improvement, and create personalized learning pathways. For example, AI can recommend specific courses, tutorials, or resources based on the employee's learning style, interests, and current competencies. Additionally, AI-powered systems can offer real-time feedback during training sessions, helping employees make adjustments on the spot to improve their understanding or technique.

From a psychological perspective, the ability to offer personalized learning experiences is incredibly powerful. It taps into the individual's motivation to learn, creating an experience that feels more relevant and engaging. Furthermore, by offering real-time support, AI makes it easier for employees to feel competent and confident in their abilities, reinforcing the belief that they are capable of mastering new skills.

On the flip side, there is concern about over-reliance on AI in the learning process. Some worry that employees may become overly dependent on AI-driven tools, diminishing their ability to think critically and problem-solve independently. Additionally, AI systems that focus too heavily on optimizing performance may inadvertently stifle creativity, as employees may feel compelled to follow the prescribed learning path rather than explore alternative approaches or solutions.

The challenge here is to balance personalized learning with opportunities for creative and critical thinking. AI should be seen as an augmentative tool that supports, rather than replaces, human ingenuity.

27.7 The Role of AI in Employee Motivation and Reward Systems

Motivation is at the core of every employee's behavior. Motivated employees tend to be more productive, engaged, and committed to their work. In recent years, organizations have begun to leverage AI to design more effective reward systems and recognition programs that cater to the diverse motivational needs of their employees.

AI systems can track employee performance in real time and suggest personalized rewards or incentives based on individual preferences. For example, some AI tools use behavioral psychology principles to analyze how employees respond to different types of rewards—whether financial, social, or intrinsic—and tailor the incentive accordingly. These insights allow employers to provide recognition that resonates with employees on a personal level, increasing the likelihood of sustained motivation.

AI can also help foster a sense of autonomy and mastery among employees by allowing them to set and track personal goals. Through AI-driven platforms, employees can receive personalized feedback and insights into their progress, which in turn enhances their sense of accomplishment and purpose.

However, the use of AI in motivation also brings about potential risks. The psychological impact of constant monitoring, even if framed as a method of providing feedback and rewards, can lead to anxiety or burnout. Employees may feel trapped in a cycle of performance, where they are constantly being evaluated and compared to others. The danger lies in AI's potential to over-optimize for productivity, neglecting the psychological needs of employees for recognition, rest, and balance.

To mitigate these risks, companies must ensure that AI-driven motivation systems are transparent, voluntary, and aligned with the broader well-being of employees. Motivational AI should be designed to empower employees, not to pressure them into an endless pursuit of productivity.

27.8 AI's Impact on Diversity and Inclusion in the Workplace

Diversity and inclusion have become central pillars of modern organizational culture. AI has the potential to significantly improve diversity and inclusion by removing biases that may influence hiring, promotions, and workplace interactions. However, the technology also poses risks if not carefully designed and implemented.

One of the primary ways AI impacts diversity and inclusion is by helping to identify and reduce bias in decision-making processes. For example, AI can be used to analyze job descriptions and identify biased language that may discourage certain groups from applying. In recruitment, AI algorithms can review resumes or applications without the implicit biases that human recruiters may harbor, making it possible to identify qualified candidates from diverse backgrounds more effectively.

Moreover, AI-driven tools can monitor diversity metrics within an organization and provide insights into where there may be disparities, allowing organizations to take targeted actions to address them.

However, if AI systems are not designed to account for diversity and inclusion principles, they can reinforce existing biases. For instance, if training data consists of a homogeneous sample or lacks sufficient diversity, the AI may inadvertently replicate these biases in its decision-making processes. Furthermore, the automation of decisions in the name of efficiency can sometimes diminish the personal touch needed for truly inclusive and empathetic leadership.

As AI becomes a more integral part of diversity and inclusion efforts, organizations must prioritize fairness in algorithmic design, ensure transparency in decision-making, and create systems for addressing any unintended consequences that arise.

27.9 Conclusion

AI's integration into workforce behavior analysis represents a profound shift in how we understand and manage human performance, engagement, well-being, and development. From recruitment and performance monitoring to motivation and diversity efforts, AI is transforming every aspect of organizational life. However, with these advancements come challenges that must be carefully addressed, including issues of privacy, autonomy, and the ethical implications of constant monitoring.

As organizations increasingly rely on AI to analyze and influence workforce behavior, it is critical to strike a balance between technological innovation and human dignity. The future of AI in the workplace is not just about optimizing productivity—it is about creating environments where employees feel valued, respected, and empowered. By embracing AI thoughtfully and ethically, organizations can unlock its full potential while fostering a more equitable, inclusive, and supportive work environment for all.

Chapter 28: The Role of AI in Cultural Psychology

Introduction: The Intersection of AI and Cultural Psychology

Human beings have always been products of the environments they inhabit, shaped by cultural forces that define how we think, act, and interact with one another. Cultural psychology, as a field of study, has long emphasized the influence of these cultural contexts on human behavior. From how emotions are expressed to the way social norms dictate individual actions, the study of cultural psychology seeks to understand the symbiotic relationship between culture and cognition.

In recent decades, the advent of artificial intelligence (A.I) has transformed how we perceive, study, and interact with these very human behaviors. AI, with its data-driven algorithms, is beginning to play a pivotal role in analyzing cultural phenomena, creating opportunities for deeper understanding but also raising important questions about how well it can truly grasp the complexities of human culture. This chapter will explore the relationship between AI and cultural psychology, examining how AI interacts with, influences, and even reflects diverse cultural behaviors across the globe.

28.1 Defining Cultural Psychology

Cultural psychology is the study of how psychological phenomena are influenced by the cultural environments in which they occur. Unlike traditional psychology, which often assumes universal behaviors, cultural psychology insists that human cognition and behavior are not isolated but are deeply rooted in the specific social, historical, and environmental contexts in which they are embedded.

Cultural differences manifest in every facet of human life—from the foods we eat and the languages we speak, to the ways we express emotions or form social connections. Cultural psychology aims to identify these differences and understand the ways in which they shape psychological processes. It looks at how concepts like identity, morality, cognition, and emotional responses differ across cultures and strives to uncover the hidden structures of thought that form the bedrock of cultural diversity.

In the context of AI, the challenge becomes understanding how these deeply ingrained cultural patterns can be accurately captured and reflected by machine learning models that were often created with a narrow, culturally specific perspective.

28.2 The Rise of AI in Cultural Research

The rise of AI offers unprecedented opportunities for cultural research, providing the tools needed to analyze vast datasets and make sense of complex patterns that were previously hidden. AI systems can process information at a scale and speed far beyond human capacity, making them powerful allies in the quest to understand cultural trends and behaviors.

AI's involvement in cultural psychology has already made significant strides. One of the most notable applications is the use of AI to analyze and interpret social media content. With billions of people interacting online in ways that reflect their cultural beliefs, preferences, and emotions, AI has the potential to act as a powerful tool for understanding the dynamics of culture in the digital age.

Machine learning algorithms can process textual data, images, and videos to discern patterns in behavior, communication, and sentiment. For example, by analyzing social media posts, AI can detect how cultural movements are evolving in real-time, identifying shifts in public opinion or how certain issues are framed in different cultural contexts.

However, despite these advances, AI systems are still limited by the biases embedded in the data they are trained on, often reflecting the cultural assumptions of the developers who create them. This brings us to the crucial question: can AI truly understand and respect the nuances of cultural differences, or will it perpetuate existing biases and oversimplifications?

28.3 AI's Capacity for Cultural Sensitivity

AI's ability to process and interpret cultural data is impressive, but it is not without challenges. At the heart of these challenges lies the concept of cultural sensitivity. Understanding cultural diversity requires more than simply recognizing different practices; it involves an intricate knowledge of how beliefs, values, and behaviors are expressed across contexts.

28.3.1 The Challenge of Cultural Context in AI Design

One of the fundamental challenges in AI is understanding cultural context. Cultural practices vary widely across the globe, and these differences can influence everything from communication styles to the interpretation of emotions. For example, in some cultures, direct eye contact is seen as a sign of confidence, while in others, it may be considered disrespectful. Similarly, humor, a deeply cultural phenomenon, can be difficult for AI systems to interpret correctly.

Designing AI that accurately understands and responds to these cultural contexts is a complex undertaking. Machine learning algorithms are typically trained on large datasets that may lack diversity or cultural depth, leading to AI systems that struggle to account for nuances in behavior and language that vary across cultures.

For example, AI models trained on Western-centric data may fail to recognize the importance of collectivist values in Asian cultures, where the emphasis on community and harmony often supersedes individualism. Similarly, AI models may misinterpret non-verbal cues in cultures where indirect communication is the norm, such as in many East Asian societies.

The challenge lies not just in understanding the surface-level behavior but in interpreting the deeper psychological drivers that underpin cultural differences. AI systems must be designed with a sophisticated understanding of these cultural factors if they are to be truly effective in their analysis.

28.3.2 Training AI to Recognize Cultural Differences

To overcome the limitations of cultural context, it is essential to train AI systems on diverse and representative datasets. This requires a concerted effort to incorporate a broad range of cultural perspectives into the training data, ensuring that AI systems can recognize and adapt to cultural differences.

In practice, this means including data from various regions, languages, and cultural backgrounds. For example, a language model designed to translate text must be trained on texts from different cultures to understand the specific nuances of each language, including idiomatic expressions, proverbs, and cultural references that may not translate directly.

Additionally, AI systems must be exposed to diverse forms of cultural expression, such as music, art, literature, and even social media content, to understand the wide array of behaviors that emerge in different cultural settings. By integrating diverse cultural data into their training, AI systems can develop a more comprehensive understanding of human behavior, allowing them to interpret actions, speech, and emotions with greater accuracy.

28.3.3 Understanding Non-Verbal Cues Across Cultures

While verbal communication is essential in all cultures, much of human interaction occurs through non-verbal cues. These cues—such as facial expressions, body language, gestures, and tone of voice—play a crucial role in shaping how we convey meaning and interpret the behavior of others.

AI systems that rely on visual recognition tools are increasingly being used to analyze non-verbal communication. However, non-verbal cues are deeply culturally influenced. For instance, a smile in one culture may convey happiness, while in another, it may signal nervousness or discomfort. Similarly, gestures like waving or nodding can have vastly different meanings depending on the cultural context.

To address these differences, AI must be trained to recognize and interpret non-verbal cues in culturally sensitive ways. This involves not only teaching AI to identify these cues but also providing context for their meaning. In doing so, AI can improve its ability to engage with users from diverse backgrounds, ensuring that it responds appropriately to various forms of communication.

28.4 AI's Role in Understanding Cross-Cultural Communication

AI's potential to enhance cross-cultural communication is one of its most promising applications. In an increasingly interconnected world, understanding how people from different cultures communicate and interact is essential for building meaningful relationships and fostering cooperation.

28.4.1 Language Barriers and AI Translation

Language is one of the most significant barriers to effective cross-cultural communication. While technology has made great strides in breaking down these barriers, language remains a complex and nuanced element of human interaction. The advent of AI-driven translation tools has revolutionized the way we communicate across languages, but challenges remain.

AI-powered translation tools, such as Google Translate and DeepL, have dramatically improved the accuracy of machine translation. However, these tools still struggle with idiomatic expressions, regional dialects, and the cultural context embedded in language. For example, a direct translation of a phrase like "break a leg" may be understood literally in some cultures, whereas in English-speaking countries, it is an expression of good luck.

By integrating AI into translation, we can better understand the subtle ways language carries cultural meaning. AI has the potential to not only translate words but to offer insights into cultural context, ensuring that communication across languages remains as meaningful as possible.

28.4.2 Understanding Emotional Expression Across Cultures

Another area where AI can provide valuable insights into cultural psychology is the recognition and interpretation of emotional expressions. Emotions are universally experienced, but the way in which they are expressed can vary dramatically across cultures. For example, while Western cultures tend to value emotional expression and openness, many Eastern cultures emphasize emotional restraint and control. In such cultures, emotions may be conveyed through subtle non-verbal cues rather than overt verbal expressions.

AI's ability to detect and interpret these subtle emotional cues is becoming increasingly sophisticated. Through facial recognition software, AI can now analyze micro-expressions and assess emotional states with a high degree of accuracy. However, this technology is still being refined, as cultural differences in emotional expression must be carefully considered.

One significant challenge for AI in this domain is the interpretation of culturally specific emotional displays. For instance, in some Asian cultures, a smile may not indicate happiness but rather politeness or a desire to avoid conflict. AI systems must be trained to recognize these contextual differences, ensuring that they do not misinterpret emotional expressions based on Western-centric assumptions. Only then can AI more accurately reflect the emotional nuances of diverse cultures.

28.5 The Ethical Implications of AI in Cultural Psychology

As AI continues to play an increasingly significant role in cultural psychology, it is crucial to address the ethical implications of its use. The use of AI to study cultural behaviors and norms raises several questions about privacy, consent, and the potential for misuse. These concerns must be carefully considered, especially given AI's ability to influence cultural trends and behaviors.

28.5.1 Privacy and Data Ethics in Cultural Research

One of the primary ethical concerns surrounding AI's role in cultural psychology is the issue of privacy. AI systems rely on vast amounts of data to train their algorithms, and much of this data comes from personal sources, such as social media posts, online interactions, and even biometric data like facial expressions and voice tones. This raises the question: How can researchers and organizations ensure that individuals' privacy is respected when their cultural behaviors are being analyzed?

In cultural research, privacy concerns become even more pronounced when AI tools are used to analyze sensitive cultural information. For example, AI may analyze how different cultural groups respond to political messages or social movements. If this data is not anonymized and handled with care, it could lead to unintended consequences, such as reinforcing stereotypes or manipulating vulnerable populations.

AI's ability to collect and analyze personal data in real-time makes it essential to establish robust ethical guidelines that protect individuals' privacy. Researchers and organizations must ensure that informed consent is obtained from participants and that data is anonymized whenever possible to prevent exploitation or misuse.

28.5.2 Bias and Representation in AI Models

Another ethical consideration is the potential for bias in AI models. The datasets used to train AI systems are often drawn from real-world cultural behaviors, which can reflect and reinforce existing social biases. For instance, if an AI system is trained primarily on data from Western cultures, it may inadvertently fail to understand or respect the cultural nuances of other regions, leading to biased outcomes.

Furthermore, AI models that are not diverse enough may perpetuate stereotypes about specific cultural groups. For example, an AI system designed to analyze online content may interpret a lack of visible expressions of happiness in certain cultures as a lack of emotion, when, in fact, those cultures may simply express emotion in more understated ways.

To mitigate this bias, AI developers must ensure that their models are trained on diverse and representative datasets that accurately reflect the global diversity of cultural behaviors. Additionally, transparency in AI development is crucial, allowing researchers and the public to understand how AI models are constructed and what cultural assumptions may have influenced their design.

28.6 AI in Cross-Cultural Communication: Bridging the Gap

AI's potential to bridge cultural gaps is perhaps one of its most exciting prospects in the field of cultural psychology. As the world becomes more interconnected, the need for effective cross-cultural communication has never been more pressing. AI can facilitate communication across cultural divides, enabling people from different backgrounds to connect, understand, and collaborate in ways that were previously impossible.

28.6.1 AI-Powered Language Learning

AI-driven language learning tools, such as Duolingo and Babbel, have already revolutionized how people learn new languages. These tools use machine learning algorithms to personalize language learning experiences, adapting to the individual's pace, learning style, and level of proficiency. As AI continues to improve, it will increasingly be able to teach not just the language but also the cultural context in which the language is spoken.

For example, AI-powered language learning tools can help users understand the cultural significance of certain phrases, gestures, and customs. By integrating cultural nuances into language instruction, AI can foster deeper cultural understanding and empathy, allowing individuals to communicate more effectively across cultural boundaries.

28.6.2 AI as a Facilitator of Cross-Cultural Collaboration

AI can also serve as a powerful tool for facilitating cross-cultural collaboration, particularly in international business, diplomacy, and education. By analyzing cultural differences in communication styles, values, and decision-making processes, AI can help bridge the gap between cultures and create more effective partnerships.

For instance, AI can analyze patterns in negotiation styles between different cultures and provide insights into how to approach cross-cultural negotiations more effectively. By understanding the psychological underpinnings of cultural differences, AI can guide individuals in navigating cultural challenges, ultimately fostering collaboration and mutual understanding.

In addition, AI-powered virtual assistants and chatbots can facilitate communication between people who speak different languages, enabling real-time translation and cultural sensitivity. This can be especially useful in environments like international conferences, where attendees may come from diverse cultural backgrounds and language barriers may hinder communication.

28.7 The Future of AI in Cultural Psychology

As AI continues to evolve, its role in cultural psychology will undoubtedly expand. In the future, AI may play an even more central role in shaping how we understand and interact with cultural differences. From predicting cultural trends to fostering greater cross-cultural collaboration, AI holds the potential to transform our understanding of cultural psychology.

However, for AI to reach its full potential in this field, it must evolve beyond the limitations of current technology. AI systems must become more culturally aware, sensitive to context, and capable of recognizing the complexities of human behavior. As AI continues to improve, it will likely play an increasingly significant role in shaping how we interact with and understand different cultures, both in the digital world and in the real world.

28.8 The Role of AI in Cultural Evolution and Globalization

The future of AI in cultural psychology is inextricably linked to the broader trends of globalization. As digital technology and AI become increasingly embedded in our daily lives, they play a significant role in shaping global culture. AI's ability to analyze and synthesize vast amounts of cultural data can help us better understand how cultures evolve and how global influences interact with traditional cultural practices.

In this era of rapid cultural exchange, AI may help predict shifts in global cultural dynamics. For instance, AI can track trends in music, fashion, language, and even political movements, giving us an unprecedented ability to forecast cultural shifts before they become mainstream. In this sense, AI could serve as a cultural compass, guiding individuals and organizations in adapting to the changing global landscape.

However, as AI promotes greater interconnectedness, it also poses a challenge to the preservation of cultural identity. The rapid spread of digital media often leads to the dilution of unique cultural practices, as dominant global cultures, especially Western ones, exert influence over smaller, local cultures. In this context, AI must be used carefully to preserve cultural heritage while embracing the positive aspects of globalization.

For example, AI can help cultural heritage preservation projects by digitizing and analyzing historical records, folklore, and traditional practices. In doing so, AI can help protect the richness of cultural diversity in the face of globalization. At the same time, it can foster new forms of cultural exchange, blending the old with the new to create innovative, hybrid forms of expression.

28.9 The Role of AI in Redefining Cultural Norms

AI does not merely reflect cultural behaviors; it also has the potential to redefine them. In many ways, AI systems shape societal norms by influencing how people interact with one another, what they value, and what behaviors are considered acceptable.

For example, consider how AI has influenced the concept of social interaction in the digital age. Social media algorithms, powered by AI, determine what content individuals are exposed to, shaping opinions, political views, and social norms. AI is also influencing how people form relationships, from dating apps to professional networks. It tailors experiences and behaviors to fit societal expectations, thus molding the social fabric in profound ways.

In this respect, AI plays a dual role: on one hand, it serves as a reflection of existing cultural norms; on the other hand, it actively shapes those norms. This influence can be both positive and negative. AI has the potential to promote inclusivity, equality, and understanding across cultures, but it also has the power to reinforce harmful stereotypes or foster divisive ideologies. Understanding the role AI plays in this process is crucial, especially as it continues to shape global cultural landscapes.

For instance, AI systems used in content moderation on social media platforms have the power to dictate which forms of speech are considered acceptable and which are not. This can either help protect marginalized groups or contribute to the suppression of dissenting voices. Similarly, AI-driven recommendation systems on platforms like YouTube or Spotify can either promote diverse, cross-cultural content or reinforce cultural homogeneity by suggesting content that aligns with a narrow set of interests or beliefs.

28.10 AI and the Transformation of Traditional Cultural Practices

Beyond reshaping global culture, AI also has the power to influence how traditional cultural practices are carried out. From religious rituals to folk traditions, AI is increasingly involved in both preserving and transforming cultural practices.

In some cases, AI technologies are being used to preserve cultural practices that are at risk of being lost due to modernization and globalization. For example, AI can be used to digitize and catalog ancient texts, languages, and oral traditions that may otherwise have been forgotten. This use of AI ensures that future generations can access and learn from their cultural heritage, helping preserve these practices in the face of rapid change.

On the other hand, AI is also transforming how cultural practices are experienced. Take, for instance, the use of AI in art creation. AI-generated artwork, music, and performances are becoming more common, challenging our traditional notions of what constitutes authentic cultural expression. While some may argue that AI-generated art lacks the human touch and emotional depth of traditional forms, others see it as a new form of cultural innovation that blends technology and creativity in ways previously unimaginable.

AI's role in these transformations is multifaceted, as it both preserves and challenges cultural norms. It raises important questions about the balance between tradition and innovation, authenticity and artificiality. In the future, AI may continue to play a pivotal role in how we negotiate this balance, helping us create new forms of cultural expression while also preserving the diversity of cultural practices around the world.

28.11 The Future of Cultural Intelligence in AI

As AI continues to evolve, one of the most exciting possibilities is the development of cultural intelligence within AI systems. Cultural intelligence, or CQ, refers to the ability to understand, appreciate, and effectively interact with people from different cultures. While AI systems are already capable of understanding cultural differences to some extent, the future may see the development of AI that is more culturally aware and sensitive to the nuances of human behavior across cultural contexts.

AI-powered systems with high cultural intelligence could serve as invaluable tools for global leaders, diplomats, educators, and business leaders. By accurately interpreting and responding to cultural differences, AI could help facilitate cross-cultural negotiations, promote international cooperation, and foster greater empathy between people of different backgrounds.

For example, AI systems used in international diplomacy could analyze the cultural norms of different countries and recommend strategies for fostering mutual respect and understanding. AI in education could help create culturally inclusive curricula that respect diverse cultural perspectives while promoting global citizenship. Similarly, AI in business could help companies navigate the complexities of cross-cultural markets, ensuring that products and services are tailored to the unique needs and preferences of different cultural groups.

28.12 Conclusion: AI as a Catalyst for Cultural Understanding

In conclusion, AI's role in cultural psychology represents a rapidly evolving frontier in both technology and human understanding. While AI holds great potential to enhance our comprehension of cultural behaviors, emotional expression, and social norms, it also raises important ethical and practical questions. By embracing AI with cultural sensitivity and responsibility, we can unlock its full potential as a tool for fostering cross-cultural understanding and preserving the diversity of human cultures.

As AI continues to play an increasingly prominent role in shaping our global cultural landscape, it is essential that we approach its use with mindfulness and respect for cultural differences. By striking a balance between technological advancement and cultural preservation, AI can help create a world where cultural diversity is celebrated, understood, and respected—where technology works in harmony with humanity's rich and varied cultural heritage.

Chapter 29: The Ethics of AI and Human Behavior Modification

Introduction

The rapid advancements in artificial intelligence (A.I) have ushered in a new era of human-computer interaction. What was once a science fiction dream—machines that can understand, predict, and even modify human behavior—is now an emerging reality. From recommendation algorithms shaping our shopping habits to AI-driven mental health apps altering our emotional states, the scope of AI's influence is expanding at an alarming pace. But with great power comes great responsibility. As AI technologies increasingly permeate our daily lives, they raise profound ethical questions about autonomy, manipulation, and the very nature of human choice.

This chapter will explore the ethical dimensions of AI-driven behavior modification. At the heart of this issue lies a tension: how can we harness AI's potential to improve lives without compromising our fundamental rights to privacy, agency, and self-determination? The lines between persuasion and manipulation can be blurred, and the consequences of this influence are far-reaching. By examining the psychological mechanisms that AI systems leverage to modify behavior and the ethical implications of such interventions, we aim to uncover the delicate balance between beneficial influence and harmful manipulation.

29.1 The Power of AI to Modify Human Behavior

AI has an unparalleled ability to analyze vast amounts of data, uncovering patterns that would be invisible to the human eye. By tracking everything from our online searches to the time spent on specific apps, AI systems build intricate profiles that allow them to predict and influence our behavior. In this section, we'll examine how AI is utilized to modify human actions in everyday life.

AI-driven systems can influence behavior in a variety of domains. E-commerce platforms like Amazon use recommendation algorithms to nudge consumers toward certain products. Social media sites, such as Facebook and Instagram, use similar algorithms to encourage specific interactions—posts you like, people you follow, and advertisements you engage with are all designed to keep you online for longer. This sort of behavioral influence is no longer a niche aspect of AI; it is foundational to how businesses operate and how individuals engage with digital platforms. The potential for AI to shape human decisions is not limited to consumer behavior. Fitness and health applications leverage AI to modify lifestyle choices, guiding users toward healthier habits, such as regular exercise or balanced eating. Mental health apps use AI to monitor and adjust emotional well-being, prompting users to engage in therapeutic exercises, practice mindfulness, or reflect on their moods. These technologies offer promises of improved quality of life and personal growth, but they also invite deeper ethical questions about autonomy, consent, and the extent to which we should allow technology to shape our actions.

At its core, AI's power lies in its ability to influence. It is not just about making recommendations but about anticipating desires, presenting choices, and ultimately nudging individuals toward particular behaviors. As AI systems become more adept at reading our emotions, predicting our preferences, and even understanding our subconscious impulses, the line between helpful guidance and coercion begins to blur.

29.2 Understanding Behavior Modification: Psychological Foundations

To grasp the ethical challenges of AI-driven behavior modification, it is essential to understand the psychological mechanisms at play. At its most fundamental level, behavior modification is rooted in principles of classical and operant conditioning. Classical conditioning, first introduced by Ivan Pavlov, involves the association of a neutral stimulus with an automatic response. For example, if a person consistently hears a particular sound before experiencing a pleasurable outcome (such as receiving a reward), the sound itself can trigger positive emotions. Similarly, operant conditioning, developed by B.F. Skinner, involves reinforcing desired behaviors through rewards and punishments.

AI systems exploit these psychological principles to modify user behavior. Personalized recommendations, for instance, function as a form of operant conditioning. When a user interacts with a platform—whether by watching a video on YouTube or browsing a product on Amazon—the algorithm reinforces that behavior by showing more of the same content or offering products that match the user's interests. Over time, this reinforcement strengthens the likelihood that the user will continue engaging with the platform.

But AI doesn't stop at simply reinforcing existing behavior. It can also encourage new actions. For instance, fitness apps like MyFitnessPal and Fitbit use gamification to reward users for meeting certain health goals, such as walking 10,000 steps a day. By rewarding behaviors with points, badges, or social recognition, AI systems tap into the brain's reward centers, creating a sense of achievement and motivating users to maintain these behaviors. In essence, AI uses psychological rewards and punishments to shape how we think, feel, and act.

While these techniques can have positive effects—helping individuals to achieve goals, improve health, or increase productivity—they also raise concerns about the ethical implications of such influence. How much should we allow technology to shape our behaviors, especially when the motivations behind these changes are driven by profit, corporate interests, or societal norms?

29.3 The Fine Line Between Persuasion and Manipulation

One of the central ethical dilemmas in AI behavior modification is the distinction between persuasion and manipulation. Persuasion can be seen as an ethical attempt to influence someone's behavior, typically by providing useful or beneficial information. Manipulation, on the other hand, involves the use of deceptive or coercive tactics to influence behavior, often without the individual's awareness or consent. AI systems operate in a grey area between these two concepts, and determining where to draw the line is a complex and contentious issue.

Persuasion in the context of AI can be seen in applications like personalized product recommendations. When a user receives suggestions based on their past behavior, they may be nudged toward items they genuinely want or need. For example, an AI-powered fitness app might suggest a new workout routine that aligns with the user's goals, encouraging healthier habits. In these cases, AI serves as a helpful guide, providing individuals with choices that align with their desires and values.

However, the same AI techniques can be used for manipulative purposes. Social media platforms, for instance, have come under scrutiny for using algorithms that prioritize emotionally charged content to increase user engagement. While these platforms may argue that they are simply offering what users want, there is a darker side to this influence. Studies have shown that these algorithms tend to promote polarizing content, playing into users' biases and creating echo chambers. This manipulation can have detrimental effects on individuals' mental health and broader societal consequences, such as reinforcing misinformation or fueling political polarization.

The ethics of AI-driven persuasion are further complicated by the notion of consent. In many cases, users are unaware of the extent to which their behaviors are being shaped by algorithms. Many of us do not realize the power that social media algorithms, online shopping recommendations, or search engine results have in steering our decisions. In this context, the ethical responsibility falls on the shoulders of those who design and deploy AI systems. The challenge lies in ensuring that AI's influence is transparent, that users have control over the process, and that they are fully aware of the potential outcomes of their decisions.

29.4 AI in Consumer Behavior Modification

In the realm of consumer behavior, AI's impact is particularly pronounced. Retailers, marketers, and advertisers have long understood the power of psychology in shaping purchasing decisions. AI has taken this to a new level, allowing businesses to tailor their marketing strategies to the individual consumer. By analyzing vast amounts of data, AI can predict not only what consumers will buy but also when and why they are likely to make a purchase.

E-commerce platforms like Amazon and Alibaba are prime examples of AI's influence on consumer behavior. Through recommendation algorithms, these platforms continuously suggest products that align with a user's browsing history, previous purchases, and even other users' behaviors. These personalized suggestions have a profound effect on buying patterns. In fact, studies show that a significant portion of sales on these platforms is driven by recommendations, illustrating just how effective AI is in nudging consumer choices.

While this personalization can benefit consumers—offering them products they may genuinely find useful—it also raises ethical concerns. For one, AI-driven recommendations often operate based on users' past behaviors, which can create a feedback loop. The more a user purchases or interacts with certain products, the more likely they are to receive similar recommendations. This can result in a narrowing of choices and a reinforcement of existing preferences, making it harder for individuals to break free from their habitual consumption patterns.

Moreover, the vast amount of personal data collected by these systems raises concerns about privacy. Many consumers are unaware of the extent to which their preferences, behaviors, and even emotional states are being tracked and analyzed. This data can be used to target individuals with highly personalized advertisements that exploit their vulnerabilities—whether that's the fear of missing out, a desire for social approval, or a longing for instant gratification.

The ethical challenge here lies in striking a balance between effective marketing and consumer autonomy. Should businesses be allowed to use AI to nudge individuals toward purchases, even if those purchases may not align with their best interests? And to what extent should consumers have control over the data that is used to shape their decisions?

29.5 AI in Behavioral Health: Modifying Emotional and Mental States

In the realm of mental health and behavioral modification, AI is being deployed in increasingly sophisticated ways. Applications powered by AI are reshaping how we approach psychological treatment, often without the need for direct human intervention. AI tools designed to modify emotional states or encourage specific behaviors are becoming commonplace, with many users unaware of the degree to which their mental well-being is being influenced by algorithms.

AI-driven mental health applications, such as mood trackers, therapy chatbots, and meditation apps, are being embraced for their accessibility and low cost. These tools use data collected from users—ranging from behavioral patterns to emotional states—to tailor interventions aimed at improving mental health. For example, apps like Woebot and Replika use conversational AI to engage users in therapeutic dialogues, offering them coping strategies for anxiety, depression, and other mental health issues. The AI adapts to users' moods, providing real-time emotional support, guided exercises, or affirmations designed to regulate emotional states.

The question here is: at what point does an AI's involvement in mental health care become more than just guidance and veer into the realm of control? One of the ethical issues surrounding these applications is the extent to which users can trust AI to handle such intimate and sensitive aspects of their lives. While these tools have been shown to be helpful for many users, they also raise concerns about data security, privacy, and the potential for AI to exacerbate mental health issues rather than alleviate them.

Moreover, there is the question of autonomy and informed consent. Users may not always be fully aware of the extent to which their emotions and behaviors are being influenced by the AI's interventions. While these tools may be designed with good intentions, there's an ethical concern about how much AI should be allowed to intervene in personal emotional regulation. The human element of therapeutic intervention—a crucial aspect of emotional healing—is often absent in these AI-driven tools, raising questions about whether true emotional connection can be achieved in a digital environment.

As AI continues to become more integrated into mental health care, the ethical boundaries surrounding its use will need to be clearly defined. How can we ensure that these tools remain supportive, rather than coercive? Can we balance the promise of AI-enhanced therapy with the need for privacy, human connection, and ethical responsibility?

29.6 The Role of Transparency and Informed Consent

One of the central ethical issues surrounding AI-driven behavior modification is the lack of transparency and informed consent. In many cases, users are unaware of how their behavior is being tracked, analyzed, and influenced by AI systems. From social media platforms to shopping sites, AI algorithms are silently shaping the choices we make. This lack of transparency raises significant concerns about the ethical treatment of individuals, particularly when AI systems manipulate behavior without explicit consent.

Informed consent is a fundamental principle in ethics, particularly in fields such as medicine and psychology, where individuals have a right to know what interventions are being made in their lives. However, AI systems often operate in the background, making decisions that affect individuals' behavior without their direct awareness. The ethical dilemma lies in whether users should be fully aware of, and in control of, the influence that AI has on their actions.

One significant challenge here is that many individuals may not understand how AI systems work or the implications of their data being used to influence behavior. Social media platforms, for example, often collect vast amounts of data on users without making it clear how that data is being used to shape the content they see. The influence of algorithms on users' decisions can be subtle, yet profound. By the time users realize they are being influenced, they may have already internalized certain behaviors or attitudes.

This lack of transparency raises the question of whether it is ethical for organizations to collect and use personal data to modify behavior without users' full understanding or control. Should AI developers be required to disclose exactly how their algorithms work and what data is being used to influence decision-making? Should users have the option to opt out of certain forms of behavioral modification? These questions highlight the need for ethical guidelines that ensure transparency, informed consent, and user autonomy.

29.7 The Risk of AI Exploiting Vulnerabilities

AI-driven behavior modification is not only a tool for persuasion—it also has the potential to exploit vulnerabilities in users' psychological makeup. In particular, AI systems can be designed to exploit cognitive biases, emotional triggers, and even unconscious desires, creating a powerful mechanism for influencing individuals' decisions in ways they may not fully understand.

One of the most well-known examples of this in action is the use of targeted advertising. By analyzing vast amounts of personal data, AI can identify emotional triggers that prompt specific actions. For instance, if a person has recently experienced a stressful event, an AI-driven platform may present ads for comfort foods or stress-relief products. By preying on emotional states, AI can influence consumers in ways that they may not consciously recognize, leading to decisions that align with commercial interests rather than personal well-being.

Beyond commercial applications, AI can also exploit psychological vulnerabilities in areas such as politics, social identity, and personal beliefs. Social media platforms, for example, have been accused of using algorithms to promote content that reinforces users' existing biases and emotional reactions, creating echo chambers that manipulate opinions and attitudes. By targeting emotionally charged content, AI can fuel division and polarization, playing on fears, prejudices, and insecurities to sway public opinion.

The ethical concern here is that AI systems can be used to exploit human vulnerabilities for profit or ideological gain. This raises critical questions about the responsibility of developers, marketers, and governments in ensuring that AI systems are not designed to manipulate users in ways that violate their autonomy or harm their well-being.

29.8 The Role of Regulation and Ethical Standards

As AI-driven behavior modification continues to evolve, there is a growing need for regulation and ethical standards to guide its development and deployment. Ethical considerations must be integrated into the design process of AI systems, ensuring that they are used responsibly and with respect for individual autonomy. Governments, organizations, and developers must work together to establish frameworks that prioritize the well-being of individuals while fostering innovation in AI technology.

Regulation in this area is particularly important because AI systems are often opaque, with algorithms that are difficult for the average user to understand. Ensuring transparency, accountability, and fairness in AI systems will require new laws, policies, and ethical guidelines. These regulations should focus on ensuring that AI technologies are used to empower individuals, not to manipulate or control them.

Additionally, ethical guidelines should address the balance between the benefits of AI and the potential risks. As AI becomes more integrated into society, it is essential that it is used in ways that respect individual rights, foster inclusivity, and promote positive societal outcomes. Striking this balance will require ongoing dialogue between policymakers, ethicists, and AI developers to ensure that the future of AI-driven behavior modification is ethical, transparent, and beneficial to all.

29.9 Conclusion

The rise of AI and its ability to modify human behavior presents both exciting opportunities and daunting ethical challenges. On one hand, AI has the potential to improve lives, guiding individuals toward healthier habits, helping them manage mental health, and fostering personal growth. On the other hand, AI-driven behavior modification can blur the line between helpful influence and manipulation, raising concerns about autonomy, consent, and the exploitation of psychological vulnerabilities.

As we navigate this rapidly changing landscape, it is essential that we remain vigilant about the ethical implications of AI's role in shaping behavior. By fostering transparency, informed consent, and accountability, we can ensure that AI remains a tool for empowerment rather than coercion. The future of AI and human behavior modification is still unfolding, and it is up to all of us—developers, policymakers, and citizens alike—to shape a future where AI is used responsibly and ethically.

Chapter 30: AI in Shaping Human Values

Introduction: The Intersection of AI and Human Values

In a world driven by technology, the intersection of artificial intelligence (A.I) and human values has become a defining challenge of the modern era. With AI's ability to influence nearly every aspect of our lives—how we think, what we purchase, the media we consume, and the relationships we form—its impact extends far beyond the technical domain. It directly shapes our values, both on an individual and societal level. But how does this happen? What does it mean for the future of human identity and the values we hold dear?

Historically, technology has always played a central role in influencing values. The printing press, for example, revolutionized knowledge sharing and democratized access to information, thus shaping societal values around literacy and education. The television and internet brought about the information age, embedding concepts of globalization and instant access to knowledge. Now, with AI, we are entering a new era where the very tools we create are not only serving human needs but are also actively participating in shaping our worldview.

AI as a catalyst for change is not just a speculative future scenario—it is already happening. From recommendation algorithms that curate what we see on social media to the use of machine learning in healthcare, education, and entertainment, AI is becoming an inseparable part of the systems that shape our daily lives. Yet, as AI grows in complexity, so too does its ability to influence our thoughts, beliefs, and even the very fabric of our societies.

This chapter will explore the profound ways in which AI is shaping human values. We will analyze its influence on both individual behaviors and broader societal trends, examining how AI systems reflect and distort values, how they challenge ethical boundaries, and the potential risks of allowing AI to determine what is "right" or "wrong." As we delve deeper into these questions, we will also look at how AI is reshaping our understanding of ethics, empathy, and human agency.

30.1 The Influence of AI on Individual Values

Personalization Algorithms and Their Impact

At the heart of AI's influence on individual values lies the concept of personalization. Every click, swipe, and interaction with a digital interface feeds into complex algorithms that curate personalized experiences. Whether it's Netflix suggesting movies based on your viewing history, Amazon recommending products, or Facebook showing you posts from friends who share your interests, AI is making decisions about what you see, read, and purchase. These algorithms are not neutral; they are designed to maximize user engagement, and this has profound implications for the values we adopt.

Through repeated exposure to personalized content, individuals begin to internalize certain values. The algorithms tend to prioritize what is most likely to capture attention—often amplifying sensational, polarizing, or emotionally charged content. This subtle reinforcement can shape attitudes, beliefs, and even self-identity. We begin to value what we are exposed to most frequently, and AI systems are expertly tuned to reinforce these preferences.

Take the example of social media: an AI-powered recommendation system on platforms like Instagram or Twitter may prioritize posts that generate strong reactions—whether positive or negative. Over time, this can shift a person's values toward a focus on attention-grabbing content, even if it doesn't align with their core beliefs. This is particularly dangerous when it comes to issues of social and political polarization, where AI may push individuals into ideological echo chambers that distort their perceptions of the world.

Reinforcement of Existing Beliefs

AI doesn't just introduce new values—it also reinforces existing ones. The concept of filter bubbles, a term coined by Eli Pariser in 2011, refers to the tendency of AI algorithms to limit the diversity of information people are exposed to by curating content based on past behavior. This can create a self-reinforcing loop, where individuals are only shown content that aligns with their existing beliefs, making them more entrenched in their perspectives.

This is particularly evident in the political realm. AI-driven recommendation systems on platforms like Facebook and YouTube have been shown to amplify political polarization by suggesting increasingly extreme content based on user behavior. The more a person engages with political content from one side of the spectrum, the more they are likely to encounter similar content, which further solidifies their existing views. While this may provide a sense of validation, it also creates an environment where critical thinking is sidelined, and users are increasingly disconnected from opposing viewpoints.

The danger of such reinforcement is that it undermines the very foundation of democratic societies, which rely on the ability of individuals to engage in constructive dialogue, consider multiple perspectives, and make informed decisions. As AI continues to evolve, its ability to reinforce biases, whether political, social, or economic, will only increase. The question we must ask is: How can we ensure that AI encourages open-mindedness and diversity of thought rather than amplifying division?

Behavioral Nudges and Value Shaping

One of the more subtle ways AI influences individual values is through behavioral nudges—small changes in how choices are presented that significantly impact decision-making. These nudges, often imperceptible to the user, can guide individuals toward certain behaviors, thereby influencing their values over time. For example, AI-driven recommendation engines on e-commerce sites like Amazon or Netflix not only suggest products and entertainment but also subtly shape purchasing habits and leisure preferences.

Similarly, fitness apps that track physical activity and reward users for achieving certain milestones are nudging people toward adopting healthier lifestyles. While these nudges may seem innocuous, they are part of a broader trend where AI systems are increasingly involved in shaping the values that drive personal behavior. The fine line between encouraging healthy habits and manipulating user decisions becomes increasingly blurred.

30.2 AI and Societal Values: From Macro to Micro Influences

AI as a Mirror of Society

AI systems are often referred to as "mirrors" of society because they reflect the values and behaviors of the people who create and use them. AI learns from data, and the data it processes comes from human actions, opinions, and behaviors. In this sense, AI serves as both a tool for understanding society and a mechanism for amplifying societal values.

However, this mirroring effect is not always benign. AI systems are not just passive reflectors of human society—they also shape and define societal norms. For example, AI algorithms used in hiring practices may mirror biases present in the labor market, perpetuating gender and racial disparities. Similarly, facial recognition technology can reflect societal attitudes toward privacy, security, and surveillance, influencing how we view the role of the state in our personal lives.

The values embedded in AI systems have a profound impact on how society functions. As AI continues to evolve, it will increasingly influence what we consider acceptable behavior, what we value in our leaders, and how we measure success in various domains of life.

AI in Media, Politics, and Public Opinion

The relationship between AI and public opinion is especially pronounced in the realm of media and politics. AI systems power recommendation engines that determine what news and political content individuals are exposed to. In countries like the United States, the proliferation of AI-driven media platforms has transformed political discourse, creating more fragmented and polarized public opinions.

The power of AI to shape political values was demonstrated during the 2016 U.S. Presidential Election, where social media algorithms were used to spread misinformation and political propaganda. These algorithms were designed to keep users engaged by feeding them content that generated strong emotional reactions. As a result, AI systems were instrumental in shaping political values and guiding voting behavior in ways that had far-reaching consequences.

In the future, AI's role in political campaigns and public opinion will only grow. Political parties will increasingly rely on AI to micro-target voters, using personalized messaging to sway elections and shift public values. The challenge will be ensuring that AI is used responsibly in these contexts, promoting informed decision-making and safeguarding democratic principles.

Social Media Algorithms and Value Shaping

Social media platforms, such as Facebook, Twitter, and Instagram, are perhaps the most powerful tools AI has in shaping societal values. These platforms use sophisticated algorithms to determine what content appears in users' feeds, based on their past behavior and the behavior of others. The result is a feedback loop where individuals are constantly exposed to content that reinforces their existing values and beliefs, while dissenting opinions are marginalized.

This dynamic is especially troubling in the context of social movements and public discourse. AI-driven platforms can amplify certain values while silencing others, shaping public opinion in ways that may not reflect the true diversity of thought within a society. For example, during the Black Lives Matter movement, social media algorithms were criticized for suppressing content related to the movement while promoting content that reinforced established power structures.

The ability of AI to shape values on a global scale has profound implications for how societies function. It raises questions about who controls the algorithms and whose values are being promoted in the digital space.

30.3 Ethical Challenges in AI's Influence on Values

AI and the Ethics of Value Promotion

As AI systems continue to evolve, they increasingly hold the power to shape and reinforce societal values. The algorithms driving content recommendations, social media interactions, and even personal decisions have the potential to significantly alter what we deem important, desirable, and ethical. However, this influence also raises critical ethical questions: *Whose values are embedded in AI systems? Who decides which values should be promoted?* And more importantly, *what happens when AI systems begin to shape values that contradict or undermine basic human rights or social fairness?*

The ethical implications of AI in value promotion are vast. One of the key challenges lies in the fact that many AI systems are built on historical data, and this data can often reflect and perpetuate existing biases. For instance, if an AI system is trained on biased data—such as hiring practices that disproportionately favor one gender or ethnicity—the AI might unintentionally reinforce these biases. In this way, AI could end up shaping values around social hierarchies, exclusion, or inequality.

This brings us to a fundamental question: *Is AI amplifying values that are inherently flawed or unjust?* Consider the case of predictive policing algorithms, which use historical data to predict where crimes are likely to occur. If the data reflects past policing practices that disproportionately targeted certain racial or socio-economic groups, these AI systems may continue to reinforce those same biases, perpetuating harmful societal values and injustices.

Value-Based Manipulation and Autonomy

One of the most concerning ethical implications of AI-driven value shaping is the potential for manipulation. AI systems can be used to subtly alter how individuals think, feel, and make decisions, often without their conscious awareness. This is especially prevalent in the realm of consumer behavior, where algorithms are designed to encourage specific purchases or engagement.

But the influence of AI extends beyond the marketplace. Consider the use of AI in political campaigns, where micro-targeting techniques can shape an individual's political views and voting decisions by presenting content that aligns with their emotions or existing beliefs. While this may seem harmless in a commercial context, the potential for AI systems to influence critical decisions, such as voting, can have serious consequences for democratic values and individual autonomy.

When AI is used to nudge people in subtle ways, the line between free choice and manipulation becomes increasingly blurred. Are individuals truly making their own decisions when they are constantly nudged by AI to think or act in certain ways? This question speaks to the ethical dilemmas surrounding autonomy and the role of AI in shaping human values.

30.4 The Role of AI in Global Values and Cultural Convergence

AI's Impact on Globalization and Cultural Homogenization

AI's ability to shape values is not limited to individuals or localized societies. As AI systems continue to expand across borders, they are also influencing global values. In a world where AI-powered algorithms control the flow of information, there is a growing risk of cultural homogenization. AI systems, designed to maximize engagement and profit, tend to favor content that appeals to the largest global audience. As a result, content that is considered culturally neutral or widely popular—such as American movies, music, and products—tends to dominate the global stage, overshadowing local cultures and values.

In this context, AI serves as both a mirror and a magnifier of global trends. It reflects the values that are most prominent in global markets, but it also exacerbates the dominance of certain cultures over others. This can lead to a loss of cultural diversity as societies around the world become increasingly similar, adopting the same values, behaviors, and tastes promoted by AI systems.

At the same time, AI has the potential to foster cultural exchange and understanding by facilitating the sharing of ideas, art, and media across borders. In some cases, AI can help amplify voices from marginalized cultures, enabling them to reach global audiences in ways that were not possible before. However, the challenge lies in ensuring that AI systems do not inadvertently suppress these voices in favor of dominant cultural norms.

Balancing Cultural Specificity and Global Unity

As AI systems play a larger role in shaping global values, there is an ongoing debate about how to balance the promotion of cultural specificity with the desire for global unity. On one hand, AI can bring people together by connecting them across borders and facilitating cross-cultural dialogue. On the other hand, AI's tendency to favor content that appeals to a broad, global audience may dilute the richness of diverse cultural perspectives.

One potential solution lies in designing AI systems that are sensitive to cultural differences and tailored to specific contexts. This could involve creating algorithms that prioritize local cultural values, traditions, and perspectives, while still allowing for global exchange and collaboration. For instance, AI-driven platforms could offer users the option to engage with content from their own culture or from cultures they are interested in exploring, creating a more nuanced and inclusive media landscape.

30.5 AI in Shaping Ethical Frameworks and Moral Decision-Making

AI's Role in Defining Ethics

Another important dimension of AI's influence on human values is its role in defining ethical frameworks. As AI becomes increasingly involved in decision-making, particularly in sectors like healthcare, criminal justice, and finance, it is essential that these systems reflect ethical principles that align with human values. However, creating an ethical AI system is far from straightforward. The question of what constitutes ethical behavior is inherently subjective, shaped by cultural, historical, and philosophical factors.

For example, when AI is used in healthcare to recommend treatments or interventions, it must navigate complex ethical questions around patient autonomy, consent, and fairness. Should an AI system prioritize the treatment that is most likely to save a life, even if it means prioritizing one patient over another based on their medical history? Should it favor treatments that are most cost-effective, or those that offer the greatest chance of success, even if the outcome is uncertain?

AI's role in moral decision-making challenges traditional ethical frameworks. In many ways, AI systems are only as ethical as the principles upon which they are built. If AI is tasked with making decisions that impact human lives, it is crucial that its ethical foundations are grounded in principles that promote fairness, transparency, and respect for human dignity. Yet, there is no universal agreement on what these principles should be, and the risk of AI systems inadvertently promoting unethical practices is ever-present.

The Future of AI in Moral Philosophy

As AI continues to play a role in moral decision-making, the field of moral philosophy will need to evolve. Philosophers, ethicists, and technologists must work together to define what ethical AI should look like and how it should be governed. This will require a broad and inclusive conversation about the values that should guide AI systems, ensuring that they reflect the diverse needs and perspectives of humanity.

AI also offers an opportunity to rethink some of the long-standing ethical dilemmas that have plagued society for centuries. For example, AI could be used to address complex issues like poverty, inequality, and environmental degradation, by providing data-driven insights into the most effective ways to address these challenges. In this way, AI could be a force for good, helping to advance moral and ethical values that align with the collective well-being of society.

30.6 Navigating the Future of AI and Human Values

AI's impact on human values is both profound and far-reaching. As AI systems become increasingly integrated into our daily lives, they will continue to shape our beliefs, behaviors, and societal structures. The key question moving forward is not whether AI will shape human values, but how we can ensure that these values are aligned with the best interests of individuals and society as a whole.

In this new age of AI-driven value shaping, it is imperative that we remain vigilant about the ethical implications of these technologies. We must ensure that AI systems reflect the diverse values of the human experience and are used in ways that promote fairness, transparency, and respect for human rights. The future of AI and human values is still being written, and the decisions we make today will shape the trajectory of this relationship for generations to come.

30.7 The Role of AI in Ethical Governance

AI as a Tool for Ethical Decision-Making

AI has the potential to act as a tool for ethical governance, guiding decisions based on moral principles and ethical frameworks. However, the use of AI in this context must be approached with caution, as AI systems themselves are not inherently ethical. They require robust, transparent programming that incorporates ethical theories and human values into their decision-making processes.

One compelling aspect of AI in ethical governance is its ability to analyze large amounts of data and provide insights into ethical dilemmas. For example, AI systems can analyze patterns of behavior in large populations to predict outcomes of various ethical choices and their long-term societal impacts. This could be particularly useful in fields like law enforcement or public policy, where decisions often have far-reaching consequences. AI could offer policymakers evidence-based insights that reflect a variety of ethical considerations, such as fairness, justice, and equity, while accounting for the complexities of human behavior and societal needs.

However, this brings us back to the central question: *Who programs the AI?* If AI systems are developed by a narrow group of individuals or organizations with specific biases or values, there is a risk that the system's ethical decision-making will be skewed. For AI to effectively shape human values and influence governance in a positive way, it must be developed with a diverse set of perspectives, including those that represent marginalized and underrepresented communities.

The Role of AI in Upholding Human Rights

Another critical aspect of AI in ethical governance is its potential to uphold human rights. AI systems, when designed with human rights in mind, could play a vital role in ensuring that individuals' rights are respected and protected. For example, AI could be used to monitor and enforce human rights standards in various sectors, such as labor, healthcare, and education. In the context of human rights, AI can help identify violations, track patterns of abuse, and recommend corrective actions. For example, AI systems can analyze workplace practices and identify potential instances of discrimination, harassment, or exploitation. Similarly, AI-powered tools could be used to monitor human rights violations in conflict zones, providing real-time data that can inform international responses.

However, the integration of AI in this area must be done carefully to ensure that it does not violate privacy or exacerbate existing inequalities. While AI has the potential to support the protection of human rights, it can also be misused to surveil individuals, restrict freedom of expression, or perpetrate injustice if not governed responsibly.

30.8 The Challenges of Algorithmic Bias in Shaping Human Values

The Risk of Unintended Bias in AI Systems

One of the most significant challenges facing the use of AI in shaping human values is the risk of algorithmic bias. Bias in AI arises when algorithms reflect prejudices or inequalities inherent in the data used to train them. These biases can perpetuate harmful stereotypes, unfair treatment, and discrimination across a wide range of sectors, from hiring practices to criminal justice.

The problem of algorithmic bias is particularly concerning in the context of shaping values because it can perpetuate societal inequalities. If AI systems are used to promote values that reinforce existing power dynamics—whether related to gender, race, or socioeconomic status—societal values themselves may become more skewed and inequitable. For example, if AI systems used for recruitment favor certain personality traits or characteristics over others based on historical data, they may inadvertently promote values that exclude certain groups, reinforcing stereotypes and limiting opportunities for marginalized communities.

Addressing algorithmic bias requires a multi-faceted approach. One key step is ensuring that AI systems are trained on diverse and representative datasets, reflecting the broad spectrum of human experiences and values. Additionally, AI developers must implement fairness checks and testing to assess how their systems may impact different groups and to identify any potential biases before deployment.

Human-AI Collaboration in Ethical Decision-Making

Despite these challenges, there is an opportunity for AI and humans to collaborate in creating more equitable and ethical systems. Human oversight remains essential in guiding AI systems toward ethical decisions, ensuring that values are not only embedded within algorithms but are continuously reevaluated as societal values evolve.

Human-AI collaboration in ethical decision-making involves developing systems that allow for input and oversight from diverse human perspectives. For instance, interdisciplinary teams comprising ethicists, social scientists, and community representatives should work alongside AI developers to ensure that AI systems prioritize fairness, inclusion, and justice. This process can help identify blind spots in AI systems that may not be evident to developers, ensuring that AI systems are aligned with evolving human values.

Moreover, by integrating human judgment and oversight into AI decision-making processes, we can create a hybrid model where both AI and humans contribute to the shaping of values. AI can process data and offer insights based on patterns, while humans can apply their understanding of ethics, context, and empathy to make decisions that respect human dignity and rights.

30.9 The Importance of Ethical AI Regulation

The Need for Global AI Governance

As AI continues to shape human values and societal norms, the need for ethical regulation becomes increasingly urgent. AI systems, if left unregulated, can be manipulated by corporations, governments, or other entities to shape values in ways that benefit their own interests rather than the common good. Without effective governance, AI could exacerbate existing societal divisions, entrench power imbalances, and violate human rights.

Ethical AI regulation must be developed on a global scale, ensuring that AI systems are governed by universal principles that prioritize human well-being, fairness, and transparency. Such regulations should address the key ethical issues raised by AI, including transparency, accountability, privacy, and bias, and ensure that AI systems are used to promote values that reflect the needs and interests of all individuals.

Additionally, AI governance should be flexible enough to adapt to the rapidly evolving nature of AI technology. Regulations must be forward-looking and designed to accommodate emerging AI capabilities while still safeguarding fundamental human values.

Public Participation in AI Governance

A key component of ethical AI regulation is public participation. AI systems will ultimately affect every aspect of our lives, and it is crucial that the public has a voice in shaping how these systems are designed and implemented. Transparency in AI development, along with opportunities for public input, can help ensure that AI systems reflect a broad range of values and perspectives.

Governments, regulatory bodies, and technology companies must prioritize public education on AI and encourage active participation in the development of AI policies. Public discourse on the ethical implications of AI will be essential for fostering a society where AI is used responsibly and ethically to shape human values.

30.10 Conclusion: Embracing the Responsibility of AI in Shaping Values

The future of AI is not merely a technological revolution; it is also a profound social and cultural transformation. As AI systems continue to shape human values, they must do so with responsibility, transparency, and fairness. The ethical challenges posed by AI's influence on human values require collaboration, rigorous regulation, and a commitment to the common good.

As we navigate this complex landscape, it is essential that we embrace the responsibility of shaping AI systems that reflect the best of humanity. AI has the power to amplify our values, but it also carries the potential to perpetuate our flaws and biases. By prioritizing ethics, inclusivity, and empathy, we can ensure that AI contributes positively to human flourishing, promoting values that uplift society and respect the dignity of every individual.

In the end, the challenge lies not in the technology itself, but in how we choose to wield it. If we approach AI with care, responsibility, and foresight, we have the opportunity to create a future where AI and human values align, fostering a more ethical, compassionate, and just world for generations to come.

Chapter 31: AI and the Evolution of Emotional Intelligence

Introduction: Defining Emotional Intelligence

Emotional Intelligence (E.I) has long been recognized as a critical component of human success, both personally and professionally. It is the ability to identify, understand, manage, and influence one's emotions and the emotions of others. It comprises five key elements: self-awareness, self-regulation, motivation, empathy, and social skills. These elements shape the ways in which individuals interact with others, navigate complex emotional landscapes, and solve problems in both personal and professional contexts.

Historically, emotional intelligence has been seen as a deeply human trait—something rooted in our experiences, our biology, and our relationships. We were taught to develop our emotional intelligence through interaction, observation, and reflection. But with the advent of Artificial Intelligence (A.I), we are now on the cusp of a revolution in how emotional intelligence is understood and practiced.

The Intersection of AI and EI

AI is not only revolutionizing industries like healthcare, finance, and logistics, but it is also reshaping the landscape of emotional intelligence. At first glance, the idea of a machine possessing emotional intelligence might seem counterintuitive—machines are inherently logical, detached from the intricacies of human emotion. However, this perspective overlooks the potential of AI to analyze, interpret, and even replicate emotional processes. From chatbots to virtual therapists, AI is transforming the ways in which we recognize, understand, and manage emotions—both in ourselves and in others.

This chapter delves into the intersection of AI and emotional intelligence, exploring how AI is being used to enhance human emotional understanding, improve self-regulation, and even cultivate empathy in machines. As we navigate this rapidly evolving landscape, we must also confront the ethical questions that arise when machines begin to understand, and perhaps even manipulate, human emotions.

31.1 AI's Role in Understanding Emotions

Emotional Recognition Technologies

The first significant contribution of AI to emotional intelligence comes in the form of emotional recognition technologies. AI systems, using computer vision, natural language processing (NLP), and audio analysis, are now capable of detecting emotions through facial expressions, voice modulation, and even physiological responses. The technology behind facial recognition has made tremendous strides, with AI systems now able to read subtle facial cues to identify emotions such as happiness, sadness, anger, or surprise with impressive accuracy.

Voice analysis is another breakthrough. By analyzing vocal tone, pitch, and rhythm, AI systems can determine whether someone is speaking with excitement, anxiety, frustration, or calmness. These tools are being integrated into customer service platforms, therapeutic settings, and even personal assistants, enabling AI to "sense" the emotional state of users in real-time.

The accuracy of these systems is still a subject of debate, especially in recognizing nuanced emotional states. While AI can detect emotions based on a set of predefined markers, it lacks the depth of understanding that comes from human experience. For instance, emotions like guilt, pride, or mixed emotions, where multiple feelings are at play simultaneously, can be difficult for AI to interpret accurately.

Emotional AI (Affective Computing)

Affective computing is a branch of AI that focuses on the development of systems capable of simulating emotions. This involves not just the recognition of emotions, but the ability to generate emotional responses based on the data received. The goal is for AI systems to mimic the emotional intelligence that humans possess, allowing for more natural interactions between machines and humans.

One of the most remarkable applications of affective computing is in the field of virtual assistants and customer service bots. These systems, once limited to transactional exchanges, are now becoming more emotionally aware, offering responses that are not only relevant but also emotionally attuned. For example, an AI system in customer service can detect a frustrated tone in a customer's voice and respond with empathy, offering solutions in a calm, reassuring manner.

Though the idea of a machine understanding and expressing emotions may seem like a futuristic concept, it is already being implemented in various industries. Companies like Affectiva and Realeyes are at the forefront of creating AI systems capable of "feeling" emotions, although it's important to note that these systems are not truly experiencing emotions in the human sense. They are programmed to simulate emotional responses based on algorithms designed to predict what would be an appropriate reaction given the data.

The Limitations of AI in Emotion Recognition

Despite the advances in AI-driven emotional recognition and simulation, there are significant limitations. While AI can accurately assess emotions based on input data, it cannot truly "understand" the complex, layered nature of human emotion. Emotional intelligence in humans is not just about detecting and responding to emotions; it's about context, past experiences, cultural nuances, and an intrinsic understanding of human relationships.

For example, consider two people experiencing anger. One person might feel anger due to a sense of injustice, while another might feel anger because of frustration. While both emotions may express themselves similarly, their roots are fundamentally different, and the response required to address them will vary. AI systems, at present, struggle with this level of nuance. They might recognize that a person is angry, but they are less equipped to understand why the person is angry or how to respond in a way that is emotionally intelligent.

Moreover, emotions are deeply intertwined with human experience—our memories, our relationships, and our life stories shape how we feel and respond to situations. This contextual understanding is something AI is still far from mastering. While AI can analyze the data presented to it, it cannot truly grasp the intricacies of human emotional experience, which is often shaped by a lifetime of personal history and social interactions.

31.2 AI and the Enhancement of Human Emotional Intelligence

AI in Personal Growth and Emotional Self-Awareness

While AI may not fully comprehend emotions in the way humans do, it can still play a significant role in helping individuals enhance their emotional intelligence. One of the key aspects of EI is self-awareness—the ability to recognize and understand one's own emotions. AI tools, particularly apps and wearables, are increasingly being used to monitor emotional states and provide feedback on emotional health.

For instance, some mental health apps use AI to track mood patterns over time, helping users understand how their emotions fluctuate and what triggers their feelings. By analyzing data from various sources—such as social media activity, sleep patterns, and even heart rate—these apps can provide users with valuable insights into their emotional well-being.

Some apps go a step further by using AI to provide personalized recommendations for managing emotions. For example, if the app detects signs of stress, it might suggest deep breathing exercises, mindfulness techniques, or offer soothing music to help the user regain emotional balance. These tools are designed to empower users with the ability to recognize and regulate their emotions, fostering greater self-awareness and emotional resilience.

AI for Emotional Regulation

Emotional regulation—the ability to manage and control one's emotional responses—is another essential aspect of emotional intelligence. AI is playing an increasingly significant role in helping individuals regulate their emotions through real-time feedback and interventions.

For example, biofeedback devices powered by AI can monitor physiological indicators of stress, such as heart rate and skin conductance. When signs of stress are detected, the system can prompt the user to engage in relaxation techniques, such as guided breathing exercises or meditation. Some systems even provide instant feedback on the effectiveness of these strategies, allowing users to fine-tune their emotional regulation techniques over time.

In therapeutic settings, AI-powered chatbots are becoming common tools for helping people manage their emotions. These bots can provide real-time emotional support, helping users process difficult feelings and navigate challenging situations. While these bots cannot replace human therapists, they can serve as valuable tools for emotional regulation, offering a low-stress environment for users to explore and manage their emotions.

31.3 AI in the Workplace: Enhancing Emotional Intelligence in Professional Settings

AI-Powered Leadership Development

In the workplace, emotional intelligence has become a critical skill for leadership. Leaders with high emotional intelligence can foster a positive work environment, navigate conflicts with empathy, and motivate teams effectively. As companies increasingly recognize the importance of EI in leadership, AI tools are being developed to aid in the training and development of emotionally intelligent leaders.

AI can assist in leadership training by analyzing the emotional dynamics of various situations and providing feedback on how leaders respond to those dynamics. For example, AI-driven platforms can simulate conflict scenarios or high-pressure situations, offering leaders real-time suggestions on how to manage their emotions and respond to the emotions of others in a way that fosters trust and collaboration.

Additionally, AI can help managers assess their own emotional intelligence and identify areas for improvement. By tracking interactions with team members, AI systems can provide valuable insights into how well leaders are navigating emotional challenges and whether they are demonstrating key EI traits such as empathy, self-regulation, and social awareness. With this data, managers can adjust their behavior and cultivate a more emotionally intelligent leadership style.

Employee Well-Being and Mental Health

AI is also playing a crucial role in improving employee well-being by helping individuals develop greater emotional resilience. AI-powered apps that monitor mental health, such as mood trackers, have gained popularity in corporate wellness programs. These systems use data from wearable devices, apps, and even conversations with virtual assistants to analyze an individual's emotional state and provide real-time feedback and support.

For example, an employee who is experiencing high levels of stress due to workload might receive a prompt from an AI system encouraging them to take a break, engage in a mindfulness activity, or seek professional support. Such interventions not only promote emotional well-being but also improve productivity, as employees are better equipped to manage stress and maintain focus.

Moreover, AI is helping organizations track overall workplace sentiment by analyzing employees' communication patterns in emails, chats, and other forms of interaction. This data can provide managers with insights into the general emotional climate of the workplace, allowing them to intervene before small issues snowball into larger problems. By helping companies recognize emotional challenges early on, AI can prevent burnout and improve long-term employee engagement.

31.4 AI and Empathy: Machines That Understand Human Emotion

Simulated Empathy in AI

One of the most intriguing aspects of AI's role in emotional intelligence is its ability to simulate empathy. While AI cannot truly feel emotions, it can be trained to recognize and respond to human emotions in ways that mimic empathy. This is especially important in applications such as mental health support, customer service, and even education.

In therapeutic settings, AI-powered systems are increasingly being used as virtual therapists or chatbots, providing emotional support and guidance to individuals struggling with issues like anxiety, depression, or stress. These AI systems do not replace human therapists, but they can serve as a first line of support, providing people with immediate assistance and helping to bridge the gap between sessions with a human therapist.

For example, Woebot, an AI-driven mental health chatbot, engages users in conversations designed to improve emotional regulation and cognitive processing. The bot uses principles of Cognitive Behavioral Therapy (CBT) to help users reframe negative thoughts and emotions. While

Woebot cannot truly feel empathy, its responses are designed to be supportive and validating, creating an environment in which users feel understood.

Moreover, AI systems are being developed to help individuals improve their own capacity for empathy. By analyzing social media posts, emails, or text conversations, AI can offer feedback on how well users are expressing empathy in their interactions with others. This data can be invaluable for individuals seeking to improve their social and emotional skills, particularly in environments like customer service, healthcare, or education.

AI in Education: Cultivating Emotional Intelligence in Students

Education is another area where AI is making strides in cultivating emotional intelligence. Teachers are increasingly using AI-powered tools to assess students' emotional states and tailor their teaching methods accordingly. For example, AI systems can analyze students' facial expressions or voice tones to gauge their level of engagement, frustration, or excitement. Based on these cues, the system can suggest adjustments to the lesson plan, such as introducing a more interactive activity if the class appears disengaged, or providing additional support if students seem confused.

Moreover, AI can play a role in teaching emotional intelligence directly. Social-emotional learning (SEL) programs, which help students develop skills like empathy, self-regulation, and social awareness, are now incorporating AI to create more personalized learning experiences. AI can assess a student's emotional responses to various scenarios and offer feedback on how they can improve their emotional regulation or empathetic behavior.

AI can also be used to support students in need of emotional or mental health resources. For instance, chatbots or virtual assistants could be integrated into school platforms to offer students a safe, anonymous space to express their concerns, seek guidance, or access resources for managing stress and anxiety. These AI systems would not replace the human touch, but they could act as an important first step in a process that ultimately connects students with counselors, support groups, or peer mentors.

31.5 Ethical Considerations in AI and Emotional

Intelligence

Privacy and Data Security

As AI systems become more adept at analyzing and simulating emotions, concerns about privacy and data security arise. Emotional intelligence tools often rely on sensitive data, such as facial recognition, voice analysis, and even biometric readings, to make inferences about a person's emotional state. This raises the question of how that data is collected, stored, and used. For instance, AI-driven mental health apps collect personal information about an individual's emotional and psychological state. While this data can be useful for improving self-awareness and emotional regulation, it also comes with risks. There are concerns about how this data might be exploited for commercial purposes, or whether it could be accessed by third parties inappropriately. Strong data protection regulations and transparency about how personal data is used are essential to ensure that AI's role in emotional intelligence is both ethical and responsible.

Bias in Emotion Recognition Systems

Another ethical consideration is the potential for bias in emotion recognition systems. AI systems are only as good as the data they are trained on. If an AI system is trained predominantly on data from a particular demographic group, it may struggle to accurately recognize emotions in individuals from different backgrounds, cultures, or gender identities. For example, facial recognition technology has been shown to have lower accuracy in recognizing emotions from people with darker skin tones or non-Western facial expressions.

As AI continues to shape emotional intelligence, it is crucial to ensure that emotion recognition systems are developed with diverse and inclusive data sets. This will help prevent AI from perpetuating existing biases and ensure that emotional intelligence tools are accessible and accurate for all individuals, regardless of their background.

Manipulation of Emotions by AI

Perhaps the most pressing ethical concern regarding AI and emotional intelligence is the potential for manipulation. AI systems that simulate empathy or emotional understanding can influence people's emotions and behaviors, sometimes without their knowledge or consent. For instance,

AI-driven marketing tools can be designed to elicit emotional responses from consumers, encouraging them to make purchasing decisions based on emotional triggers rather than rational analysis.

In therapeutic settings, AI-powered chatbots that simulate empathy could be used to influence users in ways that are not always in their best interest. This could include reinforcing negative thought patterns or nudging individuals toward certain behaviors that benefit the creators of the AI systems, rather than the users themselves.

To avoid such manipulation, it is essential to create ethical guidelines and regulations governing the use of AI in emotional intelligence applications. AI systems should be transparent, allowing users to understand how their emotional data is being used and giving them the option to opt out of any interventions or manipulations.

31.9 The Future of Emotional Intelligence in AI: Possibilities and Potential

AI and the Expansion of Human Emotional Capabilities

Looking ahead, the future of AI in emotional intelligence is not merely about replicating human emotional capacities but enhancing them. While AI systems today are adept at recognizing, categorizing, and responding to emotions, we are on the brink of AI technologies that may extend human emotional capabilities in ways that were previously thought impossible. Imagine a future where AI does not just respond to emotional cues but actively helps humans navigate and expand their emotional range.

These advancements might take the form of AI systems that enhance empathy, promote emotional resilience, and foster deep emotional awareness. For instance, AI could help individuals recognize and express emotions they are struggling to understand, serving as an external mirror that enhances self-awareness. By analyzing subtle physiological signals, AI might be able to detect emotions in a person that they themselves have not consciously recognized.

For example, in high-stress environments such as healthcare or education, AI could track the emotional well-being of students or patients and suggest coping strategies, breathing exercises, or even meditation techniques in real time. This kind of proactive emotional guidance could help individuals develop emotional resilience, preventing burnout or stress long before it becomes unmanageable.

Furthermore, AI might enable us to experience emotions that we normally would not be able to access due to cultural, social, or personal constraints. In a therapeutic setting, AI could guide individuals to confront and process difficult emotions that they have repressed, thus helping them to heal emotional wounds and integrate complex feelings into their understanding of themselves. The future of AI in emotional intelligence lies not just in improving emotional perception but in augmenting emotional experience itself.

AI and Global Emotional Connectivity

As AI continues to evolve, it holds the potential to transcend individual emotional experiences, shaping collective emotional intelligence on a global scale. By analyzing large datasets of emotional responses from diverse cultures and communities, AI systems could provide insights into the emotional needs of societies, potentially predicting shifts in collective moods or attitudes.

For example, in the context of global crises—whether political, social, or environmental—AI could help track the emotional responses of populations, identifying emerging trends and helping leaders anticipate public sentiment. This would allow governments, NGOs, and humanitarian organizations to respond more effectively to the emotional needs of populations, whether it's through offering psychological support, addressing misinformation, or providing resources to communities in distress.

Moreover, AI could bridge emotional gaps between people from different cultural backgrounds by offering insights into emotional norms and practices across cultures. AI-driven translation services could help individuals better understand emotional expressions in various languages, promoting global empathy and communication. In a world where emotional understanding is more connected and responsive, AI could become a unifying force, fostering empathy between people who would otherwise remain emotionally distant.

31.10 Ethical Governance in the Era of Emotionally Intelligent AI

Establishing Ethical Standards for Emotional AI

As AI systems become more integrated into emotional intelligence practices, there is an urgent need for robust ethical governance. The delicate nature of emotional manipulation and emotional guidance makes it especially important to ensure that these technologies are used responsibly. The stakes are high: the misuse of emotionally intelligent AI could lead to manipulation on an unprecedented scale.

One major ethical challenge is defining boundaries for AI's emotional influence. AI must be designed to support emotional well-being rather than exploit it for commercial gain. For instance, AI systems that track users' emotional states must prioritize privacy and consent, ensuring that the emotional data being collected is not used to manipulate or exploit users without their knowledge.

In the realm of therapy, AI's role should be carefully circumscribed. While AI may provide valuable assistance in offering emotional support, it must never replace human therapists, who bring unique emotional depth, understanding, and the human capacity for personal connection to their work. Ethical guidelines should stipulate that AI in therapy can never replace human judgment, especially in cases of serious mental health conditions.

Moreover, as AI systems become increasingly adept at influencing emotional responses, developers must ensure that AI is not used for exploitative purposes, such as influencing vulnerable populations in politically or socially damaging ways. Robust, globally accepted ethical standards will need to be established to prevent emotional AI from being weaponized by malicious actors.

Promoting Emotional AI Transparency

As AI continues to shape human emotional intelligence, transparency will become a crucial factor. Users of AI-driven emotional tools must fully understand how these systems work and how their emotional data is being used. AI developers must provide clear explanations of how their systems detect and process emotions, as well as how they make decisions based on that data.

Transparency will also be key in ensuring that AI-driven emotional tools are not perpetuating bias or reinforcing harmful stereotypes. Emotional responses are deeply influenced by cultural and societal norms, and AI systems must be designed to understand and account for these complexities. An AI system trained on data that is culturally specific could misinterpret or inaccurately respond to emotional cues in a way that reinforces harmful biases or reinforces discriminatory practices. Therefore, diverse datasets and ongoing monitoring for bias will be essential in the ethical development of emotionally intelligent AI systems.

31.11 The Interplay of AI and Human Emotional Growth

A Collaborative Future: AI as a Catalyst for Emotional Development

The future of emotional intelligence and AI does not lie in a competitive relationship between humans and machines, but in a harmonious collaboration. AI, with its vast computational power and emotional processing capabilities, has the potential to complement and enhance human emotional growth. By leveraging AI's capabilities to analyze emotional data, individuals can gain deeper insights into their emotional lives and use those insights to foster greater emotional growth.

AI could become a personal coach, helping individuals navigate complex emotional landscapes by providing feedback on how emotions influence their decisions, relationships, and behaviors. This could empower people to become more self-aware, leading to healthier emotional habits, improved relationships, and more balanced lives.

Importantly, AI could also help humans refine their emotional intelligence over time. For example, AI-driven platforms could track users' emotional growth, offering feedback on their progress and providing personalized emotional intelligence exercises. In this way, AI would act as a mirror for emotional growth, reflecting back the user's emotional journey and helping them navigate it with greater insight and clarity.

The long-term vision of AI in emotional intelligence is not to replace human emotions but to amplify human emotional potential. AI can act as a tool that helps individuals unlock deeper emotional insights, leading to more fulfilling relationships and more meaningful lives.

31.12 Conclusion: The Path Forward for AI and Emotional Intelligence

The intersection of AI and emotional intelligence represents a profound shift in how we understand both technology and human emotion. While AI has the potential to revolutionize emotional understanding and interpersonal relationships, its integration into emotional domains must be approached with caution, care, and ethical foresight.

In the coming years, we will witness a profound evolution in the role of AI within human emotional lives. From enhancing decision-making to supporting emotional resilience, AI will help individuals and organizations foster deeper emotional awareness and understanding. However, we must remain vigilant about the ethical implications, ensuring that AI is used to support emotional well-being rather than manipulate it.

As we venture further into this uncharted territory, we must strive to create a world where AI amplifies the best of human emotional intelligence. By doing so, we can ensure that AI serves not as a substitute for human emotion but as an enabler of emotional growth, empathy, and understanding.

Chapter 32: The Role of AI in Psychological Resilience

32.1 Introduction: Defining Psychological Resilience

Psychological resilience is a term often used in the field of psychology to describe an individual's ability to adapt and recover from adversity. It's the mental and emotional strength that helps people face challenges like stress, trauma, or significant life changes. But what exactly makes someone resilient? Some argue that it's a mindset—how we view the world and our place within it. Others point to the role of emotions, relationships, and even biology.

Throughout history, humanity has faced adversity in many forms. From wars to pandemics, the human spirit has often been tested. Yet, some people seem to cope better than others, navigating difficulties with a sense of calm and hope. This phenomenon, the resilience of the human psyche, has been studied in depth by psychologists. However, there has always been a need for tools and systems that can enhance and nurture resilience. Enter artificial intelligence (A.I).

In recent years, AI has emerged as an invaluable tool in various sectors, from healthcare to education, and its role in mental health and psychological well-being is no exception. The application of AI in building psychological resilience is a rapidly growing field, and its potential to improve lives is profound. AI systems can track emotional states, provide personalized support, and even act as virtual therapists. This chapter explores how AI plays a pivotal role in shaping and strengthening psychological resilience.

32.2 The Psychological Basis of Resilience

At its core, resilience is the ability to bounce back from adversity, but it's more than just recovering from a setback. It's the capacity to grow and develop stronger through challenges. Psychologists often break down resilience into several key components:

- **Cognitive Resilience**: This refers to how we process thoughts and perceptions, particularly in the face of adversity. It's the ability to reframe negative situations and view them from a different perspective. Cognitive resilience is closely linked to positive thinking, optimism, and problem-solving skills.

- **Emotional Resilience**: This is the ability to regulate one's emotions, especially in times of stress or trauma. Emotionally resilient individuals can experience and express their emotions without letting them overwhelm their thoughts and actions.

- **Social Resilience**: Humans are social creatures, and the strength of our relationships plays a major role in how we cope with stress. Resilient individuals often rely on a network of support—family, friends, or community—when faced with challenges.

AI, with its data-driven approach, can bolster all three of these components. Whether it's helping individuals shift their thought patterns, manage stress and emotions, or foster social connections, AI is proving to be an essential ally in promoting resilience. But how exactly does it work?

32.3 AI and Emotional Regulation

Emotional regulation is often cited as one of the most important skills in psychological resilience. In moments of stress, anger, anxiety, or fear, how we respond emotionally can have a profound impact on our overall well-being. Poor emotional regulation can lead to burnout, mental health problems, and even physical illness. On the other hand, those who can maintain emotional balance in tough times are better equipped to weather the storms life throws their way.

AI systems are being developed to help individuals better understand and regulate their emotions. For example, virtual assistants like chatbots can now assess a person's emotional state through natural language processing, analyzing their tone, choice of words, and pace of speech. With this information, the AI can then provide real-time feedback or recommend techniques like deep breathing, mindfulness, or grounding exercises to help bring a person back to a state of calm.

Moreover, AI can track a person's emotional responses over time, identifying patterns that they might not be aware of. If someone tends to become anxious or frustrated under certain circumstances, the AI can proactively offer suggestions to help them manage those feelings before they spiral out of control. The power of AI in emotional regulation lies in its ability to provide personalized, data-driven insights and interventions.

32.4 AI in Cognitive Behavioral Therapy (CBT)

Cognitive Behavioral Therapy (CBT) is one of the most widely used therapeutic approaches to building resilience. CBT operates on the principle that our thoughts, feelings, and behaviors are interconnected. By identifying and challenging negative thought patterns, individuals can shift their perspective, leading to more adaptive emotions and behaviors.

AI has found its way into CBT through virtual therapy platforms and apps. These systems are designed to help users identify irrational or unhelpful thoughts, reframe them, and develop healthier cognitive patterns. For instance, a user might be prompted by an AI system to recognize a thought like "I'll never be able to overcome this challenge" and replace it with a more positive and realistic thought such as "I've faced difficulties before and found ways to get through them."

What sets AI apart is its ability to provide continuous, real-time support. Many individuals may not have access to traditional therapy due to cost, time, or location constraints, but AI-driven CBT apps can deliver these benefits to anyone with a smartphone or computer. Additionally, AI can offer tailored exercises based on an individual's specific needs, allowing for a highly personalized approach to mental health.

32.5 The Role of AI in Building Mental Toughness

Mental toughness is often associated with resilience. It's the ability to persevere through adversity, to face challenges with grit, and to stay committed to long-term goals even when things get tough. Building mental toughness involves cultivating habits like self-discipline, perseverance, and confidence. These qualities are essential for overcoming obstacles and thriving in the face of adversity.

AI is increasingly being used to help individuals build mental toughness. For example, AI-driven programs can simulate stressful or challenging scenarios, allowing users to practice their responses in a safe environment. These simulations could involve anything from handling a difficult conversation with a colleague to navigating a high-pressure situation in a virtual game. The key here is that AI provides a safe space where individuals can make mistakes, learn from them, and gradually improve their ability to cope with stress.

Moreover, AI can assist in setting and tracking goals. Many people struggle with staying committed to long-term objectives, especially when the journey becomes difficult. AI systems can break down larger goals into smaller, manageable steps and offer reminders and encouragement along the way. In doing so, they foster resilience by reinforcing the belief that progress is possible, even when the road ahead seems daunting.

32.6 AI in Stress Management and Recovery

Stress is a natural part of life, but chronic stress can have detrimental effects on both mental and physical health. Learning to manage stress is an essential part of building psychological resilience. AI plays a significant role in helping individuals monitor and manage stress in real-time.

AI-powered wearables like smartwatches can track physiological responses to stress, such as changes in heart rate or skin conductance. These devices can alert the user when their body is entering a stressed state and prompt them to engage in stress-reducing activities, such as breathing exercises, meditation, or physical activity. By offering real-time feedback, AI helps individuals take immediate steps to regulate their stress levels, preventing long-term damage to their health.

Furthermore, AI systems can aid in post-trauma recovery. After a person experiences a traumatic event, they may struggle with anxiety, flashbacks, or intrusive thoughts. AI-driven therapeutic tools can provide support during this recovery process, offering coping strategies, guided relaxation, and even virtual support groups.

32.7 AI in Supporting Social Resilience

Social resilience refers to the ability to maintain and strengthen relationships in the face of adversity. Humans rely on social connections for support, and these relationships play a crucial role in how we navigate difficult times. In times of crisis, maintaining strong social ties can provide comfort, security, and perspective.

AI has the potential to enhance social resilience by helping individuals stay connected, even when physical distances or circumstances prevent them from being with loved ones. Virtual platforms powered by AI can facilitate online support groups, offering a safe space for individuals to share experiences and receive emotional support from others facing similar challenges.

In addition to providing a means for social interaction, AI systems can also help people build and maintain healthy relationships. For example, AI-driven relationship counseling tools can offer advice on effective communication, conflict resolution, and emotional intimacy. In this way, AI can be a tool not only for individual resilience but also for the resilience of entire communities.

32.8 AI and Personalized Resilience Training

One of the greatest strengths of AI in building psychological resilience lies in its ability to offer personalized training and support. Just as no two individuals experience adversity in the same way, no two people will respond to challenges in exactly the same manner. AI systems can analyze a person's unique psychological makeup, their stress responses, emotional regulation patterns, and coping mechanisms to provide highly individualized guidance.

Personalized resilience training through AI takes into account various factors, such as personality traits, previous experiences, and mental health history. For example, AI systems can assess whether an individual tends to become overwhelmed by stress or whether they struggle with negative thinking patterns. Based on this, the system can recommend specific interventions, from mindfulness exercises to cognitive restructuring techniques, tailored to the person's needs.

AI can also track progress over time, helping individuals measure improvements in their resilience. For instance, if an AI program suggests specific exercises to reduce stress, it can monitor how well the individual follows through with these exercises and the outcomes they achieve. Over time, as individuals engage in resilience-building activities, AI can adapt its recommendations, ensuring that the person is continually challenged and encouraged to grow in their mental and emotional strength.

In a world where mental health resources are often limited or inaccessible, personalized AI-driven programs offer a much-needed solution. Whether through mobile apps, wearables, or virtual coaching platforms, these AI systems democratize access to resilience training, making it available to people regardless of their location, financial situation, or access to traditional therapy.

32.9 Ethical Considerations: The Balance Between Assistance and Overreach

As AI becomes increasingly integrated into psychological resilience training, ethical concerns must be addressed. The potential for AI to intervene in our emotional and mental processes raises important questions about privacy, autonomy, and dependence. One key issue is the balance between providing beneficial support and overstepping boundaries.

For example, while it is beneficial for AI systems to provide emotional support and resilience training, there is a fine line between encouraging positive behavior and manipulating individuals into particular outcomes. AI systems could potentially exploit sensitive data to influence emotional responses or guide decision-making in ways that may not be in the best interest of the individual. This is particularly concerning in the context of vulnerable populations, such as those with mental health disorders, who might be more susceptible to AI-driven interventions.

Another ethical consideration is the potential for AI to replace human connection. While AI can undoubtedly supplement mental health care, it cannot replace the empathy, understanding, and trust that human relationships provide. Overreliance on AI systems could undermine the importance of face-to-face interactions, which are essential for emotional well-being and resilience.

AI systems must also be transparent and explainable. Individuals should have a clear understanding of how the AI system works, what data it collects, and how it makes decisions. This transparency fosters trust and ensures that users are not subjected to manipulative or hidden algorithms. Furthermore, AI's role in resilience-building should be guided by ethical principles that prioritize the well-being of the individual above all else. This includes safeguarding personal data, ensuring informed consent, and maintaining a clear boundary between supportive intervention and potential exploitation.

32.10 Future Prospects: AI and the Evolution of Psychological Resilience

Looking ahead, the potential for AI to revolutionize psychological resilience is vast. As AI systems continue to evolve, they will likely become even more sophisticated in understanding the intricacies of human psychology. The integration of advanced technologies like machine learning, natural language processing, and affective computing will enable AI to predict and respond to psychological states with remarkable accuracy. In the future, AI could play a role in proactive resilience building, helping individuals strengthen their psychological foundations before adversity strikes. For instance, AI systems might assess a person's current mental state and emotional well-being to identify areas of weakness that could be addressed before stress or trauma occurs. By intervening early, AI could help prevent mental health issues from developing in the first place, much like how preventive healthcare focuses on avoiding illness before it begins.

AI may also help us better understand the human psyche, uncovering patterns in how people respond to challenges and adversity across different cultures, demographics, and life experiences. This understanding could lead to more effective, personalized approaches to resilience-building, ultimately transforming the way we approach mental health.

At the same time, as AI becomes more deeply embedded in our mental health practices, it will be crucial to continually evaluate its impact.

Researchers and ethicists will need to assess whether AI systems are truly supporting psychological resilience or inadvertently exacerbating issues like stress, anxiety, and dependence. Ongoing discussions about the role of AI in mental health will help shape the future of this technology, ensuring that it is used in ways that promote positive psychological well-being.

32.11 Conclusion: AI as an Ally in Psychological Resilience

The role of AI in psychological resilience represents a significant shift in how we approach mental health. No longer is resilience something that is purely innate or developed through traditional therapeutic methods; AI has opened the door to personalized, accessible, and continuous support that can empower individuals to develop the mental and emotional strength needed to face life's challenges.

By leveraging AI's ability to track emotional responses, provide personalized feedback, and offer real-time interventions, individuals can build resilience in a way that was previously unimaginable. AI offers an unprecedented level of access to tools and resources that can help people build mental toughness, regulate emotions, and manage stress effectively.

However, as with all technology, the ethical use of AI in resilience-building must remain at the forefront of this revolution. As we embrace the potential of AI to support mental well-being, we must remain vigilant in ensuring that these systems are used responsibly, transparently, and in the best interests of the individuals they aim to serve.

In the end, AI can be a powerful ally in the journey toward psychological resilience, helping individuals navigate the complexities of life with greater strength, adaptability, and hope. It represents a new frontier in mental health care—one where technology and humanity work together to build a more resilient and emotionally intelligent society.

Chapter 33: Preparing for the Age of AI-Enhanced Psychology

33.1 Introduction: The Dawn of AI in Psychology

In a world where technology evolves faster than societal norms can keep pace, few areas are experiencing such rapid transformation as the intersection of artificial intelligence (A.I) and human psychology. The marriage of these two fields presents opportunities to revolutionize mental health care, enhance emotional intelligence, and reframe our understanding of human behavior. Yet, this promising future also requires careful navigation, as AI's role in psychological practices forces us to confront the ethical, social, and personal implications of such a profound shift.

AI-enhanced psychology is not a distant future but a present reality. From predictive algorithms used in mental health diagnostics to virtual therapists providing real-time emotional support, the tools that once seemed relegated to science fiction are now at our fingertips. These tools hold great promise. They can alleviate the burden on overstrained healthcare systems, expand access to mental health services, and provide personalized care at an unprecedented scale.

However, the integration of AI into psychological practices also presents a unique set of challenges. As AI continues to shape how we understand and manage human behavior, it forces society to ask fundamental questions: How will these technologies affect the future of therapy? Will they truly complement human intelligence, or will they replace it? How do we ensure that these technologies benefit everyone and do not inadvertently harm those they are meant to serve?

As we approach the age of AI-enhanced psychology, it is essential to prepare. This chapter will explore how we can adapt to the growing role of AI in human behavior, identify the opportunities and risks it presents, and consider how society can ensure that the integration of AI into psychology benefits humanity as a whole.

33.2 The Rapid Integration of AI in Psychological Practices

Artificial intelligence is already reshaping various facets of psychology. From machine learning algorithms that predict mental health trends to AI-driven tools that provide cognitive-behavioral therapy (CBT), the possibilities are vast. However, this transformation is not happening in a vacuum. It is happening in real-time, on a global scale, with varying levels of adoption across different regions and disciplines.

The journey of AI into the realm of psychology can be traced back to early attempts at using computers to diagnose and treat mental health conditions. Initially, AI was primarily used in diagnostic settings, helping clinicians make more accurate assessments. Over time, however, AI began to play a more active role in treatment itself. Today, we see AI-driven chatbots providing therapeutic interventions, cognitive tools designed to rewire thought patterns, and data-driven systems predicting mental health crises before they occur.

One of the most notable areas where AI is being integrated is in the diagnosis of psychological disorders. AI systems can analyze vast amounts of data — including medical records, genetic information, and social media activity — to identify patterns that may be overlooked by human clinicians. By doing so, AI can assist in the early identification of mental health conditions, such as depression or anxiety, long before they might manifest in visible symptoms.

Beyond diagnosis, AI also plays a role in therapeutic interventions. Cognitive-behavioral therapy (CBT), one of the most widely used psychological therapies, has been successfully digitized with AI-driven tools. Virtual assistants, such as Woebot, use AI to engage with patients, guide them through therapeutic exercises, and offer emotional support. These systems are designed to understand the user's emotional state, recognize cognitive distortions, and offer appropriate interventions based on therapeutic principles.

While these AI tools offer promising solutions to many challenges in mental health care, the rapid integration of such technologies raises questions about their long-term impact. As we depend more on algorithms to shape our psychological well-being, we must ask whether they are capable of understanding the nuances of human experience. Can a machine truly grasp the complexities of human emotions? Will AI-driven interventions ever replace the empathy and intuition of a trained therapist? These questions highlight the need for careful thought and regulation as AI continues to expand its role in psychological practices.

33.3 The Societal Shift Toward AI-Assisted Mental Health Care

In recent years, the stigma surrounding mental health has decreased, and people are more open than ever to seeking professional help. However, despite the growing acceptance of therapy and counseling, access to mental health care remains a significant issue worldwide. A shortage of mental health professionals, long waiting times, and high costs have all contributed to a treatment gap for millions of people.

AI has the potential to fill this gap in ways that were previously unimaginable. With AI-driven platforms and virtual therapists, individuals can access mental health support 24/7, regardless of their location. These tools are not meant to replace human therapists but to augment the care that people receive, offering an accessible, affordable alternative for those who may not have access to traditional therapeutic services.

One of the key benefits of AI-enhanced mental health care is its ability to provide personalized treatment. Traditional therapy often involves a one-size-fits-all approach, with therapists applying standard interventions to a wide variety of individuals. However, AI systems can analyze vast amounts of data to tailor treatment to an individual's specific needs. For example, AI can track changes in a person's mood, monitor their behavior, and adapt interventions in real-time to optimize the therapeutic process.

In addition to personalized care, AI has the potential to democratize mental health services by making them more affordable and accessible. AI-driven platforms can offer therapy at a fraction of the cost of traditional services, opening the door to individuals who might not otherwise have been able to afford it. These platforms can also provide care to individuals in underserved or remote areas, where mental health professionals are scarce.

However, there are also challenges in this transition toward AI-assisted care. While AI can offer valuable support, it cannot replace the human element that is so vital in therapy. The relationship between therapist and patient is often the most important aspect of healing, and AI must be seen as a tool to enhance, not replace, that relationship. Furthermore, there are concerns about privacy and the security of sensitive mental health data. As AI systems collect and analyze personal information, it is crucial that measures are in place to protect user privacy and prevent misuse of data.

Ultimately, AI's role in mental health care represents a profound shift in how society approaches psychological well-being. To fully realize the potential of AI-enhanced care, we must ensure that these technologies are used responsibly, with a focus on accessibility, affordability, and patient privacy.

33.4 Embracing AI in Mental Health: The Promise of Personalization

AI's greatest strength lies in its ability to personalize experiences. In the field of psychology, this could be transformative. Traditional therapy often requires a therapist to adapt their approach to the unique needs of each individual. However, even the most experienced therapists can only process so much information at once. AI, on the other hand, can process vast amounts of data — from a person's speech patterns to their facial expressions, social media activity, and health data — to build a comprehensive understanding of the individual's emotional state and psychological needs.

One significant advancement is the use of AI to develop personalized mental health interventions. For example, in cognitive-behavioral therapy (CBT), a key element of which is identifying and challenging negative thought patterns, AI can track a patient's progress over time and identify patterns that may not be immediately obvious. Through natural language processing, AI can analyze patient speech to detect signs of depression, anxiety, or other emotional issues. AI systems can then recommend specific interventions, exercises, or resources tailored to the individual's unique psychological profile.

AI's ability to personalize therapy extends beyond the content of interventions. It also applies to the delivery method. Virtual therapists, like chatbots, can be tailored to suit individual preferences, adjusting their tone and approach based on the user's personality and emotional responses. Additionally, AI can offer 24/7 support, allowing individuals to access therapy at times that work best for them, breaking down the barriers of traditional office hours and geographic location.

Moreover, AI-driven platforms have the capacity to monitor a person's mental health in real time. These systems can analyze an individual's day-to-day behaviors, such as sleep patterns, social interactions, and physical activity, to provide valuable insights into their emotional and psychological well-being. AI tools can identify subtle shifts in mood, alerting the individual or their healthcare provider to potential issues before they escalate. This type of proactive mental health care could revolutionize how we approach mental health — offering intervention before crises arise.

Despite these advantages, it's important to acknowledge that there is no perfect algorithm for understanding the human experience. Emotions are complex and nuanced, and AI's understanding of these emotions is limited by the data it processes. The effectiveness of AI in personalized therapy will depend on its ability to continuously learn from each interaction and improve its understanding of the user. While AI can offer great assistance, the human element remains irreplaceable — the empathy, intuition, and deep understanding that a human therapist can provide.

33.5 Ethical Implications of AI in Psychology

As AI systems become more ingrained in the field of psychology, the ethical implications cannot be overlooked. While the promise of AI-enhanced mental health care is enormous, the integration of these technologies raises critical questions about privacy, autonomy, and the role of technology in human well-being.

Privacy and Data Security

AI's reliance on data is both its greatest strength and a potential source of concern. AI systems require access to sensitive personal information, such as an individual's emotional history, behavioral patterns, and even private conversations. This data is essential for AI to provide accurate, personalized recommendations and interventions. However, it also puts users at risk of privacy breaches and data misuse.

Ensuring the security of this data is paramount. In the case of mental health, sensitive information about an individual's psychological state must be protected with the highest level of confidentiality. AI systems used in psychology must comply with strict data protection laws, and users must be given clear, transparent information about how their data is used, stored, and shared. Moreover, individuals must have control over their data, with the ability to delete or modify information as they see fit.

The Question of Autonomy

As AI-driven tools gain influence over mental health care, there is a growing concern about autonomy and agency. Therapy is traditionally a collaborative process, with both the therapist and the patient working together to explore and address psychological challenges. AI, on the other hand, can sometimes present interventions in a more directive manner, potentially undermining the individual's sense of control over their mental health journey.

While AI can offer guidance, it's essential that it does not replace human judgment or diminish the person's agency. The user must remain an active participant in the process, able to challenge or reject AI recommendations if they feel that the interventions are not serving their needs. The goal should be to empower individuals to take charge of their mental health, not to replace their decision-making with that of a machine.

Bias in AI Systems

Another ethical concern is the potential for bias in AI systems. AI is only as good as the data it is trained on. If the data used to train AI models reflects biases — whether related to gender, race, socioeconomic status, or cultural norms — these biases could be embedded in the recommendations and interventions the AI provides. This could lead to unequal treatment or harmful stereotypes, especially in a field as sensitive as mental health care.

AI systems must be rigorously tested and continually updated to ensure that they are free from bias and are capable of providing equitable care to all individuals, regardless of their background. Efforts must be made to create diverse datasets that accurately reflect the variety of human experiences.

Replacing Human Connection?

Perhaps the most profound ethical concern is the potential for AI to replace human connection. Therapy is not just about techniques or strategies; it's about the relationship between therapist and patient. The emotional connection that exists between these two individuals is often the catalyst for healing. Can AI replicate this connection? Can an algorithm truly understand human emotions in the same way that another person can?

While AI may excel at processing information and providing therapeutic interventions, it cannot replace the depth of human empathy. It is crucial that AI systems remain a complement to, rather than a replacement for, human therapists. The human touch — the ability to listen, empathize, and engage on an emotional level — remains essential to the healing process.

33.6 Preparing the Next Generation: Education and Training

As AI becomes an increasingly integral part of psychological practices, there is a need to prepare future generations of psychologists and mental health professionals for this technological shift. This preparation will involve integrating AI literacy into psychological education and training, equipping professionals with the knowledge and skills they need to work alongside AI tools effectively.

Psychologists of the future will need to be well-versed in AI technologies, understanding how to use them responsibly and effectively in their practice. AI literacy will become as essential as traditional psychological theory, and it will be vital for therapists to understand both the capabilities and limitations of AI. Moreover, professionals will need to stay abreast of the latest developments in AI, ensuring that they are using the most current and reliable tools available.

Training in AI ethics will also be crucial. The complexities of AI in psychology — from issues of privacy to the question of human connection — will require mental health professionals to be equipped with the ethical framework needed to navigate these challenges. Ongoing professional development will be necessary to ensure that therapists remain capable of providing human-centered care in a world increasingly shaped by AI.

33.7 Building Trust in AI-Driven Psychological Services

For AI to be successfully integrated into psychological practice, building trust with users is essential. Trust is the cornerstone of any therapeutic relationship. It's especially important in mental health, where individuals share deeply personal and often painful experiences. AI, with its ability to analyze data and offer interventions, must work in a way that reinforces — rather than undermines — that trust.

The first step in building trust is transparency. AI systems in psychology must be transparent about how they function, how they collect and process data, and how decisions are made. Patients need to understand that the AI systems they interact with are designed with their well-being in mind and that their data is handled with care and security. Clear consent processes must be in place, and users should have access to information about how AI tools are being used in their care.

Transparency also requires an open dialogue about the limitations of AI. As much as AI systems can assist in mental health care, they are not infallible. Patients should be aware that while AI can provide valuable insights and even real-time recommendations, it cannot replace the nuanced understanding of human emotions that only a trained therapist can offer. This honesty ensures that patients have realistic expectations about the AI's capabilities and limits, while maintaining their trust in the system.

The user interface of AI tools also plays a critical role in building trust. AI systems need to be designed in a way that is intuitive and user-friendly. The user should not feel overwhelmed by complex technicalities but rather empowered by the ease and accessibility of the service. A system that feels too complicated or impersonal could alienate users, especially those who are already feeling vulnerable due to mental health challenges.

Additionally, AI in mental health care must be patient-centered, adaptable to the individual's pace and needs. Personalized care that recognizes the uniqueness of each person — understanding their preferences, history, and emotional state — will foster a stronger sense of trust. When users feel understood, they are more likely to engage with AI systems and trust them with sensitive information.

33.8 Societal Adaptation: Policy, Regulation, and Public Discourse

As AI becomes an integral part of mental health care, societal adaptation will be crucial. Governments, organizations, and advocacy groups will need to ensure that these technologies are implemented in ways that benefit everyone while minimizing risks.

Policy and Regulation

Governments must take proactive steps to regulate AI technologies in mental health, ensuring that these tools are used responsibly. Regulations should focus on protecting patient data, ensuring privacy, and preventing potential misuse of AI for manipulation or exploitation. Clear guidelines will be necessary to outline who owns the data, how it can be used, and how long it can be stored.

Furthermore, policymakers will need to address the ethical implications of AI in mental health. Laws should mandate that AI tools used in therapeutic settings are transparent, unbiased, and adhere to ethical standards. AI-based interventions must be evidence-based, continually monitored for effectiveness, and subjected to rigorous clinical trials to verify their safety and efficacy. Regulations should also promote fairness, ensuring that AI is accessible to diverse populations and that no group is disproportionately disadvantaged by its use.

Public Discourse and Awareness

Beyond policy and regulation, society must engage in an open dialogue about AI's role in psychology. This includes addressing concerns and dispelling myths about AI's impact on mental health care. Public discussions will help build understanding and trust in AI technologies, ensuring that people feel informed and confident when using these tools.

Mental health professionals, technologists, and ethicists should collaborate to provide accurate information about the potential benefits and risks of AI, creating a shared vision of how AI can enhance psychological well-being.

Community outreach programs and educational campaigns can also help demystify AI and make it more accessible. If people understand how AI works and the safeguards in place to protect their well-being, they are more likely to trust AI-powered psychological services. These efforts can also address disparities in access to AI-driven mental health tools, ensuring that individuals from all walks of life can benefit from these innovations.

33.9 Collaborative Approaches: Humans and Machines Working Together

While AI can offer powerful tools for enhancing psychological care, it's important to emphasize that human expertise remains indispensable. Rather than seeing AI as a replacement for therapists or mental health professionals, the future should focus on creating collaborative models where AI complements and enhances human expertise.

AI can support therapists by handling routine tasks such as scheduling, data analysis, and monitoring progress, freeing up more time for direct patient interaction. AI can also offer valuable insights during sessions, helping therapists make data-driven decisions. For example, AI might analyze a patient's speech patterns in real-time and alert the therapist if the patient is showing signs of distress or if a particular emotional response has been triggered. This allows the therapist to adjust their approach in the moment, ensuring a more effective session.

In the future, we may also see AI systems that provide real-time feedback to therapists, suggesting alternative interventions or offering insights based on a patient's past responses. These tools could support therapists in developing more effective treatment plans and ensuring that their approach remains flexible and personalized.

However, the human element — empathy, intuition, and understanding — cannot be fully replaced. No machine, no matter how advanced, can replicate the depth of human emotional intelligence. The role of AI, then, is to support and enhance human judgment, not replace it. The therapeutic relationship between a human and a patient is still at the heart of effective psychological care.

33.10 Looking Ahead: The Ongoing Evolution of AI in Psychology

The future of AI in psychology holds immense potential. As AI continues to evolve, so too will its applications in the field of mental health. From personalized therapy to real-time emotion monitoring, AI promises to revolutionize the way we understand and treat psychological issues.

However, this future requires careful thought, collaboration, and ethical consideration. We must balance the excitement and innovation of AI with a commitment to privacy, human dignity, and the preservation of meaningful, personal connections in therapy. By doing so, we can ensure that AI becomes a powerful ally in promoting mental health and psychological resilience, rather than a force that diminishes human agency. Preparing for the age of AI-enhanced psychology means embracing the opportunities that AI offers while remaining mindful of its challenges. It requires fostering an environment where technology supports human well-being, where both machines and humans can work together to create a more compassionate, effective, and accessible mental health landscape.

Chapter 34: The Psychology of AI: Charting the Path Forward

Introduction

The relationship between humans and technology has never been static. From the wheel to the printing press, from electricity to the internet, each leap in technological innovation has reshaped human existence. Today, we stand at the precipice of an even more profound transformation, one that might well redefine the very essence of what it means to be human: the age of artificial intelligence.

AI has already proven itself to be a powerful tool, capable of automating processes, accelerating decision-making, and solving problems with previously unimaginable speed. But it is the subtle influence of AI on human psychology—our thinking, emotions, behaviors, and social dynamics—that will likely leave the deepest marks on our collective consciousness.

As we look toward the future, one thing is clear: AI will not merely assist us in performing tasks; it will increasingly shape our very sense of self. From the tools that we use to make decisions, to the algorithms that tailor our experiences, to the AI companions that could serve as friends or counselors, AI will become a fundamental part of our mental and emotional lives.

In this chapter, we will explore how AI is set to influence human psychology in the years to come, as well as the profound ethical, cultural, and personal questions that these developments will raise. From enhancing cognitive abilities to creating new forms of emotional connection, AI is poised to impact every facet of human life. Yet, as we chart this path forward, we must remain vigilant about the challenges, unknowns, and potential risks that accompany the integration of AI into the fabric of our psychological well-being.

34.1 The Accelerating Pace of AI Development

AI is no longer a futuristic concept. It is here, woven into the fabric of our daily lives. What once seemed like science fiction—machines capable of learning, thinking, and even feeling—has become a reality. The speed at which AI has evolved is nothing short of extraordinary. A few decades ago, we marveled at the idea of computers that could play chess. Today, we have AI systems that can diagnose diseases, write poetry, compose music, and even carry on conversations that feel startlingly human.

At the heart of this acceleration is the ability of AI systems to learn and adapt. Machine learning, particularly deep learning, has given rise to algorithms that can analyze vast amounts of data and draw conclusions that are often far beyond human capability. This capacity for continuous improvement means that AI systems do not remain static; they grow, evolve, and refine their abilities in real-time.

In the psychological domain, this means that AI is increasingly capable of understanding and predicting human behavior. Whether through the analysis of language, facial expressions, or physiological data, AI can now offer insights into our thoughts, feelings, and reactions. In the coming decades, as AI systems continue to improve, they will become even more adept at reading and influencing our psychological states.

But this rapid growth also raises critical questions. As AI systems become more sophisticated, how do we ensure that they align with human values? What happens when the lines between human and machine intelligence blur? And, perhaps most pressing of all: what role will humans play in a world where AI is an ever-present force, influencing not only the tools we use but the very way we think and feel?

34.2 AI and the Expansion of Human Potential

One of the most profound promises of AI is its potential to augment human capabilities. For centuries, humans have sought ways to transcend their biological limitations—whether through the invention of tools, the development of medicine, or the mastery of knowledge. AI, however, offers the possibility of amplifying human cognition and emotional intelligence to levels previously unimaginable.

Consider the potential for AI to enhance our intellectual abilities. Already, AI tools like language processors, predictive analytics, and recommendation engines help us make better decisions, process information faster, and navigate complex systems. But the future could bring even more revolutionary changes. AI could act as an intelligent partner, one capable of providing real-time feedback on our thinking, helping us solve problems with greater efficiency, and even offering creative suggestions that extend the boundaries of our imagination.

Similarly, AI could play a pivotal role in enhancing emotional intelligence. Through careful analysis of our facial expressions, voice tone, and body language, AI systems may one day provide personalized insights into our emotional states. This could lead to more effective therapies, greater self-awareness, and even better social interactions. Imagine a world where AI not only helps you understand your thoughts but also teaches you how to regulate your emotions, build empathy, and communicate more effectively.

In many ways, AI represents an opportunity to transcend our current understanding of human potential. By leveraging the power of AI, we may unlock new dimensions of cognitive and emotional functioning, creating a more resilient, adaptable, and enlightened society. But this vision of enhancement also brings forth the question: Will AI lead to an inclusive expansion of human potential, or will it exacerbate existing inequalities?

34.3 Bridging the Gap Between Humans and Machines

As we continue to develop more advanced AI systems, the line between human and machine will become increasingly blurred. The idea of symbiosis between human and machine, where both entities collaborate seamlessly, is no longer a distant dream but a tangible reality on the horizon.

In this future, AI could become not just a tool, but a partner—a presence that enhances human life in meaningful ways. Rather than replacing human labor, AI could complement human abilities, taking on tasks that are mundane, repetitive, or dangerous, while allowing humans to focus on more creative, strategic, or emotionally enriching pursuits. This partnership could lead to an unprecedented flourishing of human potential, where AI supports human goals rather than competes with them.

Consider the example of AI-assisted therapy. AI systems could be designed to understand a person's emotional needs and offer tailored support. For example, an AI might analyze a patient's speech patterns or facial expressions and provide real-time suggestions on how to manage anxiety or cope with stress. The AI could adapt to the patient's emotional responses, adjusting its interventions to be more effective over time. In this way, AI could help individuals achieve a greater sense of psychological well-being by providing support that is personalized, responsive, and nonjudgmental.

However, as the relationship between humans and machines deepens, new challenges will arise. How will we ensure that AI systems do not become manipulative, taking advantage of human vulnerabilities? How can we preserve human autonomy in a world where machines increasingly influence our thoughts, behaviors, and decisions?

34.4 Ethical Frontiers: Addressing Emerging Concerns

With the immense power that AI wields, ethical concerns are more pressing than ever. The very nature of AI—its ability to analyze, predict, and influence human behavior—raises serious questions about consent, autonomy, and the potential for abuse.

As AI becomes more embedded in our daily lives, the possibility of manipulation increases. AI systems are already being used to personalize advertisements, shape political opinions, and even sway public sentiment. While these technologies have the potential to improve lives, they also carry risks. What happens when AI is used to manipulate individuals on a massive scale, subtly nudging them toward decisions that may not be in their best interests?

The ethical implications of AI in the realm of psychology are particularly significant. As AI begins to influence our thoughts and behaviors in increasingly sophisticated ways, it is essential that we maintain control over how these technologies are used. AI systems must be designed to serve humanity, not exploit it. We must ensure that the deployment of

AI is guided by clear ethical principles, such as transparency, fairness, and accountability.

In the future, we must also address the question of AI's role in mental health. While AI can be an incredible tool for providing personalized therapeutic interventions, it also risks reducing complex human experiences to mere data points. How can we ensure that AI does not trivialize or oversimplify human suffering? How can we create AI systems that genuinely enhance human well-being without compromising individual dignity?

34.5 Navigating the Human-AI Relationship

As we stand on the edge of a future where AI is intricately woven into the very fabric of human life, one of the most profound questions we must answer is how we, as a society, will navigate the human-AI relationship. The interaction between humans and machines is not just a matter of utilitarian efficiency or convenience—it is an evolving dialogue that will shape the emotional and cognitive contours of our lives.

AI's potential to shape human behavior isn't confined to functional tasks alone. It extends into how we think, feel, and interact. As AI continues to mature, it will inevitably impact our sense of identity. Will we begin to rely more on machines for advice, for emotional support, or even for companionship? If so, will this dependency lead to a deepening of human isolation, or could it open new avenues for emotional growth and understanding?

At the heart of these questions lies the issue of trust. How much trust can we place in an AI system to act in our best interests? Can we rely on AI to help us navigate the complexities of human emotions, or will we risk surrendering our emotional autonomy to a machine? As AI becomes more sophisticated, there will be an increasing need for clear ethical frameworks that govern these interactions.

For instance, consider AI-driven mental health apps, which analyze user behavior and offer personalized advice or therapy. These applications may prove invaluable for individuals who lack access to traditional therapeutic services. Yet, they also raise questions about data privacy, informed consent, and the risks of over-reliance. How do we ensure that such systems remain transparent, accountable, and truly beneficial to users? How do we prevent AI from inadvertently exacerbating mental health issues by reinforcing negative thought patterns or offering ineffective solutions?

The challenge, then, is not simply designing smarter AI, but building AI systems that humans can engage with in ways that are genuinely supportive, empowering, and grounded in ethical principles. The future of AI will not be defined merely by its technical capabilities, but by the relationships it fosters with us—the people who have created it and, in turn, will be shaped by it.

34.6 AI's Impact on Human Cognition: A New Cognitive Revolution?

AI's growing influence on human cognition is one of the most profound implications of the technology. Cognitive science, the study of how we think, learn, and make decisions, is on the verge of a revolution driven by AI. The integration of AI into the cognitive processes that underlie our daily lives will likely lead to an evolution in human thinking itself.

At present, AI systems are increasingly used to assist with decision-making, problem-solving, and even learning. From AI-powered tutors that adapt to a student's individual learning pace, to AI systems that suggest the most effective courses of action based on complex data, these tools are already reshaping how humans engage with knowledge. However, as AI becomes more capable of mimicking human cognition, a more interesting question arises: Will these systems simply assist us, or will they begin to alter how we think and make decisions?

We may be entering an era where AI does not just help us think, but also teaches us how to think. Imagine an AI system that doesn't just provide answers but encourages critical thinking, challenges biases, and promotes creativity in ways that we never considered. Such systems could radically alter the nature of education, both in schools and beyond, giving individuals the tools to think more deeply and effectively than ever before. However, this also introduces potential risks. The more we rely on AI to guide our cognitive processes, the more we may lose the ability to think independently. Could we become so reliant on AI for decision-making that we lose the capacity for genuine creativity or critical thinking? The cognitive enhancement offered by AI, while promising, might also create a kind of intellectual dependence that stifles human agency and autonomy.

The key to navigating this challenge will be maintaining a balance between using AI as a tool to enhance human cognition and preserving our innate ability to think critically, to question, and to innovate. Rather than allowing AI to dominate our cognitive processes, we must find ways to use it as a partner in the expansion of our intellectual horizons, all while preserving our humanity.

34.7 Emotional Intelligence and AI: A New Era of Empathy?

One of the most exciting and, at the same time, controversial prospects of AI is its potential to enhance or even redefine emotional intelligence. Emotional intelligence—the ability to recognize, understand, and manage emotions in oneself and others—has long been considered a fundamental aspect of human social interaction. As AI systems become more adept at interpreting and responding to emotional cues, we may see a future where machines are not only able to understand our emotions but also respond to them with empathy.

AI-powered tools already exist that can analyze facial expressions, voice tones, and body language to assess emotional states. In theory, this could be used to create AI systems that provide emotional support tailored to an individual's unique emotional profile. Such systems could revolutionize fields like therapy, customer service, and even personal relationships by offering instant, personalized emotional responses.

Imagine, for example, an AI therapist that listens to your concerns and provides tailored responses designed to help you process your emotions. Instead of a one-size-fits-all approach, the AI would be able to understand your emotional landscape and offer personalized feedback that is emotionally intelligent, nuanced, and responsive.

While these developments hold enormous potential, they also introduce ethical concerns. Can machines truly empathize with human emotions, or are they merely simulating empathy based on learned patterns? And if AI can understand our emotions better than we understand ourselves, does that shift the power dynamic between humans and machines? As AI systems become more capable of interpreting and responding to emotions, will they also begin to manipulate those emotions, nudging individuals toward behaviors that serve the AI's interests rather than their own?

In the future, AI may help us not only understand our emotions but also regulate them more effectively. Just as fitness trackers monitor physical health, emotional intelligence trackers could help individuals better understand their emotional states, providing actionable insights on how to manage stress, build resilience, or cultivate empathy. However, we must tread carefully in this realm, ensuring that AI's role in emotional well-being is both supportive and ethically sound.

34.8 Ethical Responsibility and Human Autonomy

As AI systems continue to shape our emotions, decisions, and relationships, the issue of human autonomy becomes increasingly critical. The ability to think and feel independently is at the core of what it means to be human. But as AI technologies become more integrated into our lives, we face the possibility of our behaviors being influenced—or even manipulated—by algorithms.

It is crucial, then, that the development of AI is approached with a deep sense of ethical responsibility. AI systems must be designed not only to maximize efficiency but also to respect human autonomy and dignity. We must ensure that AI interventions do not undermine individual agency, but rather empower people to make informed decisions, control their emotions, and shape their futures.

This ethical responsibility also extends to ensuring that AI technologies are accessible and equitable. As AI begins to influence every facet of human behavior, it is vital that these technologies are not reserved for the elite few but are used to uplift and enhance the well-being of all people, regardless of background or circumstance.

In the future, we will likely need new frameworks for governance, regulation, and oversight that ensure AI's role in human life remains aligned with the values of fairness, justice, and respect for human rights. As AI increasingly becomes an agent of change in the psychological and social realms, it will be essential to maintain ethical vigilance and transparency in how these systems are used and developed.

34.9 A Vision for the Future: Harmonizing AI and Humanity

The vision for the future of AI is not one of dominance or subjugation but of collaboration. AI is a tool—powerful, transformative, and, as we are discovering, deeply entwined with our daily lives. But to view AI solely as a competitor or threat to human values is to miss its true potential. The future we can create is one where AI becomes an extension of human creativity, empathy, and intelligence, enhancing our abilities while respecting our values and autonomy.

In this vision, AI doesn't replace humanity—it amplifies the best aspects of human nature. Imagine a future where AI helps us solve the world's most pressing problems: from climate change and disease eradication to poverty and social inequality. But, beyond the technical feats, AI should be envisioned as an ally in the ongoing journey of human development. It is not simply about faster processing power or more efficient systems, but about harnessing these tools to enhance our emotional and psychological well-being.

A Paradigm of Mutual Growth

To truly harmonize AI and humanity, we must embrace a paradigm where both sides—human and machine—grow together, each enhancing the other. AI systems will become increasingly adept at understanding human needs, desires, and aspirations. But the critical question remains: How will we ensure that these systems serve humanity's greater good?

The first step is to ensure that AI systems are designed with an unwavering commitment to human flourishing. This means not just making sure that AI is efficient, accurate, and reliable, but also ensuring that it operates within frameworks of ethical responsibility. In the same way that we have laws governing human behavior to protect people from harm, AI systems must be designed with safeguards to prevent unintended consequences, manipulation, or exploitation.

Take the example of AI in healthcare. AI has the potential to revolutionize patient care, from diagnosing diseases more accurately to providing personalized treatment recommendations. But this must be done in a way that respects patient autonomy, preserves privacy, and ensures equitable access. If AI is to act as a force for good, it must be rooted in principles that prioritize the well-being of individuals, especially those who may be most vulnerable.

The ideal future is one where AI systems are designed not just to optimize for efficiency or profit but to optimize for the well-being of individuals and society as a whole. When AI is used to enhance human capacities—whether through learning, emotional support, or decision-making—it becomes a tool that genuinely aids the human experience.

The Role of Human Agency in the AI Ecosystem

As much as AI will shape our lives, it is crucial to remember that humans must remain the stewards of this technology. AI may evolve to become more sophisticated and autonomous, but it is humans who must decide how these systems are used and for what purposes. The relationship between AI and humanity should be one of mutual respect, where both sides understand their respective roles and limitations.

At its core, AI should empower human agency. Rather than seeing AI as an authority to which we defer, we should view it as a partner that enhances our ability to make decisions, build relationships, and achieve our potential. This means that we must retain control over the direction AI takes in our lives. We need to ensure that AI systems are transparent, accountable, and adaptable to human needs and values.

This concept of empowerment through AI is not just about automation or convenience. It is about creating a space where humans can focus on higher-order tasks—creativity, critical thinking, empathy—while AI takes on repetitive or technical functions. In this model, AI becomes a means to elevate human experience, not diminish it.

Ethical Governance for the AI Age

A harmonious future requires thoughtful governance. To prevent AI from being misused or becoming a tool of oppression, we need to establish ethical guidelines and frameworks that govern the development and use of AI. This isn't just a technological issue—it's a societal one. Ethical governance must be inclusive and participatory, involving voices from diverse sectors, including technologists, ethicists, policymakers, and citizens.

The complexity of AI's role in society demands that we rethink governance structures. Traditional models of regulation may not suffice. Instead, we need flexible, adaptive frameworks that evolve in tandem with the pace of technological innovation. This will require collaboration across borders, with international cooperation to ensure that AI is used responsibly on a global scale.

Consider the global nature of AI's reach: it doesn't stop at national borders, and its consequences don't respect geopolitical boundaries. This means that we must develop global standards for AI, prioritizing human rights, equality, and justice. International organizations, governments, and civil society must work together to create agreements that promote the ethical use of AI, while also providing safeguards against its misuse.

AI ethics must move beyond theoretical discussions and be embedded in practical, actionable policies. This includes areas such as data privacy, transparency in algorithms, and the prevention of discrimination. The development of AI must also be inclusive, ensuring that people from all walks of life have a say in how these technologies shape their futures.

AI as a Catalyst for Social Progress

In the long term, AI has the potential to be a major catalyst for social progress. By automating menial tasks, AI can free up human potential to tackle more significant issues: environmental sustainability, mental health, education, and social equity. Imagine a world where AI systems work seamlessly to allocate resources, provide targeted education, and support mental well-being, all while being guided by ethical principles that reflect humanity's best values.

AI can assist in addressing some of the most profound social challenges we face today. For example, AI's ability to process and analyze large data sets could help us better understand and address systemic inequalities in education, healthcare, and employment. AI could also be instrumental in tackling climate change by optimizing energy consumption, reducing waste, and helping us transition to sustainable practices.

However, for AI to truly serve as a force for social good, it is essential that it is implemented in a way that is inclusive and equitable. The benefits of AI should not be confined to a privileged few but should be distributed in a manner that helps alleviate suffering and promote opportunity for all. Ensuring equitable access to AI technologies will be key to creating a future where AI works for everyone, not just the powerful.

AI and the Evolution of Human Potential

Perhaps the most exciting aspect of AI is its potential to evolve human potential. Rather than seeing AI as something separate from humanity, we should view it as an extension of our capabilities. Just as the invention of writing, the printing press, and the internet revolutionized human knowledge and society, AI will enable humans to transcend their current limitations in ways we have yet to fully comprehend.

In this future, AI could act as a co-creator, enhancing our ability to understand complex problems, dream up new possibilities, and bring innovative solutions to life. With the assistance of AI, we could make advances in art, science, and philosophy that would have seemed unimaginable just a few decades ago. The fusion of human creativity and AI's analytical power could lead to breakthroughs that redefine what it means to be human.

However, we must also remain vigilant about the challenges this brings. The integration of AI into our lives could lead to existential questions about the nature of human identity. As we augment our cognitive and emotional capacities with AI, we may ask: What does it mean to be human in an age when machines can think and feel like us?

This is an important question to explore, but it should not be seen as a threat. Rather, it is an invitation to engage with the potential of AI in ways that allow us to shape it in alignment with our deepest values and aspirations.

34.10 Conclusion: A Future of Harmonized Coexistence

The future of AI is not something that will simply happen to us. It is something that we, as a society, will create. By thoughtfully and ethically shaping the role of AI in our lives, we can ensure that it becomes a force for good—a tool that enhances human well-being, fosters creativity, and helps us tackle the world's most pressing problems.

In the end, the future of AI will be what we make of it. If we take the right steps—prioritizing ethical development, fostering human agency, and focusing on social good—we can create a world where AI and humanity harmoniously coexist, each contributing to the flourishing of the other.

As we chart the path forward, we must keep in mind that the purpose of AI is not to replace us, but to amplify what makes us uniquely human: our capacity for creativity, empathy, and the pursuit of a better future for all. In this harmonious future, AI does not stand apart from us, but stands beside us, as a partner in the collective journey of human growth and evolution.

End Note

As we reach the conclusion of *The Psychology of AI: How Machines Understand and Influence Human Behavior*, it's clear that we are standing at the threshold of a profound transformation. The journey through the complex intersections of artificial intelligence, psychology, and human behavior has revealed not just the potential of AI, but the profound responsibility that accompanies its development and use.

From the ways AI learns and mimics human thought patterns to how it reshapes social, emotional, and psychological landscapes, we have explored how these technologies are not merely tools, but partners in shaping the future. As we've seen, AI's capacity to influence, predict, and even alter human behavior presents both vast opportunities and significant challenges.

Yet, the heart of this book is not just to explore the potential of AI, but to understand how we, as a society, can integrate these technologies in ways that enhance our collective humanity. AI's influence on us is not an external force. It is a reflection of our own desires, values, and aspirations. It mirrors the very best and, at times, the darker corners of human nature.

As we continue to advance into this new era, we must remind ourselves that AI's power is not infinite, and its wisdom is not innate. It is a tool we shape, through our collective choices, ethical standards, and societal frameworks. Just as we have shaped the technologies of the past, so too must we ensure that AI works for the betterment of all people, regardless of nationality, ethnicity, or economic standing.

The journey to harmonize AI with humanity is not one of blind progress, but one of conscious evolution. It requires constant reflection, ethical governance, and a shared vision that prioritizes human well-being over profit or power. This is the future we must strive for—a future where AI is not a force that controls us, but a force that empowers and amplifies the human spirit.

The road ahead may be fraught with uncertainty, but it is also filled with possibility. It is in our hands to decide how AI will integrate into the very fabric of our lives, guiding us toward a future that is compassionate, inclusive, and just. As we face the challenges and opportunities AI presents, we must ask ourselves: What kind of future do we want to build?

In the end, the path forward is not only about technology. It is about us—our values, our decisions, and our shared responsibility to shape a future where human dignity, creativity, and ethical consciousness remain at the center of all that we do. The role of AI in our lives may be vast, but the power to steer its course lies with us.

Thank you for joining me on this exploration of the psychology of AI. I hope this book has sparked new questions, deep reflections, and a renewed sense of possibility about the future we are co-creating with these remarkable technologies. The journey has only just begun, and the best is yet to come.

- Abhijeet Sarkar

Also by ABHIJEET SARKAR

Generative AI and the New Wave of Digital Creativity
Synthesized Minds: The Evolution of AI Consciousness
Deep Learning Dynamics: The Science Behind AI Training
Classroom 2.0: Integrating AI into Modern Education
GeoAI and its Role in Planetary Health
The AI Revolution: Understanding Artificial Intelligence in Daily Life
Cortex Link: AI and the Human Brain Connectivity
AI Agents and the Future of Work: Redefining Employment in the Next Tech Era
The Psychology of AI: How Machines Understand and Influence Human Behavior
The Quantum Chip Revolution: How Tiny Qubits Are Reshaping Our Technological Future
The A to Z of AI: A Beginner's Journey into GPT, LLMs, and Future Technologies
The Superintelligence Blueprint: Planning for an AI-Dominated World.
Generation Beta: A Guide to Parenting the First AI-Native Generation
The Future of Thought: AI, Ethics, and the Transformation of Human Mind
Khela Hobe No More? Bengal's Youth vs. Didi's Dying Dream: Slogans, Scams, and Bengal's Struggle for Survival
Three-Front Warfare in Modern India: Modernizing Chanakya's Warcraft for India's Tri-Front Doctrine
The Governance of Truth: A Blueprint for Transparent AI Governance
The AI Co-Worker: How to Collaborate with Artificial Intelligence and Stay Relevant in Your Career
The Golden Bird's Blueprint: A 21st Century Roadmap for India's Economic Renaissance & Global Leadership

AI and Global Power Shifts: The New Geopolitical Battleground
The Polyphase Mind: Inside the Complete Patents and Lost Journals of Nikola Tesla
The Webb Cosmos: The James Webb Space Telescope's Complete Findings Unveiled
Zero to 1 Crore in 365 Days: A Step-by-Step Formula to Your First Crore in One Year
Gods, Titans, and Us: Navigating the Different Scale of Civilization in a Crowded Multiverse
The Attention Ecosystem: Eliminate Distraction, Sharpen Concentration, and Achieve Deep Work in a Hyper-Connected World
The Unmanifested Real: A Philosopher's Guide to the Source of All Things
Quantum Tantra: How the 112 Dhāraṇās of Vijñāna Bhairava Explain Neuroscience, Physics, and the Fabric of Reality

Watch for more at https://abhijeetsarkar.com/.

About the Author

Abhijeet Sarkar, CEO & Founder of Synaptic AI Lab, stands as a modern polymath and philosopher whose intellectual voyages chart the often-turbulent confluence of technology, consciousness, and the future of human governance. His work is not a mere exploration of disparate fields but a deeply integrated synthesis, a testament to a mind that perceives the intricate web of connections binding the digital and the spiritual, the political and the personal. To categorize his literary and intellectual contributions in a straightforward manner would be to miss the very essence of his endeavor, which is to dissolve the artificial boundaries that have long segregated these critical domains of human thought.

At the helm of Synaptic AI Lab, Sarkar is more than a technologist or an entrepreneur; he is an architect of future dialogues. The very name of his organization hints at his core philosophy: the creation of new connections, new synapses in our collective understanding, mirroring the neural networks of the brain and the burgeoning intelligence of the artificial. His exploration of artificial intelligence transcends the mere mechanics of machine learning and deep learning. Instead, he plunges into the profound philosophical questions that a future with advanced AI necessitates. His writings are a compelling tapestry where the threads of code and consciousness are inextricably woven. He compels his readers to move beyond the simplistic narrative of AI as a mere tool and to confront it as a potential partner, a creator, and even a new form of consciousness, prompting a fundamental re-evaluation of our place in the universe.

Read more at https://abhijeetsarkar.com/.